D1064147

"Because He Was a German!"

"Because He Was a German!"

Cardinal Bea and the Origins of Roman Catholic
Engagement in the Ecumenical Movement

Jerome-Michael Vereb, C.P.

William B. Eerdmans Publishing Company
Grand Rapids, Michigan / Cambridge, U.K.

© 2006 Jerome-Michael Vereb
All rights reserved

Published 2006 by
Wm. B. Eerdmans Publishing Co.
2140 Oak Industrial Drive N.E., Grand Rapids, Michigan 49505 /
P.O. Box 163, Cambridge CB3 9PU U.K.

Printed in the United States of America

11 10 09 08 07 06   7 6 5 4 3 2 1

Library of Congress Cataloging-in-Publication Data

Vereb, Jerome M.
     "Because he was a German!": Cardinal Bea and the origins of Roman Catholic
engagement in the ecumenical movement / Jerome-Michael Vereb.
        p.   cm.
     Includes bibliographical references.
     ISBN-10 0-8028-2885-X / ISBN-13 978-0-8028-2885-9 (cloth: alk. paper)
     1. Bea, Augustin, 1881-1968.   2. Ecumenists — Biography.
     3. Ecumenical movement — History.   4. Catholic Church — Relations.
     5. Cardinals — Biography.   I. Title.

BX6.8.B43V47   2006
282.092 — dc22

                                                        2006003740

www.eerdmans.com

This dissertation is dedicated to Josette Kersters, who inspired it,
Dr. Edward Vereb, who supported it, but most especially to
Father Eamon McManus, who befriended it, loved it,
and whose life is consecrated to its fulfillment.

With sentiments of admiration and esteem from the author.

The dedication is likewise joyfully given to
Dr. Lester Bolonovich in sincere frendship
and gratitude for his generosity and his wisdom.

Contents

Contents

Contents

Foreword

It is now more than 40 years since the death of "Blessed Pope John XXIII," whose pontificate did so much to effect change in the modern world. Clearly, the legacy of his teaching was about a worldwide family of human beings who, created by and for the living God, seek to worship Him, to serve one another, and to assume the role of grateful stewards of the Creation. In particular, through his encyclicals *Mater et Magistra* and *Pacem in Terris* he spoke of worldwide human responsibilities, clearly indicating that every person has a place in preparing the table, maintaining the table, and enjoying the fruit of the table. Thus he wrote trenchantly:

> There is every indication at the present time that these aims and ideals are giving rise to various demands concerning the juridical organization of States. The first is this: that a clear and precisely worded charter of fundamental human rights be formulated and incorporated into the State's general constitutions. Secondly, each State must have a public constitution, couched in juridical terms, laying down clear rules relating to the designation of public officials, their reciprocal relations, spheres of competence and prescribed methods of operation. The final demand is that relations between citizens and public authorities be described in terms of rights and duties. It must be clearly laid down that the principal function of public authorities is to recognize, safeguard, and promote citizen's rights and duties. (*Pacem in Terris,* nos. 75-77)

The power of this Pope's witness to the compelling tenderness of God's merciful presence amidst the human family is, of course, located in the Gospel tradition. One has only to look at the Beatitudes of the Sermon on the Mount to verify this truth: "Blessed are the poor in spirit, for theirs is the kingdom of heaven . . ." (cf. Matt 5:1-16). Pope John's particular mission as Supreme Pontiff evolved in some of the darkest days of the "Cold War" of the twentieth century. Concern for human security and welfare led him to turn to the specific theme of Christian Unity, especially as found in the Gospel of St. John: "I pray, Father, that they may all be one, as we are One, that the world may believe that you have sent me" (17:21).

The theme of Christian Unity predominated the Second Vatican Council, but it does not stand by itself. Other themes such as liturgical reform, evangelization, reconciliation, the quest for worldwide justice and peace, and the need to continually support the truth in the modern world, also stand together with the desire for unity. Christian Unity was never conceived of in a vacuum. In 1965 when Pope Paul VI, immediate successor to Pope John, stood before the United Nations to proclaim: *"Jamais plus la guerre!"* (Never again war!), his purpose was to report on the work of the Council to all the nations of the world. His declaration remains a powerful gesture in a prolonged drama, which stems from a vision of the power of the Gospel, as specifically formulated at the mid-twentieth century, with its memory of a horrible war, religious and ethnic eradication, followed by an ever-present dilemma of a nuclear standoff between East and West. Pope Paul wrote of this again, ten years later, when he composed the monumental Apostolic Exhortation, *Evangelii Nuntiandi* (On Evangelization in the Modern World). He said: "The power of evangelization will find itself considerably diminished if those who proclaim the Gospel are divided among themselves in all sorts of ways" (no. 77).

Pope Paul went on to say: "The Lord's spiritual testament tells us that unity among His followers is not only the proof that we are His, but also the proof that He is sent by the Father" (no. 77). Then the pontiff delivered these important words:

> It is the test of the credibility of Christians and of Christ himself. As evangelizers, we must offer Christ's faithful, not the image of people divided and separated by unedifying quarrels, but the image of people who are mature in faith and capable of *finding a meeting point beyond the real tensions, thanks to a shared, sincere and disinterested search for truth* (no. 77).

In his book *"Because He Was a German!" Cardinal Bea and the Origins of Roman Catholic Engagement in the Ecumenical Movement,* Father Jerome

Vereb, C.P., examines the significance of the contemporary papal teaching of both Pope John and Pope Paul, by emphasizing the theological importance of Baptism as incorporated into "Christ the Royal Priest," with its concomitant sense of responsibility for both the Church and the world which that incorporation brings. At the same time, he locates the inception of the Roman Catholic ecumenical impetus against the pernicious background of the Germany of World War II, with its multiple tragedies and its ongoing postwar divisions. That event has inserted itself as at once a severe warning and a promise of hope, not only into the theological endeavor but also into the world of international exchange, particularly in the areas of justice and peace.

Shortly after the demise of the Nazi era, suddenly there were two Germanys! The tragedy became the icon of an imperiled world peace, and all eyes focused upon the standoff between the Soviet Union and the Allied Powers of the West, which was so evident in Berlin. German history is full of divisions among its people. The clearest example of that truth is the story of the Classical Reformation. But now, here was a new historical and practical situation which very much affected the pontificate of Pope John XXIII. For example, as a result of the divisions of the nation, the Archdiocese of Paderborn found itself directly cut in two by the Iron Curtain, providing a dilemma for Archbishop Lorenz Jaeger, who had to minister effectively in a very decidedly dual ecumenical context on either side of his diocese. His dilemma forms the topic of this work. Then came the ominous symbol of the Berlin Wall, which was erected in the middle of the Pontificate of Pope John XXIII. The exigencies of that time practically paralyzed all pastoral outreach in Germany and captured the attention of the whole world. Nuclear threat functioned as international blackmail. Drawing on the memory of these facts, Father Jerome demonstrates the interplay of contemporary theological concern against a drama of human international expediency. By doing so, he demonstrates the creative and canny vision of two German prelates, Augustin Cardinal Bea, the Jesuit biblical scholar, and Lorenz Cardinal Jaeger, Archbishop of Paderborn, who conceived a viable dream which is now a permanent reality of the Roman Curia. At first called the Secretariat for Promoting Christian Unity and now known as the Pontifical Council for Christian Unity, that dicastery has taken up and furthered much of the important projection of the Second Vatican Council and still dramatically represents a most important component in today's worldwide ministry for peace — that of "dialogue."

This book, *"Because He Was a German!"* elucidates the environment from which our new Holy Father, Pope Benedict XVI, has emerged. It is also the product of the results of the original research of Father Jerome, whose motive has been the examination of ecumenical theological issues in their historical, cultural, and social setting.

I hope that the reader will enjoy these pages, and I pray that what they signify may have a positive and lasting effect upon the world as it moves toward consistency and space through the Light of Christ. As the Liturgy for Religious Consecration states: "May God, who has begun the good work in us, bring it to fulfillment."

RENATO CARDINAL MARTINO
President, Pontifical Council
for Justice and Peace
January 25, 2006
Chair of Saint Peter

Bishop's Introduction

In one of his early autobiographical writings from long before he was elected to the See of Peter on April 19, 2005, Benedict XVI penned these words:

> The decision which comes from Christ is a "yes" of love, because this alone, precisely with its risk of suffering and losing the self, brings man to himself and makes him what he should be.

This sentence reflects long and introspective years of prayer and study as a seminarian and young priest. It comes, therefore, as no surprise that his first encyclical, *Deus Caritas Est* (God Is Love; 1 John 4:8, 16), is dedicated to the theological virtue of love. Furthermore, the Supreme Pontiff chose to promulgate this very important Apostolic document on the Feast of the Conversion of St. Paul, 25 January 2006. That very day is also the closing date of the universal week of prayer for promoting Christian Unity. Speaking at Vespers to an ecumenical gathering assembled at the Basilica of Saint Paul Outside the Walls in Rome, he stated: *"It is to the theme of love that I wanted to dedicate my first encyclical, which was published today; this happy coincidence with the conclusion of the Week of Prayer for Christian Unity invites us to consider . . . the entire ecumenical journey in the light of God's love, of the Love that is God."*

Pope Benedict's keen interest in the cause of ecumenism has been patent since his days as a Peritus at the Second Vatican Council. Previously as a student priest, the young Father Ratzinger had thoroughly familiarized himself with the details of nascent developments of the ecumenical movement in Germany and across Europe with the birth of the Catholic Conference for Ecumenical Questions in the Netherlands in the early 1950s. He is a man who was thoroughly familiar with Yves Congar, O.P., Jean Danielou, S.J., Johannes Willebrands, and the Pope's own countrymen, Romano Guardini and Hans Balthasar Fischer. In light of his ecumenical vision and in the context of the theme of charity which Pope Benedict addressed in his premier encyclical, these thoughts illustrate his compassionate and uniative heart: *"The Church is God's family in the world; in this family no one ought to go without the necessities of life. Yet at the same time, Caritas-agape extends beyond the frontiers of the Church."*

The theme of ecumenism is not superficial to the Gospel message and most especially to the proclamation of that message in our own time. Because of a lack of faith, many suffer isolation, loneliness, depression, and despair — all over the globe. The ecumenical tool of common witness can provide an antidote for individuals and for society. Terrorism and religious intolerance threaten the very notion of civilization. The Church, i.e., the universal Church, represents Christ Himself. Herein are found the component contributions of compassion, education, and the way to the Universal Fatherhood of God.

Finally, to quote Pope Benedict, "The Church's charitable organizations . . . continue opus proprium, a task agreeable to her, in which she does not cooperate collaterally, but acts as a subject with direct responsibility, doing what corresponds to her nature." This wisdom is applied universally to all the Churches and ecclesial communions within the Christian family.

The book *"Because He Was a German!" Cardinal Bea and the Origins of Roman Catholic Engagement in the Ecumenical Movement* explains the origins of the Roman Catholic Church's participation in the worldwide Ecumenical Movement. It also illustrates the atmosphere in which Pope Benedict was formed and educated. Pope Benedict's encyclical, *Deus Caritas Est,* explains the timeliness and the depth of the ecumenical endeavor for all Christians. This is so especially in these uncertain times because it ascribes to the belief that God *is* love.

WILLIAM MURPHY, S.T.D., L.H.D.
Bishop of Rockville Centre
March 25, 2006
Feast of the Annunciation

Preface

A. A Theological Reflection

As a recent theological topic, the study of ecclesiology can be said to find its contemporary origins in the early nineteenth century, amid the deliberations of neo-Scholasticism, Romanticism, and Patristic revival by practitioners of pastoral theology, such as Johann Adam Möhler (1796-1838) and Johann Michael Sailer (1751-1832). Theological deliberations regarding the meaning and purpose of the Church reached a climax, within the Roman Catholic Church, in 1964 with the promulgation by the Second Vatican Council of The Apostolic Constitution, *Lumen Gentium*. However, as the facts have shown, ecclesiology is not a theoretical subject; there are many practical aspects to it, which are illustrated particularly in the nascent German pastoral situation in which this study was inaugurated, i.e., the post–World War I era.

The Church is the vessel of the presence of God in history. One of the pioneers of the pre-Conciliar phase of this topic was Karl Adam (1896-1966), whose little book, *The Spirit of Catholicism,* has done much to awaken a consciousness of the tangibility of the topic of ecclesiology:

> Therefore, dogma, morality and worship are primary witnesses to the consciousness of the Church that she is of supernatural stock, that she is the Body of Christ. But more than this, the same consciousness determines the spirit of her ordinances and laws, the special manner and method in which she would have her supernatural life realized, and especially her conception of authority and of sacrament. We have spoken

of the supernatural life in the Church; let us now throw light on the special forms in which this life is presented. . . . Since the Church would be not else but the Body of Christ, the realization in history of His divine and human Being, therefore the glorified Christ is the proper source of her power and authority, so much so that this authority is exercised only in His name and in the true and deepest sense only belongs to Him.[1]

Adam wrote those lines in 1929 with a clear understanding that the Church is a community of believers, the solidarity of which functions in time and in place. In fact, the implication of his statement is that the Church is best understood through history. Therefore, I make no attempt to reach conclusions about the significance of ecclesiology and ecumenism through an academic exercise. The purpose and scope of this essay targets twenty years of Church History (1942-1960), and it is a process of demonstration through narration.

The Second Vatican Council has left us with an image of the Church within a human context: "The Church, 'like a stranger in a foreign land, presses forward amid the persecutions of the world and the consolations of God,' announcing the cross and death of the Lord until he come (I Cor. 11:26). But by the power of the risen Lord, she is given strength to overcome, in patience and love, her sorrows and her difficulties, both those that are from within and those that are from without, so that she may reveal *in the world,* faithfully, however darkly, the mystery of her Lord until, in the consummation, it shall be manifested in full light (L.G. 8)."[2]

According to Emile Josef de Smedt, the late Bishop of Bruges and a formidable voice at the Second Vatican Council, the mystery of the Church was presented as a display of "triumphalism, juridicism, and clericalism" until the mid-twentieth century.[3] There were some spiritual movements in the Church at that time, particularly in Europe, which converged to present a new, modern, and appropriate image of the Church. With the coming of the Second Vatican Council, a new image arose whereby the Church was identified with "THE PILGRIM PEOPLE OF GOD." The Constitution on the Church was preceded in history by the famous New Delhi Statement of

---

1. Karl Adam, *The Spirit of Catholicism* (New York: Macmillan Company, 1929), pp. 2, 3 (emphasis mine).

2. Emphasis mine.

3. Xavier Rynne, *Letters from Vatican City* (New York: Farrar, Straus & Company, 1963), p. 13. Bishop de Smedt was addressing a preparatory anticipation of the opening of the Second Vatican Council.

the World Council of Churches, which, in the words of William B. Cate, "makes all past efforts at [ecclesial] cooperation [among Christians] seem shadowy and inept."[4] The New Delhi Statement reads:

> We believe that the unity which is both God's will and His gift to His Church is being made visible as all in each place who are baptized into Jesus Christ and confess Him as Lord and Savior are brought by the Holy Spirit into one fully committed fellowship holding the one apostolic faith, preaching the one gospel, breaking the one bread, joining a common prayer, and having a corporate life reaching out in witness and service to all and who at the same time are united with the whole Christian fellowship in all places and all ages. In such wise that ministry and members are accepted by all, and that all connect and speak together as occasion requires for the tasks to which God calls His people. (no. 3)[5]

With the biblically based phraseology of the "PILGRIM PEOPLE OF GOD," the Roman Catholic Church, for its part, was at that time opening itself up to the realization of the eschatological goal of the journey and also to the historical environment in which that journey takes place, in contrast to the characterization imposed by de Smedt in his Conciliar speech.[6] That same image of pilgrimage conveyed a challenge to all Church members to hearken to the universal call to holiness, whereby each member, according to his or her capacity, searches for Christ, embraces Christ, and gives witness to Christ to the glory of the Father, for the sake of building up the kingdom in time and space, and in the hope of everlasting life.

> All the members of the Church should unflaggingly fulfill the duties of their Christian calling. The profession of the evangelical counsels shines before them as a sign which can and should effectively inspire them to do so. For the People of God has here no lasting city but seeks the city which is to come, and the religious state of life, bestowing greater freedom from the cares of earthly existence on those who follow it, simultaneously reveals more clearly to all believers the heavenly goods which are already present in this age, witnessing to the new and

---

4. William B. Cate, *The Ecumenical Scandal on Main Street* (New York: Association Press, 1965), p. 34. The language herein cited is provided by Lesslie Newbigin, whose influence on the missionary activity of the World Council of Churches is monumental.

5. *Op. cit.*, pp. 34-35 (emphasis mine). The overall draft of the 1961 New Delhi Statement was the responsibility of Lesslie Newbigin. See Günther Gassmann (ed.), *Documentary History of Faith and Order* (Geneva: World Council of Churches Press, 1993), p. i.

6. Rynne, *op. cit.*, p. 13.

eternal life which we have acquired through the redemptive work of Christ and precluding our future resurrection and the glory of the heavenly kingdom. (L.G. 44)

The exigencies which are implied in the above Conciliar quote have to do with history. The environment of history plays its part in forming the Church.[7] This study is about that fact. The implications of Karl Adam's essay on the Church, *Spirit of Catholicism,* speak about the supernatural life contained within that mystical Body, both human and divine, as an impact on history. Yet, it may not be obvious to all, nor even to a few, at first sight. This book contains much history. The general theme demonstrates that a single idea and the tenacity of an individual, even in adverse circumstances, can make a difference.

B. Reasons for This Undertaking

That individual was Augustin Cardinal Bea, who, together with his friend and collaborator, Archbishop, later Cardinal, Lorenz Jaeger, brought the question of the ecumenical mission of the Church to the attention of the great Pope John XXIII. As a simple priest, Bea was in contact with several movements of the Church which emerged in northern Europe following the First World War. Among these the Ecumenical Movement caught his attention. A multitalented man, Bea also used his biblical skills to involve himself directly in the lay movement, the missionary movement, and the liturgical movement. In this last field of study, he was personally in contact with Pope Pius XII and was able to reflect with him upon the meaning of the Church as demonstrated in contemporary liturgical reform. From biblical scholar to liturgist he became, because of the needs of the times, an ecclesiologist. Among these exigencies were the tragedies suffered by the German nation from 1918 through the Cold War, which reached a boiling point in the early 1960s. When Pope John XXIII was elected, I had my first conversation with Fr. William Abbott, S.J., and he recounted to me the fascinating events of the day when Bea became a Cardinal. Thus did Augustin Bea become the focus of my study as I saw ecumenism as a phenomenon through the events of his life.

In 1995 I found myself collaborating with Cardinal Achille Silvestrini on the production of another book, this one on the papal pilgrimages out-

---

7. Adam, *op. cit.,* pp. 36-52.

side of Italy. At the time, Cardinal Silvestrini was head of the Pontifical Congregation for the Oriental Churches. In his earlier career he had been Undersecretary of State for the Vatican, and even earlier, personal secretary to Pope John XXIII's Secretary of State Domenico Cardinal Tardini. In his youth he had very much been a part of the household of Pope John XXIII. When I mentioned to the Cardinal that I would like to obtain some background on the pontificate of Pope John XXIII which was germane to the subject of this book, Cardinal Silvestrini's response was immediate: "Why don't you go to see Archbishop Capovilla and pose the questions yourself?" Loris Capovilla had been the private secretary of Pope John XXIII, dating back to the time when that pontiff had become the Cardinal Patriarch of Venice in 1953. I was astonished at the answer. "Do you think such a thing is possible?" I queried. "Of course," he said, "I'll call him now."

Within two days I was climbing the stairs of the rather steep hill that runs alongside the Casa Roncalli, Pope John's home in the village of his birth, Sotto il Monte, not too far from Milan. I was greeted at the door by a Sister from a local religious institute. Monsignor Loris Capovilla now occupies that house, and he greeted me warmly at the door to his study. I was astonished for the second time! He looked exactly the same as when I had first met him some years before, and not very different from those days in the early 1960s when he was constantly seen at Pope John's side. A small and wiry man, he maintains a lively personality, a keen memory, and an astute sense of interpretation.

As I settled in a chair, I was struck more and more by the fact that much of the character of Pope John could be found in Capovilla's style and personality. He truly loved Pope John, and, if nothing else, that truth conveyed itself tangibly. He seemed to remember everything. As I pursued the questions that I had for him, mostly regarding the composition and content of the Pontiff's social encyclicals *Mater Magistra* and *Pacem in Terris,* I continued to hear the name Augustin Cardinal Bea. Of course, I myself was familiar with the ecumenical endeavor of the late Cardinal Bea, having spent some time as a staff member of the Secretariat for Promoting Christian Unity. At that time I worked with his first colleagues and staff members. Cardinal Bea's private secretary, Father Stjepan Schmidt, S.J., was both a colleague and a friend. In our time together, I continually pumped him for information about the early days of the foundation of the Secretariat for Promoting Christian Unity. His biography of the Cardinal has ever remained at my side since its publication in Italian in 1987.

But now, here was Pope John's secretary making continual reference to Cardinal Bea in almost every conceivable context. Obviously, Bea had been Pope John's closest advisor, as is according to conventional ecumenical wisdom. Of course, I had known Bea to be *the great* ecumenical pioneer for Roman Catholic engagement in the development of the worldwide ecumenical movement. But now, Archbishop Capovilla made reference to him in multiple contexts, which included the shape of the Second Vatican Council, international crises, social justice issues, peace endeavors such as the Cuban Missile Crisis, the revival of Latin and biblical languages, biblical studies themselves, and of course, liturgical reform. Most especially they were mutually concerned with a modern, up-to-date system of communications between the Holy See and the rest of the world, at every level. This gave me cause to wonder, "Why Bea?" The response again was immediate!

"Because he was a German," replied the prelate. *"Everything is contained in that truth."* Then there was silence. It all came clear to me: the pontificate of John XXIII, and his overwhelming hunger to dissolve the multiple disunities of the world, stemmed from the astute historical training that was at the core of his intellectual mettle. Angelo Roncalli, later Pope John XXIII, was *born* to be sensitive to history. He was conscious of his place in it, just as during his youth he was in wonder at the person of Saint Charles Borromeo and his place in the Italian history of the immediate post-Tridentine Period. He had even produced five scholarly volumes on that subject. For Pope John, Bea expressed in his very person the self-reflection of the Pope's personal understanding of his own place as Chief Shepherd in post-Nazi Europe. From that time, I became committed to looking for the theological and historical merger that verified the memory and insight of Loris Capovilla.

As pontiff, John XXIII actually grew into his ecumenical vocation so that among his final words were, "Never forget it, *Ut Unum Sint* (That They May All Be One)." Pope John's successor, Paul VI, took up the theme of discernment of the times when, in his first encyclical, *Ecclesiam Suam* (His Church), he cited the prophet Jeremiah (cf. 1:6ff.). Formulating principles of dialogue such as "gradualness" and "perseverance," he also spoke about the "historicity" of Pope John's vocation and of his own: "Our dialogue too must take cognizance of the slowness of human and historical development, and wait for the hour when God may make it effective" (*Ecclesiam Suam,* no. 77).

C. My Motives

Three motives have moved me to address this topic here in order to trace the history of the foundation of the Secretariat for Promoting Christian Unity. First, it is now more than forty years since the Secretariat for Promoting Christian Unity was founded and, as it were, attempted to find its "sea legs." It was my privilege to work for several years with members of the original staff and to enjoy their friendship, their insights, and their zealous commitment. Further, during my tenure in that Vatican dicastery, it was still known as the Secretariat for Promoting Christian Unity. As such, it still had the traces of a "movement," and even though the state of the office was somewhat primitive, there was no inconvenience, for the atmosphere remained one of freshness, vigor, and clear direction.[8] There was something revolutionary among those of my colleagues who had experienced the early days under Cardinal Bea. I have long desired to recapture in writing something of that first fervor.

Secondly, I fear that ecumenical enthusiasm is now waning around the world. Karl Barth, one of the academic heroes of the twentieth century, has consistently been clear in his approach to the Church: "God is speaking" and demands mighty decisions that are absolute and will release a veritable flood.[9] A part of that primary mission, which has been entrusted to the Church, is the mandate to unity: "I pray, Father, that they may be one, as we are one, that the world may believe that you have sent me" (Jn. 17:21). The vocation to unity is irrevocably established by Christ as the image of Christ and his Church. Hence, it must not be allowed to be lost.

Thirdly, I am extremely grateful for the education in ecumenism I received when serving as a member of the staff of the Secretariat for Promoting Christian Unity. Most of my former confreres had actually been a part of the subject of this book and the history in which it developed. One of those confreres, the late Monsignor William A. Purdy, left a challenge in his 1965 book, *The Church on the Move*, which I took personally. He wrote: "An interesting essay remains to be written on what (Cardinal Eugenio) Pacelli's (later Pius XII) sojourn in Germany contributed to German ecumenism, considered afterward, so daring, and advanced by many

8. The term *movement* is used in a sociological sense, implying spontaneity, creativity, and the clustering of people of like mind, as distinct from an institution, which connotes "the permanency of establishment."

9. Karl Barth, *The Word of God and the Word of Man* (Brookline, Mass.: Pilgrim Press, 1928), pp. 242-243.

who regarded Pius XII as something of a symbol of intransigence."[10] Purdy's premise at the time was that the pontificate of John XXIII was a natural segue from that of Pope Pius XII. To a certain extent, this dissertation attempts to provide a prolegomenon to Purdy's challenge, for it contains much history which is centered in Germany.

This work, therefore, at first written under the title *The Ecumenical Endeavor of Cardinal Bea*, tells the story of the birth of the Secretariat for Promoting Christian Unity, its historical roots and its historical sensitivity, all of which contributed to the end product of the formal recognition of the ecumenical cause through the Secretariat for Promoting Christian Unity, and later in the Pontifical Council for Christian Unity. The wider vision of an historically based Church, as distinct from the image, say, of "the perfect society," is the goal which I have intended in this narrative. In the preparatory papers for the Lund Conference of the World Council of Churches, the late Yves Cardinal Congar, O.P., made this same point. An understanding of history is of the essence for the ecumenical movement and the World Council of Churches. In order to facilitate this measure, I have attempted to return to primary sources. Some material, notably correspondence between Jaeger and Bea, is seen here for the first time in print. Certainly the Latin letter of Archbishop Jaeger to Pope John has not been previously published in full. It is found in the text and in the Appendix. The Appendix, too, by way of example, contains some primary documents relevant to the formation of the narrative, notably letters from Cardinal Bea and Cardinal Jaeger.

The publication of this book, *"Because He Was a German!"* coincides with the first anniversary of the election of Joseph Cardinal Ratzinger as Pope Benedict XVI. The choice of that name, which Paul VI had already determined would represent the development of the Christian culture of Europe, bespeaks a concern for the Europe of the present time. In order to address issues of dialogue and evangelization, ongoing problems of de-Christianization, and outright antipathy between religious families of the world, the College of Cardinals reached right into historical Germany to find a representative of the cause of unity, and especially of Christian unity, in one who had studied contemporary German theological thinking and who had actually suffered Germany's twentieth-century burdens. Hence, the title of this book, *"Because He Was a German!" Cardinal Bea and the Origins of Roman Catholic Engagement in the Ecumenical Movement*; a title which I was inclined to give it from the inception of this study.

10. William A. Purdy, *The Church on the Move* (New York: John Day Company, 1965).

D. My Collaborators

Before proceeding, it is important to indicate that I have relied upon interviews with individuals who were pioneers in the process of ecumenical exchange and establishment. I am most grateful to Archbishop Loris Capovilla, Private Secretary to Pope John XXIII; Father Stjepan Schmidt, S.J., Private Secretary to Cardinal Bea; Fathers Thomas Stransky, C.S.P., Walter Abbott, S.J., Monsignor Erich Salzmann, and the late Father John Long, S.J., all of whom shared their memories of particular incidents. The author is likewise grateful to Monsignor Eleuterio Francesco Fortino, currently under-Secretary of the Pontifical Council for the Promotion of Christian Unity, as well as Monsignor Nikolaus Wyrwoll, who provided me with direction and support during my time with the Secretariat. Alas, Monsignor William Purdy, Monsignor Richard Stewart, Bishop Jean-Francois Arrighi, former under-Secretary of the Secretariat, and Father John Hotchkin, Director of the United States Bishops Committee for Ecumenical and Inter-Religious Affairs (NCCB), are no longer with us. However, they offered guidance and advice for this story. In a special category stand Doctor Willem Visser 't Hooft, first General Secretary of the World Council of Churches; the late Doctor Paul Abrecht, formerly Director of the Church and Society sub-unit of the World Council of Churches; Bishop Basil Meeking, formerly Bishop of Christ Church in New Zealand, who was my mentor in Rome. I served with a magnificent support staff in the Secretariat. Among these were Corinna de Martini, Josette Kersters, Dr. Paola Fabrizi, Marigloria Lanni, and Sister Pierluisa Albini of the Congregation of the Daughters of St. Paul. Dr. Marjorie Weeke of the Pontifical Council for Social Communications is a great friend and guide. Jorge Cardinal Mejia provided advice and, at the time, consolation. His memories were invaluable. Finally, it was my greatest privilege to have served in the Secretariat for Promoting Christian Unity under Johannes Cardinal Willebrands. Recently, he reminded me that he is not a theologian but a philosopher, who was involved in a lifelong search for relevant language. He also reminded me that neither Cardinal Bea nor Cardinal Jaeger was a theologian. Bea was a biblical scholar, and Jaeger was a budding pedagogical psychologist. Ironically, Willebrands' reminiscences brought him to the conclusion that this great theological enterprise was entered into by men who were not professionally trained in theology. Cardinal Willebrands' leadership, wisdom and insight have affected the entire Church. His gentle personality continues to touch and inspire me to the present day.

A Note of Gratitude

First and foremost, thanks must be rendered to the Reverend Doctor Joseph Ellul, O.P., of the Theology faculty of St. Thomas Aquinas in Rome. No student could have a better instructor or director. His patience, understanding, insight, and knowledge are unparalleled. The author cannot be grateful enough that Father Ellul accepted the task of directing this dissertation. Thanks, too, must warmly be offered to Dr. Teresa Francesca Rossi, vice-dean of the theology faculty at the Angelicum, a brilliant teacher and admirable friend.

The author's gratitude is also warmly extended to the Very Reverend Doctor Charles Morerod, O.P., who has been profuse in his enthusiasm and patience. His encouragement has been a source of strength. His wisdom and his instruction are a genuine sign of hope for ecumenism's future.

Heartfelt appreciation must also be expressed to my cousin, Loretta Vereb, who provided secretarial services in organizing and recording this material. She is the epitome of fidelity and perseverance. Most of all, she gave unwavering encouragement to the completion of this task.

Many thanks are also rendered to Andrew G. Wilson, who has not only provided technical service but has also opened new doors to friendship. More than anything else, I am grateful for his buoyant spirit, which transformed every day that I worked with him.

Sincere thanks also must be expressed to my Provincial, the Very Reverend Terence Kristofak, C.P., who permitted me to study. They too go to the Very Reverend Joseph R. Jones, who acted as counselor and provincial *Ombudsman* for my many needs during the period of this writing. An expression of deep appreciation and gratitude is likewise due to the Most

Reverend Jose-Augustin Orbegozzo, C.P., an authentic biblical scholar and formerly the General Superior of the Passionist Congregation. More than any other Superior of my past, he embodies a significant and relevant spirit of St. Paul of the Cross, founder of the Passionists, and has acted always with compassion. His permissions and his advice have always led me to new plateaus.

Grateful remembrance is expressed to the late Reverend Monsignor Doctor Aloys Klein of the Archdiocese of Paderborn. Many long years ago, he led me deep into the narrative of this subject. In recent years, he led me into its archives. Always, Monsignor Klein has been a priest of great breadth, depth, and charity. From the time of our first meeting in 1978 until his recent death, he has continued to lead me deep into the subject of ecumenism. More than anyone, *he* was "present at the creation."

I am also in great debt to the faculty, students, and staff of the Seminary of the Immaculate Conception in Huntington, New York. Special thanks go to the Seminary Leadership, Monsignor Francis J. Schneider, Monsignor Robert Emmet Fagan, and Monsignor James McDonald. I must also acknowledge with gratitude and esteem my fellow faculty members — Jeffrey Pedersen, O.S.F., Academic Dean; Fr. Charles Caccavale, my patient co-editor; and my stylistic advisor, Fr. Richard Henning. Seminarians Thomas Tassone and Lee Descoteaux are expert editors, writers, and masters of format and indexing. Without their help I could not have completed this task. Elyse Hayes and her library staff of Carol Bruckner and Frances Brophy have been outstanding in their generosity and patience. So, too, have Bernadette Grodman, Beverly Malone, Rose Sullivan, and Margaret Hoenig. Finally, my Diocesan Bishop William Murphy helped introduce me to this topic almost thirty years ago. At the time, we were both junior clergy, working in different departments of the Roman Curia, but both interested in ecumenism. Since that time, his friendship and support have been unfailing and he has always been worthy of my gratitude and esteem.

Prologue

The German Context
of the Ecumenical Movement

The Challenge of Monsignor Purdy

As has been cited above, Canon William Purdy suggested that a major contribution to the worldwide Ecumenical Movement might have been forged by Roman Catholic pioneers in the Germany between the Wars. This timeframe coincided with the diplomatic ministry of Archbishop Eugenio Pacelli, who became Pope Pius XII in 1939. On February 13, 2003, the Secret Archives of the Vatican released the documents pertinent to Pacelli's dual diplomatic mission to Munich and Berlin. Missing from these are the 1931-1934 files from the Papal Nuncio's Palace in Berlin, which were destroyed by Allied bombers in 1945.[1] It is therefore impossible at this time to reconstruct a satisfactory paper trail regarding Pacelli's interaction with the Roman Catholic hierarchy and theologians. The evidence, however, does indicate that German theological thought (from Johann Adam Möhler through Karl Adam and Romano Guardini) was very much present to him when he drafted his encyclicals, *Mystici Corporis* (1943) and *Mediator Dei* (1947). His projection regarding a new and universal image of the Church would become clear later, through the ecumenical endeavor of Cardinal Augustin Bea, S.J. In 1959-1960, in concert with Archbishop Lorenz Jaeger, Bea would become the focal point for the inauguration of the Roman Catholic phase of the worldwide Ecumenical Movement. Purdy's insight was, therefore, historically accurate. It is

1. Nicole Winfield, "Vatican Speeds Up Opening Pre-WWII Archives," *Pittsburgh Post-Gazette,* February 14, 2003, p. A-6.

important, first of all, to think of Germany as a cradle for the exercise of Roman Catholic ecumenical activity.

The Roman Catholic call to Christian Unity was indeed strongest in Germany during the first half of the twentieth century. Two books from the pre-War era, *Germania Religiosa Nel 3 Reich*[2] and *Der Kampf um die Kirche im Dritten Reich,*[3] both published in the early years of the Nazi Era, prove that in the vastly growing secular world of that totalitarian regime, theological and cultural questions were, in fact, not a cause for further dispute, but rather a reason to encourage a coming together. Such an atmosphere in the Christian world of Germany, brought about a re-study of the significance of the Classical Reformation. Names such as Joseph Lortz, Adolf Herte, and Karl Adam are attached to the documentary evidence that, even as Germany was gearing up for war, a new and deeper fervor for the fruit of historical study, as a basis for the renewal of the cause of Christian Unity, was already under way.

Max Josef Metzger is likewise significant because he embodied the ecumenical sentiments of the time into a brotherhood which he called *Una Sancta* (One and Holy). His very presence in history bespeaks the themes of the call to holiness, grassroots ecumenism, the gift of prophesy and, most significantly, spiritual ecumenism, all of which would come under the category of *Lebenswelt* (the lived world).[4] This latter theme called for the association of morality and piety. Between Metzger's execution by Nazi soldiers in 1944 and the inauguration of the Second Vatican Council in 1962, no one succeeded in expressing it better than the then-very-young Hans Küng:

> Schism is a scandal. But it is perhaps a greater scandal that the majority of Christians, in all communities, even today, and including theologians and pastors, are profoundly indifferent to this scandal; that they feel the division of Christendom, at most, as a deplorable imperfection, not as an immeasurably crippling wound, which absolutely must be healed; that they are deeply concerned over a thousand religious trivialities, but not over our Lord's desire that "all may be one." Will the words and actions of the Pope be enough to awaken these sleepers?[5]

2. Mario Bendiscioli, translated and published as *Nazism versus Christianity* (London: Skeffington & Son, Ltd., 1938).

3. Waldemar Gurian, published as *Hitler and the Christians* (London: Sheed & Ward, 1936).

4. Leonard J. Swidler, *The Ecumenical Vanguard: The History of the Una Sancta Movement* (Pittsburgh: Duquesne University Press, 1966), pp. 141-66.

5. Hans Küng, *The Council Reform and Reunion* (New York: Sheed & Ward, 1961), p. 57.

It was given to the heroism and persistence of Lorenz Jaeger (1892-1975), Archbishop of Paderborn, to provide institutional protection for the Ecumenical Movement, first through the Fulda Bishops Conference and later through his own creative diocesan activities. Jaeger buttressed the talents, insights and good sense of the biblical scholar, Augustin Bea, S.J. (1881-1968), when *his hour* came.

Bea was to bring his biblical skills and his love of the *magisterium* of the Church to the Ecumenical Movement, giving it a theological base not through argument, but through demonstration. By this time, Bea was a Cardinal and had direct access to Pope John XXIII. The goodness of that old pontiff's heart somehow transcended words, jurisdictional authority and theoretical obfuscations, in order to give the Secretariat for Promoting Christian Unity a home in the Curial family at Rome. The material which follows is a narration of those events and a recall of personalities who emerged in the pre-War, the Second World War, the post-War, and the Cold War moments of twentieth-century history. These personalities promoted the idea that the unity of the Church is an essential premise of the mission of Christ (Jn. 17:21).

"He Was a German!"

What follows is also an attempt to make a contribution to the understanding of the origins of the Roman Catholic Ecumenical Movement and the particular person who animated it, Augustin Bea, S.J. When asked about the quick nomination of Augustin Bea, as First President of the Secretariat for Promoting Christian Unity, once Bea's proposal to Pope John XXIII had been assured, Archbishop Loris Capovilla, John's private secretary, replied immediately that it was *"because he was a German!"*[6] Bea carried his "Germanness" with him, but he also carried his prior proximity to Pius XII, for he was that pontiff's confessor and advisor in both personal affairs and in matters of substance for the entire Catholic Church. From this perspective, after forty years, it is possible to present this material. Much is drawn from the strength of the contemporary school of *Kerygmatic* theology, which likewise emerged in the Germany of the early twentieth century.[7]

6. Interview with the author, March 28, 2000.

7. Refer to Geoffrey Wainwright, *Doxology* (Oxford: Oxford University Press, 1980), p. 178. The term *"Kerygmatic theology"* refers most especially to that school of North European thought, in which the centrality of Christ and the good news of his proclamation is emphasized as the basis of all theological undertaking. Most specifically it was represented by Matthias Josef Scheeben, Romano Guardini and Karl Adam. Biblically based and pastorally

Now forty years later, the Secretariat for Promoting Christian Unity, once a provisional entity among Conciliar commissions, is a permanent dicastery with the distinctive title of Pontifical Council for Christian Unity. This had been foreseen by Bea, Jaeger and Pope John himself. The origins come directly from a rich and complex German history.

It may seem strange that the cradle of modern Roman Catholic ecumenism is located in German history. However, now with the availability of certain papers from the Paderborn archives, pertinent to the ministry of the later Cardinal Jaeger, it is possible to confirm that truth. In 1930, Jesuit Max Pribilla wrote a book entitled *Um Kirchliche Einheit* (Concerning Church Unity).[8] This book was a seminal study, which candidly admitted that Christian sectarian life had *no longer* any significance in Germany. In this book and numerous articles, Pribilla wrote about the Protestant discovery of Catholicism, which followed the First World War, with the abdication of the Kaiser and the collapse of the German Empire. Catholic and Protestant alike, in that period, if true to their fundamental Christian vocation, were in search of the "mystic body of Christ [*sic*]," the affirmation that Christ was the center of the worship and the life of Christianity; and that all moral doctrine was, fundamentally, a theorization of the imitation of Christ and identified with the very life of Christ.[9] Because of reliance upon sacraments and sacramentals, Catholics appeared to be more stable in those revolutionary years; but they too were caught up in the progressive disintegration of their cultural domain. What happened?

A Reformation Slogan: No Longer Tenable

When it fell in 1918, the German Empire took with it the multiple principalities and aristocratic territories that were characteristic of its constitutive elements. With that collapse, there likewise fell the principle "*Cujus regio, ejus*

---

oriented, it likewise embraces the Incarnational theology of Karl Rahner. Kerygmatic theology, for reasons to be outlined in this thesis, likewise found a special cradle in the German experience with the search for ecclesiastical truth and ecclesiological meaning or significance. The core principle of Kerygmatic theology has been stated by Geoffrey Wainwright: "It is *into the present* that the New Testament message must be preached. . . ."

8. Max Pribilla, S.J. (1874-1956), an early and outspoken opponent of the Nazis, was also a competent ecumenist. His commentary, which began as early as 1926, shows the consistency of German interest in the subject, even at the height of the Second World War. It is possible to plot his writing in Swidler, *op. cit.,* pp. 35, 76, 120-36, 192-93, 206, and 216.

9. Bendiscioli, *op. cit.,* p. 131.

religio" (To the holder of the land, the religion of the land). Naturally, there were mass apostasies from Christianity; the German population became subject to a new and different openness, favored mainly by the parties of the Left, who sought to impose a system of government by atheists. Hence, *there was a fertile field for the inception of a movement* to find a *raison d'être* for the cause of Christian unity.[10] During the twenty years between the Armistice of 11 November 1918 and the occupation of Czechoslovakia by Germany in 1938, intense intellectual activity was undertaken, although by the few, to look toward the history of Germany at the time of the Classical Reformation and to offer the public the results of those findings.[11] While the undertaking was heavily academic, the fruits were always intended to be pastoral. During that time, rumors arose. For example, in 1934, the United Press International (UPI) falsely reported an appeal to the Pope by six-hundred Lutheran pastors, who in the face of Nazism, had asked to be received into the Catholic Church. Yet, while that story was false, Cardinal Michael Faulhaber, Roman Catholic Archbishop of Munich and president of the Bavarian Bishops Conference, and Baron von Pechmann, leading spokesperson of the German Evangelical Church, were actually at the center of inaugural ecumenical activities, which indicated the mood of the times.[12] Behind all this lurked the dark, foreboding specter of the Third Reich.[13]

10. The change occurred in Catholic Luther scholarship with the appearance of an article in the *Hochland* in 1917 entitled "Martin Luther's Religious Psyche as the Root of a New Philosophical World View." Franz Xavier Kiefl, "Martin Luther's *religiösepsyche als Wurzel eines neuen philosophischen Weltbildes*," *Hochland* XV (1917/1918): 7-28: all found in Swidler, *op. cit.*, p. 21.

11. *Ibid.* pp. 19-20. For example, Max Pribilla offered the conclusion that the sixteenth century Reformation would never have taken place if the Church and her representatives had been living up to their mission. He wrote in 1929: "Protestants and Catholics, both bear guilt for the present circumstances and neither has the right to raise himself above the other." At the same time, The Reverend Doctor Paul Simon, who was to become, in the beginning of Jaeger's episcopate, both the rector of the Paderborn Cathedral and his principal ecumenical advisor, stated that "the split of (1517) would never have come if, at the time of the Reformation, the burning questions had been handled as religious questions from religious men." Also, in 1929-1931, notable theological historians, Sebastian Merkle and Hubert Jedin, debunked the popular image of Luther, offered by Heinrich Denifle, that Luther was an immoral man with an immoral motive. Along with Hartmann Grisar, Denifle depicted Luther as enraged and spiteful, "*Wildheit und Rohheit* ('Hate and Anger')." Without a doubt, all the terrible words of Luther, full of hate and anger, are actually found in Luther's writings, but the persistent complaint was raised that this was far from all that was contained in Luther's writings. That view had already been supported by the encyclical of Pope Leo XIII, *Militantis Ecclesiae*.

12. Bendiscioli, *op. cit.*, p. 126.

13. The apocalypticism of the moment is clearly demonstrated in such individuals as Fa-

The Testimony of Cardinal Willebrands

With the arrival of National Socialism in the 1930s, the theory became reality, as Catholics and Protestants alike actually collaborated with each other, to challenge the paganism of the Hitler years. According to Cardinal Johannes Willebrands and his secretary, Josette Kersters, who clearly remembered those years, *this* was the single greatest cause for the dynamic of the Ecumenical Movement, i.e., *the "life together" of Protestant and Catholic clerics in concentration camps.* According to Willebrands, the theory mentioned above "received its life and purpose from that fact." He mentioned this to the author in the presence of witnesses on September 3, 2002. In fact, in that era, the real fight was between Christianity and the materialism of atheistic and totalitarian systems, thus dramatically revealing the essential apocalyptic character of the Third Reich. At the center of that particular movement was the moral question of the validity of the oath to Hitler sworn by civil servants, members of the government, and by the military.[14] The anguish of the moment was best expressed by Pastor Dietrich Bonhoeffer, who explained to the faculty and students of Union Theological Seminary, in New York City, why, in 1933, he had to return to Germany:

> I must live through this difficult period of our national history with the Christian people of my own country. . . . Christians in Germany will face the terrible alternative of either willing the defeat of their nation in order that Christian civilization may survive, or willing the victory of their nation and thereby destroying our civilization. I know which of these alternatives I must choose; but I can not make that choice in security.[15]

In history, Bonhoeffer stands apart from Herte, Adam and Lortz who tried to find a synthesis between Christianity and Nazism, but he stands with

---

ther (now Blessed) Rupert Mayer, S.J., a highly decorated Catholic military chaplain during the First World War. Mayer was at first enthusiastic about the Nazi Party. He even addressed German crowds along with Hitler. Slowly, he learned that the aims of National Socialism were totalitarian, racist, pagan, anti-Christian and global. His courageous outspokenness about Hitler then led him to a martyr's crown. Refer to Ronald J. Rychlak, *Hitler, the War and the Pope* (Huntington, Ind.: Our Sunday Visitor Press, 2000), p. 19.

14. Mary Alice Gallin, O.S.U., *German Resistance to Hitler* (Washington, D.C.: Catholic University of America Press, 1961), pp. 26-79. Mother Gallin, herein, analyzes the anxieties of the conspirators in order to bring down the Nazi regime.

15. Cited in George Bell, *The Church and Humanity* (New York: Longmans, Green and Co., 1946), p. 187.

Pribilla and Metzger in his opposition to the government.[16] No one escaped unscathed. All were affected by the terrible events of those years. Therefore it can be said that twentieth-century Germany is, in a very real sense, the ecumenical theater in which the meaning, indeed the necessity, of the Ecumenical Movement was best expressed in palpable and very urgent terms.

The Role of Cardinal Bea in the German Drama

The reference to Max Metzger, above, indicates that he both used and popularized the term "*Una Sancta* (One and Holy)" as a kind of shorthand for the Ecumenical Movement. It also indicated that Metzger represented a *Lebenswelt,* i.e., a popular piety. The term *Una Sancta* represents the quest to disclose the sanctity of the Church, which is inherent in the four claims of the Church: One, Holy, Catholic, and Apostolic. Metzger's use of the term *Una Sancta* is not original; it dates back to the sixteenth century when it became clear that the words and actions of Luther effected not a reform of the Church but rather produced a severance from the Church.[17] Once this was realized, movements to facilitate a reconciliation sprang up under the title *Una Sancta.* In the twentieth century, Metzger applied that term to both his personal ecumenical endeavor and to his *Brüderschaft* (brotherhood).[18]

The term was taken over by Archbishop Lorenz Jaeger of Paderborn in his wartime defense of ecumenical scholars and of the Ecumenical Move-

16. The story of Adam and Lortz and that of their colleague Michael Schmaus is found in Gunter Lewy, *The Catholic Church in Nazi Germany* (New York: McGraw-Hill, 1964), pp. 107-9. They were labeled pro-Nazi and after the war were prohibited from teaching for many years. Following the publication of Lewy's book, the European press turned attention to all the members of the Fulda Bishops Conference of Germany. Naturally, Archbishop Lorenz Jaeger likewise came under the light of scrutiny. He therefore was the subject of a book by Heribert Gruss, entitled *Erzbischop Lorenz Jaeger als kirchen führer im dritten Reich* (Paderborn: Bonifatius, 1995). Gruss makes no secret that Jaeger was appointed archbishop from the position of *Divisionspfarrer* and even depicts him in Wehrmacht uniform. Gruss highlights Jaeger's efforts to keep the Church together and to ensure its integrity.

17. The term *Una Sancta* remained in continued use for four hundred years. The best example is taken from a written statement of St. Clement Maria Höfbauer, C.SS.R., who wrote in 1816: "Since I have been a papal delegate in Poland, I have become certain that the defection from the Church has come about because the Germans had, and still have, a need to be pious. The Reformation was not spread and held by heretics and philosophers, but by men who were really searching for a religion for the heart." That quotation is taken from Friedrich Perthe, *Leben von Clemens Theodor Perthes,* Vol. II (Hamburg: Herder, 1851), p. 160.

18. Swidler, *op. cit.,* pp. 144-45.

ment itself.[19] Jaeger's efforts at this time were a watershed in the development of the worldwide Ecumenical Movement. Locally oriented at first, these efforts would later, through the Fulda Bishops Conference, converge with other ecumenical initiatives. The background of the nightmare years of the Second World War provided Jaeger with the sense of urgency to carry out these initiatives. Furthermore, he *had* to act with discretion. According to the evidence given by his secretary on October 15, 2001, the subject of ecumenism addressed the issue of the entire Christian family in Germany, then under subtle but certain persecution by the Nazi Party and its philosophy. Jaeger was not free to raise directly the question he would have liked to lay on the table regarding the Christian Church in Germany at that time. He therefore acted with deftness and discretion. The matter did not end for him with the Second World War. He deepened his *Una Sancta* activities in the decade of the 1950s. Under the title *Una Sancta*, Jaeger submitted a letter of petition to Pope John XXIII on March 11, 1960, requesting a permanent body, within the Roman Curia, to promote the cause of Christian Unity, to alleviate prejudice within the Christian family and to facilitate ready access to clear and precise information for the sake of a non–Roman Catholic constituency.[20] The cause begun by Jaeger was rooted in his position of responsibility during the Second World War and it continued during the Cold War. As a Cold War issue, it found its place in the program of the pontificate of Pope John XXIII.

During the war years, Augustin Bea, S.J., was rector and professor at Rome's Pontifical Biblical Institute. He lived in extra-territorial surroundings of the Vatican, and enjoyed a marginal amount of freedom in German-occupied Rome. Although he, himself, was a German National, he did not sympathize with Nazi causes or philosophy. It is known that he protected Jews from arrest during the Roman pogrom of the Germans. He carefully followed theological and pastoral developments in his native country. It would later fall to Bea, as a Cardinal, to provide the theory upon which Jaeger's new ecumenical body would operate. Bea did not operate alone, of course. He was an heir to a rich and vibrant twenty-year tradition in which Lorenz Jaeger was the central figure, and from which he derived his sense of direction. Secondly, Bea worked as a principal collaborator of Pope John XXIII. At the beginning of those days, in a speech entitled "The Catholic Attitude toward the Problem," he outlined his ecumenical theory,

19. Interview of Monsignor Aloys Klein with the author, October 15, 2001.

20. Vicar General's Archives: Paderborn. Draft letter entitled "Beatissime pater," Archbishop Lorenz Jaeger to Pope John XXIII, unprotocoled and unpublished, March 4, 1960.

which may be considered the *declaratio* of the Secretariat for Promoting Christian Unity:

> In this connection, it is interesting to notice the Holy Father's (Pope John XXIII) words in the recent discourse at the opening of the preparatory work of the Council. He says that "one great point to be held firmly by *every baptized person*" is that "the Church remains forever his mystical Body (Christ's). He is the head, to it each of us believers is related, to it we belong." . . . For their part, separated brethren, according to the teaching of *Mystici Corporis,* are related to the mystical Body of the Redeemer "by some unconscious yearning and desire" . . . because fundamentally, even if not fully, they belong to the Church, they also have the benefit of the influence of God's grace.[21]

For this reason, Bea can truly be said to be responsible for providing the foundation for a new ecumenical consciousness regarding the Church. His vision is founded in the sacrament of Baptism and, through very capable biblical scholarship, he delivered a limpid explication of the import of the Ecumenical Movement. His terminology was neither convoluted nor inaccessible. His motto was "doing the truth in charity (Eph. 4:15)!"[22] Cardinal Bea proved an effective representative of the inaugural stage of Roman Catholic ecumenism. In Germany, many developments occurred, even during the Nazi era. As we will see, Bea maintained contacts with his native land and especially at the end of the wartime with theological developments obtained through his professional ties. It was, however, at just this right moment that Lorenz Jaeger, Archbishop of Paderborn, would provide a bridge and incentive, which in turn would spark Bea's ecumenical ministry and career.

---

21. Augustin Cardinal Bea, *Unity of Christians* (London: Jeffrey Chapman, 1963), pp. 32-33 (emphasis mine).

22. Bea's best summary of his motto contains these words: "The love of truth, without love, becomes intolerant and repels. Love without truth is blind and can not last. . . . They must be combined harmoniously, each in its place and according to its own weight. When they are united in this way, they can be effective in uniting people and creating harmony." This discourse is taken from the Second Agape Meeting of Rome in 1963, found in Stjepan Schmidt, S.J., *Augustin Bea: The Cardinal of Unity* (New Rochelle, N.Y.: New City Press, 1992), p. 576. This motto is not to be confused with Bea's Cardinalatial motto: *In Nomine Domini Jesu* (In the Name of the Lord Jesus). Maria Buchmüller, *Augustin Kardinal Bea* (Augsburg: Verlag Winfried-Werk, 1972), p. 85.

Chapter One

A Middle Eastern Prelude to Vatican Two and Its Historical Implications

Introduction

The aim of this chapter is to demonstrate the historical context of this study. In fact, before the nomination of Augustin Bea as Cardinal in late 1959, a proposal for a type of a Vatican Secretariat for Promoting Christian Unity was offered to Pope John XXIII by Patriarch Maximos IV Saigh of Antioch. While Pope John never acted on this request, the correspondence is significant in that it recalled for the pontiff that people were speaking much about ecumenism in those days. The allusion to a Catholic Movement for the Promotion of Christian Unity is fleshed out by tracing the significant ecumenical activities, ideas and persons that emerged in the first part of the twentieth century. Since Germany and its two principal representatives in this field are at the heart of this work, the German theater is the subject of Chapter Two.

Hence, Chapter One is a long, but necessary, prelude which, in two ways, provides an idea of the ecumenical atmosphere which preceded the pontificate of Pope John XXIII, as well as an examination of the ecumenical expectations of the Patriarchate of Antioch, which sought to speak about this subject on behalf of Eastern Christians. In an amazing moment, practically unremembered today, perhaps even unknown to most, the Eastern desires and Western ecumenical history coalesced into mutuality. What follows below is a narrative of this phenomenon.

Part 1: The Importance of Maximos IV Saigh

A Message of Condolence

Cardinal Augustin Bea died on 15 November 1968. In his old age, this inde-fatigable Jesuit Cardinal became the foremost figure in the foundation and development of the Secretariat for Promoting Christian Unity, prior to the Second Vatican Council. Cardinal Bea was eighty-seven years old at the time of his demise. The causes of his death were heart failure, Pfeiffer's dis-ease (mononucleosis) and pneumonia.[1] In the Cardinal's last days, Pope Paul VI visited him at Rome's Villa Stuart, a private medical clinic. When he departed, the pope was visibly moved. The two men were long-time friends, as well as intimate collaborators within the Roman Curia. Previ-ously they had served together in the household of Pope Pius XII.[2] The death of Cardinal Bea occasioned the revelation to Pope Paul that Cardinal Bea's ecumenical work was, in fact, preceded by a little-known history which had its origins in the Middle East.

Pope Paul VI was deeply grieved when he received the news of Bea's death. Among those who wrote letters of condolence to the pontiff was Maximos V Hakim, Greek Melchite Patriarch of Antioch, Alexandria and Jerusalem.[3] Maximos V's letter would contain some previously unknown information, which in itself disclosed a significant moment in the develop-ing history of Roman Catholic Ecumenism.

Patriarch Maximos V related to Pope Paul that his predecessor, Maximos IV Saigh, had written on 23 May 1959, proposing to Pope John XXIII that he (Pope John) establish a bureau to "exist in the Roman Curia as a new Congregation or special Roman Commission for the whole field of relations with Christian Churches that are not in communion with the Holy See, and for all initiatives aimed at fostering unity."[4] Maximos IV

---

1. Stjepan Schmidt, S.J., *Augustin Bea: The Cardinal of Unity* (New Rochelle, N.Y.: New City Press, 1992), pp. 692-97.

2. *Ibid.*, p. 695.

3. *Id., Le Lien. Bulletin du Patriarcat Grec-Melchite Catholique* 33 no. 5-6 (Nov.-Dec. 1968): 239-43. Herein is contained a partial quotation and a reference to the history of Patri-arch Maximos IV's letter. Schmidt, *op. cit.*, p. 328, stated: "I did not know that such a body (as the Secretariat for Promoting Christian Unity) had also been requested from other quarters." These were Bea's words.

4. "Notre Patriarcat qui, déjà en mai et en août 1959, avait proposé à Jean XXIII l'institution d'un organisme spécial permanent pour s'occuper des questions oecuméniques au sein de la curie romaine . . ." [Our Patriarchate which, already in May and August of 1959, had

had made this proposal to Pope John, regarding an ecumenical bureau, in his own name and that of the entire Melchite Synod.[5] Pope John first met Patriarch Maximos IV Saigh in Lebanon in 1954 when, as Cardinal Roncalli, Cardinal Patriarch of Venice, he visited Beirut, while on mission for the Holy See.[6]

The Foresight of the Patriarch

At the age of eighty-four, Patriarch Maximos IV would become the foremost voice to speak on behalf of the richness of the Eastern Christian tradition and of the wealth of the Patristic heritage, during the first session of the Second Vatican Council, in 1962. Refusing to make his interventions in Latin, according to Council regulations, he insisted on speaking in French, although he was fluent in Latin. He did this in order to show the diversity of languages and cultures within the Catholic Church.[7]

It is conjecture to speculate concerning the specifics and the motives of Maximos' 1959 communication. The archives are closed regarding this matter. However, the atmosphere which permitted the freedom to offer a proposal was cordial, largely because of the style of the pontificate of Pope John XXIII. Pope Paul VI explained in a memoir something of the mindset of his predecessor. Herein, Pope Paul captured Pope John's special understanding of that desire for unity which stemmed from the Christian East. Pope John had, earlier in his life, served as a Papal diplomat in Bulgaria, Romania, Greece and Turkey, countries with significant Orthodox populations. He therefore would have had sympathy for the petition of the Melchite Patriarch, Maximos IV. Here are Cardinal Montini's words about his predecessor:

---

proposed to Pope John XXIII the institution of a special and permanent organization to deal with the ecumenical questions from the bosom of the Roman Curia . . .].

5. *Ibid.*

6. Peter Hebblethwaite, *Pope John XXIII* (Garden City, N.Y.: Doubleday and Co. Inc., 1985), p. 252.

7. Xavier Rynne, *Letters from Vatican City* (New York: Farrar, Straus & Company, 1963), pp. 67, 102. The Melchite Church is dependent in its origins upon the ancient Antioch Patriarchate and over the centuries has evolved in liturgy from the Syrian to the Byzantine Rite, taking upon itself the usages of Constantinople. Affiliated with the Melchite Patriarchate of Antioch are also the Patriarchates of Alexandria and Jerusalem. Patriarch Maximos IV Saigh resided in Beirut, Lebanon. Cyril Charon Korolevsky, *History of the Melkite Patriarchates* (Fairfax, Va.: Eastern Christian Publications, 1998), pp. 2-28.

From the very first days of his pontificate the invitation to separated Christians to return to the bosom of the Church was one of Pope John's dominant leitmotifs. He understood this call to unity in terms of his duty as the good shepherd and brother to all, indeed even in terms of strict dogma: no one arrives at this sheepfold of Jesus Christ save under the guidance of the Pope; there is no salvation without fellowship with him. In his first radio message Pope John expressly invited the whole Church of the East to return, immediately and voluntarily, to the common parental household. This invitation was extended in a spirit of pronounced gentleness and humility. The first Christmas message repeated the call, again with an eye directed more toward the Orthodox Churches. The Eastern Churches also occupied the foreground in his subsequent addresses. Utterances such as: "We do not wish to hold an historical trial, our aim is not to point out who was right and who was wrong. The responsibility is shared on both sides. We want merely to say: let us come together, let us put an end to the divisions," apply specifically to the Eastern Churches.[8]

These recollections of Cardinal Montini reveal a quite narrow sense of both ecclesiology and ecumenism on the part of Pope John in the first days of his pontificate. As he lay dying, Pope John recalled to his secretary, Monsignor Loris Capovilla, the early days of his diplomatic service in Turkey, Greece and the Balkans. During that time, despite tense national situations, Archbishop Roncalli was personally moved by expressions of charity and Christian solidarity which he experienced in his first encounters with Orthodox people. Pope John's history, character, and personality seem to have provided the appropriate catalyst which would have invited the proposal of Maximos IV Saigh.[9]

However, Pope John neither developed, nor even entertained, this first and early request for some sort of bureau for Christian Unity within the Roman Curia. The reason is now known. Monsignor Loris Capovilla recalled the occasion clearly. Faithful to the Curial rules, in reference to a dicastery *per competenza* (for appropriate responsibility), Pope John passed the correspondence along to the head of the Sacred Congregation for the Oriental Churches, Eugene Cardinal Tisserant, a Frenchman, a former army officer, a scholar, antiquarian and the dean of the Sacred College

---

8. *Id., Pope John XXIII* by the Editors of Herder and Herder, 1965, pp. 113-114.

9. Jerome M. Vereb, C.P., *A Joyful Soul* (Kansas City, Mo.: Andrews McMeel, 2000), pp. 105-6.

of Cardinals. Tisserant reviewed the material and wrote across the top of each paragraph, *"No! No! No!"*[10]

The Letter of Patriarch Maximos V Hakim

Pope John did not take up the matter again until a second proposal was offered to him later by Cardinal Augustin Bea and Archbishop Lorenz Jaeger of Paderborn, in March 1960. Archbishop Maximos V Hakim published an account of his predecessor's attempt in the *Bulletin* of the Greek Catholic Melchite Patriarchate of November/December 1968. The occasion, as stated earlier, was a message of condolence upon the death of Cardinal Bea in November of that year. What follows below is taken from that documentation:

Beirut
19 November 1968

Most Holy Father:

    We have read the news of the death of the late Cardinal Augustin Bea in the press which causes us deep sadness. All of us sympathize with the pain which Your Holiness has experienced at the departure of this Eminent Collaborator of your ecumenical apostolate who has linked the views of Your Holiness and those of Your Holy Predecessor, John XXIII, founder of the Secretariat for Promoting Christian Unity. Sincerely, in my own name, and in the name of all the members of the Greek Melchite Episcopate, I offer my deep condolences to Your Holiness. It is true that Cardinal Bea was of the age of eighty-seven, but he had the clarity and vigor of a man in his full prime. He also possessed the activity and the spirit of sacrifice of an extended youth. His knowledge, his holiness of life, his obedience and his understanding made him an excellent instrument in the hands of popes, in their activity for the reconciliation of Christians.

    Our Patriarchate which, in May and again in August, 1959, had already proposed to John XXIII a special and permanent organization to occupy itself with ecumenical questions, under the auspices of

---

10. Interview of Archbishop Loris Capovilla with the author, September 18, 2001. Schmidt discusses the Greek Melchite proposal but glosses over the reason for the lack of attention to it by highlighting Bea's qualifications. Schmidt is unaware that Cardinal Tisserant provided interference to the first proposal. Pope John was respectful of the principle of subsidiarity and heeded the advice of Tisserant (cf. Schmidt, *op. cit.*, p. 328).

the Roman Curia, has been very happy with the creation of the Secretariat, and since has enjoyed with Cardinal Bea and his collaborators good relations, helping them to the best of our ability and, in return, receiving clear encouragement in our own viewpoint both during and after the Council.

Also it is with a full heart that we unite ourselves in the prayer, which Your Holiness raises to God to accompany the valiant soul of our dearly departed Cardinal that he receive the rest and reward which he has so richly deserved.

Receiving the expression of our sincere condolences, we ask the blessing of Your Holiness.

> + Maximos V Hakim
> Patriarch of Antioch, and of all the Orient,
> of Alexandria and of Jerusalem[11]

The Ideas of Maximos IV Saigh

Maximos V Hakim accompanied the publication of his letter to Pope Paul VI with a brief commentary and some extracts from the writings of his predecessor. These are taken from a note (i.e., *pro memoria*) by Patriarch Saigh, which he handed to Pope John personally in his first formal Apostolic Visit, made on 23 May 1959. To be clear, those documents consisted of a letter and a *pro memoria*. The following is a synopsis of those notes. The document begins with words which are both personal and cordial: "A humble suggestion which I confide to the great heart of His Holiness Pope John XXIII."[12]

In the first paragraph of the letter, Maximos Saigh spoke of the subject of the opportunity for ecumenism. In a tersely posed question he asked the pontiff if the actual times could not be more appropriate to engage the church in the apostolate of ecumenism. He stated that the Catholic Church represents Christ on earth. "Should not there be a permanent institution which favors the union of separated churches" [institution permanente en faveur de l'Union des Églises séparées]?" The Patriarch then made a state-

---

11. *Le Lien, op. cit.,* p. 24. The original text is reproduced in the Appendix (translation mine).

12. *Ibid.* "Une humble suggestion que je confie au grand coeur de S.S. le Pape Jean XXIII . . . ," p. 241. The phraseology of the Patriarch clearly indicates that he thought in Arabic but wrote in French. "I confide to the great heart . . ." is an Arabic anthropomorphic expression.

ment of fact: "The Catholic Church is conforming to the desires of Our Savior." The reference, although unstated in Maximos Hakim's extract, is to the Gospel of Saint John, Chapter 17:21, "May they all be one, just as, Father, You are in me and I am in You, so that they also may be in us, so that the world may believe it was You who sent me."[13]

In the next paragraph of his *pro memoria*, Patriarch Maximos Saigh stated that the question was indeed very serious and merited the highest attention. He now specified his request — "the creation of a new Congregation or a special Roman Commission, in order to deal with the relations with those Christian Churches which are not in communion with the Holy See, and all those who are working to advance union."[14] Maximos did not specify why these issues were indeed very grave and deserved the highest attention. However, tensions in the Middle East had constituted an ongoing fact of life since the conclusion of the Second World War, with religious issues facing Eastern Christians as well as Jewish and Muslim communities and states.[15] In Europe, while the Berlin Wall had not yet been constructed, the Cold War was already fueled by atheistic Communism.[16] The Cold War too was a fact of life in Asia, Latin America, and the newly emerging nations of Africa.[17]

According to Maximos Saigh's proposal, as developed in his memo, the new Congregation or Commission would rely upon experts from within the Roman Curia itself. He sought an evolution of already existing resources in personnel and material. The specifics of his recommendation will be outlined below.[18]

Patriarch Maximos Saigh concluded his personal note to Pope John in a hopeful tone. He spoke of "broadening the horizons and *enlarging the hearts*" of those who were making the earliest efforts toward an effective

---

13. *Ibid.*

14. *Ibid.*, "*créer une nouvelle congrégation ou une commission romaine spéciale* pour tout ce qui concerne les relations avec les Églises Chrétiennes qui ne sont pas en communion avec le Saint-Siège," etc. (emphasis in original).

15. For a brief first-person account of the Middle East situation, see Elias Chacour, *Blood Brothers* (Grand Rapids: Chosen Books, 1984), p. 121. A Palestinian and a Roman Catholic priest, Chacour shows great sympathy for the seeming hopelessness of religious and cultural clashes: "To me these terrified masses of Jewish immigrants were never to blame for our tragedy. They were dazed by fear, pathetically desperate to escape the heinous death camps."

16. For a fuller treatment of the Cold War and the Johannine Papacy, see Roland Flamini, *Pope, Premiere and President* (New York: Macmillan Publishing Co., 1980), pp. 16, 54-104.

17. *Ibid.*, p. 8.

18. *Le Lien, op. cit.*, p. 241.

rapprochement with brothers, *separated from the heart* of Christian unity. Such was the legacy of Patriarch Maximos IV Saigh.[19] This is but one example of his thinking in Arabic and writing in French. Maximos, as a religious figure of the Middle East, was accustomed to an anthropology which took for granted religious mysticism.

His successor, Maximos V Hakim, presumed that Cardinal Bea, the future first President of the Secretariat for Promoting Christian Unity, was at least somewhat familiar with the recommendation of Patriarch Saigh.[20] However, Father Stjepan Schmidt recorded in his comprehensive biography, *Augustin Bea: The Cardinal of Unity,* that Bea was actually unaware of "any proposals to Pope John prior to his own."[21] Patriarch Saigh's *pro memoria,* which contained references to the Orthodox context and to the composition of personnel for this proposed bureau, actually contains parallels to later correspondence between Pope John and Cardinals Bea, Tardini, and Cicognani.[22] These later two cardinals served Pope John successively as secretary of state.

A point of convergence between this proposal from Lebanon and the future proposal from Germany is the emphasis on *scholarship.* Already in this first attempt to establish a permanent curial body, Patriarch Saigh outlined the necessity of appropriate theologians and canonists. These were to be *professional academics* who were members of either the dicasteries of the Roman Curia or the faculties of pontifical universities. They were not to be of a "centralist mentality"; i.e., while schooled in their specific discipline, they should be open to making new vistas in order to envision a more unified humanity and a Church of charity. Maximos was also looking for individuals to staff this new commission whose mentality embraced an understanding of the Churches of the East so that in their reflections and in their judgments, they would reveal what was both good and just.[23] Maximos' comment is amusing: "Theologians of this category are not numerous; but, God be thanked, there are some and there will be more and more of them . . ." [Les théologiens de cette catégorie ne sont pas nombreux; mais, Dieu merci, il y en a et de plus en plus . . .].[24] As the years of the Council

---

19. *Ibid.,* pp 242-43. Since the phraseology of the text again indicates that the Patriarch was thinking in Arabic and writing in French, it is safe to say he was accustomed to using the anthropology of Oriental Christian Mysticism (emphasis mine).

20. *Ibid.*

21. Schmidt, *op. cit.,* p. 328.

22. *Ibid.,* pp. 326-32, and *Le Lien, op. cit.,* p. 241.

23. *Ibid.,* p. 241. Centralist mentality implies that all things are referred to Rome.

24. *Ibid.*

were to unfold, Patriarch Maximos Saigh and Cardinal Bea had many opportunities to interact. The Patriarch's suggestions for Conciliar preparation, and the immediate work of the Secretariat for Promoting Christian Unity in that preparation, brought praise from Maximos IV Saigh. In 1962 he wrote a note of admiration about the substantive work within the *schemata* of the Secretariat of Christian Unity for Council discussion.[25] He said that the tone of these preparatory and pre-preparatory documents was quite different from that to which the Council Fathers were accustomed. It really ought to serve as a model for all the times when the Council comes around to discussing the union of Christians.[26]

So impressed was Maximos Saigh with the ongoing work of the Secretariat for Promoting Christian Unity during the Council that, in a 1962 letter, he expressed the hope that in the post-Council years neither the Secretariat for Promoting Christian Unity nor its work would disappear from the permanent life of the Roman Curia.[27] In fact, he said: "It (the Secretariat for Promoting Christian Unity) would be as the permanent, ecumenical conscience of the Roman See and of the entire Catholic Church" [Il serait comme la conscience oecuménique permanente du Siège Romain et de toute l'Eglise Catholique]."[28] As the life and work of the Secretariat for Promoting Christian Unity evolved, Maximos Saigh was unbridled in his enthusiasm for its spirit and efficiency.[29]

Once the Secretariat was actually established in 1960, Maximos immediately wrote to Cardinal Bea, the new president, with felicitations. He conveyed his ideas regarding the future work of the newly erected body, especially for Council preparation in the specialized field of ecumenism. Obviously, from Cardinal Bea's response of 24 July 1960, much of the preliminary correspondence between the two prelates regarding ecumenism touched upon the position of the Oriental Churches. Maximos touched the heart of Cardinal Bea, who wrote movingly: "I desire fervently that the Oriental Church should be conserved in its proper character *founded upon history* and the Oriental mentality" [Je désire vivement que l'Eglise orientale soit conservée dans son propre caractère fondé sur l'histoire et sur la mentalité orientale].[30] From the time of this letter, Bea and Maximos IV Saigh remained friends and collaborators until death. It is thanks to the

25. *Ibid.*, p. 242.
26. *Ibid.*
27. *Ibid.*
28. *Ibid.*
29. *Ibid.*
30. *Ibid.*, p. 243 (emphasis mine).

synthesis of this correspondence, prepared for the journal *Le Lien,* by Patriarch Maximos V Hakim that we know of the pioneer work which preceded that of Cardinal Augustin Bea. However, Bea himself knew nothing of it. As is indicated earlier, "in fact, he explicitly stated that he was not aware of any other proposals to Pope John, prior to his own."[31]

The second paragraph of the letter of condolence of Patriarch Maximos V Hakim recalled the proposal made by his immediate predecessor. It reveals that indeed there were two interventions from the same source. The second of these was a direct appeal for a permanent ecumenical curial body from the Patriarch himself and the Melchite Synod, which has disappeared into the secret archives of the Vatican. This is the letter which received the *"No! No! No!"* of Cardinal Tisserant. That letter was dated August 1959. The earlier letter of 23 May was a personal note which Patriarch Maximos IV Saigh presented on his knees to Pope John, during his first pastoral visit to the new pontiff. It exists only in a fragmentary state in the archives of the Melchite Patriarchate.[32] The best evidence of the incident to date is the correspondence between Maximos V Hakim and Pope Paul VI. The attitude of Patriarch Maximos IV is full of love, reverence and hope.

The *pro memoria* of Maximos Saigh continued thus:

> In these our times, when people are speaking so much about ecumenism, could there not be a greater opportunity than now to establish "a permanent institution to favor the Union of the separated Churches" [une institution permanente en faveur de l'Union des Églises séparées] in conformity with the desires of Our Savior? All of this could be effected by the Catholic Church. . . .
>
> Is there not a greater opportunity than now, for example, "to create a new Congregation or a special Roman Commission" [créer une nouvelle Congrégation ou une Commission romaine spéciale] to concern itself with relations with the Christian Churches which are not in communion with the Holy See; and, which could advance toward union? This is a critical question that seems to merit the highest attention.

31. Schmidt, *op. cit.,* p. 328.

32. *Le Lien, op. cit.,* p. 240. It is customary to seal a Cardinal's quarters upon his death. His letters and papers are removed to the Secret Archives of the Vatican and are not made public for seventy-five years. Maximos Saigh was created a Cardinal in 1965. While the text of the Patriarch's communication is therefore not available, *Le Lien* indicates that there were two documents. One was a petition for a Curial Bureau and the second, an outline of the structure of such a body. For convenience, I refer to the second document as the *pro memoria.*

In this Congregation or Commission there would be an important member of the Holy Office, of the Sacred Congregation for the Oriental Churches and of the Secretariat of State. Everything that pertains to ecumenism will fall under the competence of this new institution . . . [Tout ce qui touche à l'oecuménisme sera du ressort de cette nouvelle institution . . .].

Through this new creation, *horizons would be enlarged* and *hearts would be strengthened,* as it would seem that the *first milestone had been struck,* toward the effected *rapprochement* with our brothers separated from the centre of Christian Unity ("nos frères séparés du centre de l'unité chrétienne").[33]

The remnants of Maximos IV's first appeal to Pope John XXIII will be cited later, since they have to do with the function and structure of a new Vatican bureau, but some notes can be detected now. The first of these is Maximos IV's concern for the presence of a representative of the Congregation for the Oriental Churches within the proposed Ecumenical Commission. Clearly this represents Maximos IV's desire to address primarily the question of the ongoing separation between the Churches of the East and West.[34] But this does not exclude the circumstances within the Christian community of the West. "Justification" and the other theological issues, raised by the Classical Reformation, clearly would merit input from a representative of the Holy Office.[35] Membership by the dignitary from the

---

33. *Ibid,* p. 241 (emphasis mine). Note again the Arabic pattern of thought.

34. Edward J. Kilmartin, S.J., *Toward Reunion* (New York: Paulist Press, 1979), pp. 4-10. See *Vatican Documents on the Eastern Churches: Papal Encyclicals and Documents* (Fairfax, Va.: Eastern Christian Publications, 2002). An example of the concern is found in *Allatae Sunt* (Of the Observance of the Oriental Rites) of Pope Benedict XIV, July 26, 1755. "We will declare freely that the Roman Pontiffs have carefully and tirelessly attempted to overcome the heresies which gave rise to the schism between the Eastern and Western Churches, and that consequently they have commanded Orientals who want to return to the unity of the Church to reject these errors to find out if they really belong to union with the Apostolic See (N. 17, p. 13)." Also this Pontiff set to work upon the scholarly updating of Eastern Rite usages: "The examination of this work was begun zealously under Urban VIII (1623-1644), but it was interrupted after a short time. It was taken up again under Clement XII (1730-1740), but God reserved for Us the joy of beholding the completion of this very important work. During Our Pontificate, Cardinals, Prelates, theologians, and men trained in the languages of the East devoted long hours to work and discussion. We ourselves read the discussions and weighed every matter that called for examination (No. 18)."

35. Heinrich Bornkamm, *The Heart of Reformation Faith* (London: Harper and Row, 1965). Bornkamm lists the fundamental points of the Reformation: "justification by faith; the return to the Scriptures; freedom from human and ecclesiastical intermediaries between God

Secretariat of State (the Cardinal Secretary himself, the *sostituto,* or the *assessore*) would facilitate the review of matters of practical statesmanship and public relations. Secondly, the desired Vatican bureau was intended to be *permanent* and to *actively promote the cause of Christian union (Institution permanente en faveur de l'Union des Églises séparées).*[36] Therefore, the proposed body did not exist for special occasions, nor was it intended for the General Council. *Maximos IV actually foresaw a permanent new family within the Roman Curia.*[37]

Ecumenism in the Air

Finally, Maximos IV spoke of the fact that ecumenism was "in the air" ("Dans les temps actuels òu l'on parle tant d'oecuménisme"). Here the author made reference to the worldwide Ecumenical Movement, including the various expressions of a burgeoning sense of ecumenism within the Catholic family.[38] In the text below, we shall examine the significance of "in the air." Maximos was, in particular, aware of the leadership provided by the Orthodox Ecumenical Patriarchate of Constantinople in the development of the worldwide Ecumenical Movement. He was a careful observer of all developments and trends within worldwide Orthodoxy. Likewise, as a keen theologian, he was ever mindful that the twentieth century contained a vast sea of theological riches, especially regarding such issues as the understanding of the Church, the meaning of the Church, the relevance of the Church, and challenges to the Church. He followed trends, in particular in French theological journals, and was familiar with ecumenical and ecclesiological speculative theology.

The Patriarch Maximos was a master of understatement and conveyed much through his gift for economy of words. What follows below is an overview of the reference to this above-cited phrase, "Dans les temps actuels, etc." Maximos was bringing to the attention of Pope John *the fact of an already existing ecumenical history,* which had not previously received much recognition or approval by the central Roman Catholic au-

---

and us; freedom of conscience, and therefore a freedom and self responsibility of spirit; the primacy of the majesty of God; the realization that 'God is calling us anew to his rule, his kingdom. God does not will to leave the world as it is'" (pp. 70-71). At the time of this writing by Maximos IV, Bea in fact was the consultor of the Holy Office to handle these very questions.

36. *Le Lien, op. cit.,* p. 241.

37. *Ibid.*

38. *Ibid.*

thority. Cardinal Bea was to ensure that such recognition would, in fact, take place. The text below outlines the facts of Roman Catholic participation in that ecumenical setting and gives substance to the reference of Patriarch Maximos Saigh. It likewise evidences the manner of approach of Cardinal Bea to Pope John regarding this matter. In fact, the mutual knowledge of the Patriarch and the Jesuit Cardinal gave persuasive testimony to the ultimate judgment of Pope John XXIII regarding this matter.

Part 2: Ecumenism, the Roman Catholic Church and the Twentieth Century

The Belgian theologian Piet Fransen, S.J., once wrote: "In theology, words do not entirely escape their human fate. Our times have made the discovery that even theology has a history."[39] His point helps explain the significance of Maximos IV's peculiar phraseology in his 23 May note to Pope John: "Dans les temps actuels où l'on parle tant d' oecuménisme" [In these actual times where they are talking so much about ecumenism]. This *was* "the opportune moment" from which the Melchite Patriarch would look into the future: "Il serait comme la conscience oecuménique permanente du Siège Romain et de toute l' Eglise catholique" [It will be as the permanent ecumenical conscience of the Roman See and of all the Catholic Church].[40] When Maximos was asking, "Is there not a *greater opportunity* than now?" what did he mean?

The Pre-ecumenical and the Ecumenical Phases

Before answering the above question, it is helpful to make reference to a statement of Johannes Cardinal Willebrands, the first Secretary of the Secretariat for Promoting Christian Unity, concerning the inception and development of the Ecumenical Movement among Catholic thinkers and leaders. He spoke of "the yet unknown area of ecumenism among the Catholics in the nineteenth century in a way which I would call a pre-ecumenical exploration," continuing along this way into the twentieth century, "contributing both men and ideas, expanding and modifying the approach as new insights in ecumenism arose and as the direction of le-

39. *Id.*, *Divine Grace and Man* (Rome: Desclee Co., 1962), p. 31.
40. *Id.*, *op. cit.*, p. 241.

gitimate ecclesial authority indicated."[41] The cause of ecumenism began, according to Willebrands, with an intense personal ecclesial love, expressed by certain nineteenth-century theologians and saints. In particular, at that moment, he was thinking of John Henry Newman, Ignatius Spencer, C.P., and Père Emmanuel d' Alzon, founder of the Congregation of the Augustinians of the Assumption, as heroes of the earliest part of the Ecumenical Movement.[42] Willebrands' text, which focused on the last of the above-cited figures, d' Alzon, also identified ecumenism as an historical phenomenon consisting of two parts: (1) a pre-ecumenical phase and (2) a fuller active phase in which the clear goal is "the search for unity among Christians."

The significance now becomes clear and the question is answered. When Patriarch Maximos IV proposed "une Institution permanente en faveur de l'Union des Églises séparées," he definitively, but unknowingly, signaled the end of Willebrands' first category of the pre-ecumenical era.[43] A second letter from Germany, in March of the following year, 1960, over the signature of Archbishop Lorenz Jaeger of Paderborn, would inaugurate the new era entirely. Still, much is contained in Maximos's delineation of the times as opportune: "Ne serait-il pas opportune?"

Perhaps the most concise response comes from the ecumenical histo-

---

41. *Id., Emmanuel d' Alzon and John Henry Newman* (Worcester, Mass.: Assumption College Press, 1980), p. 1. Willebrands defined this "pre-ecumenical" phase in these terms: "It was this personal, intense love of the Church especially which led d' Alzon and his Congregations ultimately to pioneer the yet unknown area of ecumenism in the nineteenth century in a way which *I would call a pre-ecumenical exploration . . .*" (emphasis mine).

42. For further reference, see S. A. Grave, *Conscience in Newman's Thought* (Oxford: Clarendon Press, 1989). The author discusses at length the meaning of the Church for each Christian individual, identifying the ecumenical necessity to discover points of convergence between the personal religious experiences of the ecumenical hero, in this case Newman, and that which is offered by the invitation of the Catholic Church. Newman had already discussed this issue in 1837, but it returned with the crises over the issue of Papal Infallibility in 1870. Grave synthesizes as follows: "Presupposed by the notion of what came to be called 'private judgment' is the notion of a divine revelation, the revelation in which Catholicism and Protestantism alike professed belief" (p. 96). For a fuller discussion of Ignatius Spencer, cf. Jerome Vereb, C.P., *Apostle of Christian Unity* (Sutton, England: Passionist Press, 1978), p. 13. Pius Devine, C.P., *Life of Fr. Ignatius of St. Paul* (Dublin: James Duffy, 1886), pp. 404-5. Spencer began a movement of prayer of the unity of Christians as early as 1839, asking for Anglican, Protestant and Catholic participation through the common recitation of the Lord's Prayer at a certain hour of the day. Also, see Richard Richards, A.A., *The Assumptionists* (New York: Assumption Provincial House, 1980), pp. 28-43. Also, Pierre Touveneraud, A.A., *Emmanuel d' Alzon: 1810-1880* (Rome: Maison Généralice, 1980), p. 22.

43. *Le Lien, op. cit.*, p. 241.

rian George H. Tavard, A.A.[44] In the introduction of his book *Two Centuries of Ecumenism,* Tavard wrote: "Since ecumenism is above all an intellectual movement, I have given special attention to the development of thought."[45] But he goes on to say: "The facts have meaning only by virtue of the concepts which they express."[46] The formation of the Ecumenical Movement is so tied to the environment, that the ideas reiterated must always be examined against the environment in which they were uttered.

Tavard illustrated this point, mid-way through his volume, when he spoke about the effectiveness of the World Council of Churches, definitively founded at Amsterdam in 1948, only twelve years before Tavard wrote his concise summary of the Ecumenical Movement.[47] Curiously, the publication of his book occurred in French and English at exactly the same time as Patriarch Saigh's pastoral visit and *pro memoria* to Pope John. Hence, in that context, Tavard's assessment of the "clear and present" effectiveness of the World Council of Churches is germane.

After his assessment, Tavard pronounced the immediate goal of the World Council of Churches to be a success! "There are lessons to be learned from this," he said. One of these was the aim of the World Council of Churches to keep the "idea of Christian Unity alive before the Churches."[48] According to Tavard, "another sign of the increasing importance of the World Council is the fact that it has aroused the *interest of the Patriarch of Moscow.*"[49] At that time, the Russian Orthodox Church had

44. Let it be noted that George H. Tavard is a true son of his founder, Emmanuel D' Alzon, a devoted member of the Congregation of the Augustinians of the Assumption. He was an instructor at Pittsburgh's Mount Mercy College, at the time of the publication of his book.

45. George H. Tavard, A.A., *Two Centuries of Ecumenism* (Notre Dame, Ind.: Fides Publishers Association, 1959), p. ix.

46. *Ibid.*

47. *Ibid.,* pp. 174-87. French Edition: *Petite histoire du mouvement oecuménique* (Paris: Éditions Fleurus, 1960), p. 183. "L'oecuménisme bâtit pour l'avenir" [Ecumenism builds for the future].

48. *Ibid.,* pp. 175-86.

49. *Ibid.,* p. 186. A fuller treatment is found on pp. 195-210. At the time of the composition of this work, the only representative of the Catholic Church in Moscow was an Assumptionist priest, attached to the American Embassy. At that time, Father Louis Dion held the position of Apostolic Administrator of Moscow. After the revolution of 1917, Monsignor Pius Neveu, A.A., was secretly ordained bishop by Monsignor Michel D'Herbigny, S.J., in 1926. He remained until 1936. Throughout the War, Father Leopold Braun remained on under Soviet rule. The continued presence of the Assumptionists kept Father Tavard informed of the developments in the Moscow Patriarchate. See Richards, *op. cit.,* pp. 87ff. Also Patrick A. Croghan, *The Peasant from Makeyevka* (Worcester, Mass.: Augustinians of the Assumption, 1982), pp. 186-90.

not yet joined the World Council of Churches. However, the World Council had effectively made inroads into the world of Communism, and more importantly, into the world of Eastern Orthodoxy, even in that patently Communist environment when the Moscow Patriarchate was completely restricted by the Kremlin. Therefore, the World Council possessed the potential to bridge an otherwise insuperable canyon.

Also, Tavard pronounced another of the benefits of the World Council of Churches: "The interest which it presents to the Catholic World."[50] While there were no Catholic observers at the General Assemblies of the World Council until well after the publication of Tavard's book, he recorded that Catholic contacts were made at all previous World Council of Churches gatherings. All in all, Tavard was optimistic about the forward role of the World Council of Churches: "Whatever may be the meaning of this new establishment, it must be recognized as a sign that the World Council of Churches will *not be a passing event* in twentieth century Christian life. Ecumenism is building for the future."[51]

Catholic Conference for Ecumenical Questions (C.C.E.Q.) and the Meeting at the Istina Centre

Maximos IV's indication of a vital and important ecumenical activity also included the cluster of theologians in North Europe, who were beginning to come together under the title C.C.E.Q. In 1949, one year after the Amsterdam Assembly, two professors of the Dutch diocesan seminary of Haarlem, in the city of Warmond, Fathers Johannes Willebrands and Frans Thijssen, established the Catholic Conference for Ecumenical Questions. The original aim of the group was to follow, among other things, the spirit and the projects of the World Council of Churches.[52] They did this from a distance because of the cautious attitudes of Roman Catholicism at the time.

Willebrands, a professor of philosophy, and Thijssen, a theologian, were both living not too far from Amsterdam during the time of the General Assembly of the World Council of Churches in 1948. This was the premier and constitutional gathering of that body. Amsterdam constitutes the major city of the diocese of Haarlem. Therefore the two priests had ample

---

50. *Ibid.*, p. 186.
51. *Ibid.*, p. 187.
52. Willem A. Visser 't Hooft, *Memoirs* (Geneva: WCC Publications, 1987), p 320.

opportunity to observe the discussions and proposals of the delegates which were reported widely in the local press and on the radio. They also took time to introduce themselves to the delegates. Therefore they began an informal but active fraternity of scholars who were interested in ecumenical questions.

The effect of this new group was instant and powerful. The *Memoirs* of W. A. Visser 't Hooft, first General Secretary of the World Council of Churches, records both the significance and passion of the moment. Less than a year after the World Council of Churches Assembly at Amsterdam (22 August through 4 September 1948), an absolutely confidential meeting occurred at the Istina Centre in Paris. Ten Roman Catholic theologians, all of whom were sympathetic to the Ecumenical Movement, met with ten other theologians of various Christian denominations who represented the interests of the World Council of Churches. Among the Roman Catholics were Jean Daniélou, S.J., Jean-Jérôme Hamer, O.P. (both of whom were destined to become Cardinals), Maurice Villian, S.M., Louis Bouyer, C.O., and the renowned philosophy professor Jean Guitton. The language of exchange was French, which is not unusual since, at that time, French Catholicism was perhaps the most vigorous in its theological ecumenical explorations.[53]

Also present was Father Yves Congar, O.P. Congar himself was destined to become a Cardinal. His presence was extremely important, since his 1937 publication *Chrétiens désunis* (Separated Christians) was already recognized as an exciting and useful handbook in the area of Catholic studies, known as fundamental theology. Formerly known as apologetics, this theological branch was now undergoing a metamorphosis with renewed emphasis upon the themes of the providence of God, the importance of Sacred Revelation, the action of the Trinity, the reality of grace and the power of the Sacramental Liturgy. Also, the inclusion of ecumenical sensitivity about these and other issues was transforming the horizon of this field.[54]

In the atmosphere of the post-antimodernist era, Congar, in conjunction with fellow Frenchmen and some brother Dominicans, encouraged renewed emphasis upon the place of biblical and patristic studies in the scope of a careful examination of the traditional exploitation of St. Thomas' *Summa Theologica*. Congar, a disciple of Marie-Dominique

---

53. *Ibid.*

54. *Id., Chrétiens désunis: Principes d'un oeccuménisme catholique* (Paris: Les Éditions du Cerf, 1937). See also Aidan Nichols, O.P., *Yves Congar, O.P.* (Wilton, Conn.: Morehouse Barlow, 1989), pp. 1-12, 14-25.

Chenu, O.P., at the Dominican Academy of Saulchoir, received his doctorate in 1931. He was convinced at the time of the completion of his studies that Saint Thomas Aquinas stood in the patristic tradition and should be counted among the Fathers of the Church.[55] Like many others of his era, he represented the efforts of Catholic academicians in the inter-war years to examine all theology in an historical context, and to undertake the current renewal of theology and the ancillary sciences, with a sense of realism which reflected the contemporary pastoral application. During the meeting at Istina, Congar was to incite further meetings by reference to the importance of historical theology. The significance of theological dialogue between the finest academicians of Roman Catholicism and the Protestant tradition was to set in motion a process which could not be put into reverse.

That Congar and Maximos IV Saigh were of the same mentality is confirmed by this journal entry of Congar on the floor of the Second Vatican Council: "It is an historic moment. On this morning of 23 November 1963, we are gathered in prayer, we listen, we attend in hope. The Church is prepared to make a definitive pronouncement in favor of dialogue" [È un momento storico. In questa mattina del 23 Novembre 1963 ci raccogliamo nella preghiera, ascoltiamo, attendiamo nella speranza. La Chiesa sta per pronunciarsi in maniera definitiva a favore del dialogo].[56]

While at the meeting at the Istina Centre, Congar represented the monumental contribution of the Dominicans to Catholic academia, a contribution for which he personally suffered, through exile from his country to an insignificant posting at Cambridge in England. Jean Daniélou, S.J. (1909-1974), represented, on the other hand, the finest of Jesuit academic renewal between the Wars. The style of his writing is so simple that it is practically journalistic. His books include: *The Presence of God, The Salvation of the Nations,* and *The Dead Sea Scrolls and Primitive Christianity.* Daniélou immediately touched a reading audience of French lay Catholics through the clarity of his writing. He was indeed widely read, since he was skilled at communicating a sense of insight which, in turn, engendered passion in the reader.[57] This, however, did not

---

55. *Ibid.,* pp. 2-6.

56. The fragment cited herein is located as part of the typed manuscript of Congar's *Mon journal du Concile* of the Le Saulchoir Library, now in the Rue de Tanneries, Paris. Access to the actual text was not yet possible at this writing. The Italian is used because this was the only fragment available.

57. *Id., The Presence of God* (Baltimore: Helicon Press, 1959). *The Salvation of the Nations* (London: Sheed and Ward, 1949); *The Dead Sea Scrolls and Primitive Christianity* (Balti-

mean that he was devoid of a speculative sensitivity, from which he devised remarkably appropriate expressions of language. Daniélou was a multi-faceted theologian whose varied theological interests were *historically based* and *pastorally oriented*. He wanted to speak to the curiosity and the skepticism of the twentieth century world; "to the interaction between theology and life." Daniélou published this *Credo* in his article in *Études* in April 1946.[58] He was once described as a combination of *ressourcement* (going back to the sources) and *aggiornamento* (bringing up-to-date). Daniélou was deeply involved in the three important projects which *were* among the Catholic miracles of wartime France, *Unam Sanctam, Source Chrétiennes* and *Théologie*.

The presence of Jean Guitton among this illustrious group of Catholic academics is indeed worthy of note. Although a layman, Guitton was a professor at the Institut Catholique with Father Daniélou. His subject was philosophy. Along with two other French colleagues, Étienne Gilson and Jacques Maritain, he focused on the Thomism of the Medieval period. The importance of a philosopher and a layman here was extremely significant, for the immediate challenge was to identify and define categories for theological exchange, which would be appropriate to the step into dialogue, which inaugurated the new ecumenical era.[59]

A consensus was reached. And thus a common language focused upon the concept of *vestigia ecclesiae* (footprints of the Church), which means that other churches and ecclesial communions have traces of the One Church. Hence the starting point for future discussion was, according

---

more: Helicon Press, 1958). Giacomo Martina, S.J., "The Historical context in Which the Idea of a New Ecumenical Council Was Born," in René Latourelle, S.J., (ed.) *Vatican II Assessment and Perspective*, vol. 1 (New York: Paulist Press, 1988), pp. 33, 67: "Professionally P. Daniélou was a historian of the early Church. However, both by family heritage and his own temperament, he was a man transformed by the zeal of the apostle, intellectually alive to every contemporary current of thought, and open to all manner of dialogue." His pastoral work led him to the chaplaincy to the Catholic students of the Sorbonne, and especially, beginning in 1941 to the École Normale Supérieure. Farsightedly and very soon he saw the signs of crises of faith which arose in the Church, and he sounded a cry of alarm in *Scandaleuse vérité* (1961). From that time on he set himself to show, without losing any of his optimism, the intellectual roots of the ambiguities of the moment and their inevitable developments — the rejection of realism, separation of religion and faith, loss of the sacred.

58. M. J. Rondeau and B. Van Hove, "Jean Daniélou," in *The New Catholic Encyclopedia*, vol. 17 (Washington, D.C.: Catholic University of America, 1981), pp. 173-75.

59. The history and details of this period, specifically contributions of laymen such as Guitton, Gilson and Maritain, are accurately presented in James C. Livingston, *Modern Christian Thought: From the Enlightenment to Vatican II* (New York: Macmillan Company, 1971), pp. 385-403.

to the participants, the common quest for a common ground, delineated by biblical, liturgical and patristic theology. The *Memoirs* of Visser 't Hooft state: "This last point was fully discussed. Père Daniélou said that our common task was to arrive at a dynamic reception of the *vestigia ecclesiae,* for these traces of the church could be developed and lead to greater agreement."[60] Thus the participants at the Istina meeting provided, quite unwittingly, the goal and style of future theological dialogues, i.e., convergence. This top-secret meeting was probably the most significant contribution toward ecumenical formation by the Catholic Conference for Ecumenical Questions, for its results had the most profound effect upon the joint concerns of Willebrands and Thijssen.

Before long the initiative of Willebrands and Thijssen facilitated the annual gathering of some eighty Roman Catholic ecumenical scholars from across Europe. The significance of Willebrands' presidency of the Catholic Conference rests upon his creativity in locating and inviting participants, who would form a network of expertise for the sake of mutual information and the promotion of the cause of unity of all Christians. Ultimately the Holy See would draw from this group both the first staff members and the early body of consultors for the Secretariat for Promoting Christian Unity.[61]

The Catholic Conference for Ecumenical Questions crossed all the frontiers of Western Europe and included other renowned participants such as: Christophe Dumont, O.P., Karl Rahner, S.J., Augustin Bea, S.J., Pierre Duprey, P.B., Emmanuel Lanne, O.S.B., Charles Moeller, Hans Balthasar Fischer, Erich Salzmann, Eduard Stakemeier, Josef Höfer and Jean-François Arrighi. Also, the Archbishop of Paderborn, Lorenz Jaeger, was a participant member. Their gatherings were semiannual. The unique characteristic of this group rested in the continued interest in the activities

---

60. Visser 't Hooft, *op. cit.,* p. 320.

61. Willebrands and Thijssen forged their initiative within a strongly pious environment. Although the Dutch Catholic Church was a tiny minority in a predominately Protestant country, it produced 10 percent of all missionary personnel throughout the world. "Both Pius XI and Pius XII had singled out Dutch Catholicism as a model Church for other nations to follow." It also possessed "the strongest opposition to ecumenism with Protestants or Socialists." John A. Coleman, *The Evolution of Dutch Catholicism, 1958-1974* (London: University of California Press, 1978), p. 2. The first support staff of female secretaries for the Secretariat for Promoting Christian Unity also came from the Catholic Conference for Ecumenical Questions. Corinna De Martini and Josette Kersters, as Ladies of the Grail, had consecrated their lives to the service of the Church by communicating the details of the ecumenical cause. Both were highly skilled secretaries endowed with great linguistic ability, remarkably affable personalities, and farsighted wisdom.

of the World Council of Churches which, from the sidelines, these Catholic scholars took very, very seriously.[62]

Endowed with a razor-sharp mind, Johannes Willebrands also possessed amazing personality skills. He spoke all of Western Europe's major languages. He could be equally at home in the halls of Vatican City or in a Dutch parish. Likewise, Willebrands shared his Dutch nationality and his friendship with the General Secretary of the World Council of Churches, W. A. Visser 't Hooft. Because of restrictions imposed by Rome, Willebrands could only enjoy a kind of "guest status" at World Council of Churches meetings. He, Thijssen and other members of the Catholic Conference attended these gatherings under the title of "journalist."

As a result of all this activity, by the time Patriarch Maximos Saigh visited Pope John XXIII in May 1959, and spoke about the atmosphere of ecumenism that was already in the air, his direct reference was to the Catholic Conference for Ecumenical Questions. The president of that Conference, Johannes Willebrands, was probably the best-informed Roman Catholic in matters regarding World Council of Churches programs, attitudes and all theological undertakings.

A Renewed Sensibility for the Church in Western Thought

As recalled by W. A. Visser 't Hooft, the Istina meeting between the Roman Catholic scholars and the representatives of the World Council of Churches produced the catch phrase *vestigia ecclesiae*.[63] The significance of the phrase and the new insight into ecclesiology were carried by the members of the Catholic Conference for Ecumenical Questions into a series of ongoing conversations. The history of the Catholic Conference indicated that the members communicated and met in order to share information and opinions. They also began informal encounters with their "opposite numbers" from the Protestant and Orthodox worlds.

Happily, the phrase *vestigia ecclesiae* was consistent with the bur-

---

62. Thomas F. Stransky, C.S.P., "The Foundation of the Secretariat for the Promotion of Christian Unity," in Alberic Stacpoole, O.S.B., *Vatican II by Those Who Were There* (Minneapolis: Winston Press, 1986), p. 64. As if by synchronicity, the 1959 meeting of the Catholic Conference for Ecumenical Questions was held in Paderborn, the archdiocese of Lorenz Jaeger. In 1959, the Catholic Conference was attempting to provide a Catholic contribution for a document to the World Council of Churches, in regard to the "Lordship of Christ." Schmidt, *op. cit.*, pp. 242, 255.

63. *Id.*, *op. cit.*, p. 320.

geoning ecclesiology of the World Council of Churches. Ecclesiology, as an issue of urgency, found its first expression at the Edinburgh Missionary Conference of 1910. That assembly, of course, was the forerunner of the World Council of Churches, ultimately and formally established in 1948 at Amsterdam.[64]

A brief reference to the nineteenth century helps highlight the question of ecclesiology. First, let it be kept in mind that the Catholic Tradition as well as the Reformation Tradition suffered from the ravages of the French Revolution. Secondly, all Christians in Western Europe were directly affected by the rise of empirical science and the ideology, sometimes ruthless in character, of the Industrial Revolution. The skepticism that grew among the masses developed into a cynicism, regarding the usefulness of the Church, the validity of philosophy, and a definite preference for the material over the spiritual. This has never been better expressed than by John Henry Newman in his *Letters on the Tamworth Reading Room.*[65]

> Science has so little of a religious tendency; deductions have no power of persuasion. The heart is commonly reached, not through reason, but through the imagination, by means of direct impression, by the testi-

64. *Ibid.,* pp. 204ff.

65. John H. Newman, "Tamworth Reading Room," in *Discussions and Arguments on Various Subjects* (London: Longmans, Green and Co., 1891). "The essence of religion is the idea of a Moral Governor; now let me ask, is the doctrine of moral governments and a particular providence conveyed to us through the physical sciences at all? Would they be physical sciences if treated as morals? Can physics teach moral matters without ceasing to be physics? But are not virtue and vice, and responsibility, and reward and punishment, anything else than moral matters and are *they* not of the essence of religion? And what department then of physics are they to be found . . . ?" Newman's best argument of all is in this sentence: "The material world, indeed is infinitely more wonderful than any human contrivance; but wonder is not religion, or we should be worshiping our railroads" (pp. 293-303, emphasis mine). Willebrands addressed this issue thus: "The rationalism of the age of the Enlightenment, the *égalité* of the French Revolution combine to produce effects in the economic and social order which thus results in secularism." Willebrands, *op. cit.,* p. 9. Conrad Charles, C.P., states in this regard: "English history following the Battle of Waterloo was characterized by the growth of Liberalism." Conrad Charles, C.P., *The Foundation of the Passionists in England: 1840-1851* (Rome: Pontifica Universitas Gregorgiana, 1961), p. 8. The environment in which Newman spoke saw the migration of entire populations from the countryside to the city, and from Ireland to England, Newman, who never passed the opportunity for pastoral contact, was aware that the stones of ancient monastic foundations have been replaced by red brick factories, producing a national sense of cynicism and numerous apostasies from the Christian faith. His own conversion to Catholicism made him look again at the very structure of faith: "Newman's sense of loneliness after he had taken the final plunge was overwhelming." See also Denis Gwynn, *The Second Spring: 1818-1852* (London: Catholic Book Club, 1944), pp. 156ff.

mony of facts and events, by history, by description. Persons influence us, voices melt us, looks subdue us, deeds inflame us. Many a man will live and die upon a dogma: no man will be a martyr for a conclusion.

According to Cardinal Willebrands, who, in the text cited above, composed a gloss on Newman's sentences:

> It was this quality of sensitivity which led Newman to both study and prayer over the meditations on the Church handed down by the Fathers (Augustine, Basil, Athanasius, Cyril of Alexandria, etc.) from the early centuries. His personal debt to the Patristic Tradition led to the study of the Anglican divines. In the *Apologia Pro Vita Sua,* he narrates that it did not happen the other way around. He did not approach the Fathers, as a means of defending the structure and theology of the Church of England, as outlined by the great Anglican writers. He went to the Fathers first, as a means of deepening his own understanding of the mystery of the Church in the face of tendencies towards secularism.[66]

After identifying Newman's two-volume *Via Media* and the *Prophetical Office of the Church* as two of the "first ecumenical documents of the modern era," Willebrands identified the period of the Oxford Movement as the inception of a new era of ecclesiological study. While much Romanticism is associated with the Oxford Movement, including its wistful poetry, Gothic architecture, the restoration of Roman vestments, and the renewed interest in ceremonial, the hard question emerged. Newman's own research led him to a principle, which he passed on to his Anglican confreres, and which they treasured even after Newman became a Catholic. At the heart of Newman's teaching, according to Willebrands, is Newman's own phraseology: "Antiquity was the true exponent of the doctrine of Christianity and the basis of the Church of England." Willebrands then went on to conclude: "Thus he made a personal study of Athanasius, Basil and Augustine to clarify for himself the *role of the Church and its clergy.*"[67]

---

66. *Id., op. cit.,* pp. 11, 13. See John Henry Newman, *Apologia Pro Vita Sua* (New York: Catholic Publication House, 1890). "I had a supreme confidence in our cause (Anglican), we were upholding that primitive Christianity which was delivered for all time by the early teachers of the Church and which was registered and attested in the Anglican formularies and by the Anglican divines" (p. 91).

67. The references to "Antiquity" are multifold in John Henry Newman, particularly in the *Apologia Pro Vita Sua,* e.g., "It was indeed one of my great difficulties and causes of reserve as time went on, that I at length recognized in principles which I had honestly preached as is Anglican, conclusions favourable to the Roman Church. Of course I did not like to con-

The Ecclesiological Emphasis of Charles Brent and Faith and Order

That same Newman-like mentality (Oxford) emerged strongly in the person of an American Anglican Bishop of the Philippines, Charles Brent.[68] Charles Brent is herein highlighted, since it was he who consistently raised the issue of ecclesiology in the first major ecumenical meetings to flow from the Edinburgh Conference of 1910. Like Newman, Brent was personally affected by the tension between the Evangelical cause and "High Church Christianity." Although not as intellectually endowed as Newman, Brent is noteworthy for his persistence in defining the ecumenical cause with the need to make more precise the study of the nature of the Church. The Assembly at Edinburgh gathered in order to wrestle with the problem of "evangelization." It was first and foremost about missionary activity as stemming from the colonial experience. At the end of the conference, Bishop Brent prophetically spoke of a "new vision," which provoked a "new responsibility." Brent's activities, his writings, and his idealism encouraged the preparation of the Faith and Order Conference of Lausanne in 1927. Brent had much to cope with in the aftermath. Nearly a decade before, he almost, but not quite, found support for this projected conference from circles within the Vatican. Tavard wrote, "while Pope Benedict XV heartily encouraged the organizers, he courteously declined their invitation." Tavard also wrote: "Nothing can make us forget that faith and order is due to the initiative of Charles Brent, a missionary bishop of the Episco-

---

fess this; and, when interrogated, was in consequence in perplexity. The prime instance of this was the appeal to antiquity. . . . Yet I was committed to antiquity, together with the whole Anglican school" (p. 205). Newman has left us many theological tools in the "principle of economy," "the principle of reserve," and "the illiative sense." But he is best remembered for this method of theology from "inside the Church"! His starting point was always history. History was not a major part of the life of theology, either Catholic or Protestant, in the nineteenth-century period, with the glowing exception of Germany, especially at Tübingen and Munich. Theologians in the Catholic world and in the Anglo-Saxon world did not quite know what to do with it. Of Newman, Ian Kerr has written: "Had it not been for his love of the patristic writings, he would no doubt have embraced a 'cold Arminian doctrine.'" Ian Kerr, *John Henry Newman* (New York: Oxford University Press, 1988), p. 23.

68. George H. Tavard, *Two Centuries of Ecumenism*, p. 98. Brent represented a particularly unique brand of Anglicanism. He was an Evangelical or Low Church Anglican, yet the principal theme that he carried to the 1910 Edinburgh Conference and to the Faith and Order Movement was one of ecclesiology. "It was a 'Low Church' Anglicanism, but anchored in the Anglican historical tradition more than that of the continental Reformation. It had, moreover, mixed in, with this a certain number of 'High Church' ideas" (p. 101).

pal Church of the United States." Because of him, Anglicanism "is there," always present in ecumenical conversation, always a reminder of the primacy of ecclesiology.[69]

Ironically, the Germans were quite distrustful of the so-called Faith and Order Movement which Brent husbanded, both at the Edinburgh Conference and the General Convention of the Episcopal Church in 1910.[70] Contrary to the emerging concept of *Volk* (German identity), German

---

69. *Ibid.*, pp. 117-18. "The pontificate of Benedict XV seems to have acted as a realistic reminder. It would be unbecoming for the sovereign pontiff to participate in ecumenical conferences if he were to join Protestants in trying to find out what kind of unity Christ intended His Church to have. To the extent that this was intended, by inviting Benedict XV [to the Faith and Order Assembly], the Holy Father could not help but answer as he did. The Protestant world is under an illusion if it imagines that the Catholic Church can change her doctrine on unity. Such a change could not conform to the truth, and there can be no rapprochement except in truth." *Ibid.*, p. 18. The above quote testifies to the very detailed research of George Tavard. The evidence indicates the practical sense of realism engendered in that pontificate, by the Secretary of State, Cardinal Pietro Gasparri, who saw to it that Benedict's written response was continually presented so as not to contain a note of condescension to Brent. The latest biography of Benedict XV, John F. Pollard, *The Unknown Pope* (London: Geoffrey Chapman, 1999), emphasizes Benedict's ecumenical and political significance, as will be cited later. On the other hand, in an earlier English biography, Walter H. Peters, *The Life of Benedict XV* (Milwaukee: Bruce Publishing Co., 1959), Benedict is seen as possessing a more ample sense of the universal Church. His vision extended to the Eastern Church as well as the Church of the West. "In Benedict's first encyclical, the blueprint of his whole pontificate, he wrote, 'immediately we begin to regard with unspeakable affection the flock committed to our care: A flock truly immense, for in one way or another it embraces all mankind. For all, without exception, have been delivered by Jesus Christ, at the price of His blood, from the slavery of sin: nor is anyone shut out from the benefits of his redemption." *Ad Beatissimi*, November 1, 1914, no. 64. "Benedict was conscious of his universal fatherhood, and there is hardly a country which did not receive some favor from him. One of the first segments of Christendom to claim his attention was that which falls within the compass of the Oriental Churches." *Ibid.*, p. 243. The pontificate of Benedict XV saw a reversal to the anti-Modernist trend within the Vatican Curia, a renewal on the part of mission and re-evangelization and the beginnings of the Ecumenical Movement among Catholics. His ministry was hampered by the lack of resolution to the Roman question. Within the period of transition from the pontificate of Benedict to Pius XI, J. Derek Holmes states: "As the attitudes of the Roman authorities toward the ecumenical movement seemed to harden, the development of Catholic ecumenism came to depend more and more on the works of individuals as Paul Couturier, Yves Congar and Max Josef Metzger." J. Derek Holmes, *The Papacy in the Modern World, 1914-1978* (New York: Crossroad, 1981), p. 30. Denis Mack Smith, *Italy and Its Monarchy* (London: Yale University Press, 1989), pp. 210-25, 267. *Id., op. cit.*, pp. 100-101. Here, the author showed the impossible isolation to which Benedict was condemned under the House of Savoy. Benedict's papacy was one of a "thwarted pontiff"!

70. *Id., op. cit.*, p. 104.

theologians at that time, in general, placed a heavier theological emphasis on the "individual in society." The war of 1914-1918 did not help, but instead hindered communications and, in fact, deepened antipathies between Germany and the United Kingdom, and indeed all the English-speaking world.

The Conference at Lausanne in 1927 was about Faith and Order. It is Tavard's judgment that by nature and orientation, the content of the original Faith and Order, i.e., the study of systematic theology, liturgical practice and ecclesial discipline, is fundamentally Anglican in approach. Faith and Order took as its principal aim the study of the issues "on which we differ, in the hope that a better understanding of different points of view, in regard to the faith and order will incite a deeper desire for unity."[71] Charles Brent, although of the Evangelical branch of Anglicanism, labored mightily to further study of the issues of the Oxford Movement. This point is exceptionally interesting. He *intentionally* sought to identify the authenticity of an ongoing quest to recover the catholic elements within the Church universal.

The history of the Faith and Order Movement has been recorded elsewhere, but the agenda of that first meeting in Switzerland bears repeating, as evidence: (1) The call to unity; (2) The Church's message to the world, i.e., the Gospel; (3) The Nature of the Church; (4) The Church's Confession of Faith; (5) The Ministry of the Church; (6) The Sacraments; and (7) Christian Unity. These issues were the very topics of the Tractarian Movement,[72] which is the major component of the Oxford Movement of 1835 and following.

Tavard recalled this phase of the pre-ecumenical movement: "Anglican doctrine is essentially ecclesiology, and this *was* the general theme of the Lausanne Conference."[73] Brent made his appeal first in 1910, the premise of which was "the finding of the unity given to the Church in Christ." The organizers of the conference "had to muster all their patience to keep repeating, day after day, that it was not a question of uniting one church but *only a seeking out of the ways of the Lord by means of doctrinal enquiries*."[74] The Faith and Order Assembly embraced the aspirations of the Oxford Movement, as represented by Newman, through "source research."[75]

---

71. *Ibid.*, p. 101.

72. *Ibid.* Gwynn, *op. cit.*, pp. 45-101.

73. *Id., op. cit.*, p. 100 (emphasis mine).

74. *Ibid.* (emphasis mine).

75. It is said of Pope Leo XIII that one would be able to detect the character of his pontificate through the name of the first individual he created Cardinal, in his first consistory. The person, of course, was John Henry Newman, the Oratorian theologian whose conversion story was carried to him by (Blessed) Dominic Barberi, C.P. At the time Leo, then Archbishop

The fruit of the Faith and Order assembly of 1927 and the memory of Charles Brent burgeoned into a strong twentieth-century emphasis upon "Resource Theology," the identification of ecclesiology as the major theological theme of the Ecumenical Movement itself, and a sense of hope. According to Tavard: "From this point of view the Lausanne Conference was the answer to the appeal made by Bishop Brent in 1910. It initiated Protestantism to a study of the unity given to the Church. This made it possible to hope for an end to Christian divisions."[76]

Not all the participants or the collaborators of the World Council of Churches, of course, were Anglicans. Certainly W. A. Visser 't Hooft was not, nor was Pastor Marc Boegner,[77] Dietrich Bonhoeffer[78] and Arch-

---

Gioacchino Pecci, was Apostolic Nuncio to Belgium. Barberi was the religious superior of the Passionists' northern mission with the provincial headquarters at Ere in Belgium. Barberi received Newman into the Church on October 9, 1845. Charles, *op. cit.*, vol. II, pp. 296-302. Ian Kerr, *op. cit.*, p. 715. Tavard confirms that Leo XIII not only admired Newman, but imbibed the lessons of the Oxford Movement: "Pope Leo XIII hereby once again proposed the basis for a Catholic ecumenism. Initially it consists in seeking points of contact between Protestants and Catholics, such as scripture and love for Christ. Starting out from here, it will bring to light the fullness of tradition, which is implied in scripture itself, and the fullness of revelation, implied in the love of Christ. Hence there is no true Catholic ecumenism without a return to the sources." Tavard, *op. cit.*, p. 90. Father Philip Hughes summarized Leo's pontificate and its importance: "Liberalism having come to stay Catholics must be shown how to live in a Liberal world, and yet live by their Catholic principles; they must learn, not only how they could survive in such a world, but how to be active loyal citizens of the Liberal state." Philip Hughes, *Popular History of the Catholic Church* (New York: Doubleday and Co., 1954), p. 257. "To examine into the nature and to promote the effects of those manifestations of His wonderous love which, like rays of light, stream forth from Jesus Christ, this, as befits the sacred office, has ever been and this, with his help to the last breath of Our life, will ever be our earnest aim and endeavour." Thus wrote Leo XIII, in *Mirae caritatis*, no. 1, May 1902.

76. *Id., op. cit.*, p. 100.

77. *Id., The Long Road to Unity: Memories and Anticipation* (London: Collins, 1970), pp. 42-43. Pastor Boegner was considered to be the foremost representative of the French Reform Church in the twentieth century. In 1914, he constructed a thesis based upon a careful study of the Reformation and the Reformers which led him to the conclusion that they saw "no unity of the Body of Christ other than invisible unity — this is a sad fact whose consequence, lies heavy on the life of the Churches and their apostolic activity. . . . I (Boegner) have adopted as my own the sentence I have already quoted from (Louis) Fillat: 'the Church will be Catholic or it will not be the Church. The Christian will be Protestant or he will not be Christian.' And in my forty fourth proposition I quoted (Alexandre) Vinet's words which have now been constantly in my mind for sixty years: *'Since freedom is only a means, Protestantism is also a means. . . . Separation is only a prelude to a new unity . . . individualism must return to Socialism, Protestantism to Catholicism, freedom to unity.'"

78. Eberhard Bethge, *Dietrich Bonhoeffer: A Biography* (Minneapolis: Fortress, 2000). Bethge indicates that Bonhoeffer was introduced to ecumenism in his first years as a pastor

bishop Nathan Söderblom.[79] They were indeed in touch with their Continental Reformation roots. However, Tavard synthesized their response in a single sentence: "Lausanne put Protestants, having a Lutheran or Calvinist background, into contact with Anglican thought."[80]

Tavard also made a telling point, indicating that the Anglo-Catholicism of the Oxford Movement was the *élan vital* of the Faith and Order Movement between the Wars. Brent came armed with his ideas to the 1910 Edinburgh Conference, which was convoked specifically for matters of international evangelization and the practical issues of missionary activity. While Brent borrowed freely from the Oxford Movement, his style was definitely "Low Church." Thus, while ecclesiologically oriented, he

---

through his superintendent, Max Diestel, who was very active in the Berlin branch of the World Alliance for promoting international friendships through the Churches. Bonhoeffer was at the time a chaplain to the Evangelical community of Germans at Barcelona. His brother Klaus was stationed in Geneva. Bonhoeffer learned through him not only of movements for inter-church collaboration but also about the League of Nations and the international labor issues that were centered there. This was about 1929 (pp. 98-99). Curiously the Bonhoeffer experience paralleled that of Pope Paul VI, who also visited his brother at the ILO in Geneva as Monsignor Montini. There he was introduced to Maurice Zundel and later to French thought and indeed that of the stirrings of the worldwide movements to unity in both the secular sphere and religious sphere. Peter Hebblethwaite, *Pope Paul VI: First Modern Pope* (New York: Paulist Press, 1993), pp. 83-114. During the Second Vatican Council, Paul took the obligation to report on the progress of the Council to the nations of the world, through the United Nations. Like Bonhoeffer, he came to an appreciation of ecumenism through what he viewed as a twentieth-century understanding of a worldwide movement toward unity. Paul's vision of the Church was that it was inserted into the human exchange of the nations of the world.

79. Bengt Sundkler, *Nathan Söderblom: His Life and Work* (Lund: Gleerups, 1968), pp. 29, 31, 45. Söderblom is largely representative of the Life and Work Movement, which ultimately metamorphosed into the Church and Society Movement, one of two components to the organization of the World Council of Churches. Söderblom took as his motto "doctrine divides, service unites." This does not mean that he treated theology superficially, but rather, his was a theology of praxis, experience and analysis. Like his fellow countryman Dag Hammarskjöld, he was a man of extreme sensitivity. He emerged into a profound piety from a period of great religious doubts and scruples. Throughout his life and ecumenical career he embraced the writing of Auguste Sabatier, *Esquisse d'une philosophie de la religion* (Paris, 1897). Sabatier was looking for that secret, the enigma of our life. In a language of compelling beauty the French Protestant theologian said that religion was "prayer of the heart," directed to *"Un Dieu intérieur,"* or even *"Un Dieu tout intérieur."* Conceived by "Protestant Christianity," this idea had made possible that liberation of personality which had allowed man to "come of age." The above-cited individuals, Boegner, Bonhoeffer and Söderblom, are significant in that each one demonstrated an awareness of the importance of Christian anthropology, i.e., the individual as subject, within the body of the universal Church.

80. *Id., op. cit.,* p. 99.

both understood and was understood by those purporting the ideals of the Classical Reformation. It could be said of Brent that he maintained the Anglican tradition and the Biblical tradition which formed the structure of his personal quest for Christian unity.[81]

The following is Brent's wisdom: (1) Christian unity is *disclosed* or *uncovered* because it is already a gift of God to the Church; (2) by its very nature the Church is rooted in the Blessed Trinity; (3) because it is rooted in the Trinity, the Church is marked as *One, Holy, Catholic, and Apostolic;* and (4) what lies ahead is definitely not a task of construction, of compromise or of constitution. For Brent, Christian unity was about the task of discovering. The sources of Christian knowledge about the Church are found in the witness of Scripture, the evidence of Martyrs and Confessors, the writings of the Fathers, and, of late, the discoveries of history, archeology and ancient Christian texts of liturgy. According to Brent, in contacts with Pope Benedict XV, Archbishop Nathan Söderblom and Max Metzger, the place to begin the task of recovering Christian Unity was not with the Classical Reformation itself, nor with the Great Eastern Schism of 1054, but with the person of Jesus.[82]

With steady patience and a burning zeal, Brent entered into the intense planning for the second Faith and Order Assembly at Edinburgh in August 1937. Despite the fact that Brent and his associates worked mightily among the Protestants of the Continent, Hitler refused passports to the Germans. Nonetheless their influence was made, for the 1937 agenda evidenced the convergence of topics which reflected both British and Continental Reformation themes. The topics were: (1) the Grace of Our Lord Jesus Christ; (2) the Church of Christ and the Word of God; (3) the Church of Christ: Ministry and Sacraments; (4) the Unity of the Church in life and worship; and (5) the Communion of Saints. The entire agenda reflected the theme of the Transcendent Church as enunciated in the ritual of the Anglican Tradition, and the theme of "Word and Sacrament"

---

81. Boegner, *op. cit.*, p. 38. "It was thus that Charles Brent, in pain and labour, gave birth to the theological branch of the Ecumenical Movement."

82. *Ibid.*, pp. 57-58, 64-66. Tavard, *op. cit.*, pp. 98-104. This reference to Christology magnifies the importance of the movement of Kerygmatic Theology, which has its roots in the writings of Friedrich Schleiermacher (1768-1834). Schleiermacher wished to stress that man does not posit his own exemplar and yet that the Redeemer is exemplary *(Vorbildlichkeit)* in that he stands in a continuum with the rest of the human race, i.e., in solidarity with them, without which there could be no communication of redemption. Livingston, *op. cit.*, p. 109. The seminal ecumenical expression of a "hierarchy of truths" is found in this point, that Christ is the center of all truth.

which entered so much into the formulae of the Evangelical and Reform Tradition.[83]

Consensus on the agenda was reached and a commitment to study this material was forged. Although the War intervened, Faith and Order continued through individual efforts, motivated by a need to return to spirituality through the intervening years. Faith and Order played its role in the World Council of Churches Assembly of 1948 and was to affiliate with the World Council Central Offices at No. 17, Route de Malagnou in Geneva, Switzerland. An Ecumenical Institute was established at Bossey, near Geneva proper, for the purpose of encouraging academic work and scholarship. The Lund Conference of Faith and Order, held in 1952, began a methodology of *doctrinal self-criticism,* which in a way provided a mandate for the whole of the World Council of Churches' future. Both as an independent body, and later, as a department of the World Council, Faith and Order would render more and more precise this mission to which it invited WCC member churches and interested observers. The Lund Conference left three issues on the table: the nature of the Church, ways of worship, and intercommunion. Some Roman Catholic theologians assisted in the preparation for this conference. Among them was Father Yves Congar, O.P., whose article "Amica Contestatio" (A Friendly Challenge) highlighted the image of "Church-as-Communion." His language would ultimately develop into *the* appropriate theological concept and component for the entrance by the Roman Catholic Church onto the ecumenical stage.[84]

The effects of the Lund Faith and Order Assembly were not to be felt directly. Many years later, in 1983, the Lima Assembly of Faith and Order endeavors released the decade-long study on *Baptism, Eucharist and Ministry.* The chair of that committee was Pastor Max Thurian of Taizé. The success of this and other Faith and Order activities was due to the strong and consistent intervention of Professor Edmund Schlink of Heidelberg, who was a friend and associate of Cardinal Bea and Cardinal Jaeger.[85]

83. *Ibid.,* p. 101.

84. *Id.,* "Amica Contestatio," in Donald Baillie and John Marsh (eds.), *Inter-Communion* (London: SCM Press, 1952), pp. 143ff. Tavard, *op. cit.,* p. 179. See, Alain Blancy, "Ecumenical Institute of Bossey," in *Dictionary of the Ecumenical Movement,* ed. Nicholas Lossky et al. (Geneva: WCC Publications, 1991), pp. 109-10.

85. William G. Rusch, "Baptism, Eucharist and Ministry," in *Dictionary of the Ecumenical Movement,* pp. 80-84. See also, Teresa Berger, "Worship in the Ecumenical Movement," in *Dictionary of the Ecumenical Movement,* p. 1110. "Theologically, the most interesting contribution to the WCC (BEM process) is undoubtedly Edmund Schlink's. He tried to

Schlink herein identified that, in the post-war situation, it was no longer possible to hold as tenable all the rituals and ecclesiastical constitutions of such a wide variety of Christian denominations. Instead, he called for a careful scrutiny of all doctrine, through extensive study of Sacred Scripture, in particular the New Testament, and its language, and a renewed analysis of Tradition, by recourse to Patristic scholarship and a deeper appreciation of the Church in history. This led to the so-called Lund Principle, for one sentence asked: "Should not our Churches ask themselves whether they are showing sufficient eagerness to enter into conversation with other Churches, and whether they should not act together in all manners, except those in which deep differences of conviction compel them to act separately?" This phrase was perhaps the most widely quoted of any Faith and Order document. Yet the impetus which that question posed became the provenance of substantial multilateral dialogues, to take place in the near future.[86]

The Confluence of Faith and Order and the Catholic Conference on Ecumenism

By 1952 and the Lund Conference, the secret meeting of the Catholic Conference on Ecumenism and representatives of the World Council of Churches at Paris had already taken place. The term *vestigia ecclesiae* had already been adopted by all twenty participants as the stated goal and methodology of their future relations and dialogue. The significance of the challenge is summed up by Père Henri de Lubac, S.J. (later Cardinal), who was aware of the meeting. Later in his life, de Lubac was to comment: "Father Daniélou (the *relator* of the principle of *vestigia ecclesiae*) does not just quote the Fathers of the Church, he goes back to one of their favorite

---

make clear the methodologic significance of worship for ecumenical conversations. He argues that dogmatic and canonical statements of different churches cannot simply be compared in order to reach agreement. Instead, they may have to be translated back to the elementary functions of Church life and worship, where they have their true source and meaning. Schlink's suggestion, if taken seriously, would have important consequences for the basis and form of any emerging consensus among the Churches. It is not with justification, however, that in the context of these important reflections on worship and ecumenical dialogue, the following sentence also occurs: 'The centrality of worship in Christian life and consequently also in the search for unity is an inalienable ecumenical conviction — though perhaps honored more with lips than acts.'"

86. Frans Bouwen, "Ecumenical Conferences," in *Dictionary of the Ecumenical Movement*, p. 329.

themes, he enters into their method and, so to speak, espouses their rhythm. This gives better proof than all dissertations put together that the thought of the first Christian centuries is still living and that if we do not live by it all the more, the fault is in ourselves."[87] De Lubac was an intimate friend and collaborator of Père Daniélou, particularly in the four major projects: *Sources Chrétienne, Témoignage, Dieu Vivant* and *Recherche de Sciences Religieuses.*[88] He shared with him the understanding of the Church as communion *(koinonia)* and the sensibility to the presence of God in history. De Lubac's work in ecumenism would lead him in later years to take a very active part in another form of ecumenism, i.e., interreligious dialogue. Here he was to use the metaphysical component of the *vestigia ecclesiae,* i.e., *veritas.*[89] This point is brought up because the concept indicates the mindset of the expectations of the times, among Catholic ecumenists. *Veritas* belongs to authenticity, i.e., the quest for what is genuinely religious and what is genuinely human.

In a certain sense, participants in the ecumenical quest at mid-century called upon their own intuitive skills. The components of such an interior vision required intellect, a sense of passion and a subjective personal mechanism to identify the honest, the good and the holy. De Lubac spoke of himself and his companions during those years, some of whom were present at the Istina meeting. Some of these had already faced concentration camps and the threat of death. Some, like Congar and de Lubac himself, faced ecclesiastical exile for long years, at the very time when their powers had reached their prime. Words like "faith" and "hope" do not quite carry the moral and intellectual strength that was exhibited by such men. Hence, in his memoirs, de Lubac quoted from a eulogy to Johann Adam Möhler: "We have an irresistible mistrust of those constructions where logic alone

---

87. *Id., At the Service of the Church* (San Francisco: Ignatius Press, 1993), p. 47 n. 5.
88. *Ibid.,* p. 94.
89. *Ibid.,* p. 119. He reported that in an international meeting of the Secretariat for Non-Believers he found himself compromised by a lack of appreciation for the religious *vestigia* or footprints of the Church which are the de facto points of convergence: "In an international meeting held in Vienna, whose theme was the examination of the great current fact of 'secularization,' I made a speech in which I distinguished a number of things that were often confused: the secular view of the cosmos coming from positive science; the secularization of human societies beginning with periods in which the church had to take upon herself the great tasks of civilization, and so on; and finally the enterprises of secularization even from within the church. This speech elicited no response and was not mentioned in the summary of the meeting; it became clear to me that the most influential organizers under the pretext of a historico-sociological analysis, were pursuing a practical end; I myself saw in it the pursuit of an illusion and the seed of a denaturalization of the Church."

and an insistence of an established system place little value on reasons of the heart and on personal commitments that give a work, just as they give life its profound unity and intrinsic rhythm, its lived logic."[90] These words patently echo the sentences from the *Tamworth Reading Room* comment of Cardinal Newman. Henri de Lubac himself, Congar, Chenu and Daniélou are the subject of Möhler's benediction! It is possible to say of them that "they loved the Church" [*Dilexerunt Ecclesiam*]!

The above reference to the World Council of Churches explains the significance of the timing of the letter of Maximos IV Saigh. Any speculation regarding Tisserant's dramatic "veto" would be futile. Perhaps it had something to do with his French origins since some of the Catholic protagonists, of the outer circle of observers of the World Council of Churches, were French. However, such a supposition could be self-contradictory, because Tisserant was the leading ecclesiastical antiquarian of Rome, and would himself be as passionately interested in discussions of Patristic writings, as well as of ancient texts, artifacts and archeological digs.[91] Perhaps Tisserant feared Patriarch Saigh's initiative, since it might signal a change in the balance of power in relations, both religious and political, in the Middle East and Eastern Europe, at least as far as the central authority of Rome was concerned. Who is to say? However, history corroborates the sentiment of Patriarch Maximos IV Saigh. The full phraseology bears repeating:

> In the very times when so much is being said about ecumenism, would it not be opportune, on the part of the Catholic Church which represents Christ on earth, to establish, in conformity with the desires of Our Savior, a permanent institution with solicitude for the union of the separated Churches? [Dans les temps actuels où l'on parle tant d'oecuménisme, ne serait-il pas opportun qu'il y ait de la part de l' Église catholique qui représente le Christ sur terre, une institution permanente en faveur de l'Union des Églises séparées, conformément aux désirs de Notre-Seigneur?][92]

90. *Id., op. cit.*, p. 142.

91. Tisserant always remained *au courant* with contemporary affairs. For example as Dean of the Sacred College of Cardinals he attended the Consultative Assembly of the Council of Europe when it gathered at Strasbourg in 1952. He sought the integration of the Church into the economic, political and cultural sphere of modern life, and pointed out the necessity of highlighting spiritual values within these parameters. Alden Hatch and Seamus Walshe, *Crown of Glory* (New York: Hawthorn Books, 1957), p. 228.

92. *Le Lien, op. cit.*, p. 241.

The proof of the veracity of that sentiment is the very existence of the World Council of Churches, with the *élan* of the Faith and Order Movement, and the Catholic response by reputable theologians.

The 1968 letter of Patriarch Maximos V Hakim was not only a memorial to Cardinal Bea, but also related to the ecumenical mentality and activity of his predecessor, Maximos IV Saigh. Maximos Saigh had died in the previous year, 1967. During his lifetime he did not receive recognition for his quiet contribution to this field. Maximos Hakim did not want his predecessor's initiative to be forgotten, for his ecumenism was neither uninformed nor opportunistic. Often considered something of "a maverick bishop" by Roman Curial members, Maximos IV was a keen Francophile, and, like all Levantines, also intellectually astute; thus, he followed the twentieth-century ecclesiastical events of the Continent of Europe with interest and enthusiasm.

The Malines Conversations and the Emergence of "Dialogue"

Among the early ecumenical initiatives to fall under the observation of this Melchite cleric was the 1921-1926 Roman Catholic dialogue with Anglicans, which had occurred at Malines, Belgium. Here five meetings were convoked under the patronage of Désiré Joseph Cardinal Mercier, the Roman Catholic Primate. The Pope at the time was Benedict XV. He had already been informed of the Faith and Order plans and of the early stirring of the Ecumenical Movement among Protestants and Orthodox. His most recent biographer, John F. Pollard, paints him as suspicious and detached about these things. However, replies to the Episcopalian correspondence, regarding these matters which came from the pen of Cardinal Gasparri, Secretary of State, were polite.[93] However, Gasparri's letters

---

93. *Id., op. cit.,* pp. 206-7. "It is all the more extraordinary that the 'Malines Conversations' of 1922-1926, between Catholic representatives, led by Cardinal Mercier, and Lord Halifax and other Anglicans, should have their origins in Benedict's reign. The answer to the puzzle lies with Cardinal Mercier, whose heroic wartime role had established him as a figure of world stature in the allied countries. In October 1919, for example, he received a standing ovation at the General Convention of the United States Episcopal Church. Though Benedict had not seen eye to eye with Mercier on the methods he used during his four-year struggle with the German occupying authorities, he had immense respect and admiration for the Belgian Cardinal. It was Mercier who proposed to Benedict in December 1920, that he should host discreet discussions in his See City between theologians from the Roman Catholic and Anglican

did, in their original draft, call for everyone to "rally around the throne of Peter."

Important contributors to the Malines Conversations were of course Cardinal Pietro Gasparri and Cardinal Désiré Mercier, both of whom put a positive spin to the arguments placed before Pope Benedict. Gasparri is rarely associated with ecumenism. Yet while he was a professor at the Institut Catholique, he followed the controversy over Anglican ordinations with such interest that he actually wrote articles on the subject. During the time of the 1896 investigation by the Pontifical Commission, Gasparri was in fact a moderate advocate of the Anglican claims at the time.[94] Gasparri's positive sympathy for Christian unity carried over from his 1896 involvement with the Anglican Orders Question to the 1920 proposal of Ferdinand Portal and Lord Halifax that there should be an Anglican–Roman Catholic Conversation that would take place for the sake of Christian Unity. According to Tavard, therefore, Cardinal Gasparri expressed Pope Benedict XV's hopes for the Malines Conversations. The purpose of the efforts made by the Sovereign Pontiff is that "the one and only church which Jesus Christ has decreed and sanctified by his Divine Blood be always carefully guarded and kept entire, unsullied, and ever overflowing with love. . . . [The Holy Father hoped that] struck by its natural beauty and all quarrels being finished, you will be able to work successfully to the end that the Mystical Body of Christ will cease being broken and scattered, and that on the other hand unity of faith and communion might finally triumph among all humanity through harmony, spiritual cooperation and concord."[95]

Gasparri possessed an ingrained sense of optimism, balanced by his continued assessment of rapidly changing affairs, in light of his native sense of realism. He therefore bolstered the mentality of Benedict XV, who throughout the entire period of the Great War was preoccupied by the fear that Orthodox and Czarist Russia would fill the *lacunae* created by the collapse of the Ottoman Empire. Benedict genuinely feared the fall of Con-

---

Churches; in fact, he originally suggested inviting representatives of the Orthodox and other Protestant Churches as well. Ironically, under Mercier's influence, the Malines initiative was more readily accepted in the Vatican than it was at Lambeth. The archbishop of Canterbury was very cautious in giving his blessings to the Conversations for fear of offending the Evangelical wing of his church. In as much as the first exploratory discussions were held at Malines, from December 6-8, 1921, it can be said that it was under the aegis of Benedict XV that the modern Ecumenical Movement was initiated in the Roman Catholic Church."

94. John J. Hughes, *Absolutely Null and Utterly Void* (Washington, D.C.: Corpus Books, 1968), pp. 20, 150-54.

95. *Id., Two Centuries of Ecumenism, op. cit.,* p. 116.

stantinople. Benedict's fears were not assuaged by the fact that the American president reduced him to a figure of suspicion. It comes as no surprise, therefore, to recall that Woodrow Wilson refused the presence of a representative of Pope Benedict at the Versailles Peace Conference of 1919. The major powers of Britain, Italy, France and the United States were only too happy to isolate him.

He imagined the Hagia Sophia cleansed of its centuries of use as a mosque, and restored as the symbol of Orthodoxy and therefore as a rival to St. Peter's Basilica. He feared the rise of two Romes and shuddered at the thought that the twentieth century would be colored by an antipathy between large Latin and Orthodox populations. It must be remembered that Benedict could not himself leave the confines of the Apostolic Palace. A simple thing such as an after-supper walk to digest his meals was denied him. With the onset of the First World War, the number of Italian soldiers, encamped right up to the walls of the Vatican, was increased so that Benedict became physically claustrophobic. Francis Aidan Cardinal Gasquet, O.S.B., an English member of Pope Benedict's Curia, recorded in his memoirs that as Benedict was dying of pneumonia, so many people crowded into his bedchamber that "the poor man died of trying to clear his throat."[96]

Mercier was indeed a formidable figure, whose appeal for dialogue simply could not go unnoticed by Pope Benedict XV. A former professor of philosophy at Louvain University, Mercier was possibly the foremost Thomist of his day. As a young professor, he was personally sent by Pope Leo XIII to Leo's favorite country, Belgium, to execute the tenets of Leo's first renaissance Encyclical, *Aeterni Patris*, in 1879.[97] Leo was proud of the young Mercier. As a Monsignor, Giacomo Della Chiesa, Benedict XV, had previously served the pontificate of Pope Leo XIII in the Secretariate of State. Benedict XV likewise admired and trusted Cardinal Mercier. When

---

96. Pollard, *op. cit.*, p. 196. Sir Shane Leslie, *Cardinal Gasquet: A Memoir* (London: Burns and Oates, 1953), p. 130. Benedict feared the Anglicanism of the British Empire and the Orthodoxy of the East. His pontificate was affected by Freemasonry and anti-Clericalism. In the post-War era he saw the specter of evil around him everywhere. Gasparri's sense of inner freedom helped to bolster Benedict's melancholy. This is not the place to judge Benedict's papacy; but, despite his depression he was innovative and truly a pontiff of world peace. The pity is that he was not recognized as such in his own time. See Gasparri, letter of 18 December 1914, cited in Tavard, *op. cit.*, p. 116. Let it be noted here that during World War I, Wilson borrowed freely from Pope Benedict's Peace Plan in order to develop his famous Fourteen Points.

97. Issued 4 August 1897 and addressed to the entire Church on the subject of the philosophy of St. Thomas Aquinas. Anne Fremantle, *The Papal Encyclicals in Their Historical Context* (New York: G. P. Putnam's Sons, 1956), p. 302.

Mercier approached Benedict about the Malines Conversations, that pontiff expressed his confidence and hope, although he also had his reservations. The actual link between the two, the Cardinal and the Pontiff, was the Abbé Ferdinand Portal, C.M., an intimate friend of Cardinal Mariano Rampolla, the Cardinal Secretary of State, whose private secretary Monsignor Della Chiesa had been. Portal therefore was not unknown to Benedict XV.[98]

The idea for the Malines Conversations had actually begun in 1889 when Portal met Lord Halifax in Madeira, Portugal. The meeting between the two was simply an accident.[99] However, in their friendship, they followed the events at Rome, which pertained to the Anglican Communion. Pope Leo XIII's Apostolic Letter, *Amantissimae Voluntatis* (1895), was written at that very time as a gesture of tenderness to Great Britain.[100] Yet, at the same time, there came the condemnation of Anglican Orders with the decree *Apostolicae Curae* (1896). Observing these seemingly contradictory events, Portal and Halifax kept their friendship alive for twenty-five years. Even the Great War of 1914-1918 did not dampen their enthusiasm to begin the formal theological conversations which marked a watershed in the history of ecumenism. The choice of Cardinal Mercier as president of the Conversations was the mutual decision of Portal and Halifax.[101] They simultaneously approached both the Pope and the Archbishop of Canterbury, Doctor Thomas Randall Davidson. All hoped that Mercier would consent to this role, which required diplomacy, intelligence, and a sense of hospitality. The end result created a precedent. These conversations proved that it was possible to maintain warm relations between the participants without making compromises. The age of dialogue had definitely begun. The mere historical fact of the Malines Conversations provided considerable hope for those who sought the resumption of religious contact with the Roman Catholic Church.[102]

98. John A. Gade, *The Life of Cardinal Mercier* (London: Charles Scribner's Sons, 1934), pp. 240-42, 285.

99. Tavard, *op. cit.*, p. 88.

100. *Ibid.* "For neither Portal nor Halifax was the question of Orders ever more than a means to an end, the device to initiate discussion, and if possible a round table conference between Anglican and Roman Catholic Theologians. Portal (1855-1927) had great influence upon Malines and, also, upon Father Courturier. His untimely death in 1927 followed that of Mercier in 1926 and brought an end to the Conversations because the two leaders were suddenly deceased." Hughes, *op. cit.*, p. 35.

101. Tavard, *op. cit.*, p. 88.

102. Tavard, *ibid.*, p. 128. Cardinal Mercier summed up the purpose of the Malines Conversations with these words: "Our Holy Father insists particularly that we keep in mind that what he expects of us above all is a work of rapprochement that consists in ground-clearing in reducing friction to a minimum, in relieving both sides of their prejudices, and in

The Reticence of Mortalium Animos

The Malines Conversations also created enough vision to carry the spirit of Christian Unity through a very dark period of ecumenical history. In 1922 Benedict XV died. His successor, Achille Cardinal Ratti, was known as Pius XI. Formerly an Archbishop of Milan, as well as a Vatican diplomat who had faced the Bolshevik attack on Warsaw, he was also a very exact librarian, historian, and linguist. He had multiple interests, including mountain climbing. In his pontificate, Ratti had to deal with the rise of Fascism, Communism, and other multiple expressions of totalitarianism. He would see the Church persecuted in Germany, Mexico, Russia and even in his native Italy. His sense of *Realpolitik* made him suspicious of just about every movement, political party, and theological innovation.[103] Thus in 1928, Pope Pius XI issued the encyclical *Mortalium Animos,* in which he warned against Roman Catholic participation in the Ecumenical Movement, which he saw as an expression of religious indifferentism. He said that participation by Roman Catholics in assemblies of non-Catholics confirms the dictum that one religion or Church is just as good as another. His fear was that ecumenical meetings were downright negotiations of revealed truths. In one passage, entitled a "Plea to Bishops for Vigilance," Pius XI precipitated an atmosphere of caution:

---

re-establishing the historic truth. Our job is to get rid of obstacles to reunion. The union as such will be wrought by grace at the hour Divine Providence shall see fit to choose."

103. Pius XI's historians, R. Fontenelle and Anthony Rhodes, are very sympathetic to the plight of Ratti's pontificate. Because of his commitment to preserving the integrity of the Church, Anthony Rhodes described Ratti thus: "It soon appeared that this mild school-master was a martinet. The diplomat, (Diego) von Bergen said: 'After he became Pope there was only one word on every tongue, *obbedire,* obey. For thirty years as an ordinary priest Achille Ratti had obeyed with an apparent unawareness that any other course was possible. Like all those who have obeyed, he instantly commanded with an apparent unawareness when authority came to him.' Beyond that, he clashed with the Nazi and Fascist hierarchy; 'he brought the overbearing and obstinate Lord Strickland, the Prime minister of Malta, to a new Canossa; and he destroyed the powerful Action Francaise party in France almost single handed.' It is to be noted that he had few counselors." Therefore what he published came from his own learning and his own pen. This author knew his secretary, the late Cardinal Carlo Confolonieri, who described Pius as very kind and devout. Anthony Rhodes, *The Vatican in the Age of the Dictators: 1922-1945* (New York: Holt, Rinehart and Winston, 1973), pp. 19-20. R. Fontenelle, *His Holiness Pope Pius XI* (London: Catholic Book Club, 1939), pp. 190-238. Eugen Weber, *Action Francaise* (Stanford, Calif.: Stanford University Press, 1962), pp. 249ff. Oddly, Pius entrusted relations with Charles Maurras, head of Action Francaise, to the Carmelite Sisters of Sainte Thérèse at Lisieux. He had a special devotion to Ste. Thérèse. Here is a curious mixture of piety and politics.

Conscious therefore of Our Apostolic Office, which warns Us not to allow the flock of Christ to be led astray by harmful fallacies, We invoke your zeal, Venerable Brethren, to avert this evil (Ecumenism). We feel confident that each of you, by written and spoken word, will explain clearly to the people the principles and arguments that we are about to set forth, so that Catholics may know what view and what course of action they should adopt, regarding schemes for the *promiscuous union into one body of all who call themselves Christians.* (No. 4, emphasis mine)

Pius XI's words were harsh. He spoke of pan-Christians, who, so far from being a few isolated individuals, had formed an entire class. They had grouped into societies of extensive membership, usually under the direction of non-Catholics, who also disagreed in matters of faith. In fact, in the end, the Pontiff pleaded for a return to the one true Church of Christ by those who are separated from it. The specific cause for such a negative encyclical is not known.[104] However, the Ecumenical Movement *was* growing. This document certainly could not have been directed against the very effective encyclical drafted by Archbishop Germanos and issued by the Ecumenical

104. The mentality of Pope Pius XI is synthesized by Philip Hughes: "Catholics can not join in reunion movements whose basis is the tacit acceptance of the principle that all the so-called Christian religions are equally Christian, or the tacit denial that there is only one Church which is truly the Church of Christ and that to this all others must, necessarily, submit." Philip Hughes, *Pope Pius XI* (New York: Sheed and Ward, 1937), pp. 167-68. In light of the historical works, cited above, pertaining to the administration of Pope Pius XI, it can be stated he faced a multiplicity of problems. Tavard indicated "Pius XI adopted a relatively inflexible position in respect to Protestant ecumenism." He also indicated however that Pius XI's biographers often pointed out he was deeply interested in unity movements. His activity in favor of the apostolate for unity had two characteristics. First, Pius XI involved himself in Orthodoxy more than Protestantism. Second, being a scholar, he had an intellectual apostolate in mind. Finally, in the very year of *Mortalium Animos,* he delivered this elocution to the Italian University Catholic Federation: "For reunion it is above all necessary to know one another and to love one another. It is necessary to know one another because it may be said that if the work of reunion has so often failed, these failures have been due in large part to the fact that neither side has known the other. If there had been mutual prejudices, these prejudices must be resolved. The errors and equivocations that exist and are repeated among the Separated Brethren against the Catholic Church seem incredible. But on the other hand, Catholics too have sometimes been lacking in a just evaluation of their duty, or because of lack of acquaintance, in friendly devotion. Do we know all the precious, good and Christian things that these segments of ancient Catholic truth possess? The separated particles of gold-bearing rock themselves contain gold. The venerable Eastern Christian bodies have preserved in their mentality a holiness so worthy of reverence that they not only merit all our respect but likewise our mutual understanding." Found in Tavard, *Two Centuries of Ecumenism*, pp. 120-21.

Patriarchate of Constantinople in 1920. It is more likely a resistance to the highly favorable press reporting of the 1927 Faith and Order Conference at Lausanne. *Mortalium Animos,* however, did not have lasting effects upon the outreach of the Anglican Communion to maintain contacts with Rome.[105]

In 1932, the Archbishop of Canterbury, the once skeptical Randall Davidson, under pressure from participants in the Malines Conversations, established a Council for Foreign Relations at Lambeth Palace.[106] As time progressed and wartime situations emerged again, representatives of this body were welcomed into contact with the Vatican Secretariate of State. Under Pope Pius XII (1939-1958), their Rome liaison was Monsignor Giovanni Battista Montini, who would later become Pope Paul VI (1963-1978).

Mortalium Animos dampened relations between Catholics and representatives of the Universal Movement for Christian Unity. This was true, in particular, in regard to relations with Protestant scholars and Protestant ecumenists. As will be seen later, the effect of *Mortalium Animos* was a matter of discussion for the Fulda Bishops Conference of Germany, even during the war years. While a severe *monitum* was in effect for Roman Catholics regarding Protestants, there developed a warmth toward Eastern Christians which bolstered another phase of the Ecumenical Movement.

Again Belgium was the scene and Dom Lambert Beauduin, O.S.B., was the central figure. Politics of course remained a catalyst in a background of rapid social change. Papal policy had, in fact, taken a new turn with the overthrow of the Czar of Russia in March 1917. It will be remembered that Benedict XV feared a pan-Orthodox alliance which would be directed from St. Petersburg, but which would have its capital in Constantinople. The Russian Revolution, at first, brought Benedict a sense of relief and the hope of a reunion between East and West. When Ratti had succeeded to the See of Peter, he was deeply moved by the plight of all the victims and, out of motives of pure charity, he organized a large-scale relief program under the direction of Father Edmund Walsh, S.J., of Georgetown University. Phillip Hughes, historian of the Ratti papacy, summed up the change in mentality concerning this new hope:

105. J. Gros, E. McManus, and A. Riggs, *Introduction to Ecumenism* (New York: Paulist Press, 1998), p. 29.

106. Kevin McDonald, "Anglican-Roman Catholic Dialogue," in Lossky et al., p. 27.

To this famine-stricken, plague-swept Russia of Lenin, Pius XI sent for the relief of the sufferers all the money he could gather, sums whose total must have reached nearly one million pounds, organizing one commission after another for the purpose of administration and help. He saw his priests murdered, churches destroyed, his commissions and his charitable advances repelled. . . .[107]

Bereft at the spurning of his charity and recalling his very fresh memory of the confrontation with the Bolsheviks, he suddenly began to unmask for the world the atheistic program of worldwide Communism. Suddenly, the relationship of the Eastern tradition of the Church became a priority for he saw it as a victim of the godlessness of Communism. It was not until 1928 that Pius issued his encyclical *Rerum Orientalium,* which he himself considered progressive, for he truly wished to help do away with mutual ignorance and scorn. Two years later, Pius would write to Cardinal Pompili a personal letter *Ci Commuovono* ("We are deeply affected") in which he expressed his tears over the true nature of Soviet atheism. By this time, Pius had already begun a program of extending himself by pointing out the riches of Eastern spirituality and their relevance for the Universal Church.[108]

The Symbol of Dom Lambert Beauduin, O.S.B.

In 1925, Pius celebrated, with all due pomp, the 16th centenary of the Council of Nicaea, in which he wished to recall the Trinitarian definition with ancient and abiding glory, while praying for the return to unity. The year before, through a gentle invitation, the Pontiff requested that the Benedictine Order foster studies, programs, and spiritual exercises, in order to heal the very profound division between the Eastern Orthodox and Roman Catholics.[109] Pius was sensitive to the role of monasticism in both

107. *Id., Pope Pius XI* (New York: Sheed and Ward, 1937).

108. *Ibid.,* pp. 164ff. The activities of Father Walsh are recorded in John B. Sheerin, *Never Look Back* (New York: Paulist Press, 1975), pp. 85-108.

109. Tavard, *Two Centuries of Ecumenism,* pp. 118-19. Pope Pius XI wrote of this matter to Archabbot Fidelus von Stötzingen on 21 March 1924. Previously Pius had reorganized the Oriental Institute in Rome in 1922. His encyclical, *Ecclesiam dei,* of 12 November 1923, stated: "The Latins must acquire a better and deeper knowledge of Eastern matters and usages." His written encouragement to the Benedictines, *Equidem verba,* used Pius' peculiar phraseology: "The world of the *unionistic reformation.*" He also stated "by your words and your writings you (Benedictines) shall work to increase zeal for unity even among Westerners,

the Eastern and Western traditions. Dom Lambert Beauduin, O.S.B., a former diocesan priest of Brussels, and also a former Benedictine professor of Patristics and Liturgy at Rome's San Anselmo University, responded with enthusiasm.[110]

Beauduin established a Benedictine Priory at Amay-Sur-Meuse with the express purpose of exposing traditional Benedictine Monasticism to the culture and Patristic spirituality of the Basilian style of the East. He did this in 1925, the same year as the Jubilee of the Council of Nicaea.[111] In 1926, he created the ecumenical quarterly *Irenikon*. Beauduin readily grasped the mystical quality of Eastern Monasticism, liturgy, and theology. When Rome criticized Beauduin for being overly enthusiastic and compelled him to resign as prior in 1928, his monastery still flourished. It moved in 1939 to a new site at Chevetogne. While Beauduin had nothing to do with the foundation of this new priory, his name and that of the Chevetogne projects were irrevocably linked. The characterization of Beauduin and Chevetogne is justifiable, since several members of that abbey were to emerge as leaders of the Ecumenical Movement among Catholics. Among those Benedictine scholars were Constantine Lialine, who made early contact with the first administrators of the World Council of Churches;[112] Olivier Rousseau, who reinforced the mission and the activities of this unique Benedictine apostolate through his liturgical research and publication;[113] and Emmanuel Lanne, the outstanding Patristic scholar and *peritus* for ecumenical questions both during and after the Second Vatican Council.[114]

---

and to make known the state of the question that separated the Easterners from us." Finally, Pius eventually issued the encyclical, *Rerum orientalium,* 8 September 1929, ordering the introduction of Eastern theology and liturgy into the curriculum of Catholic theological faculties and seminaries.

110. Sonya A. Quitslund, *Beauduin: A Prophet Vindicated* (New York: Newman Press, 1973), p. 246. Beauduin's ecclesiology rested on two fundamental principles of the Christian tradition: "The recapitulation of all humanity in Christ's humanity and the canonization of a plurality of members (parts) as seen in the symbol of the body. Although he was ready to admit that Orthodoxy, Anglicanism and Protestantism represented three distinct problems, he refused to see them in isolation one from another, which was what his adversaries demanded. . . . Malines had taught him two things: what is different in other churches from Roman Catholic tradition or custom is not *de facto anathema,* and the challenge of union, as well as the responsibility for it, is directed to every single individual — on both sides. All of his subsequent activity was coloured by this conviction."

111. *Ibid.,* pp. 111-16.

112. *Ibid.,* p. 55.

113. *Ibid.,* p. 237.

114. *Ibid.*

Beauduin's early ecumenical ideas flowed from his participation in the final sessions of the Malines Conversations. His most frequently quoted phrase: "The Anglican Church, united to Rome, but not absorbed," was controversial; but it was destined to become a part of a paradigm of ecumenism, even to this day.[115] Like other colleagues from the Dominican and Jesuit communities, Beauduin was destined to spend long years in exile for his theological reflection. He was only allowed to return to his Belgium monastic community in 1951. While in southern France, at the Abbey of En-Calcat, he met the Papal Nuncio, Monsignor Angelo Guisseppe Roncalli, who was later to become Pope John XXIII. Pope John said of him: "The true method of working for the reunion of the churches is that of Dom Beauduin."[116] Beauduin's life and work remain a hallmark of a hunger for more intense relations between Eastern Orthodoxy and Roman Catholicism. External circumstances, including exile, wartime privations, and theological misunderstandings, did not dampen Beauduin's zeal, nor that of his highly academic cluster of scholars and monks. Beauduin's story is one of academic acumen. His ecumenical commitment and his dedication to the Patristic Tradition of the Eastern Church was quite well known to Maximos IV Saigh, who was keenly aware of the details of Beauduin's life.

The Activity of Paul-Irénée Couturier

The priory of Amay-Sur-Meuse and the valiant leadership of Cardinal Mercier during the Malines Conversations were to have their influence on the French priest Paul-Irénée Couturier. In 1932, a brief stay with Beauduin's Benedictines in Belgium introduced him to his own profound yearning for the unity of Christians. In 1933, Couturier introduced the practice of a "triduum" of prayer for Church Unity in the Diocese of Lyons. In 1934, he developed the three-day devotion into an Octave of Prayer, set for 18-25 January. By 1939, the Octave was observed more universally within the Catholic Church. Couturier also successfully solicited Anglican, Protestant, and Orthodox participation.[117]

---

115. *Ibid.*, p. 73.

116. Thomas Stransky, C.S.P., "L. Beauduin," in Lossky et al., *op. cit.*, p. 91. Roncalli and Beauduin corresponded for many years prior to their meeting.

117. Geoffrey Curtis, *Paul Couturier and Unity in Christ* (London: SCM Press, 1964), pp. 52-60, 161, 226, and 236. By 1934 Couturier who had been highly influenced by the Benedictine Priory of Amay-Sur-Meuse and the example of Cardinal Mercier, had developed the devotion of the Octave of Prayer for Christian Unity (January 18-25). By 1939, the Church Unity

Today, Couturier is scarcely recognized for his importance to the worldwide Ecumenical Movement; nevertheless, it was he who introduced the term "Spiritual Ecumenism." His forerunners in movements of shared prayer for Christian Unity include Ignatius Spencer, C.P., Anglican parson Spencer Jones, and Paul Francis Watson, S.A.[118] The poignancy of the term "Spiritual Ecumenism" can easily escape the casual observer. At the time, most Roman Catholics viewed ecumenical devotion with a casual, or perhaps jaundiced eye. Ecumenism seemed to be an esoteric exercise. No distinction was properly made between Anglican, Orthodox, and Protestant denominations, and each was viewed as an anthropological, sociological, psychological, or political grouping. The value and the beauty of prayers from, say, the Protestant tradition filled Catholics with dread. Few among them knew or valued the poetry of John Donne, the music of Charles Wesley, or the sermons of George Herbert. At Christmas they were loath to sing "Away in a Manger," since it was composed by Martin Luther, or "O Little Town of Bethlehem," which came from Phillips Brooks.

By the use of the term "Spiritual Ecumenism," now actually a common phrase in ecumenical literature, Courturier anticipated by more than a decade the Daniélou phrase *vestigia ecclesiae*. The prayers of all the faithful

---

Octave was universally and annually observed. Couturier's activities included making contact with Russian Orthodox refugees throughout France and with early pioneers of the WCC. His activity also included furthering relations with the Anglican communion in the wake of the Malines Conversations. Couturier's apostolate attracted other participants and collaborators who ultimately formed the inter-confessional Association Unité Chrétienne (Christian Unity Association) at Lyons. He was in part responsible for an important ongoing Roman Catholic conversation with Reformed pastors and theologians in Switzerland and France. Dialogue began in 1937 at the Trappist Abbey of Les Dombes in France not far from the Swiss frontier. There were forty participants at each annual meeting. Originally, the methodology of this group followed a system of *compare and contrast,* for such topics as Justification, Redemption, the Sacraments and the Church. In the late 1950s, the project moved to the publication of texts of collaborative studies, in an active search for a "common theology."

118. Ignatius Spencer developed the phrase "the conversion of England through the sanctification of Ireland." It was Spencer's theory that those who were already Catholic, notably the Irish, whether in Ireland or England, possessed a very great opportunity to intensify their sensitivity to holiness and therefore provide a genuine witness of the veracity of the Catholic Church. This would serve as an attraction and effect a reunion. He also established a campaign as is cited above of the intensive use of the Our Father and Hail Mary for the cause of ecumenism. Jozef Vanden Bussche, C.P., *Ignatius (George) Spencer Passionist (1799-1864)* (Leuven: University Press, 1991), pp. 139-63. Charles Spencer, *The Spencers* (New York: St. Martin's Press, 2000), pp. 227-54. Curtis, *op. cit.,* pp. 58-61, regarding Spencer Jones, p. 59, and regarding the importance of Paul James Francis Watson, S.A., the founder and the first Father General of the Franciscan Friars of the Atonement.

throughout the whole Christian family end with "Through Jesus Christ our Lord, Amen." The Johannine Gospel is filled with instructions about prayer and therefore, in the High Priestly discourse, there is found: "Anything you ask in my name, it will be granted to you (Jn. 14:14)." Couturier found sacerdotal consensus in the liturgical practice of all Christian tradition: every denomination offers its prayer through the mediatorship of Christ.

Couturier's methods were effective. His activities included providing comfort for Orthodox refugees from Russia, who, by then, had trickled into France. He introduced himself politely to the Protestant pioneers of the future World Council of Churches, in the wake of the Malines Conversations and out of the shadows of *Mortalium Animos.* He furthered relations with the Anglican Communion. Thus, he struck up an active and ongoing relationship with the Anglican Benedictine community at Nashdom Abbey. Dom Benedict Ley came to visit him at Lyons in May 1936.[119] It was through Couturier that Sister Maria Gabriella Sagheddu, O.C.S.O., was introduced from her cloister at Grottaferrata to Nasdom Abbey. Now "Blessed," she wrote moving passages of Scripture to Dom Benedict, sending the Word of God, as it were, to him on the air, like so many petals of grace blowing on the wind. Sr. Maria Gabriella has been declared the Patroness of Ecumenism because she represents the intense mystical insight of the Abbé Couturier and because she is an image of spiritual communion through prayer.[120]

Part 3: Conclusion

Daybreak would eventually come, in 1949, with an Instruction of the Holy Office, *Ecclesia Sancta,* the first inkling of a positive incentive from the Holy See toward the Ecumenical Movement. That Instruction employed the term "Spiritual Ecumenism." It encouraged the Church Unity Octave, and it allowed for participation by Catholic experts in discussions of faith and morality with non-Catholic counterparts.

Thus, perhaps, most of all, when Maximos IV Saigh wrote to Pope John XXIII about the atmosphere of ecumenism that was in the air, he may have been referring most specifically to Abbé Couturier. Couturier had

---

119. *Ibid.,* p. 164.

120. Martha Driscoll, *A Silent Herald of Unity* (Kalamazoo, Mich.: Cistercian Publications, 1990), p. 103.

printed French pamphlets and encouraged dialogues which would not have escaped the notice of the Patriarch in Lebanon. Couturier brought ecumenism to the grass roots, to ordinary Catholics, whose daily lives were filled with the sense of ordinary devotion. Perhaps Couturier and Maximos IV Saigh could be memorialized together with Couturier's prophesy: "The visible unity of the Kingdom of God may be such as Christ wills and achieves by whatever means he wills."[121]

His biographer, Geoffrey Curtis, claims: "Any visible unity not rooted in the interior life of the growing love of God in the Holy Trinity, he (Couturier) would have regarded not only as insufficient but also as disastrous."[122] Prayer means, first of all, personal sanctification. In the case of prayer for Christian Unity, Couturier's directive was a request to God for the sanctification of each Christian community. Then, it becomes apparent to the *Orans,* i.e. the one praying, that the Gospel and prayer are, in essence, One. Curtis claims: "This criticism reveals an astonishing conception of holiness. Can members of the Body of Christ, becoming holy, fail to come close to Christ? Can they come close to Christ without coming closer to one another in the Truth?"[123]

The above narrative of this text relates numerous details from the history of what, in Cardinal Willebrands' terminology, may be cited as the "pre-Ecumenical phase" of the Roman Catholic contribution to the World-wide Ecumenical Movement. They provide ample evidence for the claim of Maximos IV that much interest and concern about ecumenism "was in the air." The details demonstrate "how a traditional society passes a watershed."[124] Facts of history do not go away. They may be inconspicuous and not in any way melodramatic, but they are there to be remembered and to be acted upon. Pope John did not act upon the advice of the Melchite Patriarch, *but he certainly remembered it* according to the testimony of Archbishop Capovilla.[125] The recall of this 23 May letter of 1959 places the circumstances of a later letter from Archbishop Jaeger, 4 March 1960, in context. When Jaeger wrote to Pope John ten months after the letter of Maximos, he likewise circumscribed the ecumenical situation by reference to already existing ecumenical activities which placed the situation in its historical environment. It remained for Cardinal Bea to transfer the data of

---

121. *Ibid.*

122. *Ibid.*

123. *Ibid.*

124. Peter Brown, *The Making of Late Antiquity* (Cambridge: Harvard University Press, 1978), pp. 2-4.

125. Interview with the author, 28 September 2001.

this history into the context of the forthcoming Vatican Council. In the words of Peter Steinfels, "Can the Church really side step the problem of historical fact? Christianity, after all, is notorious for considering itself a history-based religion."[126] These details are certainly seeds planted in the ground. In Chapter Two, we shall observe their unique and paradoxical fructification within the context of German Christianity. Through the struggles of the Nazi debut, the Second World War, and the Cold War, the idea of ecumenism took on a sense of practical urgency, which gave it impetus and brought it from seed to shoot.

Excursus: Spiritual Ecumenism

Without doubt, Paul Couturier is the pioneer of the movement of "spiritual ecumenism" in the twentieth century. Essentially, spiritual ecumenism identifies the "grass roots" efforts to express an inner sentiment of yearning for unity within the Christian family, whether through common prayer, study, or action of joint Christian witness. Règis Ladous, in an article in *The Dictionary of the Ecumenical Movement,* states: "Spiritual ecumenism consists in *identifying with Jesus' prayer* (Jn. 17:21) so that through the action of his Spirit, he himself can raise up from within each people a reconciled church capable of proclaiming the good news to all."[127] One of the first memorable efforts to solidify and demonstrate the "grass roots character" of this phenomenon was the establishment of the Religious Community at Taizé in France.

Roger Schutz, a Swiss Calvinist theology student, was a disciple of Père Couturier and imbibed his spirit, style, and teaching. Along with two other companions, he and Max Thurian, another Calvinist student, inaugurated the Taizé Community of Brothers in 1941, at a site not too far from the ruins of the Benedictine Abbey at Cluny in France. By 1944, Schutz defined Taizé as "a parable of Communion." Giving symbolic significance to the geographical location of the Community, he said:

> Taizé is like a shoot grafted onto the tree of the monastic life. No doubt there is a meaning in the fact that we are placed between Cluny and Cîteaux. On the one side, there is Cluny with its humanity, its sense of moderation and continuity. Cluny, which held such an attraction for so

---

126. Peter Steinfels, "Beliefs," *New York Times,* 20 July 2002, Section A-10.
127. Règis Ladous, "Spiritual Ecumenism," in Lossky et al., *op. cit.,* p. 948.

many Christians seeking unity within themselves and with other people. On the other side, Cîteaux, renewed by St. Bernard, with his acute sense of urgency and his reforming zeal, and refusal of all compromise of the absolute nature of the Gospel. In their footsteps, he would like to blend the sense of urgency and a sense of long continuity.[128]

The Community was destined to become an icon of spiritual ecumenism in the years immediately after World War II. Max Thurian, who later would become a Catholic, a priest, and a Canon of the Cathedral Chapter at Naples, would later serve (1970s-1980s) as the Chair of the Faith and Order Drafting Committee for the significant consensus document of *Baptism, Eucharist and Ministry,* known as the Lima Document (1982) of the World Council of Churches.

The first members of Taizé embraced a spiritual concept known as *"The Provisional,"* i.e., an ecumenical understanding of "time" where challenges, responsibilities, and acts of worship are viewed as preparatory for that moment when God will intervene in the Christian family to draw all members and all things into One in Christ. Brother Roger explained his life thus: "Christians today are living at a time when the vocation to universality common to Catholicity, confided to them by the Gospel, can find unprecedented fulfillment. Since the fourth century, few periods in history have been more decisive for Christians."[129] Although the concept was misunderstood as being "anti-establishment," it remains a seminal ideal of ecumenical spirituality. It represents the Taizé ideal of hope: the charismatic insight that all is subject to "the continuous creativity" of the Holy Spirit. "Having put your hand to the plow," advised Frère Roger, "never look back."[130]

The spirituality of Taizé was explained by its founder as early as 1941, when he composed an eighteen-page pamphlet which outlined the monastic ideal as "an image of communion." He said of these early days: "There are some texts in the scriptures which are more fundamental than others. I have always considered the Beatitudes to be essential texts and so, when it came to writing something down, I began with the three words that encapsulated the spirit of the Beatitudes: joy, simplicity, and mercy. In them was the essential of the Gospel."[131] For Schutz, these concepts were liberating

---

128. *Id. His Love Is a Fire* (Collegeville, Minn.: Liturgical Press, 1990), p. 119.

129. *Ibid.,* p. 101.

130. Kathryn Spink, *A Universal Heart: The Life and Vision of Brother Roger of Taizé* (San Francisco: Harper & Row, 1986), p. 99.

131. *Ibid.,* pp. 45-46.

and supported his understanding of the "monastic day," i.e., the embrace of the Word, and the silent watchful waiting, observing and witnessing to the activity of God Who draws all things into Unity.[132] While Frère Roger represented Taizé in terms of hope and biblical awareness, his first companion, Frère Max Thurian, searched the liturgy to represent a fresh, even innovative concept of mature Christianity. He demonstrated this in an analysis of chrismation, or Confirmation which, along with his studies on Baptism, Eucharist, and Ecumenism, set a new tone for ecumenical spirituality. In *The Consecration of the Layman,* he contributed an important statement, which surprisingly brought together the expectations of the Reformed Christians with those of Orthodox Christians:

> This fact of the "ordination of laics" by baptism in the Spirit, and then by confirmation, is very important for exorcising the Western Church of its clericalism. In the East, the distinction between "clergymen" and "laymen" is not so much marked as in the West. *The Church* is an "ordained community." This is evident in the doctrine of the Sacrament of Confirmation. For the Orthodox, confirmation has no connection with renewal of baptismal vows; it is an ordination whereby a Christian receives a "grace" which permits him to participate in the administration of all the other sacraments.[133]

Overall, in his little treatise on the subject, Thurian identified the power of the laity with that of the royal priesthood of Christ, defining it as oral witness for sanctity, the prayer of praise and intercession, and personal influence on Christian life.[134]

---

132. Schutz, *op. cit.*, p. 50, and see Mother Teresa and Brother Roger Schutz, *Seeking the Heart of God* (San Francisco: Harper, 1993), pp. 71-74: "The day will come when each one of us will know, and perhaps even will say, 'No, God did not go away. I was the one who was absent. God is with me all the time.'"

133. Max Thurian, *The Consecration of the Layman* (Dublin: Helicon, 1963), p. 90. Refer to J. M. Barkley, "The Meaning of Ordination," *Scottish Journal of Theology* 9, p. 150. Barkley indicates that Orthodoxy is primarily concerned with baptism of the Spirit *(sphragis),* the only Confirmation the Orthodox Church recognizes, and which implies "ordination" to service in the Church. The Orthodox Church has concentrated everything on baptism, i.e., "ordination of laics," as well as the initiation into its plenitude.

134. This same concept is also outlined in the Reformed tradition by Thomas F. Torrance, *Royal Priesthood* (Edinburgh: T&T Clark, 1993), p. 19. Torrance defines the Royal Priesthood as *latreia,* i.e., worship of God in spirit and truth (Jn. 4:22ff.), grounding it in the eschatological change so clearly found in the Epistle to the Hebrews (12:28). It is a short step to the ecumenical dimension, for the unity of the family of God in prayer is a symbol of the eschaton.

The foundation at Taizé was no mere experiment. In France, it demonstrated its intellectual counterpart in the "personalist movement" of Emmanuel Mounier. This philosopher and editor of the journal *Esprit* ironically used the writings of Nietzsche to strip French Christianity of "a bourgeois leisure."[135] In turn, he called for reverence of "the person" and "the community of persons" by the religious, notably by the Catholic element of society. Mounier saw no hope for the twentieth century in the heritage of the nineteenth-century concept of "progress," whether that concept be posited by either Marxist or capitalist sources:

> Whoever seeks the continuity of the Kingdom had better turn his attention away from the statistics of Massachusetts or the Ubangi, away from the epaulettes of Franco and from the prestige of Cardinal Spellman in the *Reader's Digest*. He will find . . . in the worker's quarter of Montreuil . . . three priests living in community, in shabby clothes, and around them an obscure, stammering and shocking reality . . . the Church of the year 3000 will place these solitaries on pedestals when Franco . . . will not even leave a trace in the pitiless books of History. Before burying the Christian tradition, one had better direct a little attention to its *avant-gardes*.[136]

The Taizé community was the model of Mounier's musings. Personalism has defied definition. Yet, especially in the France of the 1930s to 1950s, it stood for the most profound affirmation of the dignity of each and every human being. An intellectual *a priori*, it challenged every ideological system of the twentieth century, e.g., Nazism, Fascism, Communism, Euro-Marxism, Materialism, and Consumerism. It has also had its effect upon such Roman Catholic exponents of "essential theology" and "essential spirituality" in the twentieth century as Fathers Daniélou, Chenu, Congar, and de Lubac. Perhaps the best synthesis here is to state that consistently through his commitment to the journal *Esprit*, Mounier, the principal representative of the Personalist trend at mid-century, consistently presented a Christian anthropology, at the center of which each individual enunciates the human potential, the human religious sensitivity, and the human awareness that is unique to the human species.[137]

---

135. John Helman, *Emmanuel Mounier and the New Catholic Left, 1930-1950* (Toronto: University of Toronto Press, 1981), p. 59.

136. *Ibid.*, p. 246.

137. Reflecting on these individuals, cited above, the American Jesuit journalist John LaFarge has reflected on the personalist expression in terms of "love": Old age without love is

Therefore, writing of Taizé, founded against the darkness of Nazi-occupied France and the small, still candlelight optimism of the "personalist movement," Henri de Lubac spoke thus:

> At the very time, when some among us, as if suddenly struck by blindness, seem no longer to perceive the beauty or the benefits of the world, of the evangelic life in the Church, on the plateau of Taizé, once a nearby dependency of ancient Cluny, a swarm of young men from all the horizons of the Protestant Reformation, have gathered to lead that *life together,* a life they are rediscovering in all its freshness.[138]

Taizé grew in France from 1941 onwards, reflecting a yet unperceived thirst for spiritual unity on the marketplace level. Previously an "underground seminary" of the Confessing Evangelical Church in Germany had a very brief existence.[139] Founded and closed in 1935, it too was marked by *Life Together* and Dietrich Bonhoeffer was its spokesman:

> Human love lives by uncontrolled and uncontrollable dark *desires;* spiritual love lives in the clear light of service ordered by *the truth.* Human love produces human subjection, dependence, constraint; spiritual love creates *freedom* of the brethren under the Word. . . . The life or death of a Christian community is determined by whether it achieves sober wisdom on this point as soon as possible. In other words, *life together* under the Word will remain sound and healthy only where it does not form itself into a movement, an order, a society, a *collegium pietatis,* but rather where it understands itself as being a part of the one, holy, catholic Christian Church where it shares actively and passively in the struggles and promise of the whole Church.[140]

Bonhoeffer's words predate Brothers Roger and Max as well as Père de Lubac. He was actually on his way to India when Bonhoeffer received a call to supervise this clandestine seminary at Finkenwalde in 1935. As is of-

---

a mockery. . . . The learned French Dominican, Father Corvez, is very positive on the presence of these new occasions (within human development, to love). It belongs to the very essence of charity, he says, to its inmost structure and dynamism, to continue to grow without ceasing. And charity grows all the more rapidly as it approaches the terminus of its movement. God draws the soul all the more powerfully as the soul "approaches nearer to him by the dimensions of its charity." In *Reflections on Growing Old* (Garden City, N.Y.: Doubleday and Co., 1963), pp. 74-75.

138. Spink, *op. cit.,* p. 99.

139. Bethge, *Dietrich Bonhoeffer,* p. 289.

140. *Id., Life Together* (San Francisco: Harper & Row, 1954), p. 37.

ten noted, he was already living his Christian life "on the edge." Beginning in 1933, the year of the Nazi electoral victories within Germany, he used the radio to broadcast against Hitler. The following year, he subscribed openly to Karl Barth's condemnation of Nazi paganism and also to the Barmen Declaration, i.e., the Constitutional Statement of the Independent Confessing Church Movement, which was opposed to Hitler and to the Nazi Party's direct involvement in German Protestant life. In Bonhoeffer's desperate experience in a dictator-dominated country, there was no possibility of retreat into any sinless, righteous, pious refuge. For him, the sin of respectable people revealed itself in their flight from responsibility.[141] For Bonhoeffer, ecumenical life is *always life together* in Christ, with Christ, and against evil. While Bonhoeffer's experiment in Christian community was extinguished by the German Gestapo, the little light at Taizé continued to flicker until the end of the War. Because of it and the spontaneous efforts of individuals such as Max Metzger, Lambert Beauduin, and Père Couturier, the concept of "spiritual ecumenism" on the Continent preceded any direct institutionalized ecumenical dialogue or endeavor. This spiritual ecumenism embraces "the lived experience."

The situation was not immediately evident to the ordinary Christian at that time. Through his official biographer, Konrad Adenauer, the first Chancellor of the Federal Republic of Germany in 1945, recalled that he had foreseen Germany's defeat in the First World War:

> Early in 1918, he had remarked . . . that the war would be lost, and that also meant the end of the Monarchy. But he had not anticipated that the upheaval would take the form it did. Like many others, he did not believe the German people, with their inborn patience and submission to authority, capable of violent political outbursts. It was a Russian who had said: "When German revolutionaries plan to storm a railway station, they start by buying platform tickets." This observation was generally felt to be true; the very idea of a revolution in Germany seemed absurd.[142]

But revolution did come, like a tidal wave, lasting for a very long time, filling the land with fear and stripping every adult individual down to the ethical transparency, identified by Bonhoeffer.

---

141. *Id.*, p. 104. "Added to the fear of one's responsibility to speak, there is the fear of the other person. . . . Where Christians love together, the time must inevitably come when in some crisis, one person will have to declare God's Word and will to another."

142. Paul Weymar, *Adenauer* (London: Andre Deutsch, 1957), p. 41.

These sentiments were recorded by Adenauer, himself a Catholic, in an autobiographical reflection of Hitler's Germany. His remarks complement Bonhoeffer's meditation:

> We have reason, and we have a conscience, and both are the gift of God. In using them, as a politician, I make my contribution toward the establishment of the order willed by God. Even here in this world . . . there is a most deplorable misunderstanding on the part of many evangelical Christians who believe that with us Roman Catholics, highest and ultimate authority is vested in the Church. This is not so. With us, too, our own individual conscience makes the final decision. I should always, in any conflict, act according to what my own conscience tells me. This is the attitude which the Church expressedly demands from us.[143]

The basic claim of vengeance was a moral imperative for all Christians, although unspoken, toward a sense of responsibility in Christ. Out of fear of the Hitlerite wartime totalitarian situation, the Roman Catholic bishops of the greater German nation (thirty-five dioceses) provided little or no public incentive toward resistance, nor, for that matter, toward spiritual renewal, so thwarted were they by the Nazi regime.[144] Contemporary historians do not agree as to where the blame rests, whether in the Concordat of 1933, in the Enabling Act of that same year, or in the bishops themselves. Only Bishop Konrad von Preysing of Berlin and Bishop Clemens von Galen of Münster stood out as open opponents of Hitler. Archbishop Lorenz Jaeger of Paderborn understood something far deeper regarding the all-pervasive awareness of the German nation, that is to say, that the *spirituality* of Christian Germany, with all its complexities, was never far from the German conscience or its consciousness of *Volk*.

In his analysis of post-War Germany, the sociologist/historian Gordon A. Kreig has written that 95 percent of the population of the German Federal Republic was, at least formally, of one of the Christian denominations. He also stated that the Christians of the German Democratic Republic (GDR) were, at the time of his analysis in the late 1970s, active and professing members of their religious denomination. More impor-

---

143. *Ibid.*, p. 13.

144. Michael Phayer, *The Catholic Church and the Holocaust: 1930-1965* (Bloomington: Indiana University Press, 2000), pp. 135-39. Guenter Lewy, *The Catholic Church and Nazi Germany* (New York: McGraw-Hill Book Company, 1964), pp. 40-41. Through much of this period, the leader and spokesperson was Adolf Cardinal Bertram, Archbishop of Breslau.

tantly, Kreig gave this evidence of the perennial, yet timely, character of the German religious ethos:

> Most of all . . . perhaps, it is illustrated by the liveliness, if not acrimony, of disputes within the two principle confessions, concerning Church reform and the appropriate rule of Christianity in contemporary society. The activities and internal debates are not, of course, new. Indeed, they reflect convictions and differences that have, in some cases, existed among confessing Christians [*sic*] since the beginning of the modern era and have been exacerbated by the behavior of the Protestant and Roman Catholic establishments during the Nazi years . . . to illustrate this, we must start by going back to the Reformation, a point in time that is perhaps *less remote to the Germans than it is to us,* since they are still surrounded by its memorials.[145]

This mentality was grasped by Jaeger as a bishop and by Father Max Metzger, a kind of freelance cleric whom history now esteems as a prophet of *Lebenswelt* Christianity. Jaeger carried the issues and the sensitivities of the continued reminder of the Reformation to the table of the German Bishops Conference at Fulda, which in fact did not want to deal with him, while they were trying to keep Hitler and Himmler at bay. Jaeger, although he might never admit it, was deeply under the influence of Max Metzger, whose *Una Sancta* Brotherhood was the most telling popular ecumenical symbol in the Germany of his time. Tavard places Metzger and Jaeger side by side. The French edition of his ecumenical history should be quoted in full here, for its language possesses the pure poetry of their consanguinity:

> The convergence of ecumenical thought in Germany and in France is worth mentioning. On the spiritual level the activity of Max Metzger and Paul Couturier converge. Here and there we find the same insights and the same prophetic views. On the doctrinal level German and French theology join hands in a similar ecumenical endeavor after having followed sometimes different methods. This encounter constitutes a

---

145. *Id., The Germans* (New York: G. P. Putnam's Sons, 1982), p. 83. For a fuller discussion of this point, see Michael Burleigh, *The Third Reich* (London: Pan Books, Macmillan, 2000), pp. 256-61. Burleigh correctly identifies the Nazi era as a cynical catalyst for eventual ecumenical awareness. Understanding that a desperate logic attempted to reconcile Nazism with Christianity and played upon clerical weakness and banality, it never anticipated that thinking Christians would ultimately emerge. These heroic individuals understood that in the midst of *völkische* thought (national blood awareness), that in fact a Trojan Horse had entered the city of God.

guarantee of doctrinal maturity. This meeting constitutes a guarantee of the doctrinal maturity of Catholic ecumenism.

This convergence now is an established fact. A "Catholic Conference for Ecumenical Questions" was founded in 1952. Most of the theologians are from German, Dutch and French speaking countries. It represents a very significant development of Catholic endeavors toward ecumenism.[146]

[La convergence de la pensée oecuménique en Allemagne et en France mérite d'être soulignée. Au plan spirituel, l'action de Max Metzger et celle de Paul Couturier se rejoignent. De part et d'autre on constate les mêmes institutions et les mêmes vues prophétiques. Au plan doctrinal, la théologie allemande et la théologie française aboutissent, par des méthodes parfois diverses, à une ouverture semblable du côté de l'oecuménisme. Cette rencontre constitue une garantie de la maturité doctrinale. Cette rencontre constitue une garantie de la maturité doctrinale de l'oecuménisme catholique.

Cette convergence est maintenant un fait accompli. Une "conférence catholique pour les questions oecuméniques" a été fondée en 1952. Elle groupe des théologiens de l'oecuménisme appartenant surtout aux pays de langue allemande, néerlandaise et française. C'est là une développement très significatif des initiatives catholiques en matière d'oecuménisme.][147]

Historically, the concept of spiritual ecumenism on the Continent preceded any direct institutionalized ecumenical dialogue or endeavor. *Spiritual ecumenism embraces the lived experience.* Couturier, Mounier, Schutz, Thurian, Bonhoeffer and Max Metzger were its prophets. All recognized the priority of ecumenism's rise, from the prayers, the piety and the sentiment of the faithful. Most of all, they recognized the wellspring of the ecumenical thrust from deep inside the Church, its nature, its sense of community and its Sacraments. For Bonhoeffer, the Sacrament of the Word calls the Church to community. For Max Thurian, a Protestant of the Reformed Tradition, a Christian finds his vocation to community in the Sacraments of Initiation, Baptism and Confirmation, which confer the dignity of the royal priesthood, for it is the duty of every king and every priest to call the many into one.[148]

---

146. Tavard, *op. cit.*, p. 159.

147. Tavard, *Petite Histoire du Mouvement Oecuménique*, p. 156.

148. Max Thurian followed this procedure of reference to the Sacraments in his position as Chairman of the Drafting Committee for *Baptism, Eucharist and Ministry.* There is a

Spiritual ecumenism highlights the activity of the Holy Spirit, Who manifests Himself in the dynamic of "call!" For Mounier, the call is identified with the *Vie intérieure!* For Bonhoeffer, the call comes from the Word and stirs up the sense of responsibility. The same could be said for Max Metzger. Taizé symbolizes the community, the Church, *koinonia.* Metzger and Bonhoeffer are both associated with brotherhoods which are now tucked away in the shadows of history; Taizé shines on to speak about the significance, at once realistic and Romantic regarding people's coming-together for praise, petition, and charity. In a certain sense, Taizé demonstrates a microcosm of the Church, which after all is the purpose of any religious community.

---

reference to Chrismation in N. 14 of that document: "All agree that Christian baptism is in water and the Holy Spirit." Faith and Order, *Baptism, Eucharist and Ministry* (Geneva: World Council of Churches, 1982), p. 6. It was a revolutionary gesture for a representative of the Reformed Tradition to study the significance of the Sacrament of Confirmation which, since the time of Calvin, had been considered a sacramental.

Chapter II

The German Theater of Ecumenical Activity

Introduction

Having reviewed the pre-history of the Ecumenical Movement and the first presentation of the cause of Ecumenism to Pope John by Patriarch Maximos, it is now necessary to turn attention to the German theater of Ecumenism. Because of its Carolingian history, Reformation history, and twentieth-century history, Germany possesses a certain ecumenical uniqueness. From that heritage emerged Augustin Bea. The rich tradition of Germany, language, literature, philosophy, religious piety and religious history, endowed Bea with a specific mindset which would enable him to fulfill the role of leadership, when first appointed by Pope John to be president of the Secretariat for Promoting Christian Unity. The details of Cardinal Bea's life will be discussed in a further chapter. It is important here, however, to state that while continually affiliated with his academic position in Rome, Bea's actual professional studies in Sacred Scripture and the ancillary biblical sciences were actually undertaken in Berlin. His instructors were by and large German Protestant experts in philology, archeology, biblical history and exegetical methodology.

Prior to his transfer to Rome as a professor at the Pontifical Biblical Institute, Bea had also been the first Jesuit provincial of the Bavarian Province of his order. As such, he experienced the immediate post-war calamity of the 1920s. He felt the collapse of morale within the German nation. The experience of the transformation from the nineteenth-century Romantic mode to twentieth-century realism, in the arts and the sciences, did not escape Bea's attention or his sensibility. The link between Bea's place as a frontiersman of the Ecumenical Movement and the struggles of his German homeland was Lorenz Jaeger. It must be remembered that Bea spent most of his professional career at Rome. Especially in the post–World War II period, Jaeger kept Bea informed of religious developments in Germany. Jaeger himself epitomized ecumenical awareness in all the uniqueness of twentieth-century Germany. In order to understand Bea it is useful to turn attention to the overview of German ecumenical life and thought in the first half of the twentieth century.

Lorenz Cardinal Jaeger is also a principal protagonist of this narrative. Born at the end of the nineteenth century into the household of a blue-collar worker, he exhibited remarkable talent and was destined for the priesthood. Throughout his public ministry as an educator and a university chaplain, he dedicated himself especially to the apostolate of catechetics. Upon the death of Archbishop Kasper Klein in 1941, Jaeger was elevated to the See of Paderborn. In 1965, at the end of the Second Vatican Council, he became a Cardinal. During the Second World War, he was led by others to a renewed understanding of the importance of Reformation studies, and, in turn, he acknowledged the *Una Sancta Movement*. What follows below are primarily ecumenical aspects of his story. They are important, for he served as the first episcopal point of convergence for ecumenical trends and initiatives, which took place in the Germany of his day. He was fortunate in that three ecumenical leaders were members of his diocesan college of clergy, viz., Paul Simon, rector of the Cathedral, Josef Höfer and Eduard Stakemeier, both of the faculty of the University of Paderborn.

Jaeger's interest in ecumenism had been long-standing, and was connected with his academic interest in German language and literature. Philosophically inclined, he intended to write a doctoral thesis in the field of experimental psychology. It was one of his life's disappointments that his thesis remained uncompleted. The scope of his academic pursuits likewise included Reformation studies of sixteenth-century Germany.

The Academic Atmosphere of Early Twentieth-Century Germany

There was at this time an academic trend among religious-minded Germans to take up again issues that had been raised by Luther's rupture with Rome in 1517. The pre–Second World War and the wartime situation itself enhanced this tendency. Monsignor Heinrich Portmann, private secretary to the Cardinal Clemens August von Galen (1878-1946), Archbishop of Münster, recorded of his bishop:

> The bishop passed the evening(s) alone in his study where he read the paper or turned the wireless on for a short time. Afterwards he read either a work on religion or philosophy or a historical book on the theological controversies of the Reformation. Such works had great interest for him and he often pondered on the analogy between the Reformation and his own time, which witnessed that tragedy, which was so bitter for Germany, of renewed controversies on religion.[1]

Von Galen had little time, during those years, for the "new movements" such as the lay apostolate, the missionary movement and the revised study of the liturgy. When Peter Wust, the phenomenologist, presented him with an autographed copy of his study of "existentialism and faith" entitled, *Ungewissheit und Wagnis* (Uncertainty and Venture), von Galen threw up his hands. Such books were only for his theologians. "I talk to Almighty God in a simpler way. It seems to me that men of today like to walk on stilts." While he had no time for the so-called "new theology," the outspoken bishop, who was known as the "Lion of Münster," never put down his studies of the Classical Reformation, for he considered them ever relevant to the pastoral situation of twentieth-century German Catholic life.[2]

The Archbishop of Paderborn, Lorenz Jaeger resided only in the next diocese to von Galen. His was a peculiar diocese; it was divided completely in two by the diocese of Hildesheim. One part, with a heavy cluster of Catholics, was focused in the Western side of Germany, while the other, centered around the ancient medieval town of Magdeburg, possessed a concentration of Evangelicals. For pastoral reasons, the new Ordinary, Archbishop Jaeger, felt compelled to intensify his personal inclination to understand the issues of Reformation history.

In the first two decades of the twentieth century an anti-Catholic bias remained, as part of the residue of the *Kulturkampf* of the previous century. Here is one example. On 1 August 1917, Pope Benedict XV made an appeal to all the parties involved in the so-called Great War. That appeal included an adjustment of territories, regarding the Balkans, France, Italy, and Austria. Germany reacted negatively. Just at that moment, the Kaiser's government was overwhelmingly Protestant and pan-German in orientation. Together with the right wing of the National Liberal party and the

---

1. *Id., Cardinal von Galen* (London: Jarrolds, 1957), p. 77.
2. *Ibid.*, p. 81.

Progressive party, the chancellor, Theobold Bethman-Hollweg, accused the pontiff of being the puppet of the Western Powers. Further, he gave issue to the religious character of his political sentiments by demanding to know why *Protestant Germany* should accept a peace plan negotiated by *the Catholic leader* in the year of the 400th anniversary of the Reformation.[3] While the above indicates the abiding presence of a Reformation mentality in Germany, probably made the more intense by the exigencies of war, Catholics in general were less attentive to it in their ordinary lives.[4] The demise of the *Kulturkampf* mentality at the beginning of the twentieth century put an end to an attitude of defense and detachment, among Catholic academics, about the Church and German life. Karl Rahner, S.J., Jaeger's contemporary, recalled the era in a memoir:

> But I didn't actually experience a particularly defensive Kulturkampf mentality. Obviously in those days we Jesuits also shared in the ecclesial Roman Catholic mentality that had evolved in the nineteenth century, after the French Revolution. Intensified significantly by the Kulturkampf, this mentality became a ghetto mentality — now I don't mean this deprecatingly.[5]

Rahner then went on to mention other Catholic thinkers such as Karl Adam, Peter Lippert and Erich Pryzwara. All of these used the tools of sociology, the empirical sciences and the language of contemporary philosophy (notably phenomenology, critical history, existentialism, and personalism) in their theological quest to achieve "relevance" in pastoral life. In other words, as Catholic scholars they became involved with German thought, culture, and history. Hence they moved a few steps away from the neo-Scholasticism of the late nineteenth century. Rahner concluded his recollections of his days as a Jesuit Scholastic with this remark: "My Jesuit teachers, who came from the old days, would probably have regarded Kant and Hegel, and the whole mentality suggested by these names, as adversaries."[6]

3. Pollard, *op. cit.*, pp. 123-28.

4. Anthony Rhodes, *The Power of Rome* (New York: Franklin Watts, 1983), pp. 77-97, 239-48. John Cornwell, *Hitler's Pope: The Secret History of Pope Pius XII* (New York: Viking, 1999), pp. 69-72.

5. Karl Rahner, *I Remember* (New York: Crossroad, 1985), p. 38.

6. *Ibid.* It is interesting to note that Marxism provided a philosophical challenge to all Continental schools of metaphysical thinking at this time. See John Hellman, *op. cit.*, p. 103.

Lutheran Investigations

While Catholic studies were undergoing a mutation in Germany, Lutheran scholars were likewise raising the historical question: "What did Luther mean," for example, by the phrase "Law and Gospel?"[7] Among those who posited the question, in its historical context, was Professor Werner Elert, who published *Der Kampf um das Christentum* (The Struggle for Christianity), in 1921. Elert acknowledged that Lutheranism had undergone a series of changes; in the Age of the Enlightenment, Professor J. A. L. Wegscheider, who lived between 1771 and 1849, elided over the question of what Luther meant: "When the law speaks, the gospel is silent. When the gospel speaks, the law must hold its peace."[8] Elert employed his own term to answer his own question. He called it *Realdialektischer Gegensatz* (Real Dialectic Opposition), which he defined as "substantive opposition": one point (Law) to the other point (Gospel).[9]

According to Elert, over the years *the* fundamental Lutheran question had been relegated only to secondary or tertiary significance. Elert insisted on a return to the Gospel, but asked whether there were any preconditions to the understanding of the Gospel or does the Gospel create its own preconditions.[10] On German soil, according to Elert, only Theodosius Harnack (1817-1889), the father of Adolf von Harnack (1851-1930), "directly researched the question of the divergence between Law and Gospel in historical terms."[11]

In this particular matter, Elert was a theological opponent of Karl Barth (1886-1968), the neo-Orthodox Swiss theologian. Nonetheless, in a monograph written at the end of his life, Elert credited Barth with holding up the historical questions in terms of Luther's declaration of the sovereignty of the divine. In the flood of pamphlets and monographs on the concept of *Volk* (i.e., German national identity) which inundated German Protestantism from 1927 through 1934, Barth proclaimed the Reformation statement: "Jesus Christ, as He is proclaimed to us in the Holy Scriptures, is the one Word of God, that we have to hear, to trust in life and death, and to obey." So poignant and powerful was this rediscovery of Luther that it was made the first thesis for the Barmen Declaration of

---

7. Werner Elert, *Law and Gospel* (Philadelphia: Fortress Press, 1967), pp. 3-6.

8. Cited in *ibid.*, p. 1.

9. *Ibid.* It designates a dialectical opposition to the content *(res)* of Law and Gospel, not just in terminology *(verba)*. The antithesis is between substances and not merely forms.

10. *Ibid.*, pp. 1-7.

11. *Ibid.*, p. 2.

1934.[12] The Barmen Declaration was that synodal constitution, among German Protestants, for the establishment of "A Confessing Church," which formed in 1934 a religious bulwark against the paganism of Nazi ideology. The names most closely associated with it were Dietrich Bonhoeffer, Martin Niemöller, and Karl Barth himself. The Barmen Declaration is defined as the exposition of the fundamental beliefs of those who rejected Nazi racial theories and anti-Christian doctrine. The Confessing Church recognized itself to be at once the legitimate yet provisional Protestant Church for Germany.

In light of the above, in 1935, Barth presented a monograph, which addressed the urgent and contemporary significance of Luther and Calvin, in the classic terms of both "Gospel and Law." Barth concluded that the two Reformation figures were at one in terms of the Sovereignty of God. For him "the Law is nothing less than the necessary form of the Gospel, the content of which is grace."[13] Elert put it another way: "When God speaks in the Gospel He simultaneously expresses his demanding will and therefore it is Law. . . . When God speaks in the law it is simultaneously a promise, therefore also Gospel."[14] Throughout the 1920s, 1930s, 1940s, and 1950s, Lutheran studies progressed with a deeper and broader historical focus. Among the leading scholars were Paul Althaus, Gustav Wingren and Heinrich Bornkamm. Always their monographs included Luther's theology of the Cross, the question of Justification and the quest for the Reformation view. Bornkamm's contribution, reflecting both the predominance of existentialist philosophy and the *de facto* tragedy of post-War Germany, evidenced his Reformation anthropology:

> Luther cleared away all the differences and distinctions which he found in his church, the lower and higher degrees of perfection and holiness which can be achieved through monastic life or ascetic disciplines, the compulsion to perform individual good works by which to improve one's status before God. This is not what matters before God. Before God man is always a unity. This is Luther's fundamental contribution to our view of man. "I cannot separate myself into higher and lower, spiritual and unspiritual, divine and demonic. I am the bearer of my evil thoughts, not something evil within me, an evil part of me. I am the bearer of my yearning for the good, not some good impulses within

12. *Ibid.*, p. 3. See Franklin Hamlin Littell, *The German Phoenix* (Garden City, N.Y.: Doubleday, 1960), pp. 1-24, and Appendix B, "The Barmen Declaration," pp. 184-88.

13. For a complete synthesis of the Barthian view, see Livingston, *op. cit.*, pp. 327-36.

14. *Id., op. cit.*, p. 3.

me." Luther stated this profoundly: "It is the whole man who loves purity, and the same whole man is excited by evil lusts. . . . Thus it is that man fights against himself. . . . The glorious thing about God's grace is that it makes us enemies of our own selves."[15]

Thus did Bornkamm reflect on a little sculpture within the cathedral of Chartres, fittingly called *Adam dans la pensée de Dieu* (Adam in the Thought of God), which echoes the cry from Genesis: "Adam, where are you?"[16] Against the backdrop of a bitter political era following the collapse of the Second Reich in 1918, the German Evangelical community took up an historical quest for the Reformation view of God, the Reformation view of Germany, the Reformation view of life, and the Reformation view of death.[17] Foremost among those asking those hard questions at a critical juncture in German history was Karl Barth.[18] Years later Karl Barth visited

15. *Id., The Heart of Reformation Faith* (New York: Harper and Row, 1965), p. 109. In his introduction Bornkamm states: "For the heart is indivisible, indefinable; it is our whole self, everything belongs to it. There is such a thing as prudence of the heart, a discernment of the heart, a feeling, tender or vehement, a love, an imagination of the heart. Here and here alone it dwells. It is our whole self, but our self in a new way." *Ibid.*, p. 19.

16. *Genesis* 3:9.

17. Littell, *op. cit.*, p. 55, calls this a *Kirchenkampf*, "the struggle of the Churches." Writing of the Barmen Declaration, he quoted Professor Voegelin of Munich: "The death of the spirit is the price of progress. Nietzsche revealed this mystery of the Western Apocalypse when he announced that God was dead, and that he had been murdered. This Gnostic murder is constantly committed by the men who sacrificed God to civilization. Totalitarianism, defined as the existential rule of Gnostic activists, is the end form of progressive civilization. . . . The new dictatorships are not a wild eruption into the order and peace of Europe from uncivilized Mongolian wastes, but have arisen out of democracy itself, and it has been tendencies within democracy which have produced them." Thus did he describe the religious *angst* of post–World War I Germany.

18. Karl Barth based his ethics in the face of political *krisis* upon the priority of the transcendent God. Nigel Biggar, "Barth's Trinitarian Ethic," in John Webster (ed.), *The Cambridge Companion to Karl Barth* (Cambridge: Cambridge University Press, 2000), p. 213. Barth's role in the Protestant attempt to shake off Nazi claims on the German Evangelical Church reached its climax in the Barmen Declaration of 1934. "What we wanted in Barmen was to *gather together* the scattered Christian spirits (Lutheran, Reformed, United, positive, liberal, and pietistic). The aim was neither unification nor uniformity but consolidation for united attacks and therefore for a united march." Cited in Eberhard Busch, *Karl Barth* (Grand Rapids: Eerdmans, 1994), p. 247. Finally, H. Richard Niebuhr, *Theology, History, and Culture: Major Unpublished Writings*, ed. William Stacy Johnson (New Haven: Yale University Press, 1996), p. 67, writing of the German Church struggle indicated that Barth's objectivism, i.e., his sense of Christian realism because of original sin, is dependent upon the subject's awareness of the power of decision. Niebuhr says: "The effort of the church to define itself today is both theoretic and practical and we delude ourselves if we deal with it as though we now base deci-

Augustin Bea in Rome. He pronounced Bea to "represent a rather conventional theology."[19] This perhaps could be said of him too in 1935, and the same would be true of Lorenz Jaeger, then a priest and a secondary school teacher, as well as Clemens August von Galen, then a relatively new bishop in Münster. Yet all of them were busy, studying the Reformation. Among them at that time was a relatively obscure historian of the Catholic Theological Faculty of Paderborn named Adolf Herte, who lived between 1887 and 1970.

Adolf Herte and the New Historiography

Herte was to play a great role in preparing the path for a more active ecumenism in Germany. Herte came to the Paderborn Academy in 1921. Like many others, he was dismissed from teaching in 1945, because he was deemed to be pro-Nazi by the Allied powers after the War.[20] His undergraduate and graduate studies were taken at the University of Münster, in Westphalia. His professor was Josef Greving, who founded a journal, *Reformation History — Study and Texts,* and the Society for the Editing of the Corpus Catholicorum. It was Greving who advised Herte to observe "shifting points" of view in the writing and re-writing of ecclesiastical history. In 1915, Herte published his graduate work, which was dedicated to an examination of the writings of Johannes Cochläus (1479-1552).[21]

Herte determined that Cochläus was an illustrious theologian, whose prolific writings existed in some two hundred independent texts. Herte's

---

sion on an objective theoretic theology whether dogmatic or biblical, while other times were influenced by value-considerations." Barth reiterated the courage of Christian maturity which notes fortitude, prudence and courage as components of religious membership in an embattled Church.

19. This characterization is not intended to be derogatory. Karl Barth, *Ad Limina Apostolorum* (Richmond, Va.: John Knox Press, 1968), p. 13, wrote: "I also visited the home of Cardinal Bea on the Via Aurelia, the road that led to the northwest from ancient Rome. He is well known and rightly honoured in the non-Roman ecumenical movement, and I found him to be an undeniably good man in the service of an undeniably good cause, which, it must be admitted, he represents with a rather conventional theology. This is preferable to the cases where some others use a more modern theology to present a less worthy cause!"

20. Aloys Klein, "Adolf Herte (1887-1970): *'Eine Episode aus seiner Lutherforschung'* [An Episode from His Luther Research]," in *Theologie und Glaube,* Paderborn, Heft 4, 1989: 568-75. This remarkable little abstract covers the details of Herte's life and the importance of his scholarship.

21. *Ibid.,* p. 569.

conclusion was that the polemical character of Cochläus directly affected every German Catholic biography of Luther for four hundred years. All the negative characteristics connected with the personality of Martin Luther were recorded here, e.g., Luther's self-preoccupation, ignorant public behavior, and a false sense of obedience. To this image was added an ambiguous representation of his theology. Thus, beginning in Germany, both confessional and political conflicts and ensuing cultural biases and prejudices took on a life of their own over four hundred years. In 1935, Herte published an elaboration of his thesis that there was more to Luther and Lutheran history than was found in the first recorded impressions of Johannes Cochläus.

Herte called for the reconstitution of all historical research within Lutheran studies. Furthermore, the research ought "to penetrate the widely diverse location of the sources of the work thoroughly, and to expose its oft deeply hidden and very difficult to access roots, in a careful analysis without evasion, in order to establish the unity of the book upon a reliable basis, for the use and dignity of the commentary."[22] Herte, in short, demonstrated that for over four hundred years, every Roman Catholic biography or historical study of Luther imitated the one before it, and in fact, Lutheran studies, undertaken by Catholics, were a repetition of the records and interpretation of Johannes Cochläus. Therefore there was a need to search out primary source documents and letters and to explore anew the terrain of the historical period of the Reformation.

The lives of Lorenz Jaeger and Adolf Herte crossed in 1943. Jaeger had been Archbishop of Paderborn for almost two years when Herte developed his doctoral dissertation still further. In 1943, despite the shortage of paper, Herte published a three-volume work entitled *Das katholische Lutherbild im Bann der Lutherkommentare des Kochläus* (The Catholic View of Luther within the Lutheran Commentary of Cochläus).[23] Only one edition of seven hundred copies was made. Most of these perished in the fire bombings, which destroyed much of the city of Münster. The work received the necessary ecclesiastical imprimatur from the very careful bishop, Count von Galen of Münster. By this time, Professor Eduard Stakemeier of the Paderborn Academy had appeared on the scene, and

---

22. *Ibid.* p. 569. "Das weitverzweigte Quellengebiet des Werkes restlos zu durchdringen und seine oft tief verborgenen und vielfach so schwer zugänglichen Quellen in sorgsamer, keinem Zweifel ausweichender Analyse aufzudecken, um so das Eigengut des Buches sicherzustellen und eine zuverlässige Grundlage für die Ausnützung und Würdigung der Kommentare zu schaffen."

23. *Ibid.*, p. 570.

along with Otto Schoellig of the Freiburg faculty, called the work of Herte "exceptional."[24] This opinion was shared by other Church historians and theologians. It was also shared by the Evangelical Reformation expert, Karl August Meissinger.

Meissinger was so impressed by the quality of Herte's research that he volunteered a review for the Catholic publication *Theologie und Seelsorge* (Theology and the Care of Souls). Meissinger pointed out "how invaluable was this work and the commentary on Cochläus' *Commentarii de actis et scriptis Martini Lutheri* (The Commentary on the Acts and Writings of Martin Luther), which was published three years after Luther's death as the first Catholic, comprehensive contribution to Luther research."[25] Both the work of Herte and Meissinger's review in a Catholic journal came to the attention of the very conservative Archbishop of Freiburg, Doctor Conrad Gröber (1872-1948).[26]

Writing of the incident some forty-six years later, Professor Aloys Klein indicated that the nerves of all the members of the Fulda Bishops Conference were very frayed because the war began to go badly for Nazi Germany. All questions of ecumenism, even academic contact with members of the Evangelical Church, were considered an innovation and, therefore, under the circumstances, dangerous.[27]

24. *Ibid.*, "Ausnahmefall."

25. *Ibid.*, "einen umfassenden Beitrag des protestantischen Lutherforschers."

26. Gröber's reputation in the history books of this era is unfortunate. He is portrayed as naively sympathetic to the Nazis as well as being fastidious, nervous, conservative and one who communicated a sense of his neurosis to the Fulda Bishops Conference. Guenter Lewy, *The Catholic Church and Nazi Germany* (New York: McGraw-Hill Book Company, 1964), p. 294, paints this portrait. "As late as March 1941 Archbishop Gröber, in a pastoral letter abounding in anti-Jewish utterances, had blamed the Jews for the death of Christ and added that 'the self-imposed curse of the Jews, His blood be upon us and upon our children' has come true terribly until the present time, until today."

27. Since the late 1860s, the German bishops gathered annually in the city of Fulda at a former Benedictine abbey. This however did not include all of the bishops of Germany. Prior to 1938, the eight bishops of Bavaria were organized into an independent body. The Freising Bishops Conference was then under the leadership of Cardinal Michael von Faulhaber, the Archbishop of Munich. The Austrian hierarchy existed under Theodore Cardinal Innitzer until 1938. With the Austrian *Anschluss*, the entire membership was organized into the Greater German Bishops Conference of Fulda. The organizational unity of the German episcopate was continually a point of criticism. Later a permanent Secretariat was established to provide continuity for deliberation and action. Three Cardinals took their turn as chair of the annual August meeting, von Fulhaber, Innitzer and Adolf Bertram of Breslau. Cardinal Bertram was primarily responsible and the bishops mostly wrote to him to post items for the agenda or to voice a complaint. Although Bertram was the first bishop "to sound the alarm" by criticizing

Hence on 18 August 1944, while Adolf Cardinal Bertram, Archbishop of Breslau and co-president of the Greater German Bishops Conference, was preparing the agenda for the usual Fulda Bishops Conference Assembly. Archbishop Gröber wrote to him:

> Already for several months, I have closely studied the work of Adolf Herte. . . . I recognize the great diligence of his other work, on the part of this very renowned writer. Nonetheless, I regret the appearance of these three volumes, because they do not do justice to Cochläus or to the Catholic view of Luther. I can call upon the judgments of the recognized historians of the Reformation time. However, I remained quiet at first. When the second volume of the 1944 Catholic journal, *Theologie und Seelsorge* arrived [I became upset]. . . . That article about a Catholic view of Luther, by State Professor K. A. Meissinger, referred to Herte's book in such a style which causes me to propose that a Commission of German bishops be established to take the position of the *Una Sancta* efforts. I have given the Archbishop of Paderborn, the Ordinary of Professor Herte (Jaeger), an extract from the above writing.[28]

---

as grave error the Nazi one-sided glorification of the Nordic race and the contempt for Divine Revelation posited by Alfred Rosenberg, he was destined to walk a fine line in keeping the bishops in order and the Gestapo at bay. Lewy categorized the conference as follows: "The background of the bishops was notably similar though some were of noble families and others were of humble origin, all of them had distinguished themselves during their studies for the priesthood and many had engaged in advanced theological study in Rome. Nearly all had then become professors or heads of Seminaries before being appointed Church officials and eventually bishops. Only one Bishop, Preysing (later Cardinal) of Eichstätt (later Berlin), had also studied a secular subject, law, and had come to the priesthood at a more advanced age. . . . Most of the other members of the episcopate were excellent theologians or administrators but possessed only limited understanding of political matters. Their average age was slightly above sixty; their outlook on politics had been shaped by Imperial Germany before World War I. Many were still convinced monarchists; all had a basically conservative outlook and were distrustful of liberalism and democracy." The war took its toll on their lives. Archbishop Kaspar Klein (1865-1941) of Paderborn and Cardinal Joseph Schulte (1871-1941) died while the war was at its height. Cardinal von Galen and Cardinal Bertram died at the end of the war, as did the Apostolic Nuncio, Caesere Orsenigo (1873-1946) of Milan. Lewy, *op. cit.*, pp. 8, 11-13.

28. Klein, *op. cit.*, pp. 570-71. During the wartime deliberations, the term *Una Sancta*, taken from the cause of Max Metzger, was used as a kind of jargon for ordinary ecumenical issues. "Schon vor mehreren Monaten habe ich das Werk von Adolf Herte über 'Die katholische Lutherbild im Banne der Lutherkommentare des Cochläus' in drei Bänden eingehend studiert. Ich anerkenne den grossen Fleiss des von mir seiner übrigen Arbeiten wegen sehr geschätzten Verfassers. Trotzdem bedauere ich die Erscheinung diesen drei Bände, denn sie werden weder dem Cochläus noch dem 'katholischen Lutherbilde' gerecht. Ich kann mich dabei auf das Urteil von anerkannten Historikern der Reformationszeit berufen. Trotzdem schwieg ich vorerst, bis

Archbishop Jaeger was advised by Cardinal Bertram that his services were necessary for the Fulda Bishops Conference. Jaeger was both a member of the two-man *Una Sancta* Commission as well as Herte's bishop. The dispute with Archbishop Gröber, although tiresome, would prove to be personally enriching for Jaeger, for he gained a new and exciting perspective on the history of the Reformation when he learned the shocking fact that Herte had uncovered four hundred years of Catholic historical inertia regarding the treatment of Luther's life and work. Everybody had been writing the same book over and over! No one had added so much as a new insight to the original data assembled by Cochläus.

Jaeger lost no time in responding. He did not wait for Cardinal Bertram's letter. Clearly and directly, the research by Herte represented his life's work, which, in fact, had been extant for years but unacknowledged. The work was judged worthy of publication in 1935. The publication belonged to the realm of academic research. Further, in 1943, Jaeger himself had won the approval of the Fulda Bishops Conference for the establishment of a "committee for questions concerning reunion in faith" (Referat für die Fragen betreffs Wiedervereinigung im Glauben).[29] In fact, that commission consisted of Jaeger himself and the Archbishop of Vienna, Cardinal Theodor Innitzer (1875-1955).

In point of fact, Jaeger had been inured, both by the circumstances of his life and his previous attempts at ecumenism within the scope of the Fulda Bishops Conference. Jaeger thought of himself as something of a scholar of German history, although an amateur. He therefore deemed the protest of Archbishop Gröber as not a theological matter and, therefore, not germane to a judgment by the Bishops Conference. Since Herte's work was a matter of history, it should be judged as such by competent historians. Jaeger also knew well his partner on the ecumenical commission. Cardinal Innitzer was always complaining to him that he was afraid of air raids and did not like to travel. This was Innitzer's way of dismissing ecumenical questions as superfluous to a wartime situation. Finally, Archbishop Gröber did not seem to be aware that the Commission he called for already existed.

---

mir heute das Heft 2, 1944 der katholischen Zeitschrift 'Theologie und Seelsorge' zugestellt wurde. . . . Dieser Artikel zum katholischen Lutherbild von Lic. Dr. K. A. Meissinger referiert über Hertes Buch in einer Art und Weise, die mich veranlasst zu beantragen, dass von seiten des deutschen Episkopats eine Kommission eingesetzt wird, um zu der Art und Weise dieser Una- sancta- Bestrebungen Stellung zu nehmen. Sr. Exzellenz dem hochwürdigsten Herrn Erzbischof von Paderborn habe ich als dem Ordinarius von Prof. Herte von obigem Schreiben in Abschrift Kenntnis gegeben."

29. *Ibid.*, p. 571.

In the meantime Gröber wrote again to both Cardinal Bertram and Archbishop Jaeger. The date of this second letter was 28 August 1944, a few hours before the Conference:

> What the three volume work of Herte, in opposition to the Catholic Church, means, can be deduced from the fact that the Evangelical World Conference immediately bought one-hundred copies, after its appearance, as I have already learned from Münster. Does Professor Herte perhaps now believe that even the Protestants express their own *mea culpa* at the echo of his book? And what has been accomplished? The opposition of the two churches then refers only in a very subsidiary capacity to the judgment of the person of Luther. People can be in agreement in regard to the judgment of the Reformer, and yet disagree in matters of faith. I myself would not wish to disturb Protestants, as to dishonour their own four-hundred year past, as the Catholic past has been damaged by the work of Herte. I do not know the giant work of Professor Herte. I admit however that renowned Church historian is correct who said: "Three volumes would not have been enough; thirty pages would have been plenty." These (historians) write truly factual matters and are not prejudiced, as is, unfortunately, often the case with Herte. Every Catholic reader is dazzled when innumerable folios and tracts, from over four-hundred years, are excerpted to cleanse Luther's *Gestalt* from all reproach, while on the other hand, famous Catholic names (i.e., biographers of Luther) sink into the shadows of prejudice or even forgery of Luther.[30]

30. *Ibid.*, pp. 571-72. "Was das dreibändige Werk Hertes im Kampf gegen die katholische Kirche bedeutet, ist wohl daraus zu entnehmen, dass die evangelische Weltkonferenz sofort 100 Exemplare nach der Erscheinung des Werkes aufgekauft hat, wie ich von Münster erfuhr. Glaubt Professor Herte vielleicht, dass nun auch die Protestanten als Echo auf sein Buch ihr eigenes mea culpa sprechen? Und was wäre damit erreicht? Die Gegensätze der beiden Kirchen beziehen sich doch wahrlich nur ganz nebensächlich auf die Beurteilung der Person Luthers. Man kann sich in der Beurteilung des Reformators einig sein und trotzdem in den Glaubenssachen trennen. Ich selber würde es den Protestanten nicht zumuten, ihre eigene vierhundertjährige Vergangenheit selber so zu entehren, wie die katholische Vergangenheit durch das Werk Hertes geschädigt worden ist. Ich verkenne die ungeheure Arbeit Professor Hertes nicht. Ich gebe aber jenem bedeutenden Kirchenhistoriker recht, der gesagt hat: 'Drei Bände wären nicht notwendig gewesen, dreissig Seiten hätten genügt'. Diese aber wirklich sachlich geschrieben und nicht voreingenommen, wie es leider bei Herte oft der Fall ist. Es blendet jeden katholischen Leser, wenn unzählige Folianten und Traktätchen aus vier Jahrhunderten exzerpiert werden, um die Gestalt Luthers von allen Anwürfen zu reinigen, während andererseits berühmte katholische Namen in den Schatten der Voreingenommenheit oder gar der Fälschung des Luterbildes versinken."

The incident of protest is important, for it indicates the emergence and the strength of scientific history, with adherence to the canons of the professional historian as opposed to a profane approach albeit hagiography or polemics which had so characterized the landscape of Roman Catholic–Lutheran exchange for centuries. From 1935 to 1944, the work of Adolf Herte followed again a careful analysis of the resources and a genuine establishment of the principle of *hermeneutic*. The interpretation of history requires the authentication of data and the willingness to follow the laws of evidence. Archbishop Gröber protested the work of Adolf Herte, in language that may exhibit a tone of paranoia and the style of bluster. Cardinal Bertram became confused, and seemed willing to pass the matter on to Cardinal Innitzer, who would chair the forthcoming session of the Fulda Bishops Conference.[31]

Archbishop Jaeger prevented Cardinal Bertram from passing off the responsibility to Innitzer, by indicating that he had located an expert in the matter of ecclesiastical historiography, in the person of Dr. Friedrich Zöpfl of Dillingen. Zöpfl required only two and a half pages of Herte's work, in order to clarify what this study of Cochläus was actually about. This was a work of historiography! It was neither a new life of Luther nor a new presentation of Luther's theology. The judgment of Zöpfl is as follows: "It will always remain a title of honour of Catholic scholarship that it first courageously broke the spell (of prejudice), and put aside the public testimony, and adopted the criterion of historical truth in respect to the person of Luther. It does so in the trust, therefore, that now also Protestant research and scholarship can reciprocate and will treat with respect the treatment of Catholic personalities, happenings and phenomena on the basis of actuality, correctness, truthfulness, and courtesy, and that, in this way, the dialogue within the Christian confessions will be fruitful and blessed."[32]

To reinforce his defense of Herte, Jaeger then turned to Father Matthias Laros, a local pastor and a Doctor of Canon Law. Laros cited Canon 1393 §2 of the 1917 code and found Herte not only to be in confor-

---

31. Normally the Fulda Bishops assembled in August.

32. Cited in Klein, *op. cit.*, p. 573. "Es wird immer ein Ruhmestitel der katholischen Forschung bleiben, dass sie zuerst mutig den Bann gebrochen und auch der Person Luthers gegenüber öffentlich Zeugnis für die geschichtliche Wahrheit abgelegt hat. Sie tat es im Vertrauen darauf, dass nun auch die protestantische Forschung und Lehrverkündigung bei Behandlung katholischer Persönlichkeiten, Geschehnisse und Dinge auf den Boden der Sachlichkeit, Gerechtigkeit, Wahrhaftigkeit und Ritterlichkeit treten werden und dass sich auf diese Weise die Aussprache zwischen den christlichen Bekenntnissen fruchtbar und segensreich gestalten werde."

mity but expressed wonder at this marvelous piece of scholarship![33] Laros had a dread of what might happen and warned Jaeger not to let the bishops "thrust a 'dagger in the back' *(Dolchstoss aus dem Rücken)* of our most scientific pioneer and to advise them to protect Herte's work."[34] Professor Geheimrat Merkle, an historical theologian of Würzburg, was contacted and spoke to Jaeger in the strongest possible language to defend Herte from any negative judgment from the Fulda Bishops Conference. An unfavorable judgment would militate against due recognition to Professor Herte, to the cause of Catholic scholarship, to historical scholarship, not to mention an unnecessary blight on the Paderborn Academy, for which Jaeger was responsible.[35]

Joseph Lortz, who had by this time published his two-volume history, *Die Reformation in Deutschland,* in 1939 and 1940, was also contacted. Lortz submitted no written report; instead he gave an oral evaluation directly to Cardinal Bertram. However, it was noted that he pronounced Herte's work to be a marvel. In a later book, Lortz would cite Cochläus, who together with John Eck attempted "to shake unsuspecting Catholics out of their lethargy to make them realize that there was no question here of reform, within the old Church, but of something new and irreconcilably hostile to the Church."[36] Lortz was very much a scholar of German history, as well as of ecclesiastical history. His understanding of Cochläus' warnings against the establishment, some four hundred years earlier, may very well have been the cause of his positive but confidential report to Cardinal Bertram. In the end no negative impediment was imposed upon Herte regarding his teaching and writing.

Aloys Klein, who wrote of this incident, was lavish in his praise of Herte's scholarship and its significance: "The Catholic Church and Reformation History research has, until the present, waited, in vain, for a similar work of scholarly research to the work of Herte, on the part of Evangelical

---

33. This canon states the *materia* of heretical writing. "Examinatores in suo obeundo officio, omni personarum acceptione deposita, tantummodo prae oculis habeant Ecclesiae dogmata et communem catholicorum doctrinam quae Conciliorum generalium decretis aut Sedis Apostolicae constitutionibus seu praescriptionibus atque probatorum doctorum consensu continetur" [Examiners in carrying out their duties must avoid all personal considerations and have only before their eyes the dogmas and the ordinary Catholic doctrinal teaching, which is contained in the general counsels or the prescriptions and constitutions of the Apostolic See and with the consent of the approved doctors].

34. *Ibid.,* p. 574.

35. *Ibid.*

36. *Id., The Reformation: A Problem for Today* (Westminster, Md.: Newman Press, 1964), p. 209.

Christians. Adolf Herte . . . was motivated 'to seek understanding, to extract the poison from the (four-hundred-year old) confessional atmosphere, and to heal old wounds.'"[37] Herte's goal was to widen the circles of culture, within the Confessions, as well as to assure a sense of fairness, in the field of research. Just as he attempted to elicit a sense of impartiality before the facts on the Catholic side, Herte sought a similar professional behavior on the part of Protestant scholars as well.

There were some brief but important conclusions to this incident: (1) The protest of Archbishop Gröber enlisted the commitment of Archbishop Jaeger, not only as Herte's Ordinary and as the supervisor of the Paderborn Academy, but also in his role as co-chairman (with Cardinal Innitzer) of the Fulda Bishops Conference Ecumenical *Una Sancta* Commission, and thrust him to the forefront of this issue. (2) The matter at hand involved many people as *periti*, viz., Zöpfl, Laros, Lortz and Merkel, who unanimously, but individually, advised the Conference of Bishops that historical work in authenticating sources and laying the facts of history on the table of history is not for the judgment of bishops. Scholars only can judge scholars.[38] (3) Herte laid down the challenge for academic dialogue between Catholic and Protestant students of Reformation history. The fact that Professor Karl August Meissinger responded so favorably was a sign that this invitation to conversation had been heard. Truly, Herte was an ecumenical pioneer.

Scholarship of Joseph Lortz

If Adolf Herte was identified by fellow scholars as "an ecumenical pioneer" who set the rules of the quest for Christian unity in terms of scholarship and a professional approach to history, Joseph Lortz was his companion. His already cited *magnum opus, Die Reformation in Deutschland,*

---

37. Klein, *op. cit.,* p. 575. "Die katholische Kirche und Reformationsgeschichtsforschung hat bis heute vergeblich auf eine dem Werk Hertes ähnliche wissenschaftliche Untersuchung auf seiten der evangelischen Christenheit gewartet. Adolf Herte war . . . geleitet, 'Verständigung zu suchen, die konfessionelle Atmosophäre zu entgiften und alte Wunden zu heilen.'" The questions to which Monsignor Klein referred were: a Reformation study of the Mass, devotion to Mary, the Sacraments, indulgences, biblical exegesis. Above all, it is a challenge to a study of the Papacy in the Church.

38. This is in reference to the rules of evidence within the specific field of academic historical scholarship. The charism of the bishop pertains specifically to the teaching of religious doctrine.

contains a more positive character than any previous Catholic presentation of the topic. Lortz explained himself only thirty years later, in a freer political and academic atmosphere, when he produced a foreword to the English language text. He wrote, "Furthermore I want to state that this book does not give a complete history as such. It deals, as the title says, with the events in Germany, the country of the origin of the Reformation, and with its centre, the personality of Martin Luther, the genius who initiated what later became an all-European tragedy."[39] Lortz's history of Luther, especially after the initial publication of Herte's work in 1935, bore little of the polemical style of the previous Roman Catholic studies, all of which were written from an apologetical point of view, using the tools of the German historico-critical analysis. This scholar sought not only to identify the Reformation topics, but also to see them in and against the environment in which they developed. As a Catholic, he took very seriously the theological themes which he deemed to have shaped the most significant moment in German religious history, i.e., Luther's rupture with Rome. Because the Reformation was a political, philosophical, cultural, as well as a religious event, Lortz's perspective in writing *was* an innovation; he was critical of historical data but never polemical.

Lortz's work was characterized by a particularly unique style. Unlike other historians or biographers, he did not follow a chronological process, beginning with, say, Luther's birth in 1483, moving to the Ninety-five Theses of 1517, and concluding with Luther's death in 1546. Instead he took particular historical topics such as "political and ecclesio-political interaction," "the effect of the Reformation upon Humanism," and the person of "Luther himself" as a dramatic character on the stage of history. In a way he provided both a prototype for and an historical antecedent to John Osborne's play of the 1960s.[40] Lortz wrote:

> Luther is an ocean of powers, impulses, perceptions and experiences. His eloquent power of imagery is incomparable, as is his power of pathos. The richness of his utterances is almost entirely the result of *ad hoc* decisions arising out of totally different situations, the utterances of one subjectively inclined and insufficiently controlled by a system. He himself saw and admitted the Vulcan-like quality of his work. . . . Luther worked entirely from experience. Self-confidence, sense of mission, arrogance, peremptoriness, strength of will — all at the level of

---

39. Joseph Lortz, *The Reformation in Germany*, vol. 1 (London: Darton, Longman and Todd, 1968), p. vii.

40. John Osborne, *Luther* (New York: Dutton-Plume, Plume Imprint, 1994).

genius — all compelled the situation of the moment to take on, for him, the character of crisis.[41]

Lortz called this style of historiography "viewing." By this term, he summed up his method of not examining one text, one sentence, or even one word outside the context in which it was expressed.[42] Secondly, Lortz's scholarship was deliberately undertaken in light of the theological and ecclesiological situation of the interwar period. He wrote, however, after the war:

> Never since 1517 have prospects for such a dialog between the Churches been better than they are today. This is due partly to developments in the area of historical scholarship, partly to developments in the strictly religious field. Because of the work of the last forty years, we have a more adequate knowledge of a world that saw the end of the Middle Ages and the early years of Luther. This has helped to correct erroneous presentations of the late medieval period as well as the development of the "Luther legend" among the latter's contemporaries and succeeding generations. The research of Catholic scholars such as Paulus, Denifle, Merkle, and Grisar, together with those of the Protestant historian Otto Schell, have contributed significantly to the collapse of the Luther legend.[43]

It is interesting to note that Lortz diverted from scholarship as the strictly pivotal point of dialogue. He was convinced of the importance of academic evidentiary factors regarding history. He cited three of them, the first of which came from his own life experience *(Lebenswelt)*: "We cannot overlook the common experiences of the Churches. . . . Above all the martyrs and confessors of both Churches in the concentration camps of Hitler and Himmler have been a most important factor in the Church Unity Movement because of the sacrifices made in common."[44] The second concerns those who survived World War II, who "unlike their predecessors," are totally aware of the un-Christian character of division among Christians. Thirdly, evolution has taken place in the world of religion in the West: "Protestant Churches of today are independent both of the Reformation and of questions of justice or injustice of that movement."[45] But prob-

---

41. Lortz, *The Reformation in Germany, op. cit.,* pp. 169-70.
42. *Ibid.,* p. 171.
43. Lortz, *The Reformation: A Problem for Today, op. cit.,* p. 18.
44. *Ibid.,* p. 19.
45. *Ibid.,* p. 21.

ably the strongest conclusion that Lortz drew in his post-War reflection was that the principle that governed Germany for four hundred years, *Cujus regio, ejus religio,* was totally and unabashedly pagan. He said: "For the heart of Christianity is dogma, truth which can be known and clearly stated." Curiously he added: "When we aim at furthering mutual understanding and seek to contribute to an eventual *rapprochement* of the Churches, we must start not with tolerance in matters of dogma but with intolerance. Tolerance in matters of dogma makes the search for truth impossible." Finally, that ecumenism was an indispensable commodity of the time is evidenced by this statement: "The union of Christian Churches is an absolutely indispensable condition for the necessary rechristianization of the West." That Lortz would be precisely in that position at the time of his death, he could not have known. He too was deprived of his lector's pulpit, for he was deemed a Nazi sympathizer in the Hitler era.[46]

By 1933, when the Concordat between the Vatican and Nazi Germany was signed, and the Enabling Act of 5 July was promulgated, thus dissolving the Catholic Centre Party, Lortz was described by his contemporary, Waldemar Gurian, as being representative of a certain brand of Catholic academics who regarded "political Catholicism as having been necessary and highly meritorious but, nevertheless, an abnormality, demanded by the times."[47] Lortz was conscious that he lived in a peculiar period, during which (before the Great War) the Catholic Church was likened to a ruin, projecting out of the Middle Ages into modern times.[48]

The Catholics were confused and frightened of offending the orthodoxy of their faith, but they felt also that they were living in a time when a defensive Catholicism had left them with a lackluster Catholicism, which was unspiritual and devoid of cultural content. Further, Germany felt itself to be quite paradoxically one yet two.[49] Writing directly at the moment of the rise of the Nazi Party, after a painful and humiliating depression of unemployment, physical and national hopelessness, as well as that "political game of musical chairs" which was known as the Weimar Republic, Gurian stated soberly: "No other people has been so deeply and lastingly affected by the religious cleavage that took place in Western Europe in the sixteenth century as the German — the people among whom it took its rise. But no people is so divided by religion as the German. No, the determining

46. *Ibid.*, pp. 12-21, 191.

47. Waldemar Gurian, *Hitler and the Christians* (London: Sheed and Ward, 1936), p. 135.

48. *Ibid.*, p. 15.

49. *Ibid.*, p. 1.

factor is not so much the present-day cleavage of the German people into two opposing halves, as is its peculiar historical development."[50] It is this mentality which drove Lortz to join others in presenting the facts of the Reformation in a new and compelling light so that the wounds of the Reformation might be healed. In this, by enunciating the fact of "the Christian creeds and the German nation," he joined Herte by promoting a brand of ecumenism within a local, cultural, and national context. Already known and accepted for his textbooks on Church history for secondary schools, he had none of the difficulty of Herte when he published his two-volume history of the German Reformation. He was criticized neither for his method nor his motive.

Just as Lortz recognized the complexity of Luther's personality as well as the multivalent politics of his nation and his times, Lortz's greatest contribution was his clarification that the causes of the Reformation were multiple and deeply rooted in history. In the early pages of his first volume he stated in dramatic fashion that the Reformation was nothing less than a tapestry. His quote deserves to be cited in full:

> The age of the Reformation was marked by a complexity and diversity of life, hitherto unknown. In a measure, likewise unknown until then, personalities of second and third stature appeared on the stage of history and drew the masses into the course of events. The great precondi-

---

50. *Ibid.* For the history of the impact of the Weimar Republic on Christianity, see Stewart A. Stehlin, *Weimar and the Vatican, 1919-1933* (Princeton: Princeton University Press, 1983). "The central character was Archbishop Eugenio Pacelli who was Nuncio," Dorothy Thompson, the American journalist for the *New York Times,* stated. She went on: "In knowledge of German and European affairs and in diplomatic astuteness the Nuncio was without equal." Robert Murphy, former U.S. undersecretary of State, was in Germany as an American diplomat in the 1920s, where he had known Pacelli. Later, after Pacelli had become pope, Murphy was granted an audience with his old colleague. They talked of old times and how they underestimated Hitler in the mid-1920s, since both Murphy and Pacelli had at first reported to their governments that Hitler would never come to power. Pacelli held up his hand for Murphy to stop, laughed and said, "In those days, you see, I wasn't infallible" (pp. 318-19). This thought was shared not only between Murphy and Pacelli. Most Europeans realized too late that they had underestimated Hitler. Sadly, even German citizens themselves could not believe that they had been participants in diabolic schemes. Refer to Roger Boyes and Adam LeBor, *Seduced by Hitler* (Naperville, Ill.: Source Books, 2001), pp. 7-8. "Harold Laski, the left-wing British scholar-seer of the London School of Economics, thought that Nazism was a spent force. Exhibiting an unerring capacity to get the major issues hopelessly wrong, Laski predicted that Hitler was destined to spend the evening of his life in a Bavarian village, reminiscing in a beer garden about how he had nearly ruled the Reich." Also see Burleigh, *op. cit.,* p. 145.

tion of all modern history: numbers, numbers of individuals, that is, caught up in the historical process, and in turn reacting upon it in some way or other, and upon each other in a variety of ways, is indeed a characteristic of Reformation history. The history of the preaching friars, of theology, of the mercenaries, of the peasants' wars, provides an indication of this factor. An even better indication lies in the fact that this period was the first to be decisively touched by that power which first made possible any sort of real public opinion, any spiritual mass-movement — the art of printing.[51]

In sum, according to Lortz, inquiry into the *causes of the Reformation* is essential to the study of the Reformation. The full significance of this fact appears when it is recognized that "the Reformation period was heir to the close of the fifteenth century — a period of countless interwoven antitheses. These antitheses, for their part, were the result of centuries-old dissolutions and rebuildings, and as such not only characterize or even dominate the image of life at that time, but also make this whole life an antithesis from its very foundations upwards."[52]

Lortz challenged the quest for an immediate causation of historical events. He painted a larger picture of broad significance. He spoke of history, as detached, and the role of the historian as professional, i.e., necessary but not judgmental: *"Demonstration of a deep historical logic does not decide concerning truth or error, merit or guilt,"* he wrote.[53] In his treatment of the background of the Reformation, Lortz was aware that he was addressing the observer as well as the student. To the observer he spoke the truism that the actual causes of the Reformation were not immediately self-evident. He warned: "It is time now to do justice to irrational factors . . . only then will sufficient light be cast on Luther's responsibility for the Reformation Schism."[54]

To the student of the Reformation, he spoke from an historical point of view, and his conclusion was paradox: "this acceptance of dogma, and loyalty to the externals of the church tend to be the last things to go, but once they do begin to go, their decline is very rapid. Suddenly they seem to

51. *Ibid.*, p. 5. For a fuller treatment, see A. G. Dickens, *The German Nation and Martin Luther* (London: Edward Arnold, 1974), pp. 102-15.

52. *Ibid.*

53. *Ibid.*, p. 4 (emphasis in original).

54. *Ibid.*, p. 14. "The Reformation was a battle for the authentic form of Christianity; its emergence was not a self-evident fact; less still was it self-evident that the struggle was to be resolved by the greater part of western Christendom turning against the Church."

lose their meaning. One day staunch Catholicism is there and is being emphatically lauded; the next day it is gone."[55] His principal theme was then expressed:

> And yet it is precisely here that the mysterious element in the subsequent Reformation Schism becomes evident. The church was still the dominant power of the time, the acknowledged guardian and leader, the moulder, so men thought, of both public and private life. Proof of this can be adduced from many sides. The Christian faith was still the central point of all life, and it was taught and dispensed by the priests of the Roman Pope; in science, theology, philosophy, law, as in social life, including the administration of justice, and charitable activity, the leadership of the clergy was not seriously called into question. Even the life of the state seemed conceivable only on a foundation of church order.[56]

Herein lie the lessons of Lortz's research, and they had a profound effect upon Archbishop Jaeger, who by that time was now acquiring new titles, the Champion of Herte, the Paderborn Academy President, the *Una Sancta* co-chairman and the ecumenist. As war was raging and bombs fell upon his city, Jaeger listened as Lortz lectured. The Reformation is evidentiary. It is complex. It is paradoxical. It is more than one grand event in church history. Because men and women in the West had been living with the presence of the Church for more than a millennium, they could not therefore conceive of themselves, nor their environment, without it. Even when the liturgy, the language, the discipline and the ecclesiastical jargon changed, and changed quickly, there was still a metaphysical entity, the Church, to which even the dissenter adhered. Hence Lortz's final point was the need to lay the question of ecclesiology on the table. Dialogues about this matter needed convergence. Lortz claimed that the man Luther must be set on his own historical stage. In a brief but trenchant exposition, Lortz made his point, which of itself was to be valuable in the ecumenism of post-War Germany:

> In the monastery, Luther's main source of spiritual nourishment was the Bible. It was not as though he flouted the will of superiors in reading the Bible, as some formerly thought. Rather it was the monastic rule itself, which prescribed the reading of the Bible and which, in the practical order, provided him with the whole Bible, bound in red

55. *Ibid.,* p. 16.
56. *Ibid.,* p. 17.

leather, for reading and study. It was then that something unusual happened: Luther applied himself with unusual vigor to the Book of Books, and the Bible answered his needs to such an extent that there resulted that extraordinary inner relationship between Luther and the Bible, which he later compared correctly to a marriage.[57]

According to Lortz, the Bible was the source of Luther's inspirations. This means that Luther had, after some years, memorized much of the Bible. He was fond of citing it spontaneously within his lectures. The Bible played an overwhelming role in his academic life and in the monastic training and the monastic theology.

Lortz asked also: Is it perhaps that Luther was a bit one-sided in his outlook? "In his later years, Luther never tired of pointing out that in the Catholic Church, there was nothing but *hypocrisy* and that Catholics taught that grace and salvation could be earned through a man's own works."[58] Through juxtaposition, Lortz put the old Luther back into the monastery, on the very day when he received the Augustinian habit and pronounced his vows. He compared the book of meal prayers with the monastic ritual and the Holy Rule. Lortz found in these circumstances that *every* printed word of the text conspired to say that *grace is everything* and the religious, left to himself, is helpless. After all, how do all these ceremonies end but with the words: "May *God* who has begun this good work in you bring it to perfection"?[59]

Lortz then said: "Luther's entry into religious life in the monastery was *not* done in a framework of hypocritical ceremonies; these ceremonies were permeated by the doctrine of grace . . . but Luther had not made this doctrine his own, though it was quite obviously present in those prayers."[60] Thus Lortz provided a critical pathway, should there be any future dialogue between Catholics and Evangelicals. The experience of Luther must be traced through the facts, into the words he spoke, and behind those, into the words he first studied and prayed. Therefore, Lortz placed the Bible within the context of the Church, and that within the context of the church of Luther's day.

"Furthermore," wrote Lortz, "Did his theology really give Brother Martin a thoroughly Catholic foundation?" Having asked the question, Lortz then answered it: "Luther had *not* made this doctrine his own,

---

57. Lortz, *The Reformation: A Problem for Today, op. cit.,* p. 116.
58. *Ibid.,* p. 117.
59. *Ibid.* (emphasis mine).
60. *Ibid.*

though it was quite obviously present in those prayers. It seems that he was simply blind to it. It would seem that from other sources he had somehow gotten the erroneous idea that man had to rely on his own powers to effect a reconciliation with God."[61] This notion dominated all his thinking so that he was unable to break out of the closed circle. Lortz then went on to elucidate the downright contradiction of Luther's personal experience, which is the cornerstone of the Reformation itself. According to Lortz, on the one hand, Luther railed against the Catholic Church for hypocrisies in practice. Yet, "he has left us a number of accounts of his First Mass."[62] By pointing to the evidence, Lortz demonstrated that Luther sought and was overwhelmed by "the nearness of the awesome majesty of God, who is addressed in the canon as the living and true God."[63] *Sanctus* (Holy) was Luther's seminal prayer. If he could say nothing else but this, *satis* (it would be enough)!

According to Lortz, where else did Luther get this word, this expression of a great surge of adoration, but from the Church itself, which, though fragile and cracked, was still the vessel of the presence of God. Lortz, a Catholic historian, took seriously the facts and experiences of the life of Luther, and he placed them in a non-polemical way within the context of both remote and proximate history and then presented the two confessions, Evangelical and Roman Catholic, with the conundrum that must be resolved if the German character were ever to achieve peace of soul.

The record of political commentator Waldemar Gurian, who observed Lortz on the occasion of the signing of the 1933 Concordat, presented the image of a man who was conscious of his "Germanness," the reality of politics, and the history of the German Church. In a certain sense, Lortz's knowledge became his burden, and in those years from 1933 to 1945 he could be compared to Milton's *Samson Agonistes*. The end of the War saw him as a pathetic figure, a famous priest professor, yet labeled with Nazi identity. Still, his insights and perhaps the subjectivity of his personality, as well as those of Herte, contributed much to the academic foundations of Evangelical–Roman Catholic dialogue and became an inspiration to Archbishop Lorenz Jaeger, who was to inaugurate it.[64] Jaeger

---

61. *Ibid.*, pp. 117-18.

62. *Ibid.*

63. *Ibid.*

64. Bishop Stählin, the Lutheran co-founder of the dialogue, was obviously admired by Lortz, *The Reformation: A Problem for Today, op. cit.*, p. 16, who quoted him: "It is not permissible to fight for anything but the truth in fullness of the Gospel and for the purity and unity of the one, holy, universal, and apostolic Church."

had been in a state of bereavement since he received his episcopal appointment to Paderborn, for he felt that his elevation had compromised his desire to continue the study of German life and letters. He found, however, that actually he was not divorced from his books. He discovered that the history and the effects of the Reformation itself were to color the rest of his episcopal ministry. Indeed, as founder of the Johann Adam Möhler Institute and as the bishop patron of the Paderborn Academy, he was always a part of university life.

Karl Adam and the Sense of National Compunction

In 1935, Waldemar Gurian published in Switzerland a small book entitled *Der Kampf um die Kirche im Dritten Reich* (The Struggle about the Church in the Third Reich) (in England known as *Hitler and the Christians*), in which he made three points: (1) the crisis of the German people, not only in the rise of the Third Reich, but also over the past four hundred years, had dealt with the "cleavage of the German people into two opposing halves as its peculiar historical development"; (2) the effect of this split has been that each of the two Christian denominations, viewing the situation from different angles, at different periods — has stigmatized the other as "anti-Reich" and as "imposed upon its adherents by the powers that be"; (3) the effect of such a cleavage has produced an ongoing, psychological quest for "realization of the German soul."[65] Although Christianity and the genuine German mission "have been indissolubly wedded," the German people because of the power of princes had not been free to believe as they wished.[66] The principle of *Cujus regio, ejus religio* is demonstrated in the figures of Maurice of Saxony, Bernard of Weimar, Frederick the Great and, of course, the "Iron Chancellor," Otto von Bismarck.[67] Throughout the four hundred years the pan-German dream best expressed itself in poetry, music, politics and religion. Realistically, the best that ever occurred was "the form in which the idea of toleration gained a footing in Germany not merely as a philosophical *Weltanschauung* (world view) but as a political reality, (which) was the governmental system of the House of Hohenzollern, which in itself was intolerant."[68] Thus did Gurian also de-

---

65. Gurian, *op. cit.*, pp. 1-3.
66. *Ibid.*, p. 2.
67. *Ibid.*
68. *Ibid.*, p. 4.

scribe the mentality of religious academics in the early Nazi era. In general, one is left with the impression that he was demonstrating a not-yet-enunciated mandate to return to the sources of the Reformation itself. While Gurian's practical motives were sociological and historical, he clearly understood the theological importance, for the focus of his examination was *Kirche im Krisis* (the Church in crisis).[69]

The bishop who enunciated these sentiments and brought them together under the heading of the Ecumenical Movement was Lorenz Jaeger. Within the wartime Fulda Bishops Conference, there were many varying figures. As has been cited, history recognizes Clemens August von Galen and Konrad von Preysing, who died in 1950, as the most outspoken of the German bishops against Hitler. (For his heroism von Galen was beatified in 2005.) As also noted, Archbishop Conrad Gröber of Freiburg was narrow-minded theologically, and nervous publicly, having unsuccessfully and humiliatingly attempted an accord with the Nazis, regarding the Youth Groups and Catholic Lay Organizations, only the day before the Night of the Long Knives, 30 June 1934.

Cardinal Michael von Faulhaber of Munich, although at the time he protested to Secretary of State Eugenio Pacelli about the persecution of Jews, likewise continued "that for the time being it was impossible to oppose the Government on the racial question because of the threat that it would present to his Catholic followers."[70] According to Professor Ronald Rychlak,[71] who is otherwise favorable to the Church, von Faulhaber helped shape Pacelli's future thinking, regarding the Church in the German crises. The president of the Bishops Conference, Cardinal Adolf Bertram (1859-1945), of Breslau, was a diplomat with a mission. He challenged the ambiguity of Nazi propaganda, which used such abstruse terms as "positive Christianity." "For us Catholics," he stated, "[this term] cannot have a satisfactory meaning since everyone interprets it in the way he pleases." History has not judged Bertram with great sympathy, for he was only a diplomat. His ability to discern ambiguities made him the perfect spokesman to pronounce them. Archbishop Lorenz Jaeger of Paderborn brought to the conference a sense of mission for the *Lebenswelt*. The issue he brought to the table continually was that of the meaning of the Church, specifically as a community of believers in

69. *Ibid.*, p. 9.

70. Rychlak, *op. cit.*, p. 77.

71. *Ibid.*, p. 77. Also see Cornwell, *op. cit.*, p. 83. Faulhaber had been informed in 1917 that "in the year of the 400th Jubilee of Luther's anti-papal Wittenburg Thesis, Catholicism should be seen as a focus of a Christian cultural and intellectual revival." Munich would be the heart of such a revival since it was the center of Catholic Bavaria.

Jesus Christ. His perception, his vision, and his logic led him to a cause, which seemed to his colleagues to be esoteric — the cause of ecumenism.[72]

While the cause of ecumenism may have seemed superfluous during the Hitler years, its relevance was demonstrated dramatically after the war by no less a theologian than Karl Adam of Tübingen. A renowned scholar of both Christology and ecclesiology in the German inter-war period, he was presently suffering the humiliation of the deprivation of his professorship, because of his pro-Nazi sympathies before the War. Now, over a three-day retreat, Adam addressed a packed audience in the Stuttgart Evangelical Church. These lectures were, in part, derived from Adam's own ever-developing ecclesiology, as well as Lortz's and Herte's studies of the Lutheran Reformation. The discourses were as popular as they were poignant with the allusions to the Cold War, and the tragedy of the Hitler War. At this stage, when news of the Berlin airlift signaled a definite threat to the German mind and spirit, Adam's language was a clarion call in regard to the relevance, even the urgency, of ecumenism in Germany:

> We Christians have just passed through a time when religious disunity drove us to the very brink of the abyss. The set of Godless men hating Christ as the Son of David, almost succeeded in rooting out from the German people not merely this or that Christian denomination, but the very substance of Christianity itself . . . for German Christianity it has become a vital question, a choice of "to be or not to be" for the Christian substance in our people, and so in the heart of Europe. We know that organized anti-Christianity lies in wait beyond our frontiers. We must recognize that there is in our midst something evermore dangerous, carrying a far greater menace of ruin — the vacuum that has been left in the German soul: an emptiness, a fearful emancipation from all memories, traditions and ideals of Christianity, making room for every demon of heart and mind and preparing the soul to receive every and any gospel, not only the gospel of the cross. How can German Christianity hold its ground against its Anti-Christianity without and within, how can it arm itself against the gate of hell, when it is split to its very core? When conscious

---

72. See Gordon C. Zahn, "Catholic Resistance? A Yes and a No," in Franklin H. Littell and Hubert C. Locke (eds.), *The German Church Struggle and the Holocaust* (Detroit: Wayne State University Press, 1974), p. 228. "Perhaps one might fault the bishops for a failure of vision and commitment, perhaps even for a failure of courage when the chips were down. In strictly pragmatic terms one can see that their decisions in favour for restraint were 'dictated' by precedent circumspection. What is more, they were probably quite correct in their pessimistic assessment of the prospects of success for any more determined stand they might have taken or advised."

of the disunity, it cannot even pray with a clear conscience to our Lord Jesus Christ when it can no long summon up the power to bear witness in one, united confession to our Lord and Saviour.[73]

The language of this text, of course, revealed Adam's concern for the German tragedy. But it also underscores his entire systematic work, in which he intimately identified the Church with Christ. The mandate of Christ has become the mandate of the Church, not only through the teaching of Scripture, but in the data of history: "Let all be one (Jn. 17:21)." He also spoke of theological substance, which he highlighted within the text. After years of struggling with the quest for the German soul and, simultaneously, the quest for the soul of the Church, it had now become obvious to him that *Christian substance* was not to be found in *Volkische* (national racial identity).[74]

Throughout the Nazi era, including the six years of world war, Augustin Bea resided in Rome. His position as rector of the Pontifical Biblical Institute, however, did not isolate him from events in Germany. As has previously been indicated, Pope John XXIII's selection of Bea in 1960 to be the first head of the newly created Secretariat for Promoting Christian Unity was directly related to his German nationality. This point will be

---

73. Karl Adam, *One & Holy* (New York: Sheed & Ward, 1951), pp. 3-4 (emphasis mine).

74. See Robert Anthony Krieg, *Karl Adam* (Notre Dame: University of Notre Dame Press, 1992), p. 60. Much of this concept of *Volk* is also found in the writings of Romano Guardini specifically, *"The Spirit of the Liturgy"* (New York: Sheed & Ward, 1951); also see Robert Krieg, "Romano Guardini's Theology of the Human Person," *Theological Studies* 59 (1998): 457-74, and Robert Krieg, "Karl Adam, National Socialism, & Christian Tradition," *Theological Studies* 60 (1999): 432-56. Karl Adam is the foremost representative of the so-called new theology in Germany. Influenced by the school of theological ideas and such prophets as Friedrich Nietzsche, Max Scheler, Wilhelm Dilthey, and Karl Mannheim, Adam challenged the Catholic community to a new awareness to its surroundings, the building of community, a new awareness of symbols in communication and the establishment of a point of "engagement" by the mature Christian. His major works in ecclesiology and Christology are eminently readable. Unfortunately, by 1933, his enthusiasm to provide convergence between the German people and the Christian religion demonstrated itself in an article entitled "Deutsches Volkstum und katholisches Christentum" (German Identity and Catholic Christianity). The article was partially published. At the beginning of Hitler's regime, he argued Catholicism and Nazi doctrine were "reconcilable in principle." He found his point of entry in the concept of *"Volkische,"* i.e., "National-Racial Identity." He found a certain mutuality in national platform statements about common destiny, civil obedience and marriage and the family. The "Night of the Long Knives" (June 30, 1934) disenchanted Adam along with others, including Michael Schmaus, Joseph Lortz and Adolf Herte. He blundered into public statements. It was too late. After the war he was branded as a pro-Nazi sympathizer.

clarified in the next chapter. Bea was ideally placed, between his German origins and his Roman residence, to both appreciate and express the ideals of Karl Adam. The above-cited sermon of Karl Adam personifies Augustin Bea and his future mission, for Bea represents the struggle of being a German, since it involves the German context of a church divided by the Classical Reformation. Ecumenism, likewise, is the search for the soul of the Church.

Chastened by war and by personal humiliation, Adam shared Jaeger's sense of *Lebenswelt* and looked upon the theological implications of "real life." Therefore, Adam published his lectures in a little book called *One and Holy*. *One and Holy* was a deliberate memorial to the late Max Metzger and to the vision he exhibited in the early days of the *Una Sancta* movement. His words were also prophetic. In regard to the enormity of the task of Christian reunion, he said:

> For there are hindrances and difficulties. Reunion is not a matter of simple will, but also of hard thinking and energetic action. More precisely, we need a kind of good will which is ready to abandon deep-seeded prejudices and habits of thought for the sake of eternal truth, and is willing to go unconditionally to the very ground of truth itself. The way is a way of blood and wounds, both for the Catholic and the Protestant, though differently for each of them.[75]

These words penetrated, as is exemplified by the thirty-three-year-old Hans Küng, the German-speaking Swiss theologian. Although stated above, it bears repeating: "Schism is a scandal. But it is perhaps a greater scandal that the majority of Christians, in all communities, even today, and including theologians and pastors, are *profoundly indifferent to this scandal;* that they feel the division of Christendom at most, as a deplorable imperfection, not as an immeasurably crippling wound which *absolutely must be healed;* that they are *deeply concerned over a thousand religious trivialities* but not over Our Lord's desire that 'all may be one.'"[76]

Karl Adam's parallel statement came directly from the depths of a sense of national despair:

> Whatever belief in the Son of God-made-man has remained alive, the Christian conscience has been pierced by the overwhelmed reproach and accusation of the High Priest's prayer to the Father on the eve of

---

75. *Id., One and Holy,* pp. 5-6.
76. *Id., The Council Reform and Reunion, op. cit.,* p. 57 (emphasis mine).

his Passion . . . "that they all may be one, as Thou, Father, in Me and I in Thee!"[77]

From the pulpit in Stuttgart, Adam reproached Christians for such a cruel wounding of the Holy Body of Christ, the Church, and for the neglect of centuries when these festering divisions among Christians remained unhealed. Based upon the neo-Romantic *Lebenstheologie* (life theology) at the turn of the twentieth century, as he wrote about Christ and the Church, Karl Adam confronted also the history and the destiny of the German people. While the ramifications of his thought were optimistic at the dawn of his career, in his retirement he exuded a sense of sober responsibility for his nation, and for his Church. He now saw the Church as wider than the Roman Catholicism which he sought to interpret. As he called for national healing, he called the nation to heal the Reformation. Thus, he presented a challenge both urgent and mighty. Along with Herte and Lortz, Adam preceded the Ecumenical Movement specifically within the German context. At mid-century, Adam's words from the pulpit in Stuttgart, concerning the urgency and the contemporaneity of the ecumenical challenge, must have moved many. Certainly the influence of Karl Adam did not escape Jaeger, for Adam was a giant of twentieth-century theology. Karl Adam is renowned for his pioneering efforts in twentieth-century fundamental theology but most especially for the Christocentric ecclesiology which he propounded in his treatise *The Spirit of Catholicism,* in which he enunciated concretely the already popular concept of the Mystical Body of Christ at a time prior to the encyclical *Mystici Corporis.*

According to his historian, Robert Krieg, Karl Adam showed remarkable attentiveness to "the origins of Christianity in Jesus Christ" — origins which are accessible to us "only through biblical and ecclesiastical tradition."[78] Herein lies the ideological connection between Adam and Bea. As Professor Walter Kasper expressed in 1976, Adam was a pioneer of the contemporary use of biblical studies in Christology. Kasper himself, as well as Hans Küng and Edward Schillebeeckx, would later follow a trend set by Adam. Adam's understanding of the Christological significance of the economy of salvation depends on the New Testament in order to highlight the humanity of Jesus Christ. According to Kasper, this methodology was "astounding."[79]

---

77. *Id., One and Holy,* p. 1.
78. *Id, Karl Adam: Catholicism in German Culture, op. cit.,* p. 103.
79. *Ibid.*

The biblical approach which Adam forged first appeared in his seminal work *Das Wesen des Katholizismus* (The Spirit of Catholicism) in 1924. This was a pastoral work which stressed ecclesial-mindedness, an openness to the times and, most importantly, the unity of scientific thorough-mindedness. This last characteristic is based upon a priority given to the evidence of the New Testament. He wrote: "So the Church possesses the Spirit of Christ not as a collectivity of single individuals but as a compact, ordered unity of the faithful, as a community that transcends the individual personalities, and expresses itself in a sacred hierarchy."[80] The concept of the Mystical Body appears early on in that work: "Christ the Lord is the real self of the Church. The Church is the body, permeated through and through by the redemptive might of Jesus. So intimate is this union of Christ with the Church, so inseparable, natural and essential that St. Paul in his epistles to the Colossians and Ephesians, explicitly calls Christ the Head of the body. As the Head of the body, Christ makes the organism of the Church whole and complete. And Christ and the Church can no more be regarded separately than can a head and its body (Col. 1:18; 2:19; Eph. 4:15ff.)."[81]

It is not certain when Bea became aware of the theological method of Karl Adam. As the evidence will show, he was certainly aware of theological trends in Germany by 1949 when he joined the staff of the Holy Office. As a biblical scholar, Bea would reflect both the insights of Adam and his own scriptural propensities when he came to address the subject of ecumenism through a process of harmonizing the Scriptures. Certainly the concept of the Mystical Body of Christ was a predominating theological theme which spoke to the exigencies of post–World War I Germany. Adam wrote thus: "Moreover [the Western individual] because he has renounced the fellowship of the Church, the *communio fidelium,* the interrelation and correlation of the faithful has severed the second root of his life (the first being union with Christ), that is to say, his fellowship with other men."[82]

Max Metzger and the *Una Sancta* Movement

Karl Adam dedicated his little book *One and Holy* to the memory of Father Max Metzger, the foremost symbol of the *Una Sancta* movement. The

---

80. *Id., The Spirit of Catholicism,* trans. Dom Justin McCann (New York: Macmillan, 1929), p. 9.

81. *Id.,* Sheed and Ward edition (London, 1929), p. 17.

82. *Ibid.*

Nazis eventually executed Metzger in 1944 for his courageous attempt to hasten the conclusion of the Second World War. His crime consisted in an appeal to the Lutheran archbishop of Uppsala, in neutral Sweden, to intervene to end the war. Betrayed by a Gestapo spy, he was condemned to decapitation, after a mock trial. Active as a liturgist, and a proponent of biblical spirituality, as well as the lay apostolate, "his pastoral activity in Germany" from 1920 to 1940 could be called "innovative." Metzger founded a society, Welt Friedensbund vom Weissen Kreuz (The World Peace League of the White Cross), in 1917, and later, a *Brüderschaft* (*Una Sancta* Brotherhood) in 1928. Both societies attempted dialogue with the Lutheran Churches, especially with those Evangelicals of the "High Church" mentality. Aware of more universal efforts at unity among non-Catholic Christians, he was an observer at the important Faith and Order Conference at Lausanne, Switzerland, in 1927. This conference inspired him to the specific adoption of the term *Una Sancta,* which actually had been, in effect, in the very broadest sense, an expression of attempts at church unity since the days of the Reformation itself. By use of this term, Metzger, as much as any other, emphasized the role of "spiritual ecumenism" in the quest for Christian Unity. It was he who made it the jargon phrase for all German ecumenical activity, keeping the concept of holiness *(Sancta)* continually before the eyes of the hierarchy and the faithful.[83]

After the Lausanne Conference, with the support of Charles Brent, Metzger attempted an appeal to Pope Pius XI in that same year. He petitioned the pope to permit a Roman Catholic presence within the Universal Movement for Christian Unity. He did this in a written report on the Conference and its possibilities. His report was not received at Rome![84]

In 1939, already previously arrested on Nazi suspicions of political implications in his religious preaching, Metzger wrote to the newly elected Pope Pius XII from jail. Pius had earlier been Apostolic Nuncio in Germany, and Metzger counted on his understanding of the German ethos, and of the possibilities which his pontificate held for world peace. He was never sure that his letter, posted from Switzerland, had ever reached its destination. However, during the wartime conversations of the Fulda Bishops Conference, Archbishop Jaeger referred to Pius XII's knowledge of the existence of the *Una Sancta* movement and its activities. Metzger called for the acknowledgement of faults on both sides, not only on the part of those engaged in actual belligerency, but also on the part of those who had contributed to the

---

83. Swidler, *op. cit.*, pp. 141-66.
84. *Ibid.*, pp. 47-49.

popular state of mind that preceded the war and had escalated attitudes in regard to it. He recalled for the pontiff the little-known fact that Pope Adrian VI, as early as 1522-23, had sought a General Council of the Church, to which Protestant leaders and theologians would be invited, along with their Catholic counterparts, to heal Europe of its many ideological and religious divisions. That proposed sixteenth-century council never occurred.[85]

In the face of such an indigenous impassability, Metzger proceeded to propose to Pope Pius XII a commission of twelve outstanding Catholic theologians in conjunction with an equal number of Protestant counterparts in preparation for such a council. These twenty-four partners would select topics to serve as a basis for secret conversations. These themes would constitute a fundamental report which would be the basis for a council of healing and peace. Metzger foresaw that the "instrument of harmony" would be dialogue.[86]

Despite the fact that Archbishop Jaeger was never comfortable with Metzger's personality, seeing him as an eccentric, Jaeger used Metzger's terminology, *Una Sancta,* as his own appellation for the Ecumenical Movement.[87] Surely no one could take offense at the quest for holiness and the cause of unity.

After the War, Jaeger used Metzger's specific model of "conversations" regarding theological issues as the pattern of ecumenical dynamics within his diocese. In 1947, the first "conversation" of "controversial theology" occurred under Jaeger's supervision. The group consisted of twelve participants from the Roman Catholic side and twelve from the Lutheran.

---

85. *Ibid.,* p. 28.

86. *Ibid.,* pp. 155-58, note especially p. 156: "I know that your Holiness grieves especially over the disunity of the Body of Christ . . . much has already been attempted in this direction during recent years."

87. Interview of Aloys Klein with the author, 15 October 2001, and Swidler, *op. cit.,* p. xxi. Despite his personal reservations about Metzger, "the *Una Sancta* movement nevertheless apparently continued to have the whole-hearted support of Archbishop Jäger [*sic*] and others of the German hierarchy. On July 28, 1948, Jäger wrote to Matthias Laros (his canon lawyer) 'that on the part of the German Episcopacy ways are being sought to be able to continue the *Una Sancta* work without disobeying the existing ecclesiastical prescriptions.'" *Ibid.,* p. 212. Needless to say, Archbishop Gröber was as usual out of step. "For years [he] opposed energetically the liturgical movement and had refused Metzger permission to lecture on Christian reunion." In 1947, a major *Una Sancta* conference was planned for Constance in Switzerland. The conference had to be cancelled at the last minute by prohibition of the French military authority. Archbishop Gröber forbade the passage of the participants from Germany, France, Holland and Switzerland through his diocese and so informed the French. *Ibid.,* p. 182.

The idea of theological conversations is not limited to Metzger's conciliar proposal. More importantly, Metzger's plan was aimed most specifically at the local level. It formed part of a threefold program at the heart of his quest for Christian unity, stemming back to 1937-1938. His plan first sought friendship as a goal, whereby clergy of varying Christian traditions would meet to form ties of understanding and mutual sympathy, i.e., become friends. Clergy were engaged in the common cause of promoting the Gospel, and of providing sustenance and consolation to the faithful. According to Metzger, could they not do the same for one another?

The second phase of Metzger's plan encompassed instructions and gatherings, lectures and publications. This step concerned communication and information. Metzger's intuition, in this matter, identified ignorance as the mother of prejudice. Were knowledge to become available, the barriers of bias would fall. Finally, in the third phase of his plan, he proposed a system, which today would be termed "dialogue." Quoting from Leonard Swidler's *Ecumenical Vanguard* is perhaps the most succinct way of representing the method which was to become a reality some twenty-five years later:

> The third form of the *Una Sancta* circles was what Metzger considered possibly the most effective of the three types. This should be a discussion group of carefully chosen, mature people of different confessions; the number should not exceed thirty so as not to destroy the intimacy of the discussions. He (Metzger) insisted that the choice of the location of the discussion was important, that it should be psychologically conducive to a friendly exchange of opinion; parliamentary forms were ruled out. He thought there should be two short simple talks by persons of different churches of twenty to forty minutes in total on the theme to be discussed at some length afterwards by everyone. He highly recommended that the meeting be opened and closed with a common prayer or reading from Scripture; prayers such as the Apostles Creed and Our Father were obvious choices. "Catholics ought not to shy away from praying the ancient ecclesiastical doxology at the end" of the Lord's Prayer.[88]

If Adolf Herte, Joseph Lortz and Karl Adam stand as the academic representatives of the Catholic pre-ecumenical phase in Germany, Max Metzger would be its practical symbol. In 1947, three years after his death,

---

88. *Ibid.*, p. 152. The above methodology forms to this day the pattern of international bilateral ecumenical dialogue as originated by the SPCU.

ecumenical conversations began between twenty-eight distinguished theologians, half of them Lutherans and the other half Catholics, under the leadership of Archbishop Jaeger and the Lutheran Bishop Wilhelm Stählin of Oldenburg. Some fifteen years later, Augustin Bea would personify the dreams and aspirations of these above-cited ecclesiastics and scholars.[89]

Jaeger was a member of the reconstituted West German Bishops Conference at Fulda. Jaeger was designated again to become the bishop officially in charge of German ecumenical affairs. He had first used the language of *Una Sancta* in 1942 when he came to the conference. He was now the heir to the language and the dream of Max Metzger.

By the conclusion of the Second World War and the collapse of the Nazi regime, the emergence of a concern for the affairs of Christian unity could no longer be thwarted. This was immediately grasped and presented by Archbishop Jaeger to the German Bishops Conference. Leonard Swidler explained the entire mentality in the following paragraph:

> Germany has long been the focus of intellectual, cultural and other kinds of fermentation in the world — for evil as well as good. This one was good. The name given to this fermentation in Germany towards Christian unity is the *Una Sancta* Movement. It is to be distinguished from the ecumenical movement, which has broader historical roots but which did not, until Vatican II, substantively include Roman Catholics. The Catholic-Protestant dialogue was the essence of the *Una Sancta* Movement, which became the vanguard of Roman Catholic involvement in ecumenism. The term *"Una Sancta"* (coming from the Nicene Creed, *"Credo in . . . unam, sanctam . . . ecclesiam"*) (I believe in . . . one, holy . . . church) was used by a number of people interested in re-unification work, particularly in the decades following the First World War. But the term *"Una Sancta* Movement" seems to have crystallized only as a result of the work done by Father Max Metzger and to have gained general currency only after he founded his *Una Sancta* Brotherhood (a society which embodied clerics, religious and laity alike in the cause of the reunification of Christians) in 1938.[90]

It is this distinction of a Catholic concern for the cause of Christian Unity as apart from — but not unconnected to — the worldwide Ecumenical Movement that characterizes the post-war efforts of Lorenz Jaeger, in

---

89. Schmidt, *op. cit.*, p. 320. This point is clearly evidenced by the *positive reaction* from every quarter of Germany to Bea's nomination as a Cardinal in 1959.

90. *Ibid.*, p. xii.

the cause of Christian Unity. This *Una Sancta* Movement was both German and Roman Catholic in its initiative, and had as a specific goal, the provision of an appropriate atmosphere for meetings and organized conversations. It was theological in scope, and called upon the wisdom, talents and training of disciplined theologians. In his lifetime, Metzger had only two such meetings, one in 1939 and another in 1940. That such events took place at all, given the extraordinary atmosphere of wartime Germany, was remarkable. The topic of discussion for the 1940 assembly was especially noteworthy. It was simply called "The Church!" It was attended by seven Protestant pastors and fourteen Roman Catholic clergy.[91]

The wartime atmosphere provided an opening in which the topic of the Church would be welcome news to religious people suffering the confusion and oppression of the Nazi era. In his memoir of those times, *My Thirty Third Year,* Gerhard A. Fittkau, a German priest arrested by invading Russian soldiers, described his "shared prayer time" in captivity. His partners in this improvised service of worship were the Orthodox wife of a Russian diplomat, herself a prisoner, and a male Lutheran pastor. These words are the summation of the situation in which Fittkau found himself:

> It does no good now to sit around blaming the separation we inherited. What we have to do is dig down to the root evil that caused the separation — the weakening of faith within the Church. If the sufferings we are going through now will tear that root out of our hearts and let our faith grow mature and strong, then maybe those same sufferings will be the instrument of uniting us all again in Christ. Only in Christ and through Christ can the lost unity be restored.[92]

These words were spoken while the war was yet raging. His comment continued: "Our little congress was independently getting at the very heart of the 'ecumenical movement' which at the same time was taking a new lease on life in Christian countries."[93] He concluded with his own theological premise that while "ostensible unity" had been broken in history, the Church, on the contrary, had never lost that fundamental unity which constitutes the Mystical Body of Christ.[94] In this, Fittkau verified Metzger, who lived his life in the vanguard of a renewed Catholicism in a twentieth century between the wars.

---

91. *Ibid.,* p. 153.

92. *Id., My Thirty Third Year: A Priest Experience in a Russian Work Camp* (New York: Farrar, Strauss, Cudahy, 1958), p. 218.

93. *Ibid.*

94. *Ibid.,* p. 130.

His many pastoral interests of the Germany of 1920-1940 anticipated a mind-set only to be discovered by others in the Church with the convocation of Vatican Council II. Metzger founded both a society and a movement, which sought unity between the Reformation and Catholic Churches.[95]

In the wake of the Second World War, the *Una Sancta* movement intensified on both the Protestant and Catholic sides, as German Christians assessed themselves as being covered with sorrow and shame. The Evangelical pastor Martin Niemöller, someone who was labeled a "white martyr" of the Hitler era, appeared before the United States military government officials to explain what had happened to the churches in Germany after 1933. He outlined for them the truth that the German state is based on Christian principles and therefore is verifiably a German state *if* the government is composed of Christians, but if there be no Christians at the helm, Christian principles have not the slightest chance to influence Christian events.[96] Niemöller wrote in 1946:

> We Christians in Germany are indigent. The era of suffering which lies behind us ate up our resources; moreover, we have become tired, and from our inmost being rises the prayer that Elijah prayed: "It is enough now, O Lord, take away my life!" . . . Guilt for the past rests on us — a guilt that is terrible in the eyes of men, terrible also and enormous in the eyes of God. We are trying today to testify to our people that God's grace is greater and is more powerful than all the sin that has seized power over us; we believe that God — for Christ's sake — forgives our sins and He is willing to forgive sin and send a blessing which will provide new powers — powers which should not be expended in the future on the self-centered goals set by our human hearts, but in the service for which all mankind today is waiting, namely, the service of brotherly love and of peace among men.[97]

95. Swidler, *op. cit.*, pp. 63, 146, 149.

96. See Leo Stein, *Hitler Came for Niemöller* (Gretna, La.: Pelican Publishing Company, 2002); Clarissa S. Davidson, *God's Man* (Westport, Conn.: Greenwood Publishing Group, 1979); Martin Niemöller, *God Is My Führer* (New York: Philosophical Library, n.d.). Martin Niemöller was a much-decorated naval officer and was in the Kaiser's service. He was a major factor in the Barmen Declaration. He was also the virtual spokesman for the Confessing Church, which was totally anti-Nazi. His official titles were Chairman of the Pastorals Emergency League, a member of the Council of the Evangelical Church of the Old Prussian-Union (the biggest United Church in Germany), and a member of the council which was the legitimate governing body of the German Evangelical Church (the DEK). After the war, Niemöller was a leading spokesperson for ecumenism.

97. Stewart A. Herman, *op. cit.*, p. ix.

There is considerable evidence of a conversion in wartime Germany from a secular and self-centered society to one that was now open to the Word of Christ. For example, the *Marburger Presse* headlined: "End of State Churchism." The article made reference to the election of a new Protestant bishop of Kursheen, which pointed to several new trends within the Protestant Church of Germany. Among these were a renewed appreciation of the Sacrament of the Lord's Supper (a movement deemed an expression of favor for the Church of Rome), a spontaneous desire on the part of the Church *to be churchly,*[98] and finally a new historical look at Luther. Professor Stewart W. Herman, writing on the scene and at the time (1945-1946), recorded: "It was the original intention of the Luther Reformation in Germany to retain the office of bishop, but the circumstances of the times, chiefly the temporal power of the Pope and the physical frailty of 'Protestants' led to the fatal practice of looking to the local lord as the overseer — or bishop — of the church."[99] Herman went on to explain that it was presently being realized, in 1946, that in history such a practice led more and more Protestants away from the call to holiness and looked to the importance of the state's preferential position, and establishment, based upon the arbitrary conduct of princes. The martyred pastor, Dietrich Bonhoeffer, had earlier recorded these same sentiments as a young cleric when he wrote movingly of his visit to the Church of Rome, and simultaneously expressed his desire that "the Protestant Church should have remained but a sect," for this would have spoken to Luther's desire for holiness, which was at the heart of the Reformation.[100]

Herman also wrote: "Today the whole German Church seems to be conscious that the total collapse of the total state has presented it with an opportunity for reformation, such as it has not possessed since the days of Martin Luther."[101] Herman's observations dovetail with Martin Niemöller's witness. A survivor and acknowledged religious opponent of Hitler, his heroism gave him the status of a prophet among Protestants of post-War Germany. There was a hunger for a *communio sanctorum,* to which the total church in Germany, in all its human weakness, gave vent in its groaning:

> In the course of the last twenty years, Christendom has become increasingly aware of the blessed fact that the church of Jesus Christ on earth

---

98. To be churchly implies the restoration of the arts, of piety, the wearing of vestments or church garb by the clergy and the renewal of ritual.

99. *Ibid.*, p. 154.

100. Bethge, *op. cit.*, p. 61.

101. *Ibid.*, p. 155.

is *one,* over all national frontiers and that we neither dare nor can segregate ourselves by nationalities. Even though, the Body of Christ may possess both strong and feeble members, each of these members has been called to the service of the entire body and the body cannot dispense with a single one of them. The Church in Germany today may rightly be regarded as a decidedly feeble member; nevertheless, if the Lord of the Body so wills, her service will be accounted of use to the whole![102]

The above-cited text, by a Protestant ecclesiastical journalist, summed up the current quest for the *"Holy."* He recalled that the Reformers, Luther, Calvin, Melanchthon, etc., never dropped the use of that term. They always spoke of "Holy Mass, Holy Church, Holy Scriptures, Holy People!" In this moment of vulnerability, a cold sense of dread clutched at the heart of German ecclesiastics who realized that their sermons and their parishes had for too long been at the disposition of the State. "To be churchly" is to be "holy." While Protestants struggled with their national, ecclesiastical heritage, Jaeger acted. He may not have appreciated the personality of Max Metzger, but, as the proverb states, "imitation renders consent." Jaeger's contribution to the post-War crisis was, therefore, not in words but in actions.

Jaeger's secretary, Aloys Klein, recalled that the first participants slept together in a barrack-like room; their beds were composed of rusty box springs and their mattresses had been bloodied by prisoners who were ultimately executed. By this time (1947) the Fulda Bishops Conference had confirmed, within the newly restructured hierarchy, all of Archbishop Jaeger's previous and present ecumenical work and made him "Bishop Responsible" for the *Una Sancta* work. Jaeger's task was to keep the bishops and Rome simultaneously informed of German interconfessional developments, a task he willingly accepted from 1948 until his death in 1975.[103]

There is no question that Max Metzger, his courage, creativity, and persistence, all of which focused around the idea of "Spiritual Ecumenism," was the prophet of his era, even though he went to his death applauded by none. If not convinced of the man, Jaeger was convinced of the cause. He picked up the banner which had fallen into the dust. Yet, the words of Metzger's letter to Pope Pius XII appear quite moving as they echo down the hollows of history: "Is all this I lay before Your Holiness

102. *Ibid., op. cit.,* p. xi.
103. Joseph J. Link and Josef A. Slominski, *Kardinal Jaeger* (Paderborn: Verlag, Bonifatius-Druckerei, 1966), pp. 30-31.

too daring? I know that it goes far beyond what can be counted on to succeed. . . . Church history and world history, alike, will raise a memorial to the wearer of the triple crown (papal tiara), who begins this work on a generous scale and to the one, who may, finish it later."[104] How prophetic were his words!

1945: A Challenge for the Fulda Bishops Conference

At this point, it is both necessary and beneficial to assemble a few facts before proceeding further. Some have already been mentioned. Yet, in bringing these items together, it is possible to set the stage for the important role of Lorenz Jaeger at the table of the Fulda Bishops Conference.

First, much of the pontificate of Pope Pius XII focused on Germany because of the Second World War. In 1917 Pope Benedict XV had sent the young Archbishop Eugenio Pacelli as his diplomatic representative to the German Empire of Kaiser Wilhelm II. Pacelli remained in Germany not only through the close of the War but almost through the entire life span of the Weimar Republic.[105] As Secretary of State from 1930 until he was elected to the See of Peter in 1939, he was much preoccupied with Germany. In 1933, Pacelli was heavily involved with the negotiations for a new Vatican-Reich Concordat.[106] In 1943, the German *Wehrmacht* Forces occupied the City of Rome and Pius found himself eyeball-to-eyeball with Ambassador Ernst von Weizsacker over the issue of the neutrality of the Vatican and the condition of the City of Rome.[107]

---

104. Swidler, *op. cit.,* p. 158.

105. Stewart A. Stehlin, *op. cit.,* p. 13. Pacelli's appointment followed the sudden death of Archbishop Giuseppe Aversa, who was accredited to the Court of the Kaiser and the German states *(länder).* The most important of these for the Vatican was Bavaria.

106. Cornwell, *op. cit.,* pp. 130-56. Admittedly a slanted view, Cornwell nonetheless gathers the essential facts. A more contemporary narrative is found in Gurian, *op. cit.,* pp. 119-56.

107. John Weitz, *Hitler's Diplomat* (New York: Ticknor & Fields, 1992), p. 289. Ernst von Weizsäcker was in a most embarrassing position as a Secretary of State in the Foreign Ministry and Ambassador to the Vatican. "He hated his chief, von Ribbentrop, as well as Adolf Hitler, von Ribbentrop's chief. He could not stomach the Foreign Minister's arrogant dilettantism, lack of diplomatic skills, and his absence of courage in dealing with Hitler. Von Weizsäcker's immediate concern was for the men working in the ministry, most of whom he considered honorable." That he had to stand before Pope Pius XII and mouth the dictates of Joachim von Ribbentrop was the supreme humiliation of his life. See also Vincent A. Lapomarda, *The Jesuits and the Third Reich* (Lampeter, Dyfed, Wales: Edwin Mellon Press,

Pius XII remained continually informed about the German situation both during the War and immediately after. Individuals, many of whom were friends and contacts made by Pope Pius during the time of his ambassadorship to Germany, wrote to him to inform him of issues such as refugee priests, the hardships suffered by the survivors of the war, and the need for material sustenance. While Archbishop Lorenz Jaeger was not to be numbered in this category, he too began the practice of writing directly to the pope about these same issues. For his efforts, he often received a direct and very personal response from the pontiff's own typewriter. Through all this time, the Fulda Bishops Conference did not miss a meeting. However, the War had in fact brought a shift in the religious mentality of the Christian people yet once again. Just as after the First World War, when the aristocracy fell, taking with it the Reformation principle of *Cujus regio, ejus religio,* now responsibility for the support of Hitler and the lack of resistance to the Holocaust affected the German nation profoundly. The issues *now* were guilt and shame.[108]

After the War, Pius was still very much concerned for Germany. Ten years before his death a German Catholic named Gertrude Luckner founded a circle, which was both philo-Semitic and pro-Israel. Miss Luckner was distraught about the guilt of the Holocaust and the fate of the quarter million Jewish Holocaust survivors. She sought papal approval for her work. Instead of a blessing, she received a *monitum* (a formal warning) from the Holy Office, charging her with promotion of religious indifferentism (the belief that one religion is just as good as another). Fraulein Luckner, herself a victim of Nazi concentration camps, protested. In 1950 Pius sent two members of his household, Jesuits Robert Leiber and Augustin Bea, to carefully scrutinize Miss Luckner's Freiburg group. Bea returned to tell the Pope there was nothing to the charges against Miss Luckner and her circle.[109]

From 1943 on, the German bishops had to fend for themselves before

---

1989), pp. 215-29. This latter book records the clandestine activities of the Jesuits during the German occupation of Rome. Prominent among them were members of Pius XII's own household.

108. Regarding the impact of the Second World War, Ronald J. Rychlak, *op. cit.* p. 243, presents this telling sentence regarding the pope: "For Pius, reminders of the war years were particularly disheartening. Not only did the war reveal humans at their most evil, but the suffering was not confined the way it had been in previous wars. World War II was unlike others before it, a war between entire nations. Women and children figured very high among the death rolls."

109. *Op. cit.,* pp. 176-77.

public opinion. They were isolated from direct contact and support from Pius, since he and they were now completely surrounded by Nazi threats. After the war, the same repercussions of guilt and shame were obvious. Why had they not been more forthright in their challenge to the Hitler regime? Certainly no German bishop went to prison and no German bishop was executed while countless ordinary clergy were rounded up and thrown into Dachau. Historian Michael Phayer summed up the situation of the Fulda Bishops Conference by citing Konrad Adenauer: "Who also believed that Catholics — flock and shepherds alike — bore responsibility for the Holocaust. 'I believe,' he wrote before his re-entry into politics, 'that if the bishops altogether had publicly taken a stance from the pulpit, a lot could have been avoided. That didn't happen and there's no excuse for it. *If the bishops had been taken to the concentration camps or to jail,* it wouldn't have hurt anything — on the contrary.'" Adenauer kept his opinions to himself, but they found expression in modified form in the essays of Jesuit Max Pribilla.[110]

With odd analogies, the bishops struggled to put a good face on their behavior under Hitler's rule. For example, Cardinal Josef Frings, who succeeded Cardinal Bertram as president of the conference, upon the latter's death, tried to make a defense by comparing the bishops to surviving soldiers on the battlefield.[111] One bishop whose aristocratic origins had already earned him Hitler's hatred did speak out boldly from the pulpit:

> Is the reason why the Gestapo has been instituted to replace the ordinary courts, the fact that the Gestapo's actions in the Reich are not, unfortunately, themselves subject to juridical revision? No German citizen has any defense against the power of the Gestapo. I repeat that he is utterly defenceless. Not one of us is certain, though he be the most loyal, the most conscientious citizen, though he knows himself innocent, I say that not one of us is certain that he will not any day be dragged from his house and carried off to the cells of some concentration camp.[112]

> My brethren, the name of an Evangelical pastor, who in the last war risked his life for Germany as a submarine commander, and has for years now been deprived of his liberty, is known to all of you. We have the greatest respect for his courage and the fortitude with which this es-

110. *Id., op. cit.,* p. 136.
111. *Ibid.,* pp. 143-48.
112. Heinrich Portmann, *op. cit.,* p. 233.

timable German confesses to his Christian belief. So you will see from this last example that the demand which I make open today is not confined to denomination or for Catholics only, but something *which effects all Christians; it is a request for something fundamentally human, religious and national.*[113]

These words came from Bishop Clemens August Count von Galen. Von Galen was created a Cardinal in 1946 and died shortly thereafter. The stately 6'7" von Galen was warmly remembered twenty years later in 1966 by Rabbi Fritz Steinthal. Von Galen went in search of Steinthal after the 1938 pogrom. Steinthal wrote that the Jews were spiritually strengthened by the bishop's conduct and by those he influenced.[114]

But von Galen's neighbor in Westphalia, Archbishop Lorenz Jaeger, did not enjoy any post-War accolades. It must be remembered that Jaeger was a military chaplain on the Russian front when he was notified that he had been elected Archbishop of Paderborn. The election as bishop came from the Cathedral Chapter, which was very aware that it had to receive the approval of the government, according to the terms of the Concordat of 1933. Jaeger had served on the German side during World War I as a common fighting soldier. He had an impeccable war record, and during the years of his priestly ministry that ensued, he was a revered teacher and spiritual director of boys and young men. These were reasons which would indeed pass muster at the Reich headquarters in Berlin. His election also had to be approved by the Supreme Pontiff, Pius XII. Jaeger protested the election and the papal appointment. He was very aware that besides leaving incomplete the dream of his studies, he was compelled by circumstances to walk a tightrope in the shadow of Hitler.[115] Professor Michael Phayer, an American scholar of twentieth-century Church history, explained: "They [the German bishops] had to be careful, Bishop Jaeger said, because a 'political split' had affected the entire German people . . . many members of our Church, who had been blinded and misled by a deceitful propaganda, would have been driven all the more into the arms of National Socialism by too sharp a language."[116] Whether or not Jaeger collaborated with the Na-

---

113. *Ibid.*, pp. 233-34. Of course, von Galen spoke of Pastor Niemöller, who was arrested in 1937 and imprisoned until the end of the war. This statement pronounces the situation of an ecumenical martyrdom that is, i.e., witness between representatives of two denominations against the powers of evil.

114. Phayer, *op. cit.*, p. 17.

115. Link and Slominski, *op. cit.*, pp. 14-17.

116. Phayer, *op. cit.*, pp. 146-47.

zis, either wittingly or unwittingly, was to remain a point of controversy until the end of his life.

In 1995, Heibert Gruss compiled the evidence and published it under the title *Erzbischof Lorenz Jaeger als Kirchenführer im Dritten Reich* (Archbishop Lorenz Jaeger as a Church Leader in the Third Reich).[117] According to Gruss, Jaeger did everything in his power to protect the authenticity of the Christian faith against the propaganda of Doctor Alfred Rosenberg, who claimed in his book, *The Myth of the Twentieth Century,* that the Nazi party represented progress itself.[118] Jaeger was aware that he had to play with subtleties in order to sustain the integrity of the Church. Toward that end, the opportunity did arise when he was approached by the hierarchy of his own ecclesiastical province, as well as that of Cologne, and asked to raise the issue of ecumenism before the other diocesan ordinaries at their regular August meeting.

Three facts are discernible. One is the fact that during the hiatus created by the death of Archbishop Klein, the ecumenical question *(Una Sancta)* was discussed and brought to the fore by scholars and prelates of Paderborn. These individuals would have, in fact, been among those who had elected him in Chapter. Secondly, it is clear that the atmosphere at Fulda was perpetually tense during those years and no innovation was welcome. Finally, Jaeger showed exceptional courage in his persistence that *Una Sancta* questions would indeed be discussed for the good of the church.

Towards that end, Jaeger attempted to place the question of ecumenism on the table of the Fulda Bishops Conference in 1942. On 5 August, Jaeger wrote to the president of the conference, Adolf Cardinal Bertram, that he deemed it opportune to institute an "ecumenical seminar." Cardinal Bertram of Breslau responded within three days that he did not deem it "opportune." The implication according to Jaeger's secretary was fear. Any innovation by seeking dialogue with Lutherans or other Christians of the Reformation would raise the suspicion of the Reich Chancellery and bring down the fury of Hitler's police upon the Catholic Church. This judgment is correct, for already it had been noted by Waldemar Gurian in 1936 that an attack on the Church's hierarchy would strike at the heart of Catholicism.[119] As early as 1934, one year after the Concordat was signed by Vati-

---

117. Gruss, *op. cit.,* pp. 346-47.

118. *Ibid.* Also cited in Rychlak, *op. cit.,* pp. 336-38. Based upon Rosenberg's recommendation, new holidays were instituted over holy days, e.g., Hitler's birthday, summer solstice, Beer Hall Putch anniversary, etc. They hoped to establish a ceremony of naming rights to replace baptism.

119. Gurian, *op. cit.,* pp. 119-56.

can Secretary of State Cardinal Pacelli and Adolf Hitler, the bishops issued a pastoral letter dated June 7 in which they complained of neo-pagan doctrines and tendencies.[120] It was evident from their reference to the "Myth of Blood" that the bishops specifically targeted the Führer's deputy for *Weltanschauung*, Alfred Rosenberg. Twenty days later, Bishop von Galen, in company with other German bishops, personally informed Hitler of the duty of the bishops to protect Catholic faith and morals and to ward off the attacks made on Christianity and the Church. Hitler received von Galen graciously, but he obfuscated. His promises of detachment from the philosophy of Rosenberg were merely straw and hay.[121]

Gurian predicted seven years before the 1942 Fulda Bishops Conference:

> The struggle for the Church in the Third Reich is a struggle for the soul of the Church. It is not, as the National Socialists continually proclaim it to be, a struggle for political strongholds which are not the Church's business. . . . The real object of the Reich Concordat (1933) is not the guarantee of stipends, of State-controlled theological faculties, of the positions in common law held by ecclesiastical bodies. All these things are the means to a final end, the preaching of the Catholic doctrine in Germany.[122]

Then Gurian made a startling statement for the times: "In the case of the Evangelical Church its adherents are not fighting for any particular past or for the retention of some particular Christian terminology, but for the realization of the *true essence of the Christian Church*, which precludes compromises (tantamount to betrayal) with those powers which are attempting more or less adroitly . . . to set earthly values and regimes in the place of Christ."[123]

Lorenz Jaeger: Ecumenist, Creative and Courageous

Among the German hierarchy, Lorenz Jaeger was the pioneer bishop to bring the ecumenical questions before the Episcopal Conference in Germany. He was a complex man! In his thinking, Jaeger was coldly logical,

---

120. Lewy, *op. cit.*, p. 122.
121. Lewy, *op. cit.*, p. 125.
122. *Id.*, pp. 157-58.
123. *Ibid.*, p. 158 (emphasis mine).

but he had a warm heart. In the early days of his ministry, he treated his clergy with military rigor. However, as time went on, he was warm and open to them, especially when they were confused or in trouble. He came from blue-collar stock, but he was at home with members of the working class and with the aristocracy as well. Hitler did not like the aristocracy and they suffered from him. Jaeger on the other hand made himself available to all. Monsignor Klein recalled that on his pastoral visits or Confirmations, he would call in to see a widowed baroness or the family of a *Landgraf*.[124] He wrote letters profusely, working at his desk late at night; he mixed lofty theological insights with diocesan gossip. His letters revealed him always as a "man on the go."[125] His secretary remembered Jaeger as a man of genuine piety. He always traveled with a rosary in his hand. He made at least two retreats per year with the Benedictines, availing himself of the beauty of their liturgy.

Upon the death of Archbishop Kaspar Klein of Paderborn in 1941, the Cathedral Chapter assembled and elected Jaeger. The dean submitted his name to the Holy See and to the German Government for approval. Jaeger, however, declined. But, according to the terms of the Concordat of 1933, the Holy See, once it had received the nomination, had to consult with the government.[126] The German Government readily gave its approval. Jaeger accepted under pressure from the Nuncio, Caesare Orsengno. The Nazi Administration considered only Jaeger's clean war record as an embattled soldier in two military campaigns. At a later time, some historians would claim that Jaeger had expressed pro-Nazi sympathies and that this was the reason for the swift confirmation of the appointment from the *Reichskanzlei* in Berlin. The accusation is false, and that Jaeger at all should have accepted this particular bishopric under such circumstances was indeed an act of heroism. For one thing, Heinrich Himmler controlled his mountain *Schloss* for the SS not far from Paderborn. It was here the elite Waffen SS

---

124. Interview with Monsignor Klein and author, 15 October 2001.

125. Please see Appendix for examples.

126. In 1933, the German government concluded a concordat with the Holy See. The existing partial concordats with the Länder (Bavaria, Prussia, Baden) under the Vychiark Constitution did not provide adequate guarantees for Catholicism. W. A. Purdy, *The Church on the Move, op. cit.*, p. 43. Admittedly John Cornwell, *op. cit.*, p. 179, is a controversial source; however, he is clear in the effect of the Concordat on the Fulda Bishops Conference which found itself as a body reduced to inertia. "In response to the Bishops pastoral letter, Hitler declared . . . that he was not against Christianity in itself, 'but we will fight it for the sake of keeping our public life free from those priests who have failed their calling and who should have become politicians rather than clergymen'."

took their oath to Hitler for life, on a dagger, "for blood and honour."[127] Against such an oath Jaeger made his own motto, *Vita et Pax,* "Life and Peace." Jaeger's interest in the cause of ecumenism, along with his episcopal ministry, began in terrifying circumstances here and grew along with his sensibility to the significance of history. Once he assumed his seat in the Fulda Bishops Conference in 1942, he began to raise questions and make proposals which made his brother bishops nervous, given the atmosphere of terror in which they lived.[128]

On 5 August 1942, the scarcely fifty-year-old Bishop Jaeger sent a letter to the Fulda Bishops Conference, in which he requested that attention be paid, by the bishops, regarding the enclosed document: "Considerations in Regard to the Ecumenical Questions." He stated that it appears necessary, that the bishops at the impending Fulda Bishops Conference should, from within the very well meaning but frequently unwise and unrequited desires in this regard, *undertake the cause of Christian unity in Germany.*[129] Later the matter was presented at the conference. Adolf Cardinal Bertram, Archbishop of Breslau, was chairman of this assembly of the Fulda Bishops Conference. He coolly expressed his thanks for Jaeger's efforts. At the same time, he clearly expressed his reservations against each of the petitions which had been offered by the Archbishop of Paderborn. The Cardinal would not entertain the proposal on the part of the Fulda Bishops Conference to institute an "Ecumenical Seminar."[130] If the individual Bishops wish to do something like this, that was their choice. Then the Cardinal President warned Jaeger of the dire circumstances:

The National Socialistic *Weltanschauung* would seek the complete annihilation of the Catholic Church in Germany as its presumed singular

127. Richard Rhodes, *Masters of Death* (New York: Alfred A. Knopf, 2002), p. 17. "Himmler had refurbished a Saxon Castle, Wewelsburg, for his SS leadership, which he considered 'A Knightly Order.' Situated on a bluff of the Almay River near Paderborn in Western Germany, it looked out grandly across the Westphalian Plain." In fact, this pagan temple of outrageous ritual had once been a chapel of the archbishops of Paderborn.

128. Cornwell, *op. cit.,* p. 138. The bishops by this time felt that they had made a devastating acquiescence after the Enabling Act of March 1933. Combined with the Concordat of that same year, the bishops had reached a stalemate in regard to their ability to shepherd the flock.

129. "Es begann," *op. cit.,* p. 331. "Es erscheint mir notwendig zu sein, dass der Episkopat in der bevorstehenden Fuldaer Bischofskonferenz Stellung nimmt zu den vielen gutgemeinten, aber häufig unklugen Versuchen Unberufener, die, 'Wiedervereinigung' der Konfessionen in Deutschland anzubahnen."

130. *Ibid.,* p. 332.

powerful enemy. "More than any ecumenical speech, (the gospel admonition) of the Mass, for the anniversary of the consecration of a bishop, with its five fold admonition in regard to the future, *Vigilate!* (Beware), for its part, is worth due consideration." (cf. Mk 13:33-37).[131]

Thus despite the written warning of Cardinal Bertram, Jaeger *did* bring the question to the floor on 18 August 1942. The *Una Sancta* Movement "became the point at issue." Fear of reprisals deferred the matter of immediate discussion regarding *Una Sancta,* although the reason given was lack of time. Some of the bishops even shouted at Jaeger. "Sit down!" "Shut up and sit down!" The conference secretary even deleted his remarks, but in 1943, when the next Fulda Bishops Conference was assembled, the subject matter returned to the floor. Jaeger requested that his comments from the previous year be read back into the record.[132] Further, he indicated that he had taken counsel with local bishops, most especially his own neighbors.[133] He noted on that occasion that the political situation was not the only sign of the times. He regarded as "deeply rooted" the changes in Evangelical theology, which included: (1) its present disengagement from Liberalism; (2) the sense of the essence of the Church; (3) the new high regard for Sacred Scripture, as the Word of God, by recourse to exegesis; and (4) the very evident, passionate search for truth.[134] These are Jaeger's direct words:

> Thus since the question of truth has already moved to the centre, the discussion with Catholicism must begin with it. The reality therefore is that this discussion will no longer be carried out in the bias of party spirit, and of striving to outdo one another, but to discover the truth, that many Evangelical theologians earnestly and sincerely strive to attain. . . . Catholic theologians have the obligation to help these Evangelicals, in their search for truth, with all the means at their disposal![135]

---

131. *Ibid.* "Die nationalsozialistische Weltanschuung strebe die vollständige Vernichtung der katholischen Kirche in Deutschland als des vermeintlich einziger starken Feindes an. 'Mehr als allem ökumenischen Gespräch gilt demgegenüber die in der Messe des Anniversarium consecrationis episcopi fünfmal vorkommende Mahnung, 'Vigilate!'" (Vg. Mk 13:33-37).

132. Interview of Monsignor Klein and author, 15 October 2001.

133. Klein, "Es begann," *op. cit.,* p. 333.

134. *Ibid.,* p. 333.

135. *Ibid.* "Dadurch, dass die Wahrheitsfrage wieder in den Mittlepukt gerückt ist, musste von selbst das Gespräch mit dem Katholizismus beginnen. Das Wesentliche dabei ist, dass dieses Gespräch nicht mehr im Geist der Parteilichkeit und des Kampfes um jeden Preis

Jaeger further indicated that the Holy Father, Pope Pius XII, was personally interested in the *Una Sancta* Movement.[136] At this time, greater Germany contained a single united hierarchy of thirty-nine dioceses, which included Bavaria, East Prussia and Austria. A tiny ecumenical commission was established with Archbishop Jaeger and Cardinal Theodore Innitzer of Vienna as "The Bishops Responsible." Their work was hampered by Innitzer's disinterest.[137] The chaotic conditions of the war impeded their contact with other bishops and theologians through the postal service.

At that moment in time, Jaeger laid the cause of ecumenism before the Fulda Bishops Conference under the title of *Una Sancta*, which became the code name for the German Ecumenical Movement. An example of the persistence of the cause of ecumenism came with the publication of the encyclical *Mystici Corporis* on 29 June 1943.[138]

Consternation broke out among the German Protestants since the encyclical brought into question exactly who is a member of the Church. Papers were prepared and delivered by theologians such as Josef Höfer, Karl Rahner, and Romano Guardini. By the end of the 1944 Fulda Bishops Conference, the participants were charged with preparing a kind of *votum* (opinion) which included some special assigned area of expertise, as well as an evaluation of the ecumenical implications of Pius XII's encyclical. The work was under the supervision of Archbishop Jaeger. Throughout the war years, from his nomination as bishop in 1941, Jaeger kept the substance of ecumenism alive among the German bishops, and so convincingly did he present and argue the questions that the topic remained on the floor from that day to this.[139]

Immediately at war's end, Jaeger converted the ruins of Hardehausen into the first German center for ecumenical dialogue. Hardehausen had

---

geführt wird, sondern dass sich viele evangelische Theologen ernstlich und aufrichtig bemühen, die Wahrheit zu finden."

136. Cf. Swidler, *op. cit.*, pp. 155-57. This reference to Pope Pius XII is indeed interesting since Max Metzger was never certain that his letter to Pius had ever reached its destination. Later reference by Pius to the *Una Sancta* in Germany indicates that it was a jargon for ecumenism.

137. Theodor Cardinal Innitzer was a highly chastened individual after his warm welcome to Adolf Hitler in Vienna following the Austrian *Anschluss*. After having led the Austrian bishops into a profession of loyalty to the Führer, he was all but forced to retract. Historians of this period are unanimous in concluding that he did not enjoy favor with Pope Pius XII. See Rhodes, *The Vatican in . . .* , *op. cit.*, p. 150. The endorsement of Hitler by Church leadership caused confusion for the faithful.

138. Klein, *op. cit.*, p. 337.

139. *Ibid.*, p. 338.

once been a monastic abbey (originally founded in 1140 from the Cistercian foundation, a Zistezienserkloster).[140] This monastery, which had experienced a millennium of changes, had finally hit rock bottom when, in 1944-1945, it was used by the German Gestapo as a particularly heinous annex to Buchenwald Concentration Camp.[141] In April 1945, the American authorities handed it back to the diocese of Paderborn.[142] Jaeger sought dialogue with Bishop Wilhelm Stählin, Protestant bishop of Oldenburg. He was fortunate in having the Reverend Dr. Paul Simon as rector of the Paderborn Cathedral. Simon had been the leader of a precedent-making Catholic-Protestant theological meeting in Berlin in 1934. In fact, he had actually organized that meeting. Simon was the immediate successor of Max Metzger. As head of the *Brüderschaft Una Sancta*, he enlisted the assistance of the Benedictines of Niederaltaich Abbey to edit and publish the journal *Una Sancta*. Simon died after the initial meeting of what became the Jaeger-Stählin Circle, the biannual Catholic–Evangelical Lutheran Theological Conversation of twenty-four theologians.[143]

In 1957, Jaeger established the Johann-Adam Möhler Institute in Paderborn, for the purposes of ecumenical research, dialogue and publication. This multi-form institute continues sharing resources with both the State Academy and the diocesan seminary of Paderborn.[144] With the announcement of the Second Vatican Council on 25 January 1959, Jaeger could not hide his joy:

> As soon as we shall have arrived at, agreed upon and demonstrated the best solution in relation to the new developments of our time, we can show the Separated Brothers the sure way for that unity, which they themselves long for.[145]

But Jaeger was realistic and he knew the Evangelical and Reformed mentalities, which were at best suspicious of the invitations of Pope John. It was this that compelled him, according to Monsignor Klein, his secretary, to

140. Georg Pahlke and Wilhelm Pohlmann, *Hardehausen: Wir gehen durch das alte Kloster* (Paderborn: Bonifatius, 1984), p. 25.

141. *Ibid.*

142. *Ibid.*

143. Swidler, *op. cit.,* pp. 21, 31, 58, 136.

144. *Ibid.,* p. 21, *op. cit.*

145. Cited in Wittstadt, *op. cit.,* p. 182. "Sobald wir die besten Lösungen festgelegt, vereinbart, aufgezeigt haben werden, auch im Verhältnis zu den neuen Forderungen der Zeit, wir den getrennten Brüdern den sicheren Weg für jene Einheit aufzeigen können, die sie selbst ersehnen."

prompt the letter which Cardinal Bea handed to the Pope on 11 March 1960. Prior to that, he wrote Father Augustin Bea on 20 February 1959, that the West German Bishops Conference had been very busy in the preparations for the upcoming council. Jaeger went on: "I have reported about the response which the proclamation of this Council has had upon both Catholics and Evangelicals. Already reaction here can be summarized: On the Catholic side, exuberant, full of hope . . . while on the Evangelical side, the reaction is characterized by restraint if not actually negative."[146] Jaeger's collaboration with Bea, Höfer and Stakemeier, in presenting a proposal for a Secretariat for Promoting Christian Unity, remains the subject of this examination. Jaeger was created Cardinal only on 22 February 1965, by Pope Paul VI, who on the occasion called him the "hidden Father of Catholic ecumenism."[147] He died of cancer on 1 April 1975, almost two years after his retirement as archbishop. He had served the Archdiocese of Paderborn for thirty-four years. He was the sixty-fourth bishop of Paderborn. His immediate predecessor had been the prelate who had ordained him a priest, Archbishop Kaspar Klein. The first Archbishop of Paderborn in an unbroken chain at Paderborn was Hathumar (806-815); he had been appointed by Charlemagne![148]

The Genius of Lorenz Jaeger

When Archbishop Jaeger sent his first letter to the Fulda Bishops Conference on 5 August 1942 asking that attention be paid to ecumenical questions, he accepted an inherited responsibility. Other bishops meeting within his region, during the interim between the death of Archbishop Klein and Jaeger's own ordination to the episcopacy, drew up a statute for recommendation before the entire Fulda Assembly. If the content of the statute had not at all appealed to Jaeger, he never would have presented it. Gifted with remarkable personal qualities, including a sense of theological discipline, an appreciation of the value of history, as well as the persistent and diplomatic sensitivity native to his character, Jaeger succeeded where every-

146. Jaeger to Bea, 20 February 1959, Vicar General's Archives, Paderborn. "Ich habe berichtet über das Echo, das die Konzilsankündigung auf katholischer und evangelischer Seite gehabt hat. Kurs zusammengefasst, ist die Reaktion hier in Deutschland auf katholischer Seite überschwenglich hoffnungvoll . . . während auf evangelischer Seite die Reaktion betont zurückhaltend oder auch direkt negativ ist."

147. Interview of Monsignor Aloys Klein with the author, 15 October 2001.

148. Anonymous, *Die Erzdiözese Paderborn, op. cit.,* p. 54.

one else had failed from his region. It became his task to lay the ecumenical question before the congress. In this, Jaeger displayed his military training. He entered the fray not with a plan, but rather with a vision. Herein lies the difference. A plan might well be rigorous and constrictive. A military leader who is wedded to a plan is doomed to fail. But an officer with a core thought, who is able to adapt to new and unanticipated circumstances, is much more skilled at confronting every new obstacle or leaping over every hurdle.

Jaeger's ecumenical career might have had a successful but short run if limited to only the wartime years which ended in 1945. Thereafter, he established a dialogue between evangelical and Roman Catholic Christians, founded the Möhler Institute, expanded his ecumenical horizons to include interest in both the World Council of Churches and the Catholic Conference for Ecumenical Questions, and inaugurated new friendships, including one with Augustin Bea, which would ultimately have successful results. Lorenz Jaeger was a remarkable man, whose military acumen fortified his ecumenical ministry: he knew the difference between "a plan" and "planning"!

Conclusion

In the first chapter we saw that the ecumenical cause of East and West came together, at a certain fortuitous moment, expressed by Patriarch Maximos IV Saigh, on 23 May 1959. In this chapter, the focus has embraced the concept of the local church, specifically that of Germany. By drawing attention to the new situation in the inter-war years and during the entire Hitler period, we are enabled to observe many trends, movements and confluences at a particular point of history. The darkness of the Nazi years highlighted the hidden tensions within the Fulda Bishops Conference, as was evidenced in figures such as Archbishop Gröber and Cardinal Bertram. At the same time we can observe the prophetic character of Max Metzger, the courage of Max Pribilla, to whom we made brief allusion, but most especially the persistence of Lorenz Jaeger.

It can be said that German Roman Catholic ecumenical awareness telescoped through the person of the Archbishop of Paderborn, as was evidenced by his insistence in keeping the *Una Sancta* issue before the Fulda Bishops Conference. But perhaps the greatest contribution was Jaeger's support for the cause of Adolf Herte, the ecclesiastical historian. Along with Joseph Lortz, Herte demonstrated and emphasized the importance of historical scholarship as a hermeneutic in achieving an understanding of the Church.

At this time, German scholarship was important for the possibilities which it unveiled. Problems which had become so immured in the tension of Roman Catholic–Lutheran relationships could now be placed within and against the entire scope of Church history. What previously had been situated only in theory now assumed a tangibility because it could be seen in the light of both its particular and wider history. The particularities of questions no longer seemed so abrasive or threatening. Roman Catholic and Lutheran ecclesiology could be capable of reconciliation, provided that the perspectives of an honest historiography were to prevail. The overall work of Lortz and Herte tossed aside the detritus of polemic to uncover genuine personalities, in Reformation characters like Martin Luther, Martin Bucer, and Philip Melanchthon. Associated with their manner and thinking was an authentic quest for holiness. If taken to its logical conclusion, this process of ecumenical study was, in essence, for these twentieth-century scholars, an exercise in Spiritual Theology. Spiritual Theology itself is focused upon the person of Christ. So far as we conform to Christ, we become conformed to the Church. One need not fear the discoveries of history. This was the great lesson of the early struggle for ecumenism in the twentieth century.

The object of history is not the enumeration of facts alone but also the identification of civilizations as vessels of culture. The late Rabbi Abraham Heschel wrote: "No religion is an island!" If that premise is accepted, then its conclusion is obvious. Religion *is* at the base of all culture. Religion contributes to culture; it flows from culture and finds its expression in cultural language, usages, customs and forms. In his analysis of culture, Heschel places a particular emphasis on the unique character of the period we have outlined: "Nazism in its very roots was a rebellion against the Bible, against the God of Abraham." In so speaking Heschel clarified that Nazism was a denunciation and condemnation of the possibility and reality of divine revelation. He went on: "Realizing that it was Christianity that implanted attachment to the God of Abraham ('Revelation') and involvement with the Hebrew Bible in the hearts of Western man, Nazism resolved that it must both exterminate the Jews and eliminate Christianity, and bring about instead a revival of Teutonic paganism."[149] This was the very

---

149. Abraham Joshua Heschel, "No Religion Is an Island," in Harold Kasimow and Byron L. Sherwin (eds.), *No Religion Is an Island: Abraham Joshua Heschel* (Maryknoll, N.Y.: Orbis Books, 1991), p. 4.

point over which Karl Adam anguished from his Stuttgart pulpit when he lectured about the urgency of ecumenism under the threat of the godlessness of the Cold War: "Nazism has suffered a defeat but the process of elimination of the Bible from the consciousness of the Western World goes on."[150] The German bishops may have found some comfort during those times through their connection to the wider Church through the papacy, but there was no escaping their responsibility. Responsibility means that one *is* in the dilemma and *must* do something about it. Clearly what was required now for the particular circumstances regarding the possibilities of a united Church was a figure who was an ecclesiastic, a scholar, a German, and a man of the Bible. This is the most appropriate description of the Jesuit Augustin Bea, whose story is now taken up.

150. *Ibid.*

Chapter III

Augustin Bea: Cardinal of Ecumenism

Introduction

The ecumenical character of the pontificate of Pope John XXIII is well known. Certainly his summons of a General Council of the Church included the dimension of the recovery of Christian unity. Not only did the pontiff make his announcement regarding the Council at a ceremony concluding the week of Church Unity Octave, but he affirmed it in his first encyclical, *Ad Petri Cathedram,* of June 29, 1959: "Now we want to speak of that unity which is closest to our heart and with which this pastoral office entrusted to us by God is most particularly concerned. We refer to the unity of the Church (32)." Naturally, the questions arise: Did Pope John know Archbishop Jaeger? Did Archbishop Jaeger play a part in the ecumenical scope of the projected Second Vatican Council? According to the verbal testimony of Archbishop Loris Capovilla, private secretary to Pope John, the answer is in the affirmative.[1] Jaeger had long been in the habit of writing to the pope directly. As we have seen, Jaeger corresponded with Pope Pius XII regularly. His topics included wartime and post-War conditions in Germany, as well as certain theological questions. From the start of the new pontificate, Jaeger likewise directed his personal thoughts to Pope John XXIII.

Furthermore, Jaeger was personally represented in Rome by a priest of his diocese, Monsignor Josef Höfer, who was serving as Ecclesiastical Counsel for the Bonn Government. It was another German, however, who

---

1. Interview with the author, March 16, 1999.

was to become known as *Der Kardinal der Einheit,* "The Cardinal of Unity." This was the biblical scholar Augustin Bea. Pope John had only shaken hands once previously with Father Bea during a brief and informal visit to the Holy Office. Still, he named him to the Sacred College of Cardinals in November 1959. It was not until January of 1960 that the new Cardinal and the pontiff would have anything remotely resembling a serious conversation. Thus, in a somewhat ephemeral atmosphere, began a new and important phase in developing the ecumenical sensitivity of the Catholic Church. Here below follows a brief outline of the life, work, and spirit of Cardinal Augustin Bea.

Augustin Bea: Jesuit and Scholar

Augustin Bea was born 23 May 1881 as the only son of a middle-aged couple in Riedböhringen. His father was a carpenter. And together his parents ran a small farm. As a youth he was delicate and seemingly he suffered from tuberculosis.[2] From 1887 until 1900 he attended the ordinary grammar school and *Gymnasium* at Riedböhringen and Sasbach, both near Baden. Feeling himself called to both the religious life and the priesthood, Bea examined the Benedictine and Capuchin Religious Orders, but ultimately felt himself called to be a Jesuit. At the time, the German Jesuits were living in exile as a result of the *Kulturkampf.* Not only Bea's father, but other relatives objected to his choice. However, he formally entered the Society of Jesus in 1902. Prior to entering the Jesuit novitiate at Blijenbeek, the Netherlands, he took three semesters of theology at the University of Freiburg. Professed in 1904, he continued his studies in Holland. He showed a propensity for ancient and modern languages, which was acknowledged by his superiors, when they sent him for a summer school of philology at Innsbruck. Having taken up his theological studies at Volkenburg, he was ordained a priest in 1912 by Archbishop Jürgens of Bombay.

The following year, Bea undertook the study of Oriental Languages at the University of Berlin. Here his professors were mainly Protestant biblical experts. Curiously, he also began his Tertianship in 1913. According to Jesuit tradition, Tertianship does not normally begin so close to the date of ordination, nor is it coupled with external studies. With the outbreak of the Great War in 1914, he was appointed the first superior of the Houses for Scholastics at Aachen. In 1917 Bea enjoyed a brief interlude in the class-

---

2. Schmidt, *op. cit.,* p. 31.

room, again at Volkenburg where he also was student prefect. Due to his health, Bea never served as a military officer during the War.

At the War's end, the Jesuits were allowed to return to Germany. Thus, from 1921 to 1924, Bea served as Provincial Superior of the Bavarian Province, with headquarters at Munich. In 1924, he moved to Rome as professor of Biblical Theology at the Gregorian University, and simultaneously Superior of the Faculty House, on the Via della Pilotta. At the same time he began his long career as professor of the Old Testament at the Pontifical Biblical Institute. In 1930, he was absent from Rome for one entire year while he reformed Jesuit university life in Japan and China on behalf of the Jesuit General Wlódimir Ledóchowski. Upon his return, he resumed the dual rectorship as local Superior of the House and Dean of the academic programs at the Pontifical Biblical Institute. He held that posting until 1949.[3]

In 1945 Pius XII summoned him as his personal confessor. Because the pontifical household was, by and large, German speaking, a German Jesuit was appointed not only to hear the pope's confession, but also to make himself available as confessor to the sisters who served as housekeepers. Weekly, sometimes more frequently, he spent a half-hour with the Pontiff. In 1949, Pius XII appointed Bea to the important position of German Language Consultor in the Holy Office, and he remained a consultor there, as well as confessor to Pope Pius, until the latter's death in 1958. Bea stayed in the Holy Office until his own nomination as Cardinal by Pope John XXIII in 1959. According to a close collaborator and student of Bea, the Jesuit Biblical scholar and consultor made "significant contributions to Roman documents" *prior* to his nomination as Cardinal.[4]

For example, in 1941, he was a participating member of the Special Committee of the Pontifical Biblical Commission which rendered a favorable report in regard to critical Biblical scholarship. In 1943 he assisted Pope Pius XII in drafting the encyclical *Divino Afflante Spiritu,* which became a charter for Catholic Biblical scholars. The encyclical encouraged the return to original texts, the knowledge of ancient languages, and the use of textual criticism. In this encyclical, Pope Pius XII praised the fruit of biblical archeology, four years before the discovery of the Dead Sea Scrolls. At this same time, Bea also contributed to a landmark response to the Archbishop of Paris, Cardinal Emmanuel Suhard, regarding the latter's inquiry into the question of primordial history.[5] In 1950 he devised an innova-

---

3. Bernard J. Leeming, *op. cit.,* pp. 13-26.

4. *Ibid.*

5. Schmidt, *op. cit.,* p. 122. In 1948 Bea, along with G. Paste, was summoned by Pope

tive program for Biblical studies in seminaries. All of this work, as well as his future ecumenical career, may have been linked to his 1935 experience at Göttingen. Here he sought the personal approval of Pope Pius XI to attend and participate in a seminar, which was organized and sponsored, by and large, by Protestant, Jewish and secular biblical scholars. Fearing a negative reaction from the Pontiff, he approached him in his capacity as rector of the Pontifical Biblical Institute. Pius, a scholar and student of languages, replied warmly: "But of course, you must attend!" He therefore participated openly in the Alten Testamentarisch Kongress (Old Testament Congress) of German Scripture scholars. This created a precedent![6]

Bea joined the Vatican dicastery of the Holy Office, as German language consultor, in March 1949.[7] A few months later, this congregation issued the first positive document, regarding the Ecumenical Movement, *Ecclesia Catholica*.[8] This instruction allowed scholars to attend meetings with non–Roman Catholic counterparts in order to discuss doctrinal and moral questions. It encouraged the "Spiritual Ecumenism" advocated by Father Paul-Irénée Couturier and Max Metzger, emphasizing the importance of the Week of Prayer for Christian Unity. Finally, this document, although cautious, spoke positively of efforts, especially among academics, to address the question of unity within the Christian family.

While serving in the Holy Office, Bea was directly in contact with the only Vatican department that had exclusive authority in all questions concerning other Christians, i.e., "heretics" or "schismatics," as they were then called. According to Father Schmidt: "We can go further and say that

---

Pius XII to provide a response to Cardinal Suhard of Paris from the Pontifical Biblical Commission to a series of requests regarding the clarification of the authorship of the Pentateuch and the appropriate exegesis of the first eleven chapters of the book of Genesis. At the time, the biblical directives that were in effect stemmed from the age of Pope Pius X. These bore the title *Instructions of the Pontifical Biblical Commission*. Pope Pius XII was inclined towards abolishing the responses. Father Schmidt records: "Father Bea had managed to persuade him that this was not a wise step, because if he did, people could claim that any other Instruction of the Pontifical Biblical Commission had only temporary validity." Bea encouraged instead a positive orientation preferring the path of providing "deeper explanation of the elements of the problem and indicating the direction in which a solution should be sought." Emmanuel Suhard, *Priests among Men* (Notre Dame: Fides Publishers, 1960). Suhard died in 1950 leaving the pastoral letter *Priests among Men* as his principal literary legacy. Although he did not live to see its publication, the letter calls for a renewal of priests in their ministry and is noteworthy in that it relies upon the teaching of Scripture and not the precepts of theological abstractions.

6. Schmidt, *op. cit.*, p. 97.
7. *Ibid.*, pp. 138-45.
8. *Ibid.*, p. 138.

it was Bea's experience in this context that convinced him of the need of the Holy See to set up another department — be it a commission or a simple office — to which such brethren could turn without difficulty and fear."[9] Further in that same position, as consultor for the Holy Office, he was assigned particular responsibility for German affairs. This made him aware of the general state of theology in post-War Germany.

Ecumenism was now a new and tangible theological exercise, which had been fueled by common Christian collaborative resistance to the Nazis during the Second World War. Following the War, many mutual efforts eventuated in Germany. An *Una Sancta* desk was now part of a reorganized Fulda Bishops Conference. The Jaeger-Stählin Group, i.e., a joint Roman Catholic–Lutheran dialogue, was now meeting annually at Hardehausen, as noted above, with Lutheran Bishop Wilhelm Stählin as the counterpart to Archbishop Jaeger. This is still known as the Jaeger-Stählin Group. Finally, the Johann Adam Möhler Institute, an ecumenical study center endowed with a rich library, was established within the walls of the Paderborn University. All of this was the result of the remarkable ecumenical empathy and creativity of Archbishop Lorenz Jaeger.[10]

The Spirituality of Cardinal Bea

Throughout his religious life, Augustin Bea was accustomed to keeping a spiritual journal. The evidence of the diary is that in his private prayer and meditation, Father Bea was equally Ignatian and Biblical, much after the fashion of Carlo Maria Cardinal Martini, S.J., lately the Archbishop of Milan.[11] Bea himself was so dedicated and consecrated a Jesuit that he squirmed at the singularity imposed upon him with the Red Hat.[12] All during his life, his retreat notes state that the vow of obedience is the most precious gift one can render to God. For the Religious, obedience is the "gift of one's own will."[13] According to the Ignatian tradition, the religious state

9. *Ibid.,* p. 237.

10. *Ibid.,* pp. 143-45.

11. A good example of the prolific writings of Cardinal Martini is *Promise Fulfilled* (Sherbrooke, Quebec: Mèdias Paul, 1994).

12. *Ibid.,* p. 303.

13. *St. Ignatius of Loyola: The Spiritual Exercises and Selected Works,* ed. George E. Ganss, S.J. (New York: Paulist Press, 1991), p. 303. The primitive documents of the Society of Jesus include the first sketch of the Institute of the Society of Jesus. It is the evidence of the Constitutions for the College, Rules for Scholastics, Rules for Priests and the Letters on Obe-

creates a "particular affinity for love" between Christ and the consecrated soul. In this loving dedication to Him the soul becomes more especially able to join in union with Christ and the Church. Bea called this experience his *missio*. In his retreat notes, as a Jesuit, he defined himself primarily as an apostle, i.e., *one who is sent,* whether into the classroom or into the pulpit, to proclaim the truth of the unitive love of the Father for the Son and of the whole Trinity for all the creation and for all God's children. As for himself, he wrote the following:

> It is above, here ["The Crucified One, Synthesis of My Exercise"], that I see that *love* is not affection or gentle feelings, but *sacrifice,* that goes according to the degree of humility. The Heart of Jesus is circled with a crown of thorns that has the cross over it, and it is pierced with a spear; this is *authentic* and solid love.[14]

When meditating on the Passion while on retreat in 1950, Father Bea wrote:

> Truly, I have borne few heavy crosses in my life; now at the end of my days, I am almost concerned and pained by this, when I think of that true love for the Saviour is really shown only by sharing in His cross: Or maybe He still has a heavy cross in store for me for my last years. Whatever the case may be, whatever He may send me, I shall accept it with supernatural joy from His hand. Hail, O blessed cross![15]

Commenting on Cardinal Bea's spirituality, Father Schmidt, secretary and literary executor, spoke of Bea's core grace as "trust in God." This gave him courage. Schmidt quoted further from Bea's diary:

> The fundamental fact that I must remember in all difficulties and storms — whether of a personal nature or whether concerning the Church or the Society — is that the Lord is always present with His power and goodness. I am never alone, and the Church is never alone. "*I am* with you until the end of the world." This must give me great

---

dience: "All should keep their resolution firm to observe obedience and to distinguish themselves in it not only in matters of obligation but also in the others, even though nothing else is perceived except the indication of the superiors' will without an expressed command. They should keep in view God Our Creator and Lord, for whom such obedience is practised and they should endeavour to proceed in a spirit of love and not as men troubled by fear" (No. 547).

14. Schmidt, p. 278. Alongside this Ignatian category of *missio,* Bea would later develop the concept of *Fachmann* (one who is called to a special expertise).

15. *Ibid.,* p. 278.

calmness and serenity in all situations. Storms and difficulties can take various forms: Sickness, and inability to work, misunderstandings, etc.; in the end, the name is unimportant. . . . Here the only correct attitude is *trust* . . . a trust that is accompanied by *prayer,* work, struggle . . . that bears in mind that the Lord is in the boat with us.[16]

Making a distinction between "passive" trust and "active" *trust,* Schmidt cited Bea's further reflection that God's intervention "does not dispense me from faithful use of all *human means:* study, advice, method, prudence, care and attention: as though everything depended on me, and only on me. I am an instrument, and the instrument must use all its inherent quality. Disappointments and setbacks must not depress me . . . everything of value in the kingdom of God has been won at the price of much patience and self-denial."[17] Clearly Bea's spiritual vision embraced a sense of Divine Providence and a prayerful, watchful discernment for the will of God that is notably Ignatian.

Cardinal Bea and Pope John XXIII: A Shared Spirituality — a Shared Mentality

Normally, the retreat annotations of a Biblical scholar are personal and, to the outsider, may appear superfluous. However, the spirituality of Cardinal Bea takes on added significance in light of the fact that Angelo Giuseppe Roncalli was elected as Pope John XXIII on October 28, 1958. Much has been written about Pope John's spirituality elsewhere; however, both Cardinal Bea and Pope John were not only the same age, but their common sensibility of a vital, active and personal engagement by a senior cleric provided them with a common atmosphere of mutual comfort and personal exchange.[18] Both men followed an Ignatian road map, to which they re-

16. Cited in *ibid.,* p. 280 (emphasis in original). Such sentiments are recorded by Bea's fellow Jesuit, John LaFarge, *op. cit.,* pp. 129-30, who wrote: "Old age, too, is the time when we need the *courage* to love. The courage, let us say, to think more *(mas)* of other people, rather than less; to go out of one's self, rather than to withdraw and close the curtains and brood." All of the italicized words are basic Ignatian concepts. Father LaFarge's point is that old age brings with it a treasure chest of courage from which the Christian is able to dispense freely.

17. Schmidt, *op. cit.,* p. 280. LaFarge, *op. cit.,* p. 131, also shares the same Jesuit sentiment. Again, under the *titulus* of courage, he calls it "courage of inquiry."

18. Augustin Bea, *St. Paul on the Essence of the Importance of Interior Life* (Mequon, Wis.: Notre Dame of the Lake Press, 1963), p. 17. Bea's spirituality was particularly fueled by his continued study of the Hebrew Scriptures and by a personal dedication to the writings of

ferred in their later private conversations. Capovilla confided that Roncalli's favorite bedside book was *The Folly of the Cross* by Raoul Plus, S.J. It was from this text that Pope John drew a self-understanding in light of the mystery of the Redemption:

> When it was a case of offering sympathy and making amends (for the sufferings of Jesus), then the sinner was regarded chiefly as one who should be reproved and reproached for his sins, and for whom loving acts must be made to satisfy the yearnings of the love of Christ. Now, no longer does wrath fall upon the sinner; it is realized that he must be saved and that our Lord alone is not sufficient. Christ vouchsafes to be insufficient so as to make use of us. It is for us to bring him the assistance of our humble self-sacrifice, the *complement* of our collaboration. . . . *I desire to do this:* Christ chooses to act as if he were not all-powerful. Therefore the Cyrenean and St. Veronica must come to his aid. . . . *It is my duty:* without my intervention, souls will be deprived of the measure of redemptive grace which would have assured their sanctification or their final salvation.[19]

Here is another expression of the call to courage. Thus, too, Roncalli, like Bea, was engendered with a sense of *missio,* finding his opportunities wherever God put him, even in old age.

Capovilla expressed the importance of this spiritual convergence when he recorded the words of Pope John, after his initial meeting with the new Cardinal: "*This Cardinal Bea is a man and a Religious of great worth!* Only to look at him inspires trust; so learned, and humble, ascetic and studious, capable of descending from his professor's chair to teach simple catechism; this is the stuff of which a shepherd is made. I felt inspired to open myself to him in confidentiality and I did so. *He will be very useful to me.*"[20]

The date of that first conversation was 9 January 1960. After their initial chat, Bea remarked to his secretary, Father Schmidt: "We understood

---

St. Paul. "After so decisive and solemn a pronouncement, the question arises — *Why is so profound an interior life essential to the Apostolate?*" (emphasis in original). In short, the answer to the true aim of the apostolate is to pour in and fasten spiritual life in souls. As Christ came "that they may have life more abundantly (Jn. 10:10)," that by faith they may become sons of God (Jn. 1:12), conformable to the image of his Son (cf. Rom. 8:29); this is the aim of every apostolate. Clearly, Cardinal Bea was a genuine contemplative in action, placing his spiritual duties alongside his apostolic commitments.

19. Cf. R. Plus, S.J. (Westminster, Md.: Newman Press, 1949), p. 103 (emphasis mine).

20. Cited in Mario Begnini and Goffredo Zanchi, *John XXIII: The Official Biography* (Boston: Pauline Press, 2001), p. 370 (emphasis mine).

each other perfectly!"[21] To Father Walter Abbott, S.J., a *Biblicum* student and a future member of Bea's Secretariat staff, Bea commented: "The Pope told me some of the things he wants to do; and you know, *I think I can help him!*"[22] Bea's spirituality is significant in that it would endear him to Pope John. For later he recorded:

> My personal contacts with Pope John were always a spiritual feast for me. He allowed me to penetrate his profound religious life and observe how his judgments and activities welled up from this hidden spring. . . . I never left an audience that had been granted to me without having been profoundly impressed by his character. He had such a breadth of vision. He was so tolerant and indulgent, yet so strong and inflexible in his principles and plans . . . it has been well said by a writer who knew the situation that the council was first an act of faith on the part of Pope John and the fruit of his trust in God. No other explanation corresponds to the facts. He succeeded in inspiring others with his faith and *courage.*[23]

Mutual recognition of a common spirituality between Bea and Pope John found its point of convergence in the oft-quoted phrase, "To speak the truth in love (Eph. 4:15)." This phrase would become the motto for the new Secretariat for Promoting Christian Unity. The Biblical dictum itself is an expression of courage. If Pope John admired the spirituality of Cardinal Bea, it was because he himself was a spiritual man, in exactly the same way. When asked about the Pontiff's most salient virtue, his secretary, Loris Capovilla, replied without hesitation: "His humility! Pope John was not judgmental. He lived on a spiritual plane and, perhaps naively, he believed everyone else did too!" Certainly, Pope John discerned that same virtue in Cardinal Bea.[24]

There are currently many biographies of Pope John XXIII. One of the most recent, by Thomas Cahill, refers to Pope John as *Il Papa Bono,* "the very good pope." It was this "goodness" that made him *disponibile,* accessible even to his enemies. Cahill recalled, for example, the dismissive comment from the imperious Monsignor Domenico Tardini at the Vatican Secretariate of State during the reign of Pope Pius XII: "Questo non ha

---

21. Schmidt, *op. cit.,* p. 324.

22. Walter Abbott, an early member of the staff of the Secretariat for Promoting Christian Unity, was likewise interviewed by the author at Assumption College, Worcester, Massachusetts, 22 August 1980 (emphasis mine).

23. Schmidt, *op. cit.,* p. 745 (emphasis mine).

24. Interview of Loris Capovilla with the author, 9 September 2000.

capito niente" [This chap understands nothing].[25] Yet ultimately, John made this individual his first Cardinal Secretary of State. As with Bea, people were apt to misjudge Pope John's simplicity as stupidity and timidity.

This quality, *disponibilità,* a type of courageous holy humility, became John's fundamental ecumenical characteristic. This could likewise be said of Bea. Both were open to new ideas. Both loved people. Both distinguished errors from individuals. Both were committed to a ministry of "the intensity of personal ties!" Pope John wrote of himself:

> Things have been said about me that greatly exaggerate my merits. I humbly introduce myself. Like every other man on Earth, I came from a particular family and place. I have been blessed with good physical health and enough common sense to grasp things quickly and clearly. I also have an inclination to love people, which keeps me faithful to the law of the Gospel and respectful of my own rights and the rights of others. It stops me from doing harm to anyone; it encourages me to do good for all.[26]

The source of humility is strength, which is nothing less than the full acknowledgement of the presence and the gifts of the Holy Spirit, who can and does overcome all obstacles. This is an ecclesiological spirituality. "The Book of Acts describes how the Church is brought to the center of the world through the very power of God. . . . What is true of the Church as a whole is also in a sense true of each member insofar as he or she is in Christ; '. . . *And your life is hidden with Christ in God.* When Christ who is Our Life appears, then you also will appear with Him in glory (Col. 3:4).'"[27] The "hiddenness of Christ in God" was not only the mutual subject matter of Bea's and Pope John's meditations, but also they both adopted the phrase as a motto. The ecclesial significance of the phrase clarifies the biblical expression, for the Church, which has as its whole life "the being *in Christ* Himself." "Before the beginning of time, the Father knew His chosen ones by name (Is. 43:1)." And He called them to be *One* in His Son, entrusting each to Him in advance. Generation after generation, the Spirit of the Son comes to them taking them with Him into His Exodus, and bringing them back to the Father. This is a pneumatic spirituality of trust, *for it is confident of the hiddenness of God's ways,* whereby the

---

25. Thomas Cahill, *Pope John XXIII* (New York: Lipper/Viking Book, 2001), p. 132.
26. *Ibid.,* pp. 155-56.
27. Gilles Pelland, S.J., "A Few Words on Triumphalism," in Latourelle, S.J. (ed.), *op. cit.,* p. 110 (emphasis mine).

Redeemer-Lord is gradually making ready His final victory over death and evil. The Ignatian "humility" to which Pope John and Cardinal Bea ascribed envisions a Church Triumphant because the very spirit of Jesus binds it together into one single body and gives it the very strength of God amidst the concrete, albeit often chaotic, circumstances of human history.[28]

The Curial Activity of Cardinal Bea

When Pope Pius XII summoned Augustin Bea as his confessor, he also discovered Bea's wisdom and Biblical expertise. Some indications of this we have seen earlier in the chapter. At the same time, Bea became privy to the *élan* and policies of papal thought. Therefore, he observed that conscious of the sufferings of Catholics in this wartime situation, and perhaps more so in Germany, Pius sought to raise the matter to higher ground. By 1940, Pius had become alarmed by Hitler's attempt to nationalize the German Protestant Churches. His fear was certainly a factor when in 1943 he issued a papal encyclical about ecclesiology entitled *Mystici Corporis*.[29] Bea was not present for the drafting.

---

28. *Ibid.,* p. 112. Also see Louis J. Puhl, S.J. (ed.), *The Spiritual Exercises of St. Ignatius* (Chicago: Loyola Press, 1951), p. 69. Ignatius distinguishes three kinds of humility in the *Exercises*. The third kind of humility, i.e., the most perfect, prioritizes "the praise and glory of the Divine Majesty." It likewise identifies itself with poverty, foolishness, and simplicity. Bea and Pope John left ample evidence of the primary place of Ignatius' influence in their personal writings. It is easy to see why they converge.

29. Other pastoral problems faced Pius XII at that time. For example, "During the 1940s, French Catholics in particular had become increasingly aware of the fact that industrial workers and the urban proletariat were largely indifferent or hostile to the claims of Christianity and the Church. This evidence of *de-christianization* coupled with an apparently ever increasing shortage of priests suggested the necessity of adopting more radical methods of evangelization." Holmes, *ibid.,* p. 184. Holmes, p. 191, said the encyclical *Mystici Corporis Christi* endorsed ecclesiological ideas that had begun and developed in the nineteenth century particularly under the influence of Johann Adam Möhler. "The Church was the mystical body of Christ visible, indivisible and organically compact. The Church established by the preaching of the Gospel and the Redemption of the Cross and spread throughout the world following the gift of the Spirit at Pentecost was entrusted with the sacraments of Christ as the means of salvation. But the Pope also emphasized that the church was identical with the Roman Catholic Church as well as the hierarchical nature of ecclesiastical authority. He warned against the notion of an invisible church of all men of goodwill in mystical union with Christ which might be contrasted with the visible institutional Roman Catholic Church led by the Pope. This encyclical marked a crucial stage in the Church's understanding of the rôle of the laity, though it was not entirely free from those clerical and authoritarian sentiments which were typical of Pius XII."

By 20 November 1947, when Pope Pius XII issued his encyclical *Mediator Dei*, "On the Sacred Liturgy," Bea was a permanent member of the small papal household. The key sentence of the entire encyclical reads thus: "The sacred liturgy is consequently the public worship which our Redeemer, as Head of the Church, renders to the Father, as well as the worship which the community of the faithful renders to its Founder, and through Him to the Heavenly Father. It is, in short, the worship *rendered by the Mystical Body of Christ in the entirety of its Head and members* (No. 20)" (emphasis mine). In the wake of the Second World War, Pius needed to encourage prayer, both public and private, to combat the worldwide cynicism, skepticism, and disbelief that emerged from the ashes.[30] Within the text, there are twenty-five references to *Mystici Corporis*. The encyclical enhanced the understanding of the relationship of the individual Christian to the Jesus of history, and to the "pneumatic" or *glorified Christ*. Pope Pius composed this significant sentence which Bea would recall with such frequency twelve years later: "Nor is it to be wondered at, that the faithful should be raised to this dignity. By the waters of Baptism, as by common right, Christians *are made members of the Mystical Body of Christ the Priest,* and by the 'character' which is imprinted on their souls, they are appointed to give worship to God. Thus they participate, according to their condition, in the priesthood of Christ (No. 88)" (emphasis mine). Theologically and liturgically, this encyclical encouraged pastoral renewal.[31] A rising sense of ecclesiology accompanied the remaining years of Pius XII's pontificate, reaching a climax with the renewal of the Holy Week services, which unilaterally made the entire body of the faithful familiar with and sensitive to the meaning of the phrase "the Paschal Mystery of Christ."[32] To this work Bea contributed directly.

---

30. *Ibid.,* pp. 189-90.

31. Very much this encyclical, coupled with liturgical reform in 1947, 1949, 1951, and 1953, as well as Pope Pius' address to the International Conference on Pastoral Liturgy, regarding the real presence of the Blessed Sacrament, had a profound effect regarding "a new awareness of the rôle of the laity." *Ibid.,* pp. 190-91.

32. The term "Paschal Mystery" reached a point of liturgical popularity at mid–twentieth century. It is connected to the concept of "Mystery Theory" enunciated by Dom Odo Casel of Maria Laach Abbey in Germany. The term "Paschal Mystery" is thought to originate with the Austrian Canon, Pius Parsch. Between Casel and Parsch, the historical-liturgical approach became prominent in this branch of study. Dom Damasus Winzen, O.S.B., synthesized this point: "The true unity of [ancient liturgical] texts is rather to be found in the sacramental mystery which they surround. Every mass is the feast of our redemption through the death of Jesus and of his exaltation unto glory as the Lord." This is the definition of Paschal Mystery. The sentence by Winzen is found in the foreword to Dame Aemiliana Löhr, O.S.B., *The Mass*

By 1948, the year following *Mediator Dei,* the Sacred Congregation of Rites and Sacraments, at the specific direction of the Pope, inaugurated what was known as the "Pian Commission."[33] It is generally acknowledged that this body actually had its roots in 1945, with the arrival of Augustin Bea, as the papal confessor. From that time, Bea had advised the pontiff of the importance, for pastoral reasons, of liturgical and Biblical reform. Specifically, he had in mind the publication of a new Latin version of the Psalms, which the Pontifical Biblical Institute finished rather quickly in 1945, under commission from Pius XII.[34] This work "helped to ripen in the Pope's mind the idea of a reform of the entire liturgy"; "the new Psalter would simply be the first building block in the new edifice."[35] In a personal memoir, the late Archbishop Annibale Bugnini, C.M., whose entire life was dedicated to liturgical reform, synthesized in a single page the earliest pre-Conciliar papal developments for modern liturgical reform, beginning in the 1940s. For example, in 1942, Pius called for a private draft from Dom Pio Alphonso, O.S.B., a member of the Propaganda faculty, for sweeping liturgical reform. His two-page paper, entitled "General Norms," called for the recodification of liturgical times and feasts. It came to nothing.[36]

But, in 1946, Father Josef Löw, C.SS.R., an Austrian, submitted a plan to Pope Pius XII for the reorganization of the Sacred Congregation of Rites. The two chief points to be immediately developed concerned the Liturgical Year and the presentation of the Divine Office. From 28 May 1948, an active twelve-man commission functioned almost weekly. This commission took as its charter the encyclical *Mediator Dei.*[37]

---

through the Year (London: Longmans, Green, 1958), pp. iii-x. In her preface, Dame Aemiliana spoke of the effect of *Mediator Dei* upon a full theological understanding of the liturgy as a discipline. An exponent of Dom Odo Casel, she explained: "My work is an attempt to approach the *Mysterium Ineffabile.*" It is the evidence of T. M. Schoof, *A Survey of Catholic Theology, 1800-1970* (Amsterdam: Paulist Newman Press, 1970), p. 124, that Pius XII provided a religious and theological revival through the topics of Christ (kerygmatic theology), Church (ecclesiology and ecumenism) and the liturgy (pastoral *praxis*) by way of the two major documents of his pontificate, *Mystici Corporis* and *Mediator Dei.* Movements regarding these topics found both incentive and confirmation of their validity in the midst of Fascism and other totalitarian expressions.

33. Annibale Bugnini, *The Reform of the Liturgy: 1948-1975* (Collegeville, Minn.: Liturgical Press, 1990), p. 7.

34. Schmidt, *op. cit.,* pp. 101-5. It has often been suggested that the translation was Bea's idea. Having collected evidence from Tardini, Leiber and Bea himself, Schmidt testified that the entire project was the idea of Pius XII.

35. Bugnini, *op. cit.,* p. 7.

36. *Ibid.*

37. *Ibid.,* pp. 7-9.

Immediately, Pope Pius XII appointed Bea a member of this commission. Therefore, from 1948 until 1958, Bea assumed a pro-active position in liturgical reform. At the first meeting of the commission, he informed Clemente Cardinal Micara, the president, that the liturgical reform entrusted to this body would take a very long time. He submitted a report indicating that the necessary revisions of Scripture for sacred liturgical use would go on for five years and beyond. Throughout this working period, meeting almost every single week, Bea acted as the committee's liaison to the pope. Bea submitted a weekly report to Monsignor Giovanni Battista Montini, Undersecretary of State, to guarantee a written record for the archives. Bea's work in the commission lasted right through the election which brought John XXIII to the See of Peter in 1958. In many, many ways, it was a forerunner to the important work taken up by the Second Vatican Council.[38]

In his memoir of Cardinal Bea, Father Schmidt recorded that Bea was, during this period of 1945-1958, closely and intensely aware of the development of Pope Pius' thought about the Church, the liturgy, the evolution of theology, as well as moral problems concerned with developments in science and technology. Using his Biblical expertise, Bea contributed to Pius' pronouncements to the faithful. Bea later admitted at a press conference that he had been privy to the musings and theological direction of the Pope whom he served in many capacities and to whom he was loyal for the rest of his life. Because of Bea's ready access to the papal apartments, Archbishop Bugnini called him "the go-between." It should come as no surprise, therefore, that Bea would notice and later describe for Pope John XXIII the significance of Pius' major encyclicals *Mystici Corporis* and *Mediator Dei*: "Let the faithful consider to what a high degree they are raised by the Sacrament of Baptism (*M.D.*, No. 88)."

Josef Höfer Becomes the Theological Friend of Bea

As Schmidt remembered, Father Bea immediately recognized the importance of "a mutual identity among Christians based upon the authenticity of Christian baptism into the royal priesthood of Jesus Christ."[39] He un-

---

38. Schmidt, *op. cit.,* p. 104. According to Schmidt, the Council saw itself as carrying forward the liturgical and biblical *ressourcement* of the 1950s in the overall field of liturgical and biblical studies. Paul VI saw to a later revision not only of the Psalter but of the entire Vulgate, based on the earlier rules of Pope Pius XII.

39. Schmidt, *op. cit.,* p. 324.

derstood this point when the encyclical *Mediator Dei* was issued in 1947. When Bea was appointed to the office of Consultor for German theological matters in the Holy Office in 1949, he carried his point of view to discussions pertaining to the first positive "Instruction regarding the Ecumenical Movement," entitled *Ecclesia Sancta.*

Bea's ecumenical perspective was vastly broadened when, in 1954, Chancellor Konrad Adenauer appointed Josef Höfer to Rome as a member of the first German Embassy Staff to the Holy See. His title was Ecclesiastical Counsel. The appointment came when Höfer was Dean of the Catholic Evangelical Faculty at the University of Munich, where he taught the Christian foundations of culture. Because of his official capacity, Bea often called upon him not only for advice and information pertaining to his own work regarding developments within German theology, but also in order to understand well the political and cultural situation of the two Germanys.[40]

It is important to note that Höfer was both a contemporary and a

---

40. Anonymous, "Daten zum Lebenslauf von Josef Rudolf Höfer" (Data for a Curriculum Vitae of Josef Rudolf Höfer), Vicar General's Archives, Paderborn (publishing information not available), pp. 743. While in Rome, Höfer was no mere errand boy. His ability to combine theology and diplomacy was patent. He lived in a time when the Church was directly attacked by the anti-clericalism of Communism, Nazism and secularism. All of these attacked ecclesial truth and custom, relegating them to the title "Utopian." Even with the rise of Hitler, he was able to declare, especially after the scales of the *Cujus regio, ejus religio* norm fell away, that there was an *awakening* of the Church of twentieth-century Germany of his day. Through his early writing, Josef Höfer, "Die katholische Wirklichkeit im Licht der Enzyklika *Mystici Corporis,* im Ergebnisbericht der Werktagung des 74," *Deutschen Katholikentags Passau in Altötting,* Vicar General's Archives, Paderborn 1950, pp. 20-65, was able to identify *a longing after unity in the Spirit of Christ,* which began to exercise itself in the anti-war movements and religious devotion right through the wartime period. After the War, he declared that *the Church and its hierarchy must become a sign* that is elevated to the impaired vision of the nations. Even before any official teachings encouraged ecumenism, Höfer courageously pronounced that the ecumenical task must take root "from the ground of this year, beginning now, 1950." Clearly one can see the reason Adenauer created a post for him in the German diplomatic service: he was a man of vision and effected what he dreamt. Also see Anonymous, "Daten zum Lebenslauf . . . ," pp. 574-75. During wartime, he vehemently opposed the predominating Schopenauer principle of human dignity as being subject to the will to power. In the first *Una Sancta* meeting, 1943, it was he who foresaw the priority of providing clarity regarding the theology of Baptism, citing Cor. 1:3, 22:23 and John 14 and 17. In this, he anteceded and paralleled Bea in the reference to Baptism and the use of Scripture. As a German he was aware of the fall of the Westphalian principle, *Cujus regio, ejus religio,* in 1918, and therefore appealed to the possibilities of unity of the One, Holy, Catholic, Apostolic Church as both a valid Johannine theme and as a current remedy to German disunity. He saw this as a Catholic ecumenical task springing from the German soil.

protégé of Archbishop Jaeger. Both were ordained priests for the Archdiocese of Paderborn by Archbishop Klein. Both were dedicated to Reformation studies and the burgeoning theological science of ecumenism. Both had a direct contact with the unique structure of that venerable See. It is appropriate to state, once again, that the Archdiocese of Paderborn was uniquely divided into two sections — one in the West, around the city of Paderborn, with a majority Catholic population; and the other in the East, around the city of Magdeburg, with a predominately Evangelical population. At that time, the Magdeburg section was behind the Iron Curtain and inaccessible to its archbishop. Höfer never forgot his experience as parochial vicar in the predominately Lutheran surroundings. Now, he was ever more mindful of its present surroundings. He always found it to be an immediate pastoral task to explain the Roman Catholic Church to those who were unfamiliar with its beliefs and practices. Fundamentally, Höfer always believed his first ministerial mandate was to be catechetical. It was indeed incumbent upon him to explain the truths of his Catholic faith. Since this mission was intensified by the fact that Magdeburg was in Soviet-dominated Eastern Germany, he was aware of the uniqueness of his diocesan bishop. Lorenz Jaeger was pastor of the one German diocese that, by its very structure, represented historical Germany and all the present exigencies of Cold War Germany.

Historically, Josef Höfer is associated with the theological concept of the Mystical Body of Christ, as developed in post-Napoleonic Germany. This concept was reintroduced in 1830 by Johann Michael Sailer, Bishop of Regensburg, who attempted to insert a new "age of belief" into a world secularized by the French Revolution. Theologians who came after Sailer placed emphasis on the uniqueness of the Church as an institution in history, delineating it from political structures. It is a sociological entity, yes, but also a spiritual reality, which is *greater than its juridical delineations*. It is, at once, temporal and eternal, therefore it is an *eschatological reality*.[41] A legal understanding of the Church dominated all the controversies dur-

---

41. In Germany the perception of the mystical nature of the Church was intensified through the influence of Romantic theology and its principal prophet Friedrich Schleiermacher, who wrote in his autobiography, *Aus Schleiermachers Leben im Briefen* (London, 1860): "It was here that I awoke for the first time to the consciousness of the relation of man to a higher world. . . . Here it was that the mystic tendency developed itself, which has been of so much importance to me, and has supported and carried me through all the storms of scepticism." Cited in Livingston, *op. cit.*, p. 97. It was Schleiermacher's contribution that Christian anthropology is founded upon the potential premise that man is made to experience the eschatological dimension of ultimate reality.

ing and after the Reformation and the Enlightenment.[42] It reached a climax in the nineteenth century.

Despite nineteenth-century controversies with German Jesuits over the renewed pastoral expression of this biblical concept, the view of Sailer prevailed.[43] His work influenced German theology, even in the aftermath of the decree of Vatican Council I, of 18 July 1870, *Pastor aeternus,* with its model of institutional ecclesiology. Germany became a center of renewed ecclesial exploration, not out of a sense of political commitment, as was the case in France at this time, but from a mostly theological concern. The representative figure was Ignaz Döllinger (1799-1890), a layman, who in the Munich Congress of Catholic Scholars (1863) denounced Scholasticism as ahistorical and undynamic, and therefore unmeaningful to the lives of the faithful. Döllinger identified the subject of the Church as the primary topic of the Christian vocation, and called for a sharpening of critical tools regarding Sacred Scripture, Church history, and theological exploration.[44]

Josef Höfer, from his seminary days until his death in 1974, espoused the very vital notion of the Church as the Mystical Body of Christ, as was expressed in Matthias Scheeben's *Mysteries of Christianity* (1865). This book embraced the theme of ecclesial unity amidst a diversity of ecclesial expressions.[45] In the twentieth century, Karl Adam would give it prominence in his *Spirit of Catholicism* (1929):

> The conviction that the Church is permeated by Christ, and of necessity organically united with him, is a fundamental point of Christian teaching. From Origen to Augustine and Pseudo-Dionysius and thence to Thomas Aquinas, and thence onto our own unforgettable (Johann Adam) Möeller (1796-1838), this conviction stands in the centre of the Church's doctrine. Her teachers delight to repeat in ever new forms those expressions of Augustine wherein he celebrates the Mystical Oneness of Christ and the Church: The two are one, one body, one flesh, one and the same person, one Christ, the whole Christ.[46]

42. Holmes, *The Triumph of the Holy See, op. cit.,* p. 145.

43. The *somatic* implication inherent in the biblical language is particularly expressive, for it indicates the identity of the personality with the body. One does not say for example "My body is tired." One says, "*I* am tired." The *ego* is identified with the condition of the bodily state. Thus is the person of Christ likewise connected to the Church.

44. Livingston, *op. cit.,* pp. 272-73.

45. Cited in Livingston, *op. cit.,* p. 81 (emphasis in original). Matthias Scheeben, *Die Mysterien des Christentums* (Freiburg: Herder and Herder, 1865). "The aim of Romanticism was *inclusiveness,* and for this reason the romantic spirit is difficult to define simply."

46. Id., *Spirit of Catholicism, op. cit.,* pp. 17-18.

It was Adam's intention to recover the ancient ecclesiology of the Patristic age.[47] That he succeeded is the positive judgment of Cardinal Walter Kasper:

> In *The Spirit of Catholicism,* Adam taught [us] to understand anew the Church as the Mystical Body of Christ as the *living community pulsing with the life of Christ,* as the Catholic Church in the encompassing sense of the Word, because [Catholicism] speaks a full Yes to the whole of Scripture, to the whole person, to one's body and to one's soul, to nature as to culture.[48]

After World War I, while copies of *The Spirit of Catholicism* were translated into multiple languages, other theologians examined the concept. Romano Guardini published *The Church and the Catholic* and *The Spirit of the Liturgy,* both in 1928. In 1931 Peter Lippert drafted *Die Kirche Christ;* in 1933 Emile Mersch produced *Le Corps Mystique du Christ,* and in 1937 Sebastian Tromp, S.J., released his *Corpus Christi quod est Ecclesia.*

Tromp is especially noteworthy, for it is more than the conventional wisdom that he had a direct hand in the preparation of the encyclical *Mystici Corporis.*[49] That such an encyclical was necessary in the midst of the tragedy of World War II is obvious. Pope Pius appealed to the image of the Church as a transcendent community, over and against the horrible reality of warring nations. His vision is identified with Christ:

> In the course of the present study, Venerable Brethren, we have thus foreseen that the Church is so constituted that it may be likened to a body. We must now explain clearly and precisely why it is to be called not merely a body, but the Body of Jesus Christ. This follows from the fact that Our Lord is the Founder, the Head, the Support and the Saviour of this Mystical Body (No. 25).

The encyclical was widely praised at its publication, and both encouraged and bolstered the study of ecclesiology. Yet, *Mystici Corporis* had its critics. Among them was Josef Höfer, who held that the encyclical was mono-Christic in scope, in that it did not show sufficient attention to the dynamic action of the Holy Spirit, who is not confined to the action of love within the Godhead, but who reaches deep into the creation and draws all

---

47. Krieg, *op. cit.,* p. 40.
48. Krieg, *op. cit.,* p. 52 (emphasis mine).
49. Martina, in Latourelle, *op. cit.,* p. 16. Interview of the author with Father Peter Gumpel, S.J., on July 3, 2003, confirms Tromp's role in drafting the encyclical.

persons into Christ, who is the Mediator through whom all pay reverence, obedience and worshipful praise to the Father.[50]

Höfer's comments, first expressed at the original meeting of the *Una Sancta* Mixed Commission in 1943, resulted later in a highly technical article which appeared in the German Catholic encyclopedia of 1948 and a newspaper article of 1950 titled "Die katholische Wirklichkeit im Licht der Enzyklika *Mystici Corporis,* im Ergebnisbericht der Werktagung des 74" [The Catholic Reality in Light of the Encyclical *Mystici Corporis,* in the Concluding Report of the Workgroup of 74]. Likewise, he highlighted the problem of paragraph No. 22 of that same encyclical. This rose to become *the* central ecumenical question: "Who is a member of the Church?" "Actually only those are to be included as members of the Church who have been baptized and profess the true faith, and who have not been so unfortunate as to separate themselves from the unity of the Body or been excluded by legitimate authority for grave faults committed (No. 22)."

Höfer felt that this statement, while soundly based in the principles of Christology, does not take into consideration the new dispensation of the *glorified Risen Christ, in which the Holy Spirit is active to assemble the body of the Church*. He sought an inclusivity which had not yet been addressed by magisterial authority. Höfer deepened his insight while serving the Fulda Bishops Conference as a member of the Mixed Commission on *Una Sancta* Affairs. Here he first addressed his reservation regarding paragraph 22. He carried the quest to find an answer for this *lacuna* with him to Rome, where he presented it to Father Bea at the Biblicum. He declared later in life that it was he who made Cardinal Bea an ecumenist. Continued discussion of this topic with Bea was how he did it.[51] Bea, the scholar, never forgot the question nor its import.

In 1958, Bea laid down his principal responsibilities. Having left the rectorship in 1948, he now resigned his professorship at the Pontifical Bibli-

---

50. Wittstadt, *op. cit.,* p. 190. Höfer had continued to advise Cardinal Jaeger about the importance of sacramental theology. Jaeger held that the Church, as Sacrament, and the seven sacraments should be the principal theme of the theological life of ecumenism. He stated that "Protestants are very anxious to have a sacramental Church." With Höfer's direction he attempted to prod the Fulda Bishops Conference to present these same themes to the Pre-Preparatory Commission of the Second Vatican Council. As regards ecumenism, he stated that the question of the *Regale Dominium Christi* is very important for ecclesiology. Further, the teaching concerning the Holy Spirit as the animating and enlightening principle of life of the *Corpus Christi Mysticum* should be strongly emphasized so that the magisterial authority of the Church may be interiorly grounded.

51. Schmidt, *op. cit.,* p. 404.

cal Institute. With the death of Pope Pius XII on October 9, 1958, Bea no longer served as confessor and counselor in the papal apartments, and he all but ceased his activities regarding liturgical reform. The only position which he continued to fulfill was that of Consultor to the Holy Office. It seemed of little personal significance to him, when on January 25, 1959, Pope John XXIII announced his plans to convene an Ecumenical Council. He read the details of preparation in *L'Osservatore Romano.* His only responsibility then was to prepare the weekly *votum* for the Holy Office. Suddenly things changed! Father Schmidt recorded the important moment:

> At about 9:30 that day (Monday, 16 November 1959), a car from the Holy Office came to take him to the usual meeting of consultors. While he was sitting in the car, outside the Pontifical Gregorian University, on the other side of the square, waiting to collect another consultor, Father Franz Hürth, a car with a Vatican registration drew up outside the Biblical Institute, and an official of the Secretariat of State, Monsignor Angelo DiPasquale, got out and told the doorman that he had to speak to Father Bea. "He just left. . . ." "Ah: the car's still outside the Gregorian University," he was told. Monsignor DiPasquale walked over to the car and told Father Bea that he had to talk to him. "I'm afraid it's not possible right now, Monsignor. I have to be at the Holy Office meeting, and we're late already." "But I've come from the Holy Father," answered the other. When Bea got out of the car, Monsignor DiPasquale handed him a large, sealed envelope with the words: "My congratulations and best wishes, Your Eminence. But not a word until 1 p.m." And he took his leave.[52]

The ecumenical career and endeavor of Cardinal Bea had begun.

As the foremost representative of the quality of ecclesiastical service offered by the Biblicum, he took seriously the value of Biblical Theology and was an exponent of St. Thomas Aquinas: "Theology therefore does not accept its principles from the other sciences, but through revelation, directly from God" [Non enim accepit (theologia) sua principia ab aliis scientiis, sed immediate a Deo per revelationem] (*S. T.* I, q. 1, a.2, ad 5). Biblical theology consists of the scholarly examination of themes offered by Sacred Scripture. Bea also followed the horizontal line in his reference to the magisterium, as is seen above, from his advice to Pope Pius XII in the preparation of the text of a response to Cardinal Suhard regarding the authorship of the first eleven chapters of the Book of Genesis: Never annul

---

52. Schmidt, *op. cit.,* pp. 299-300.

the previous directions of the magisterium, instead go deeper into them, in order not to relativize the value of previous papal documents. He followed his own advice when he presented the ecumenical problem to Pope John.

Thus, in the end, it is possible to diagnose the *ratio* of the statement of Monsignor Capovilla regarding Bea the representative of a nation where Catholic and Protestant labored together to discover the possibilities of reconciliation. Jaeger, as bishop of the local Church, bore the Catholic ecumenical burden in Germany for many long war-torn years, practically alone. Höfer identified the *lacuna* of *Mystici Corporis* — the need to refine for the sake of a *Spirit-given inclusiveness* in the Universal Church. The long-suffering struggles of a diplomatic life, dedicated to both a sense of history and to the reconciliation of peoples molded John XXIII into a refined paragon of pure goodness and openness. He was, as it were, the rich soil, into which the farmer dropped the good seed (Matt. 13:1-23). Bea was the farmer gifted with discretion and wisdom, drawn from the number of his years and from his experience. The seed was the Biblical theme of Baptism. But before addressing that point, it is necessary to observe the development of events, as history would unfold to come to that precise moment, when it is possible to see how this seed would develop to the full flowering that was to become the Secretariat for Promoting Christian Unity.

Conclusion

The fourteen years of Bea's direct service to the pontificate of Pope Pius XII are extremely important for understanding his future role as ecumenical pioneer. For one thing, he was close to the pontiff at the time of the promulgation of the encyclical *Mediator Dei*. As has been stated, he immediately recognized the importance of the authenticity of Christian baptism into *the Royal Priesthood of Jesus Christ*. Afterward, the pontiff assigned Bea to work in the Holy Office as Consultor for German theological affairs. The consequences of this appointment, of course, are immediately obvious in that eventually he came into contact with Archbishop Jaeger and the ecumenical developments of Germany. Less obvious, but equally important, was Bea's work on the so-called Pian Commission for the sake of liturgical revision.

This activity brought to his consciousness the very important theme of the *community at worship*. Because of his biblical expertise, he directly became involved with the revised Latin translation of the Psalms, and later the reform of the Breviary. The recitation of the Divine Office, associated with the daily reverential use of the Breviary, is an act of ecclesial worship of God which is the sanctification of the entire day. To recall the point raised above by the late Dom Damasus Winzen, O.S.B., "The true unity of the texts is rather to be found in the sacramental mystery which they surround." The evidence is that Bea convinced Pope Pius that a reform of the entire Liturgy would be necessary for the pastoral restoration of the image of the Church, identifying it essentially as a universal praying community. Archbishop Bugnini indicated that it was the consensus of the Pian Commission that the new Psalter would simply be the first building block for the new structure. It was Bea's task to synthesize and carry back and forth between pontiff and commissioners the essence of those ideas.

In those years, there were no less than four liturgical reforms. The most significant of these was the restoration of the Easter Vigil in 1951 and, later, the entire Holy Week Liturgy in 1955, centering on the theme "Christ has risen from the dead, death overcome by death; He has given life to those who dwelt in tombs." Dame Aemiliana Löhr, O.S.B., wrote: "Again and again the verse is sung, made holy by the tremendous mystery it contains, and by centuries of use. It is the finest, the best-beloved, the best known, the most popular, and most familiar formula for the Church's transparent joy at Easter."[53] Dame Aemiliana ascribes the restoration of this hymn to the prudence of Pope Pius XII. The restoration recalls the central theme of *baptism*. For, "In ancient times, it was above all those to be baptized whose longing was pitched forward toward the coming night."[54]

Bea played a direct hand in practically every phase of liturgical reform at this time. The circumstances gave him ample opportunity to reflect upon the significance of baptism and its immediate effect. This he identified with the royal priesthood of Christ and of the shared ministry of prayer and worship, which is the common heritage of all the baptized. Furthermore, the grace of baptism is rooted in the risen and glorified Christ, and therefore is pneumatic, in that it flows from His "Lordship" upon all those who have been initiated through the saving waters into the Pilgrim People of God and thus been "made members" of the Mystical Body of Christ the Priest.

A second aspect is his contact with Monsignor Josef Höfer. Höfer, as we have seen, carried with him from Germany a decade-old preoccupation with the theological concept of the Mystical Body of Christ. In the last days of the war, with the promulgation of *Mystici Corporis*, he criticized the text

53. *Id. op. cit.* p. 40.
54. *Ibid.*, p. 43.

as being mono-Christic in nature. He sought instead a Spirit-given inclusiveness. He posed the question over and over: Who is a member of the Church? He identified for Bea as well as for Jaeger that the mindset of the ordinary Roman Catholic excluded schismatics and other Christians from Church membership. Again, the answer to his repeated statement of the question eventually would come from a reexamination of the biblical theme of Baptism. Apart from Bea's formal tasks in the fifteen years before he became cardinal, he received an abundance of riches from his membership on pontifical commissions and his very valuable friendship with Höfer. This experience gave him ingress to what really was the heart of the question: Who *is* truly a member of the Mystical Body of Christ? The resolution to that question was necessary before the concept of ecumenism could be developed from a Roman Catholic perspective. It would be Bea's gift to place it in a wider ecclesial context. It would be safe to say here that by his involvement with biblical and liturgical renewal, his reflections upon the implications of *Mediator Dei,* and his discussions with Josef Höfer, that Bea provided himself with ample instruments to undertake this task. Thus fortified, Bea entered into the forum of ecumenism.

Chapter IV

The Correspondence of Jaeger and Bea

Introduction

This chapter will document the extensive correspondence between Father Augustin Bea and Archbishop Lorenz Jaeger. Passing reference will be made to Josef Höfer and Eduard Stakemeier. The chapter includes Jaeger's ecumenical concerns at the end of World War II, the rise of ecumenical sensitivity in Germany, and the so-called Rhodes Incident of the World Council of Churches in 1959.[1] While this period was filled with local matters of interest to the German scene, the leitmotif is the presentation of Jaeger's ecumenical interest.

A General Council of the Church was summoned in 1959. With the onset of preparations for the Council, an ancillary theme emerged, i.e., the need to offer clear, precise and ready information primarily through a Vatican Press Bureau. Jaeger specifically proposed the establishment of just

---

1. Because of the particularity of the situation of the extremely serious misunderstanding in the August 1959 meeting of the executive bodies of the World Council of Churches and two Catholic observers, who attended in a private capacity, throughout the remainder of this text, the Rhodes Incident will be identified in uppercase. The Rhodes Incident identifies a misunderstanding between World Council of Churches leadership and Monsignor J. Willebrands and specifically Father Christoph Dumont, O.P. In the course of an executive meeting in August 1959 on the island of Rhodes, Dumont arranged for a private tea with the Orthodox. In that he was a guest himself, Dumont's gesture was deemed inappropriate. Ultimately, it was interpreted as an affront to the World Council and to the Orthodox themselves. From this vantage point in history, Dumont's invitation was totally innocent. The World Council of Churches' authorities fumed that the Vatican was seeking to ingratiate itself. This was totally false.

such an office for the sake of the "Separated Brethren" *(Getrennten Brüder)*. For Jaeger, the interest of the German-language Churches of the Reformation was a primary concern, as was the possibility of their attendance and participation in the General Council in some form. These thoughts he would share with Augustin Bea.

The date of Bea's public nomination was 16 November 1959, as has been noted. In the semi-public Consistory, which preceded Bea's reception of the Red Hat on December 14, Pope John stressed the fact that he promoted Bea to the Sacred College in recognition of "his special service to the Church."[2] In the course of the ceremonies connected with the elevation of the Cardinalate, he took possession of his titular Church, that of St. Sabas on the Aventine Hill, where he delivered this message: "This Church is a symbol of the unity that is the great desire, not only of the church of Rome and its children, but also of so many non-Catholic Christians, indeed of humanity itself, which longs more than ever today to leave its splintering behind it and reach for unity — although it will never do so without Him who prayed to the Father 'that they may all be one just as We are One.'"[3] Thus, it is evident that from the inauguration of his cardinalatial ministry, Bea possessed an ecumenical mission. He would express this to Pope John when first they met on January 9, 1960. Bea's ecumenical interests were sparked by other sources, Monsignor Josef Höfer, as well as long-standing professional contacts with the Lutheran biblical scholars of the German universities. The flame was certainly fanned by his ten-year correspondence with the Archbishop of Paderborn, Lorenz Jaeger.

Jaeger and His Correspondence

Apart from his personal commitment to the Ecumenical Movement, there are many notable qualities in Jaeger's life which stand out. Aloys Klein, who was his closest and longest-trusted secretary, explained them.[4] They included his piety, his priority of the pastoral, his concern for priests, and his generosity. Most notable of all was his propensity for study. In this, he was disciplined, consistent and creative. When he was eventually elevated to the Red Hat in 1965, he was heartily applauded. Even earlier, when it was rumored that he might head a Vatican dicastery at Rome, he wrote

2. Schmidt, *op. cit.*, p. 307.
3. *Ibid.* p. 311.
4. Interview with the author, 16 October 2001.

emphatically to Monsignor Höfer that he would not accept. He simply could not leave Paderborn. When he died, he was genuinely mourned. Over his tomb in the Paderborn Cathedral crypt, his memorial is composed of five bronze medallions. The most moving of these is the "Open Hand."

That medallion refers to his spirit of charity, which was evidenced in the pastoral letter which he wrote to his diocese in October 1946. The air raids around Paderborn in the final days of the War were terrible. German heavy industry had already been located there because it was a land of iron and coal. He reported sadly that not even a hotel or guesthouse remained standing. The center of the town square had been devastated and even a wing of the Cathedral had taken a direct hit. His pastoral letter began: "In the forefront for the care of souls, the radiant and immediate enunciation of faith is intimately related to the exercise of Christian Charity. We have no greater real means to win the world for Christ, than to show Him how we love one another. I need not emphasize to you how many there are who are in misery and suffering, awaiting the Saviour who alone can heal them. The parish charity in the city and the country must be enlarged, in partnership with the other agencies, especially with and for the youth."[5] Jaeger went on with great practicality and with no embarrassment whatsoever to list what he was talking about. Here are some examples: country cooking, sewing rooms, kindergartens, bathing establishments, home bathrooms, house laundries, workshops for handiwork, night shelters, railway facilities for mothers with children, functioning employment agencies, co-ops for gardening and a missing persons bureau. The City of Paderborn fell within the Western Zone of Occupation and Jaeger did not hesitate to present himself before the Anglo-American authorities, to care for his flock. In this letter, he was inciting his parishioners toward neighborly courtesy in order to assist in the care of one another.

The last of his very evident qualities is Jaeger's dedication to his correspondence. While much of it remains inaccessible, at this date, it is possible to observe the great number of portfolios which contain his personal and of-

---

5. "Caritasdienst in der Stadt Paderborn," 15 October 1945, Archives of the Vicar General, Paderborn. "Im Vordergrund der Seelsorgsarbeit muss sich mit der lichtvollen und zeitnahen Glaubensverkündigung DIE ÜBUNG DER CHRISTLICHEN CARITAS verbinden. Wir haben kein wirksameres Mittel, die Welt für Christus zu gewinnen, als wenn wir ihr zeigen, wie wir einander lieben. Ich brauche euch nicht erst zu sagen, wieviel Not und Leid auf den Heiland wartet, der allein sie heilen kann Die Pfarrcaritas in der Stadt und auf dem Lande muss unter weitester Beteiligung aller Kreise, nicht zuletzt auch der Jugend, ausgebaut werden."

ficial letters. Truly, the amount of writing that he generated was enormous. This is especially true of his continued contact with Rome by post.

Already in 1942, when he had been bishop for less than a year, he wrote to Pope Pius XII, congratulating the pontiff on the third anniversary of his "papal coronation."[6] Pius replied personally, speaking of the tragic events occurring in Germany at that time. Pius mentioned how many faithful German Catholics had come to receive his blessing; the pontiff hoped that his blessings would also extend to the non-Catholic neighbors within Germany, bringing them benefit and strength. The pope lamented the current atmosphere of unbelief and hate in which the Church must exist and he encouraged trust in the Love of God, who, from this cauldron of suffering, can lead His Church to new truth.

Jaeger's Vatican Correspondence

Pius wrote again on 18 January 1946, thanking Jaeger and his diocese for the Christmas greetings, which had been extended. Pius commented upon the tragedy of the War and the disastrous effects it had upon German civic, religious and cultural life. The Pope commended the Archbishop for his zeal for the displaced priests, who had wandered into his diocese as a result of the war: "Oft times we think in love and hope upon a Germany, securely constituted by recourse to the restoration of unity of the Catholic religion, gleaming with the variety of its rich, original talent, strengthened, in gentle force, through the gentleness of the Gospel."[7] The Pope concluded with a reminder of the Christian virtues, e.g., wisdom, fortitude, truth, courage, holiness, love of the cross, prayer, vigilance against evils of the time, all of these in conjunction with the bishop's duty to strengthen the brethren. The advice corresponds to Jaeger's genuine love for the entire Church of Paderborn.[8]

---

6. "Papstkrönungstages." The letters of both Pius and Jaeger, typed, corrected and signed in their own hand, are found in the Vicar General's Archives, Paderborn.

7. Pius to Jäger, January 18, 1946, Vicar General's Archives, Paderborn. "Oftmals denken wir in Hoffnung und Liebe an Deutschland, das, festgegründet durch Wiederherstellung der Einheit der katholischen Religion, glänzend durch die Mannigfaltigkeit seiner reichen ursprünglichen Begabung, gekräftigt in milder Kraft durch die Sanftheit des Evangeliums."

8. *Ibid.* For the most part, the correspondence is in German. It is noteworthy to observe this correspondence for it has been stated that Pius XII discouraged correspondence with diocesan bishops. Each typed his own letters, sometimes badly.

Two years later on 12 May 1948, Jaeger wrote to Pope Pius XII, informing the Pontiff about a new development within German Protestantism. He was doing so in light of his responsibility for correspondence with Rome pertaining to the *Una Sancta,* having held the appointment since 1943. The letter is based upon a memorandum which the President of the Evangelical Church Chancellery, Doctor Hans Asmussen, had forwarded to the Council of the Evangelical Church of Germany. Asmussen, who played a very significant role in Protestant opposition to Hitler, was seeking to unite the Lutheran Reform Churches with the Lutheran Unionists in the Evangelische Kirche Deutschland (EKD). For his efforts, Asmussen was dismissed. Still Jaeger was convinced that such a union would be good for ecumenical relations in Germany. Asmussen had been and still was very close to the *Una Sancta* Movement.[9]

By 1951 there was evidence that correspondence had already eventuated between Jaeger and Father Bea. In 1945, as stated earlier, Pius XII had indeed appointed Bea as his *beichtvater,* "Spiritual Father."[10] Thus, Bea had easy access to Pope Pius XII. By the beginning of 1949, Bea relinquished the post of rector of the Pontifical Biblical Institute, but he remained professor there until 1959. However, in the year of his resignation as rector, he was appointed Consultor for German Affairs within the Holy Office. Therefore, because of his capacity as correspondent to Rome for *Una Sancta* affairs, Jaeger began to share ecumenical developments with Father Bea. Thus, their correspondence began at first haltingly, eventually their letters became more chatty and more frequent. For example, Bea's letter of March 23, 1951, bore upon the subject of the treatment of those Lutheran clergy who had come into the Catholic Church.[11] Jaeger commented in reply: "It is very fortunate that the Holy Father has remained steadfast in his promise to open the way to the priesthood in connection with the former Lutheran pastors, in cases where they possess a true priestly calling and can become useful to the Church."[12] Jaeger expressed his 100 percent agreement with

9. Jaeger to Pius, 12 May 1948. Vicar General's Archives, Paderborn. This letter is available in draft form, containing many corrections made in Jaeger's hand.

10. Schmidt, *op. cit.,* pp. 163-64. As was stated above, Pius chose a German for this position since his household staff was German speaking. The confessor therefore was designated to serve the Sisters and the Pope. The first was Father F. van Laak, S.J., who died in 1941. He was succeeded by Father A. Merk, S.J., who died in 1945; when the Pope appointed Bea he observed: "I hope that this one lasts." Bea and Pacelli had known each other since the early 1920s when Pacelli was Nuncio to Munich and Bea was Jesuit provincial of Bavaria.

11. Bea to Jaeger, 23 March 1951, Vicar General's Archives, Paderborn.

12. Jaeger to Bea, 31 March 1951, Vicar General's Archives, Paderborn. "Sehr erfreulich

Bea that these individuals should be instructed, formed in Catholicism in a Religious Order House. There they would get a better grounding in the Catholic faith.

On 19 March 1951, Jaeger wrote to Bea, wherein he indicated that he was in the midst of preparing a report for the Plenary Session at Fulda, regarding the *Una Sancta* desk. He also informed Bea of the death of his personal theological advisor, H. H. P. Grendel, and he invited Bea to fill that post. "After all, you [Bea] know the mind of the Holy Father and of the Holy Office about these matters . . . you know, on the other hand, the German circumstances."[13]

In light of the above, Jaeger was asking Bea's opinion about the situation concerning the conversion of Lutheran pastors and their admission to Holy Orders. At present, there was an urgent issue before him, for a local Lutheran pastor had recently resigned his post, converted to Catholicism, and was seeking a place in the seminary. There were others — one from Berlin, one from Jena and still another coming from Ohomatz. The Bishop of Mainz already had seminarians who were former Lutheran clergy, and was disposed to promote them to Orders. Jaeger was asking about the groundwork to be done, so that the *status quaestionis* could be forwarded to the Holy Office. Jaeger confided that he had kept Josef Höfer informed about his last meeting with the Evangelical theological professors. That meeting was highly successful and gave rise to evidence that the Protestants must revise their positions, so that they could really enter into a truly scholarly discourse with Catholic theologians.[14]

On 11 April 1951, Jaeger wrote to Bea again. His letter talked about the definition of the doctrine of the Assumption. Jaeger was delighted to report that opposition in Germany to the proclamation had lessened. German Evangelical theologians had taken to their textbooks and became aware that Luther himself had venerated Mary under that title. Famous Lutheran theologians had regarded that such veneration was taken for granted, until the seventeenth century. He spoke of the "Mary book" of Doctor Hans Asmussen, and he spoke also about the Stuttgart Preaching Academy *(Predigt)*, as warmly greeting the definition and in turn contribut-

---

ist, dass der Heilige Vater grundsätzlich an der Zusage festhält, den konvertierenden Pastören den Weg ins sacerdotium zu öffnen, falls sie ein echte priesterliche Berufung mitbringen und für die Kirche nutzbringend verwendet werden können."

13. Jaeger to Bea, 19 March 1951, Vicar General's Archives, Paderborn. "Sie kennen die Meinung des Heiligen Vaters und des Heiligen Officiums in diesen Fragen. . . . Sie kennen anderseits die deutschen Verhältnisse."

14. *Ibid.*

ing to the silencing of the objectors. In that same letter, Bea stated that renowned Lutheran theologians were in agreement. "The situation is such that we can understand well the best theologians of the Lutheran confessions, because there is encountered, in every respect, a great reverence for the person of the Holy Father and the knowledge concerning the ordinary teaching content with regard to the decisive truths of the faith. They reverence the Church of Rome as their Mother and as regulative of their own theological work and teaching."[15]

However, according to Bea, other Churches of the Classical Reformation were more attached to the Reformation itself and, therefore, were more separated from Catholicism than the ordinary Lutherans. Here, Bea was demonstrating his knowledge of German Protestant Church history, where he stated that the renewed proposal to bring back the Old Prussian Union, the so-called "Unity Church," created by the Prussian king between Lutherans and Reformed, especially in the Rhineland and Westphalia, would be a disaster! This proposal would be a mismatch dogmatically. The only thing that would exist in common would be a certain connection with Luther.[16] It would allow for pulpit hospitality. Its history is more political than doctrinal and, in the past, had outright refused union with the other Lutheran denominations. In the aftermath of the war, where regionalism became more acute again, since Germany was divided into Eastern and Western sections, the Old Prussian Union would attempt to use whatever influence it could from Westphalia, the Rhineland and Hesse; undoubtedly, according to Bea, they would resent the closeness between Protestants and Catholics even more so than in the past.

The letters between Jaeger and Bea continued throughout the 1950s. They always began with terms of endearment and deference. While seeking Bea's counsel, Archbishop Jaeger acknowledged him as more than a simple Jesuit. True, Bea was endowed with many intellectual gifts, a winning personality, which made him respected but not feared in Rome, and therefore it might be said of him that he was a "man of contacts." Klaus Wittstadt, whose article on Lorenz Jaeger remains so far the most comprehensive treatment of the subject, stated that in these years of correspondence, Jae-

---

15. Jaeger to Bea, April 11, 1951, Vicar General's Archives, Paderborn. "Die Lage ist so, dass wir mit den besten Theologen des lutherischen Bekenntnisses uns gut verständigen können, weil dort eine grosse Ehrfurcht vor der Persönlichkeit des Heiligen Vaters durchweg anzutreffen ist und das Wissen um den gemeinsamen Lehrgehalt hinsichtlich der entscheidenden Glaubenswahrheiten. Sie verehren die Kirche Roms als Mutter und als Regulativ für ihre eigene theologische Arbeit und Lehre."

16. "Ein Zurückgehen auf Luther," in *ibid.*

ger in turn became counsel to Father Bea.[17] Before long, both would share the office of bishop and the title of cardinal together, although briefly. Yet it must be stated that the ecumenical awakening in Rome effectively arrived from Germany, communicated by one German to another. To Bea's intelligence and *Romanità* (sense of Rome) must be added Jaeger's persistence and fortitude. After all, he had directly handled these matters (the *Una Sancta*) as a German bishop for almost twenty years. Besides being German, he was also a man of experience and, in his own lifetime, wisdom.

A Change of Papal Administration

While this correspondence was taking place, Pope Pius XII died on 9 October 1958. His successor, Angelo Giuseppe Roncalli, the Cardinal Patriarch of Venice, was elected at 4:50 P.M. on 28 October 1958. A new style of papacy had begun. At the inception of the conclave, before the call *"Extra Omnes,"* Monsignor (later Cardinal) Antonio Bacci, the papal Latinist, gave the sermon "de eligendo pontifice" [concerning the election of a pope]; the historian Peter Hebblethwaite called Bacci's words prophetic:

> We need a pope gifted with great spiritual strength and ardent charity . . . he will need to embrace the Eastern and the Western Church. He will belong to all peoples, and his heart must beat especially for those oppressed by totalitarian persecution and those in great poverty . . . may the new Vicar of Christ form a bridge between all levels of society, between all nations — even those that reject and persecute the Christian religion. Rather than someone who has explored and experienced the subtle principles belonging to the art of discipline and diplomacy, *we need a Pope who is above all holy, so that he may obtain from God what lies beyond natural gifts. . . . He will freely receive and welcome the bishops,* "whom the Holy Spirit has chosen to rule over the church of God (Acts 20:28)." *He will be prepared to give them counsel in their doubts, to listen and comfort them in their anxieties and to encourage their plans.*[18]

Bacci's memoirs record his intention to formulate his address specifically to the conclave: "I remember that my address was well received by the press. Some wrote that I had clearly and precisely drawn the portrait of

17. *Id., op. cit.,* p. 187.
18. Hebblethwaite, *op. cit.,* p. 281 (emphasis in original).

John XXIII. In fact I had simply presented to the Cardinals the ideal figure of a Pope that the present age demanded. So the merit was not mine."[19]

Hebblethwaite called Bacci's comments *revisionist,* in that he was calling for someone who would be everything that Pius XII was not. Hebblethwaite also noted that, with a few words, Bacci invited the Cardinals to choose someone who would be accessible to the bishops of the world. Secondly, he would be a bridge between East and West, which at that time was the world of the Cold War, and which at that time focused upon a divided Germany. Hebblethwaite noted that during the invasion of Hungary in 1956, Pius XII had expressed both his outrage and his impatience through three encyclicals, over as many days.

For his part, Roncalli was different; he stunned all onlookers.[20] First he presented to his electors an already prepared address in which he announced to them that he would be simple, serene, pastoral, and "John." This name had not been used for five hundred years. To the crowd waiting outside in the square, he was a relatively unknown figure, but Mario Begnini, an author of the Italian official biography, stated: "The anguish that vibrated in the voice of Pacelli . . . almost ethereal, was unknown to Roncalli. The voice of the new Pope descended on the crowd in blessing — warm, very human, melodious, in truth quite beautiful. It was a friendly paternal voice."[21] The conclusion of both Begnini and Hebblethwaite was that the new Pontiff possessed a strong independent personality.

While Begnini and his co-author, Goffredo Zanchi, remained silent about the discussion of a projected Council of the Church within the Conclave, Hebblethwaite believed that there was enough evidence to indicate that "many Cardinals, including Alfredo Ottaviani and Ernesto Ruffini, visited Roncalli's cell on the night of 27 October to provide encouragement and comfort."[22] They already knew he was going to be elected. Perhaps not for motives of *aggiornamento,* but rather out of *Romanità,* they proposed a General Council.

Whether or not such a conversation ever took place in the 1958 Con-

---

19. *Ibid.,* pp. 280-81.

20. *Ibid.*

21. Begnini et al., *op. cit.,* p. 276.

22. Hebblethwaite, *op. cit.,* pp. 283 and 310. Cardinal Ottaviani stated: "In the last days of the conclave I went to visit the Patriarch in his cell and said: 'Your Eminence we have to think about a council.' Cardinal Ruffini, who was also present, was of the same opinion." From *Epocha* interview, 8 December 1968. Suffice it to mention here that two earlier attempts to summon a council after each World War had been inaugurated by Pope Pius XI and Pope Pius XII, respectively. They did not come to fruition.

clave cannot now be verified. However, Roland Flamini recorded an incident, which can be authenticated in the papers of Cardinal Domenico Tardini, who was made Secretary of State and Cardinal only after the 1958 Conclave:

> Pope John used to use another anecdote to describe how the idea came to him in an inspirational flash on 20 January 1959, during an audience with Domenico Cardinal Tardini, his Secretary of State. They were discussing, he would say, the troubled state of the world, and the Church's need to set an example of peace and concord before men when suddenly, "without having given it any prior thought," as he put it in his private diary, *"Un Concilio!"*

Tardini's response was immediate and enthusiastic: "Si! Un Concilio!"[23]

The topic of conversation according to Flamini was that, in the midst of complexities of Cold War politics, religion was failing, and that to combat growing indifference, not only the Catholic Church but all Christian Churches needed to seek ways to bring back freshness to Christianity. According to John, the idea of a council was "Un Balzo Inavanti" [A Leap Forward]. Therefore, only five days later, in the presence of a handful of Cardinals, Pope John proclaimed the Council in the Basilica of St. Paul's Outside the Walls at the conclusion of the Week of Church Unity Octave, as it was then called, on the feast of the Conversion of St. Paul, 25 January.[24]

From its inception in 1908, the Occasion of Church Unity Octave presented the world with a concept of ecumenism. For many, there was confusion between "return" or "reunion." At the time of Pope John's proclamation of the Council, it was still *not yet clear.* The public events of 1959 were to be about world unity, the urgency of which *was* clear, against the terrifying threats of the Cold War. On that occasion, without eliminating his themes, John effectively conveyed a message of unity. Political commentators Roland Flamini and Giancarlo Zizola believed that the political crisis between East and West weighed heavily upon the shoulders of the pontiff, along with his sensitivity to a growing relaxation into secularism, agnosticism, and even atheism in Europe. Both Cardinal Willebrands and Archbishop Capovilla confirmed for the author *viva voce* that the above inter-

---

23. Roland Flamini, *op. cit.*, pp. 9-10. Begnini is more subdued in his report taken from Tardini's diary: "Important audience. Yesterday afternoon His Holiness reflected and meditated on the program of his pontificate. 'For my part, I like what is new and good.'" See also Hebblethwaite, *op. cit.*, p. 294.

24. Flamini, *op. cit.*, p. 10.

pretation is correct. Pope John was to confirm his message about unity in even more explicit terms on 29 June 1959, with the encyclical *Ad Petri Cathedram* (At the Chair of Peter). Pope John would, it seems, grow into a more precise theological focus upon reunion in the remainder of his pontificate, as will be evident on the occasion of the visit of the Archbishop of Canterbury in late 1960.[25]

The Ecumenical Character of the Later Bea-Jaeger Correspondence

Through these days of transition and innovation, Jaeger and Bea continued to correspond. For example, Jaeger wrote to him, twice, on 13-14 August 1959. By this time, Jaeger enthusiastically responded to the idea of the Johannine Council, which was not yet quite precise in either scope or methodology.[26] Jaeger was in the process of mustering enthusiasm and participation from the other members of the Fulda Bishops Conference. Bea apologized for not having responded earlier, since he was on retreat. The letter from Jaeger contained, like his entire previous correspondence, many questions which were all mixed together.[27] Bea responded as follows: First, he regarded that the most important consideration to be taken up by the pre-Preparatory Commission of the Council to be the *doctrina de Ecclesia* (the doctrine of the Church).[28] Within that consideration, perforce, would be the place of bishops. It *must* be established that bishops, more than before, are summoned to lead the universal church, as well as particularly in their own dioceses. The question of dioceses is not the issue, but the Ordinary of the diocese should be consulted. Bea's opinion also extended to Rome. "This centralization is certainly not a blessing for the Church. With it is connected another issue, namely the composition of the *Curia Romana,* especially the

25. *Ibid.,* pp. 6-16. Flamini interprets the pontificate of John XXIII in terms of the politics of standoff between Russia and the West. Therefore return and reunion are important as political dynamic. A similar view is held by Giancarlo Zizola, *The Utopia of Pope John XXIII* (Maryknoll, N.Y.: Orbis Books, 1978), pp. 100-14.

26. *Ibid.,* p. 293. "In the midst of all this activity, on 25 January 1959, came as a bolt out of the blue when Pope John XXIII announced that he was planning to convene an Ecumenical Council. . . . It is well known that this announcement raised many hopes, but also gave rise to certain misapprehensions, or at least reflections and conjectures on its ecumenical aim." Jaeger's response is noted in the letter of Jaeger to Bea 14 August 1959, Vicar General's Archives, Paderborn.

27. Jaeger to Bea, 14 August 1959, Vicar General's Archives, Paderborn.

28. Bea to Jaeger, 15 September 1959, Vicar General's Archives, Paderborn.

Congregations."[29] Of necessity, each Congregation should be headed by an appropriate expert, even though he not be a Cardinal, since every Congregation consists also of a board of Consultors. These must come from the international forum. It is also easier that the out-of-town Cardinals who are appointed to an appropriate Congregation could come to the preliminary meetings as needed, once or twice a year, especially if the matter discussed involves care of the Universal Church. It would not be a bad idea if the Fulda Bishops Conference were to say something in this regard.

Bea's concern about ecclesiology expanded also to the *Regale Dominium Christi* (The Royal Lordship of Christ). Further, he called for a presentation of the doctrine of the Holy Spirit as the guide and illuminating principle of the *Corpus Christi Mysticum* (The Mystical Body of Christ). This should be strongly accentuated so that the "Teaching Authority of the Church" can be grounded from within.[30] Here we see evidence of Bea's growing awareness of the dynamic pneumatological element of the essence of the Church. Perhaps, this is a result of the influence of Höfer. Questions of the constitutive elements of the meaning and activity of the Church now began to become a part of his correspondence. This would appear later in his work in preparation for the Council where he raised the questions of charism, the role of the local bishop, collegiality of bishops, and the Royal Priesthood of the faithful People of God.

The second part of Bea's response to Jaeger's 13-14 August letters dealt with the project of a vernacular translation of the Roman Canon of the Mass. Jaeger had apparently asked for Bea's opinion of a model of a translation of *die deutsche evangelische Messe*. Bea's response, on 15 September, stated that in fact a manuscript had arrived by post. He found *das Exemplar* (the projected text) to be "not altogether fortunate. I have marked the emendations, which came somewhat in question, in the copy . . . with red ink, at least when the authors sought to reproduce faithfully the canon of the *'missale Romanum.'"*[31]

A third example of the rather typical correspondence between Bea and Jaeger is contained in the 15 September letter which dealt with Jaeger's

---

29. *Ibid.* "Diese Zentralisation ist sicherlich nicht zum Segen der Kirche. Damit hängt noch ein anderes zusammen: die Zusammensetzung der römischen Kurie, besonders der Kongregationen." On November 1, 1958, Archbishop Giovanni Battista Montini (the future Pope Paul VI), Archbishop of Milan, said exactly the opposite.

30. *Ibid.*

31. *Ibid.* "Der Übersetzung . . . ist nicht überall glücklich. Ich habe in das Exemplar . . . mit Rotstift die Änderungen eingetragen, die etwas in Frage kämen, wenigstens wenn die Herren den Kanon des Missale Romanum treu wiedergeben wolle."

local project of composing a catechism. Bea wrote, on that date, that the most important thing is naturally the catechism itself. "I have long thought about this matter from every angle, but I am of the opinion, *salve meliore iudicio* ('saving your better judgment'), that, here, once again, it is a question of an illusion, to which the people of the 'compilation' would not be the first (to succumb). The catechism itself is not a place for creative writing. Consequently it is much too long and too spotty. One can think, it seems to me, only about a lecture on the *Confessio Augustana*." Here, Bea was referring to the subject of atheism (atheists were the targeted audience of address), which is not a topic for long discursive writing. Jaeger's letter to Bea must have indicated to him that his project was intended, as a catechism, to be a handbook for Protestants. That being the case, the drafted text did not meet the standards and Bea found himself thinking that he was reading an essay regarding the *Confessio Augustana*. In point of fact, Bea had just read a major part of a recent book by the Lutheran scholar Max Lackmann on Catholic unity. While Bea found that it had some merit, he actually found it boring.[32]

For his part, Archbishop Jaeger had been beside himself with joy with the proclamation of the Council on 20 February 1959. Klaus Wittstadt recorded him as saying, "As soon as we have determined the best resolution and shall have developed the agreed-upon procedures, in relation to this new advancement of our time, we *can* advance the Separated Brethren upon the sure way of that unity which they themselves perceive."[33] This became Jaeger's personal ideal. As an ecumenical scholar, a true leader and an administrator, there he focused his eye. Thus, he wrote to Bea early on 20 February 1959 sharing the haste with which the Fulda Bishops Conference ran to the table to begin preparation for the upcoming General Council of the Church. "I have," he stated, "reported about the atmosphere which the announcement of the Council has had upon the Catholic and

---

32. *Ibid.* No doubt he is referring to Max Lackmann's 1959 *Katholische Einheit und Ausburger Konfession*, which exists in English translation as *The Augsburg Confession and Catholic Unity* (New York: Herder and Herder, 1963). "Ich habe mir die Sache lange hin und her überlegt, glaube aber, salvo meliore iudicio, dass es sich hier wieder einmal um eine Illusion handelt, die bei den Herren der 'Sammlung' nicht die erste wäre. Der Katechismus selbst ist sicher keine Gesprächsgrundlage. Dafür ist er viel zu weitläufig und zu buntscheckig. Mann könnte m.e. nur an ein Gespräch über die Confessio Augustana denken."

33. Wittstadt, *op. cit.*, p. 182. "Sobald wir die besten Lösungen festgelegt, vereinbart, aufgezeigt haben werden, auch im Verhältnis zu den neuen Forderungen der Zeit, wir den getrennten Brüdern den sicheren Weg für jene Einheit aufzeigen können, die sie selbst ersehnen."

Evangelical side. The reaction here in Germany is summarized in brief: On the Catholic side exuberant! Full of hope! . . . while on the Evangelical side, the reaction accentuates restraint! or is even directly negative!"[34]

Jaeger's lectures were filled with the topic of the Holy Spirit, pointing out "the pneumatic dimensions" of the *Magisterium,* now about to meet in Council. He wrote: "Great skill will be needed to so balance all pronouncements, in reference to the forthcoming great event, that the great hope in the work of the Holy Spirit in the Church is nourished in believers, so that all pronouncements, nonetheless, remain realistic and not lead to pessimism, [but] will always have recourse to prayer, so that the Holy Spirit awakens the readiness of hearts, and, all the more, the yearning for unity in all of us."[35] Thus Jaeger was conveying a pastoral expression of his own deep personal faith and piety. On 19 June 1959, he carried this theme still further in a public diocesan discourse in which he disclosed the prophecy that the Council would fan the flames of a desire among Christians for reunion: "In the Holy Spirit the great hope lies grounded upon which the believing Christian approaches the Council. That which according to human reckoning is impossible, is possible to the Spirit of God. He [the Holy Spirit] knows ways and means to the unity of Christians, which are still closed to us. In this hope, all can believe in Jesus Christ as true Son of God and Redeemer, and join in the (wonderful) prayer (from the liturgy): 'You who have gathered together the people of all time to the unity of faith, send out your Spirit and all will be made new.'"[36] Jaeger's words reveal at once his pneumatic confidence as well as his lifetime of exposure to the

---

34. Jaeger to Bea, 19 June 1959, Vicar General's Archives, Paderborn. "Ich habe berichtet über das Echo, das die Konzilsankündigung auf katholischer und evangelischer Seite gehabt hat. Kurz zusammengefasste, ist die Reaktion hier in Deutschland auf katholischer Seite überschwenglich hoffnungsvoll . . . während auf evangelischer seite die Reaktion betont zurückhaltend oder auch direkt negativ ist."

35. Wittstadt, *op. cit.,* pp. 182-83. "Es wird viel Klugheit brauchen, alle Äusserungen zu dem grossen kommenden Ereignis so abzustimmen, dass in den Gläubingen die Grosse Hoffnung auf das Wirken des Hl. Geistes in der Kirche genährt wird, das aber alle Äusserungen durchaus realistisch bleiben und ohne in Pessimismus zu machen, immer zum Gebet aufgerufen wird, damit der Heilige Geist die Bereitschaft der Herzen wecke und die Sehnsucht nach Einheit in uns allen mehre."

36. *Ibid.* "Im Heiligen Geist 'liegt die grosse Hoffnung begründet, mit der der gläubige Christ dem Konzil entgegensieht. Dem Geist Gottes ist das möglich, was nach menschlichem Ermessen unmöglich ist. Er kennt Wege und Mittel zur Einheit der Christen, die uns noch verborgen sind. In dieser Hoffnung können alle, die an Jesus Christus als wahren Gottessohn und Erlöser glauben, einstimmen in das Gebet': 'Der Du die Völker aller Zeiten zur Einheit des Glaubens versammelt hast, sende aus Deinen Geist, und alles wird neu geschaffen.' "

twentieth-century German "Kerygmatic theology" which begins all things and sees all things through the primacy of Christ.[37] In the same time period, Jaeger's closest associate in ecumenical work, Professor Eduard Stakemeier, publicly and frequently represented the thinking of his diocesan bishop and patron, Monsignor Jaeger.[38]

Stakemeier had been instructed to keep the Archbishop in touch with Monsignor Willebrands, President of the Catholic Conference for Ecumenical Questions. In fact, through 1959, preparations were being made to host the Catholic Conference for Ecumenical Questions in Paderborn. The task at hand was assisting the World Council of Churches/Faith and Order in preparation for a document on the "Lordship of Christ." In this time period, Stakemeier traveled to the Benedictine Abbey at Maria Laach to address the monks and clergy with a lecture entitled "The Council Which Has Been Announced and the Unity of Christians." He stated on behalf of Jaeger: "The Council *should* serve the reunion of Christendom."[39] On 13 August 1959, Jaeger wrote to Bea the first of his two above-mentioned letters. Bea obviously did not respond to the first letter completely. For his part, Jaeger, in that text, complained about the shortness of time allotted for drawing up the *lineamenta* for the Preparatory Commissions for the Council. This was at the time of the pre-preparatory phase of the Council. Jaeger thought the deadline much too close since the questions had been received

---

37. Lackmann, *op. cit.*, p. 120. The concept of Christology likewise pervaded the Evangelical Church at this time, e.g., "The New Testament and the ancient Catholic Church obviously understood Christ as a human member of a new humanity. . . . This is a humanity which is enabled by Christ (not in and of itself) to answer God and to be responsible to God. Christ, the Incarnate Word, is the *hypostasis* of the original, divinely intended dialogue between God and man."

38. See Livingston, *op. cit.*, pp. 96-112. Hervé Savon, *Johann Adam Möhler: The Father of Modern Theology* (Glen Rock, N.J.: Paulist Press, 1966), pp. 27-33. For three years now, Stakemeier had been the Director of the Johann Adam Möhler Institute, a Roman Catholic Ecumenical Research Center, which had opened its doors in 1956, honoring the highly regarded nineteenth-century expert in Controversial Theology, Johann Adam Möhler (1796-1838). Möhler has been spoken of before in this thesis. Jaeger considered him to be the icon of theological dialogue, in an ecumenical context. Möhler was identified with Catholic innovation and said to be the leading *relator* of German liberal theology. Möhler had allowed himself to be influenced by Friedrich Schleiermacher and Hegalianism. Completely unpolitical in character, Schleiermacher's goal was the pastoral interpretation of doctrine and therefore he sought to apply experimental, historical and imaginative categories of contemporary Europe as opposed to the scholastic contributions of Thomas Aquinas, Bonaventure, William of Ockham, John Duns Scotus.

39. Wittstadt, *op. cit.*, p. 184. "Das Konzil soll der Wiedervereinigung der Christenheit dienen" (emphasis mine).

by the hierarchy in mid-July and the responses were due by early September. There were only six weeks for working time, and this period covered the span of the European summer holidays.

Jaeger was, in fact, saying that the rubric imposed by the Central Commission was downright laughable. All of Europe takes a one-month holiday in August. Who would be there at the post office, let alone in the Central Commission itself, to receive all of these filled-out rogatories by 1 September? Jaeger had a few more things to say in that letter. First, he did not like the rumors coming forth, which stated that "The majority of Roman officials do not look too friendly upon the Council and endeavor to render it as innocuous as possible. . . . Such gossip is not good and severely damages the Church, above all, in the eyes of people of different faiths. It would be well if the Holy Father would soon make known the exact themes of the coming Council."[40]

It was in part that Bea responded in his 15 September letter with suggestions of ecclesiology and the office of bishops. Bea's letter also contained a prophecy in that he foresaw a definite place for the laity in the deliberations of the Council.[41] At the moment, Cardinal Ottaviani was thundering about "the approaching danger of rampant laicism."[42] For his part, Jaeger could also see "the Laity as true members of the Pre-preparatory Commission." Still, Jaeger remained exuberant when he wrote, "Despite the *prima vista* unfavourable assumptions, in which the preparations for the Second Vatican Council begin, there should nevertheless be no great disappointment on our part."[43] This was a man with a vision and one filled with great optimism about it. Almost a year later, on 15 May 1960, he briefly stated what he always believed: "This Council is not a matter which would pertain to and enliven the inner life of Catholicism only, but it is a matter which affects Christianity in its entirety, in its depth and concerns Christianity as a whole."[44] And then the bomb dropped!

40. Jaeger to Bea, 13 August 1959, Vicar General's Archives, Paderborn. "Die Mehrheit der römischen Beamten sei dem Konzil nicht freundlich gesonnen und darum bestrebt, es zu einer möglichst harmlosen Angelegenheit zu machen. . . . Solches Gerede ist nicht gut und schadet vor allem in den Augen der Andersgläubigen der Kirche sehr. Es würde gut sein, wenn der Hl. Vater recht bald die genauen Themen für das kommende Konzil bekanntgeben würde."

41. Bea to Jaeger, 15 September 1959, Vicar General's Archives, Paderborn.

42. Wittstadt, *op. cit.,* p. 183: "überhandnehmenden Laizismus."

43. *Ibid.* "Trotz der prima vista ungünstigen Voraussetzungen, unter denen die Vorarbeiten für das II. Vatikanum beginnen, sollte unsererseits keine Enttäuschung laut werden."

44. *Ibid.* "Das Konzil ist keine Angelegenheit, die nur den Katholizismus innerkirchlich angehen und erregen würde, sondern es ist eine Angelegenheit, die die ganze Christenheit aufs tiefste bewegt und die Christenheit als ganze angeht."

The Rhodes Meeting and Its Aftermath

On 21 October 1959, Jaeger wrote to Bea that he had just returned from a month of conferring the Sacrament of Confirmation. He was grateful for the information Bea passed on to him about the German Catechism, etc., and he also spoke of a terrible misunderstanding which occurred on the Island of Rhodes, involving two members of the Catholic Conference for Ecumenical Questions, World Council of Churches' Officials and Orthodox representatives.[45]

In August 1959, a meeting of the Central Committee of the World Council of Churches had assembled at Rhodes. Monsignor Johannes Willebrands and Father Christophe Dumont, O.P., were likewise present as "observers." Because of the restrictions imposed by the protocols of the World Council of Churches and the Holy Office directives, both priests could, on this occasion, only enjoy the status of "journalists." In the course of the gathering, Dumont attempted to arrange a friendly encounter with the Orthodox representatives who were present. This initiative occasioned a misunderstanding among the administrative authorities of both the World Council of Churches' General Secretariat and the Central Committee. These authorities interpreted Dumont's friendly gesture as an attempt to entice the Orthodox from their commitment to membership in the World Council of Churches. Ensuing confusion precipitated the cancellation of a special Orthodox–Roman Catholic meeting already scheduled for Venice within two months.[46]

Among the small but growing number of Roman Catholic experts in ecumenical affairs, the Rhodes Incident produced much sadness. It likewise fanned the flames of an already existing desire to have a Roman Catholic bureau, at the Vatican, to "intervene in official terms to clear up such misunderstandings in the future." Archbishop Jaeger, in turn, had written to express his anguish to Father Bea on 21 October, and later on 8 November 1959. The news of the mishap at Rhodes had produced such ill feelings within the Holy Office, which had, in turn, postponed indefinitely, and practically annulled, the theological meeting of Father Dumont and Monsignor Willebrands with the Orthodox in Venice. The same negative attitude likewise threatened Willebrands' projected meeting with the Protestants in Assisi around the same time. Jaeger bemoaned "that in Rome sufficient knowledge of the German situation and of the psychological condition of

---

45. Jaeger to Bea, 21 October 1959, Vicar General's Archives, Paderborn.
46. Schmidt, *op. cit.,* p. 322.

German Protestantism is not available" [dass in Rom keine genügende Kenntnis der deutschen Situation und der psychologischen Gegebenheiten im deutschen Protestantismus vorhanden sind].[47] Jaeger typed the letter himself and began very formally: "Sehr verehrter, hochwürdiger Herr Pater Bea" [Esteemed and Most Reverend Dear Father Bea]. Jaeger then reported:

> An unfortunate mishap appears to have descended upon the efforts of the good Professor Willebrands. First came the breakdown in Rhodes. Here, this morning, in the press, the news came that the Holy Office has postponed indefinitely, and practically annulled, the proposed theological meeting of P. Dumont and Professor Willebrands with the Orthodox in Venice, and even the planned meeting of Willebrands with the Protestants in Assisi. I do not perceive what is being played out here.[48]

Bea responded with a long missive on 3 November 1959.[49] After greeting the Archbishop, he indicated that he had spoken recently to the Reverend Doctor Hans Heinrich Harms, a World Council of Churches official for Faith and Order matters. Harms was in Rome at the time. During the course of their long conversation, they discussed the Rhodes Incident. Dr. Harms was of the opinion that the relationship of Rome with the World Council of Churches *had* been severely affected by the Rhodes Incident.

---

47. Jaeger to Bea, 21 October 1959, Vicar General's Archives, Paderborn.

48. *Ibid.* See Schmidt, *op. cit.*, p. 323. "Ein rechter Unstern scheint über den Bemühungen des guten Professor Msgr. Willebrands zu ruhen. Erst kam die Panne in Rhodos. Heute morgen geht hier durch die Presse die Nachricht, das HI. Offizium habe das für 1960 von P. Dumont und Professor Willebrands in Aussicht genommene Theologentreffen mit den Orthodoxen in Venedig und ebenso das von Villebrands geplante Treffen mit den Protestanten in Assisi auf unbestimmte Zeit vertagt und damit praktisch annulliert. Ich durchschaue nicht, was da gespielt haben mag."

49. On 21 October 1959, Archbishop Jaeger wrote to Father Bea, who was then in retirement at the Pontifical Biblical Institute. This letter was a response to Bea's letters and *votum* of 15 September, regarding the preparation of the German Catechism. Jaeger had been away for a month on his autumn Confirmation tour. His letter spoke of the effect Bea's *votum* had had on Pastor Max Lackmann. All of this pertained to the above-cited preparation of a German catechism. Jaeger likewise reviewed Lackmann's abstract of the same subject as well. He wrote: "I shall inform you further, as soon as I have an answer from Pastor Lackmann [about this project]." He also reported: "The leading men of the 'Assembly' (Evangelical) wish to meet in mid-November, to attend to, as Pastor Lackmann writes, 'the preparation of the Council!'" So beyond Jaeger's expectations and first report, the German Protestant theologians had indeed progressed in their enthusiasm for the Council.

Bea's entire letter was long, but was filled with passion. In this letter, Bea began to take the lead. The news of the Rhodes Incident had obviously upset him very much. He indicated that he took the time to inform himself about it. Somehow, in the intervening time, while Harms[50] was visiting Rome, Bea had come into contact with him. A few lines from this letter are very telling:

> We [Bea and Harms] talked naturally, in detail, about the entire Rhodes Incident, which, alas, has caused such a stir! Doctor Harms also thought that the relationship between Rome and the World Council had become very clouded. He did not talk [to me] about Visser 't Hooft, although I mentioned the name. It appears to me that the role of Visser 't Hooft is to seek to discover the thing that is causing the crises. He will obviously, under all circumstances, keep the Orthodox in the World Council, and now he has arrived at the position that he is happy whether or not they are willing to go to Venice or Assisi.[51]

In another paragraph, Bea indicated to his correspondent that some of the confusion on the part of the Roman Catholics, who were still trying to digest the significance of the Rhodes Incident, stemmed from the fact that they did not know the World Council of Churches' players. He mentioned there were self-contradictory interventions, for example, by a Greek Metropolitan, named Iacovos, on 2 and 29 September. In fact, *there were two* Orthodox bishops present with the same name. Both represented the Ecumenical Patriarchate but in different capacities. At any rate, General Secretary Visser 't Hooft was not under the "strict admonition" of Greek Metropolitan Iacovos of 29 September ("Nicht hinter der scharfen Erklärung des Jacovos vom 29 September steht.")[52] The next paragraph is likewise telling.

---

50. Harms was already an official of the World Council of Churches and was destined to become moderator of the Faith and Order Commission of the World Council from 1967 to 1971.

51. Bea to Jaeger, 3 November 1959, Vicar General's Archives, Paderborn. "Wir sprachen natürlich eingehend über die ganze Rhodos-frage, die leider so viel Staub aufgewirbelt hat. Auch Dr. Harms bedauert, dass das Verhältnis Rom-Weltrat dadurch sehr getrübt worden ist. Über Visser' t Hooft sprach er nicht, obwohl ich den Namen nannte. Mir scheint, dass bei Visser 't Hooft die treibende Kraft in der Krise zu suchen ist. Er will offenbar unter allen Umständen die Orthodoxen beim Weltrat halten und hat es nun auch glücklich erreicht, dass sie weder nach Venedig noch nach Assisi gehen wollen."

52. *Ibid.* In this instance, the phrase "strict admonition" signifies "not accountable to."

Anyhow, what is behind the action that the Holy Office had somehow taken, in reference to Venice and Assisi, I do not know. Neither did Doctor Harms know anything about it. He said that he himself had called off the Assisi meeting, since the Orthodox had explained that they would not come. Even if the Orthodox had refused to go to Venice, therefore the meeting in Assisi would naturally have been groundless also. The Holy Office, at least, could have recorded these things. Nonetheless, one sees in the posture of the Orthodox, that the efforts of Geneva to hold them was completely successful, so favourable beforehand, was the atmosphere in which the (unofficial) conversation at Rhodes had taken place. The continuance of the Orthodox in the World Council is a matter of life and death for its "ecumenical" character.[53]

In the same paragraph, in uncharacteristic language for him, Bea put some blame on Rome and indeed upon his fellow Jesuits: "The confusion, to which Vatican radio contributed its part, demonstrates therefore two things."[54]

The first of the two needs, delineated by Bea, encompassed clarity, objectivity, and authenticity; in short, he wanted to see a "Press Office" *(Sala Stampa)* at the Vatican. "The Vatican must have a 'Press Office,' the head of which would be responsible for *everything* that emanates from the Vatican, in the *Osservatore Romano,* on the radio, and on the television."[55] Bea indicated that, in fact, this was proposed by the Secretary of State, Domenico Cardinal Tardini, only a few days before in a kind of press conference where he spoke of the needs for the Council. Tardini foresaw the need for a press bureau set up specifically to clarify the deliberations

---

53. *Ibid.* "Was Assisi und Venedig betrifft, war mir nicht bekannt, dass das HI. Offizium irgendwie eingegriffen habe. Auch Dr. Harms weiss nichts davon. Er sagte mir, dass *er* selbst das Treffen von Assisi abgesagt habe, da die Orthodoxen erklärt hatten, dass sie nicht kommen würden. Ebenso hätten sich die Orthodoxen geweigert, nach Venedig zu gehen, womit die Zusammenkunft in Venedig natürlich gegenstandslos geworden sei. Das HI. Offizium hätte also höchstens diese Tatsachen registrieren können. Aber man sieht aus der Haltung der Orthodoxen, dass die Bemühungen von Genf, sie bei der Stange zu halten, vollen Erfolg hatten, so günstig vorher die Stimmung bei dem (inoffiziellen) Gespräch [sic] in Rhodos gewesen war. Das Verbleiben der Orthodoxen im Weltrat ist für dessen 'ökumenischen' Charakter eine Lebensfrage."

54. *Ibid.* "Die Verwirrung, zu der auch das Vatikanische Radio seinen Teil beigetragen hat, zeigt allerdings zwei Dinge."

55. *Ibid.* "dass der Vatican notwendig eine *Pressestelle* haben müsste, deren Chef verantwortlich wäre für alles, was im Osserv. Romano, im Radio, im Fernsehdienst, vom Vatikan ausgeht."

and decisions made by the Council Fathers. Bea confided that he had approached the German Bishops Conference with such a suggestion sometime previously, in the hope that they would present this need.

The second concern of Bea was the so-called official "Office for Experts" *(offizielle Gutachterstelle)* concerning the question of Protestantism and the Ecumenical Movement. Bea stated what he was looking for and it was all positive in character, i.e., "concerning what we have in common" [was damit in Zusammenhang steht, betreffen].[56] It is interesting to note that Bea had come around to an idea that was previously passed onto him by Jaeger. Bea focused upon the Churches of the Classical Reformation as the principal interest of this new office, *über die Fragen die den Protestantismus* (concerning the issues of Protestantism). He also emphasized the goal of convergence.

While at this time he had not moved away from a theology of "return," he was beginning to demonstrate the inauguration of a new theological process, which sought "convergence." A bureau of this kind did not exist at all. Bea named a group of individual experts in Rome including a Monsignor Hudal and Fathers Boyer, Witte, and Dambariena. He also included himself. What Bea was asking for was innovative, "a new kind of 'Secretariat,' which assembles information and disseminates it; and, (also) gives inspiration, information, etc." He wrote: "It appears to me that we would require much sooner an 'office' [*Amt*], a kind of Secretariat." Bea had spoken recently to Charles Boyer, S.J., to see if *The Center Unitas* could not be oriented toward this direction. Boyer was favorable, but how was the plan to begin to formulate? Bea thought that the best way to broach the recommendation for an official Church organ to carry out the above-outlined task would be from a national Bishops Conference.[57]

Bea's recommendation made sense. Not only was the time ripe, but Bea had detected from his conversation with Doctor Harms that "without further ado, within German Protestantism there remains a remarkable desire for unity and he himself informed me about the case of [the New Testament form critic, Professor Martin] Dibelius." Also, of course, at that time, the Bishops were being consulted for the preparations for the Council. Bea's aspiration was to have the Bishops Conference of Germany recommend to Rome the foundation of an appropriate bureau to acknowledge the development of the Ecumenical Movement. The recommendation was both expedient and timely. The scope of the new body was not historical

---

56. *Ibid.*
57. *Ibid.* "mir scheint, wir würden viel eher ein "Amt," eine Art Sekretariat brauchen."

but contemporary. Seemingly, Bea looked with some yearning at the scope and function of the World Council of Churches, for he wrote to Jaeger: "Opposite the exemplary organization of the World Council [of Churches] . . . a corresponding Catholic organ would be a pressing need." However, Bea knew Rome well, for he wrote at the end of this paragraph: "But it will not be set in motion here, if a strong push from outside does not come."[58]

After dealing with some lesser matters, Bea signed off to Archbishop Jaeger. He did so with growing enthusiasm for the Ecumenical Movement. In light of the entire letter, his closure was more than a polite "Hail and farewell" [*ave et vale*]: "But if I can be, in some way, useful to Your Excellency and, the common task, I am always happy to be at your disposal." *Bea was now a committed ecumenist.*[59]

Jaeger's response to Father Bea came on 8 November 1959. His reference to the August Rhodes Incident came after a discussion of the unique situation in Germany in which he had to work. In fact, as earlier indicated, part of his diocese was in the Eastern Zone (DDR), and for one and a half years he had been prohibited from entry. This would have been a particularly tense time for him, for Berlin, the city in which he had to meet his clergy, was now moving toward the center of world attention in the Cold War situation. Ever the ecumenist, the first part of his letter was somewhat chatty. He spoke of the shifting relations between the Land Churches (Lutheran), the Evangelical Church and the Reformed of the Union Church. He wrote from his unique perspective: "The entire life of Protestantism [in Germany] is distinguished by a nervous unease and a convulsive stirring to imitate the Catholic Church in all things. The reaction to every move and every communiqué of the Church, is, at present, exceedingly intensive. Severe pronouncements of Evangelical Church leaders and pastors, of such a kind, occur again as no longer have been heard for years." In other words, along with the political difficulties of the nation, Jaeger was reporting to Bea that there was an outbreak, yet again, of anti-Catholicism.[60]

---

58. *Ibid.* "ohne weiteres zugegeben, dass bei den deutschen Protestanten die Einigkeit ganz bedeutend zu wünchen ubrig lässt, und hat selbst auf den Fall Dibelius hingewiesen. . . . Gegenüber der musterhaften Organisation des Weltrats . . . wäre eine entsprechende katholische Stelle ein dringendes Bedürfnis. . . . Aber man wird sich hier nicht in Bewegung setzen, wenn nicht ein kräftiger Anstoss von aussen kommt."

59. *Ibid.* "Aber wenn ich Ew. Exzellenz und der gemeinsamen Sache irgendwie dienlich sein kann, stehe ich immer gerne zur Verfügung."

60. Jaeger to Bea, 8 November 1959, Vicar General's Archives, Paderborn. "Das gesamte Leben des Protestantismus ist gekennzeichnet durch eine nervöse Unruhe und das krampfhafte Bestreben, es in allem der katholischen Kirche gleichzutun. Die Reaktion auf jede

In a long and telling narrative, Jaeger likewise reported on the pastoral problem of mixed marriages. He wrote: "They certainly know that thick book, concerning the question of mixed-marriage, which was published by the Confession Information Institute of the *Evangelical Bund* in Benshein. All Protestant Pastors, Lutherans, as well as Reformed and United, have been stirred up." Jaeger's anger was scarcely veiled. He saw many Catholic partners of mixed marriages as weakened. Their vulnerability was embellished by continued house visits by Protestant pastors, who made it a point to accompany the Baptism of the first child and the enrollment of that child in the Evangelical School with continued pressure. Jaeger wrote: "It is a pity, in contrast, that our clergy are so very indifferent. Perhaps the time for such intense home visitations is lacking as a result of their commitments."[61]

Then Jaeger turned his attention towards the Rhodes affair. There seems to be in that correspondence a harsh judgment regarding Wilhelm Visser 't Hooft, the General Secretary of the World Council of Churches. At any rate, his opinion about motives and reactions regarding the Rhodes affair revealed that Jaeger himself was something of a religious political insider:

> In regard to the Rhodes Incident, I agree with you that the entire maelstrom would have been made known to Visser 't Hooft, because he must hold the Orthodox by the handle at any price. *The continuance of the Orthodox in the World Council is a question of life and death for Geneva.* At best, it illustrates the agreement that Visser 't Hooft had obtained in reference to the Ecumenical Institute *Hochschule* [high school, referring to the Ecumenical Institute] in Bossey. Visser 't Hooft inaugurated the Church Leadership function of the Executive of the World Council there. Obviously, Visser 't Hooft wishes to make the World Council "suitable for presentation" [*Hoffähig*] as a genuine dialogue partner to Rome. To establish it, he assembled a community of 173 united Churches in the World Council, so that it [the World Coun-

---

Massnahme und jede Verlautbarung der Kirche ist z.Zt. überaus heftig. Es fallen wieder derart scharfe Äusserungen von evangelischen Kirchenführern und Pfarrern, wie man sie seit Jahren nicht mehr zu hören bekommen hat."

61. *Ibid.* "Sie kennen sicherlich das dicke Buch, was zur Frage der Mischehe herausgebracht worden ist von Konfessionskundlichen Institut des Evangelischen Bundes in Benscheim. Alle protestantischen Pfarrer, lutherische wie refomierte und unierte, sind aufgeputscht worden. . . . Leider ist unser Klerus alldem gegenüber viel zu gleichgültig. Vielleicht fehlt auch, infolge der Arbeitsüberlastung, die Zeit zu solch intensiven Hausbesuchen."

cil] should not "remain empty." In the middle of this surprising development and the suddenly egressing complications of our time, fast decisions are demanded. It must be decided now if the Church will be left out of these experiences and out of the opportunity to contribute its proper perspectives, or if the World Council could give directives to the Church in certain questions.[62]

I suspect that the development, for which Visser 't Hooft strove so zealously cannot be so clearly traced. The Conference at Rhodes, with the arrangements of the International Mission Council in the World Council of Churches, [and] furthermore, the ungrounded severe action of Visser 't Hooft concerning the unfortunate announcement of the Press Agency about the meeting [*Sprach* — conversation] of Professor Willebrands and Father Dumont, with the Orthodox are together only steps along the way to the goal which Visser 't Hooft had in mind. He wishes within the Ecumenical World Council to create a counterpart to *the universal Church of Rome.* We must also in the near future learn to do several things, since Visser 't Hooft is an exceedingly clever and astute Church politician, who is endowed with an enormously great measure of strength and organizational skill. The Vatican should keep this danger in mind, and establish at Rome an official *Gutachterstelle* [a bureau of experts], *which must be affiliated with a Press office.*[63]

62. *Ibid.* "Zu der Rhodos-Affäre bin ich mit Ihnen der Meinung, das der ganze Wirbel von Visser 't Hooft bewusst gemacht worden ist, weil er um jeden Preis die Orthodoxen bei der Stange halten muss. Es ist der Verleib der Orthodoxen im Weltrat eine Lebensfrage für Genf. Am besten beleuchtet das der Vertrag, den Visser 't Hooft vor der ökumenischen Hochschule in Bossey gehalten hat. Visser 't Hooft forderte dort kirchenleitende Funktionen für die Exekutive des Weltrates. Offenbar will Visser 't Hooft den Weltrat 'offähig' machen zu einem echten Gesprächspartner für Rom. Zur Begründung führt er ann [*sic*], die Gemeinschaft der 173 im Weltrat zusammengeschlossen Kirchen dürfte nicht 'leer bleiben'. Inmitten der überraschenden Entwicklung und plötzlich auftretenden Komplikationen unserer Zeit erforderte es schnelle Entscheidungen. Es müsse [*sic*] jetzt entschieden werden, ob es den Kirchen überlassen bliebe, aus diesen Ereignissen ihre eigenen Folgerungen zu ziehen, oder ob der Weltrat in gewissen Fragen den Kirchen Direktiven geben könne" (emphasis mine).

63. *Ibid.* "Ich meine, deutlicher könnte sich die Entwicklung gar nicht abzeichnen, die Visser 't Hooft zielsicher anstrebt. Die Konferenz von Rhodos mit der Einordnung des Internationalen Missionsrates in den Weltrat der Kirchen, ferner die unbegründet scharfte Reaktion Visser 't Hoofts auf die unglückliche Meldung der Presseargenturen über das Gespräch von professor Willebrands und Pater Dumont mit den Orthodoxen sind alles nur Schritte auf dem Wege zum Ziel, das Visser 't Hooft vorschwebt. Er will im ökumenischen Weltrat das Pendant zur Universalkirche Roms schaffen. Wir werden in den nächsten Jahren uns noch auf mancherlei gefasst machen müssen, denn Visser 't Hooft ist ein überaus kluger und geschickter Kirchenpolitiker, der mit einen ungewöhnlich grossen Mass von Kraft und

With this letter Jaeger painted a sinister picture of Wilhelm Visser 't Hooft. He picked up on the hint thrown to him by Bea in his previous letter of 3 November — "Rome will act if an outside source shows initiative and prods a decision." It is as if the two clerics detected a lack of compulsion in the Roman style of decision making, i.e., one of offense and defense. Having presented the problem of potential leadership in the ecumenical world, Jaeger then called for the solution with the official *Gutachterstelle,* i.e., the bureau of experts, which must be affiliated with the Press Office.

The third component of this now developing vision of unity for the Church was the need for a *Fachmann,* or a "leader expert"! The urgency of a proper leader in ecumenism was now underscored by the evidence that Archbishop Jaeger was becoming increasingly suspicious of the World Council of Churches and its *Fachmann,* Doctor Visser 't Hooft. Jaeger then went through a list and dismissed Père Boyer as too old, and Professor Witte as perhaps not competent enough in organization and publicity matters. "Anyway," he said, "a single person cannot, above all, carry out such an office." He then went on to speak of potential resources from the German sector, from the Johann Adam Möhler Institute, and from Herder Correspondence. From the French, he proposed the Centre d'Istina. In times of rapid social change, one must attempt to keep up with every new development. Finally, he returned to the concept of *Gutachterstelle,* the proposed Vatican-based official bureau of experts.[64]

In the meantime, Bea was informed of his elevation to the rank of Cardinal on 16 November. Amidst piles of letters and telegrams of congratulations, Bea took the time to respond on 30 November to Jaeger's letter of 8 November. This reply further broadened the scope of Jaeger's aspiration. Bea was definitely in sympathy with Jaeger's thought. Specifically, Bea used here the word "promotion" of Christian unity for the first time, which implied not merely the representation of facts or diplomatic intervention, but rather the creative fostering of the ecumenical endeavor. Thus, he recognized the validity of the movement, already inaugurated by Orthodox, Anglicans and Protestants, and he endeavored to broaden the ecumenical thrust in such a manner that the Roman Catholic world could participate.[65]

---

organisatorischen Geschick ausgestattet ist. Der Vatikan sollte diesen Gefahren ins Auge sehen und eine offizielle Gutachterstelle in Rom einrichten, der eine Pressestelle angegliedert sein müsste" (emphasis mine).

64. *Ibid.* "Ein einzelner Mann kann überhaupt ein solches Amt nicht verwalten."

65. Bea to Jaeger, 30 November 1959, Vicar General's Archives, Paderborn. "Promotion of Christian Unity" was to become part of the official title for the new dicastery, which he would propose.

His words show his skill at Curial protocol: "The most important thing," he wrote, "is certainly the question of a representation of the ecumenical movement in Rome. As soon as the celebrations are over [those associated with receiving the Red Hat], I shall speak directly to the Holy Father about it. Just as a *'Commissio pro-Russia'* was created at the time, so such a one *'pro promotione oecumenica'* [*sic*] could be set up now." At that point, Bea had not yet had his first private audience with Pope John XXIII. They had not even previously known each other. Bea was aware, however, that, as a Cardinal, he would enjoy personal access to the Pope.[66]

Pope John XXIII imposed the Red Hat upon Augustin Bea on 14 December 1959. For that occasion, the Cardinal Secretary of State prepared a brief: "German . . . biblicist, was confessor to Pius XII."[67] All three points were significant, as will be seen. While the Pope's interest in internationalizing the Roman Curia and reorganizing the Pontifical Biblical Commission was important, Bea brought his German nationality and all that it implied, and particularly his biblical expertise, to the ecumenical question. The third point of Tardini's memo revealed the homage John wished to pay to the memory of his predecessor, Pope Pius XII. There were, of course, other German Jesuits who had served that Pontiff, viz., Robert Leiber, who was private secretary to Pius, and Wilhelm Hentrich, who was the librarian of the Papal Apartments. Lieber was also a professor of history and theology at the Gregorian University. Of the three, Pope John chose Bea. It was not known in Rome that Bea had developed a personal interest in ecumenism that would now be disclosed. Out of two disparate events, the Rhodes affair of August 1959 and his elevation as the Cardinal Deacon of St. Sabas, Bea emerged as *Fachmann* for ecumenism.

The Rhodes event should not be looked upon from hindsight as a negative affair. It sparked a sense of urgency and of realism. Truly it was the catalyst event which brought about more ecumenical action than had been previously anticipated from the Catholic Church. Clearly the memory of it stayed with Bea, for in 1961, when he was publishing so prolifically, he spoke of the Rhodes Incident favorably. Here, the non-Catholic world accepted and welcomed the forthcoming Vatican Council. It is obvious that the misfortune of Monsignor Johannes Willebrands and Father Dumont

---

66. *Ibid.* "Das Wichtigste ist wohl die Frage einer Vertretung der ökumenischen Bewegung in Rom. Wenn die Festlichkeiten vorüber sind, werde ich einmal direkt mit dem Hl. Vater darüber sprechen. Wie man s. Zt. eine "Commissio pro Russia" gebildet hat, so könnte man jetzt eine solche 'pro motione oecumenica' machen."

67. Schmidt, *op. cit.,* p. 308.

provided Bea with much food for thought. For so it seemed, the fallen apple contained seeds for a new tree.

The Cardinalate, Bea, and Jaeger

As already stated, in the midst of the correspondence between Jaeger and Bea regarding the foundation of a *Gutachterstelle,* the bureau for ecumenical affairs at Rome, Bea found himself nominated Cardinal. Just when he thought he had reached retirement, a whole new world opened for him. It is worthy to note here that Jaeger himself was also being talked about in Rome as a possible candidate as Cardinal, to be elevated in the very consistory which gave the Red Hat to Augustin Bea. He, too, was talked about as a potential permanent member of the Preparatory Commission for the General Council of the Church, with the specific responsibility of spokesman for ecumenical questions.

On 21 November 1959, Höfer wrote to Jaeger from the German Embassy in Rome: "You, yourself, came to the forefront of suitable candidates in regard to the question. At the same time, it was commonly realized that you would then have to leave Germany, where a comparable replacement would be difficult to find."[68] Jaeger's reply followed on 26 November 1959: "The naming of Bea has resulted here in universal joy, but I believe the one most so is myself. It would have been completely impossible for me to give up Paderborn and go to Rome. And even if a command came, I would have had to decline it because I am simply incapable of adjusting to the Roman scene. I regard the election of P. Bea, especially in light of the coming Council as extremely fortunate."[69] Jaeger already saw, in the selection of Bea as Cardinal, the elevation of one of the great leaders of the Council.

At this point, Jaeger had personally taken up the cause of the Council

68. Höfer to Jaeger, 21 November 1989, Vicar General's Archives, Paderborn. "Sie traten selbst in der Vordergrund der in Frage kommenden Persönlichkeiten. Gleichzeitig wurde gewöhnlich bedauert, dass Sie dann Deutschland verlassen müssten, wo ein angemessener Ersatz schwer zu finden sein würde."

69. Jaeger to Höfer, 26 November 1959, Vicar General's Archives, Paderborn. "Die Ernennung P. Beas hat hier allgemeine Freude ausgelöst, aber ich glaube, die allermeiste bei mir. Es wäre für mich ganz unmöglich gewesen, Paderborn aufzugeben und nach Rom zu ziehen. Und selbst auf einen Befehl hin hätte ich mich weigern müssen, weil ich einfach ausserstande bin, auf dem römmischen Parkett mich zu bewegen. Ich halte die Wahl P. Beas gerade im Hinblick auf das kommende Konzil für ausserordentlich erfreulich."

with fervor in his own country. He began and finished a book about this Council, comparing it to its predecessor, Vatican Council I. He hoped that the Johannine Council would be very different in style and form. In this book, too, Jaeger stated that in the history of the Church, there actually exists no set pattern for a General Council. One outstanding sentence sums up the book's theme: "Equally, a Council's form depends upon the prevailing relationship between the Church and its environment, for clearly, the Church exists in the actual world, not in a vacuum." Jaeger's propensity for ecclesiastical history is evident. The first four chapters demonstrate a multiplicity of styles, as they focus upon the previous twenty Councils. The specific ecumenical goal of the anticipated Vatican Council climaxed the theme of Jaeger's concluding chapter: "Knowing then that the unity of Christians is not the work of human prudence, and organizational ability, but is a gift of God's grace, we turn in faith, and confidence in prayer to the Paraclete, the soul of the Mystical Body, the Church, and the deepest principle of its unity."[70]

While Jaeger was writing his book, he and Stakemeier conducted lecture tours throughout Germany favoring an ecumenical theme within the Second Vatican Council. For example, on 29 March 1959, Jaeger's Easter message to his diocese touched on the theme of *Einheit* (Unity): "Just as the Apostles wanted to safeguard the unity [of the Church], so also those who came after, the Bishops, have only this pressing wish: to safeguard the unity of Christians and to unite the separated Christians again."[71]

On 19 June 1960, Jaeger presided at an open forum on ecumenism and the Council at the Benedictine Abbey of Maria Laach. He began with a briefing for both Catholic and Evangelical journalists. This press conference actually became a substantial talk, entitled "Das Ökumenische Konzil als Repräsentation der Gesamtkirche" (The Ecumenical Council as Representative of the Universal Church), in which he covered a multiplicity of subjects and in which he also spoke of the various types of Councils in their history and in their etiology. He essentially perceived the role of Bishop-in-Council as being responsible for the entire Church. He also perceived the twin themes of this, and every Council, as being *Einheit und Verbindung*

---

70. Lorenz Jaeger, *The Ecumenical Council: The Church in Christendom* (New York: P. J. Kennedy and Sons, 1961), p. 184.

71. "Und wie die Apostel die Einheit der Kirche zu wahren wussten, so haben auch deren Nachfolger, die Bischöfe, keinen dringenderen wunsch, als die Einheit der Christenheit zu Bewahren und die getrennten Brüder wieder zu vereinigen." Lorenz Jaeger, *Der Geist der Einheit: Eine Österliche Betrachtung zur Konzilsankündigung*, 29 March 1959, Vicar General's Archives, Paderborn. (Draft, p. 2.)

(Unity and Cohesion). By their consecration, bishops should be disposed to the dynamic of the Holy Spirit, Who is both *life giving and leading (belebt und leitet),* a very important ecclesiological distinction, in that the magisterial role of the local church and of the universal church go hand in hand. Therefore, all must be acutely aware of the expectation to develop an appropriate vision for the future.[72]

At the conclusion of the 1960 Church Unity Octave, Jaeger published an article for his diocese concerning the forthcoming Council, from the perspective of unity. Within that context, he stated that the leitmotif of all Conciliar preparations was about Church Unity and catholicity. Jaeger concluded by saying that the catholicity of the Church means that it possesses the fullness of truth, which, until the end of the world, can always be articulated in a fuller and fuller manner. Jaeger identified the corollary task for the Church as the maintenance of a sense of watchfulness as Sacred Revelation and Redemption unfold in culture and civilization.[73] To illustrate this, Jaeger concluded that article with a moving passage from the German Catholic poet, Gertrude von Le Fort:

> I was at home in the temples of your gods.
> I was dark in the stains of your fields.
> I was in the towers of your astronomers.
> I was with the single woman.
> I was the desire of all time.

> [Ich war heimlich in den Tempelen ihrer Götter;
> ich war dunkel in den sprüchen all ihrer Weisen.
> Ich war auf den Türmen ihrer Sternsucher;
> ich war bei den einsamen Frauen, auf die der geist fiel.
> Ich war die Sehnsucht aller zeiten.][74]

By use of this last poignant and familiar phrase, from *Hymns to the Church* (*Ich War die Sehnsucht Aller Zeiten* — "I Was the Desire of All Time"),

---

72. *Id.,* "Das Ökumenische Konzil als Repräsentation der Gesamtkirche," Undated and Unprotocoled, Vicar General's Archives, Paderborn.

73. *Id.,* "Das Konzil als Darstellung der Einheit und Katholizität der Kirche" (The Council as a Depiction of the Unity and Catholicity of the Church), 25 January 1960 (released 31 January 1960), Vicar General's Archives, Paderborn.

74. Miss von Le Fort composed these poems before her entry into the Church, in 1925. A feminist and philosopher, she was a friend and colleague of Edith Stein. She also was a native of Westphalia. See *Id., Hymns to the Church* (New York: Sheed and Ward, 1953), p. 21. Also translated in England as *The Holiness of the Church.*

Jaeger demonstrated how much Christ loves the Church! From that time on, Jaeger took over the project of responsibility for the written part of the collaborative project — between himself and Bea — to see established a permanent body, within the Roman Curia, for the sake of Christian Unity. As archbishop of a local church, and as founder and president of the Ecumenical Institute dedicated to Johann Adam Möhler, not to mention the two full decades as the lone episcopal voice in Germany, in which he squarely involved himself with ecumenical work, his sincere direct appeal would look mighty before the eyes of Pope John XXIII.

Thus when Augustin Bea was named Cardinal on 16 November 1959, the plan to effect the goal of a permanent Curial body was under way. However, until then, Bea had no idea how he was going to achieve the impossible. He possessed an admirable reputation in Rome. Still, he was all but helpless within the context of the Roman Curia. His nomination to the Red Hat *gave* him the necessary *prestige* and *entrée* into the chambers of the Pope. He became the *Fachmann* for whom he himself was looking. The first issue was the need to repair the misunderstanding at Rhodes. Besides hurt feelings, a sense of embarrassment, and the cancellation of the Venice and Assisi encounters, the mutual desire of both Jaeger and Bea was to avoid further misfortune, misunderstanding, and humiliation for the Church. Their collaboration, *coupled with their sense of history and their appreciation of scholarship,* expressed a realistic sensitivity for the work and activity of the universal movement for Christian Unity, as epitomized in the World Council of Churches. November 1959 might well go down in history as "the Ecumenical November"! Within those thirty days, a sense of *Realpolitik* emerged, along with the idea of formulating a letter to the Pope presenting the issues, the mood, and the need to become more precise about the cause of Christian Unity. In the midst of his celebrations, reception of the Cardinal's regalia, and ceremonial preoccupations, Bea never let the idea slip out of mind: *He had committed himself to a task and he would see it through.* The work on the letter of 4 March 1960 to Pope John XXIII began then.

Conclusion

It is important and interesting to note that as early as 1951 Jaeger identified the uniqueness of both Bea's person and his position. He wrote to Father Bea: "After all, you know the mind of the Holy Father and of the Holy Office about these matters. . . . You know, on the other hand, the German circumstances."[75] *The German circumstances* include many factors. First, Germany was the cradle of the Classical Reformation. Second, because Germany had been divided into multiple kingdoms, principalities, duchies, and otherwise independent territories, it did follow the principle, laid down by the Peace of Westphalia of 1648, thus guaranteeing a multiplicity of expressions in religious polity, culture, and practice. Third, this principle was solidified by Otto von Bismarck in 1870 at the inception of the German empire; it collapsed, however, in 1918 with the abdication of the Kaiser.

Individual initiatives for the sake of Christian unity were then ignited, and were popularly known as *Una Sancta* activity. In the early twentieth century, scientific historical scholarship pertaining to Reformation history manifested itself both before and during the Second World War. In the War-time period, Ecumenism found its German patron in Archbishop Lorenz Jaeger of Paderborn.

Jaeger's activity did more than encourage individual ecumenical initiatives; he sponsored them. Germany experienced what may very well be described as the worst cataclysm to befall any nation in human history. In the years between 1933 and 1945, it was dominated by a vicious, pagan, totalitarian regime. Germany was defeated by a coalition of Allies, who were determined to level the nation. For the Holocaust itself and the death of six million Jews, it stood alone, disgraced and in shame. Then, a greater humiliation was imposed, a division into a Communist and free zone. Yet it was expected that life would go on as normal under such circumstances. In the light of this history, the theologian Karl Adam presented a poignant ecumenical challenge:

> Does what we have been saying mean that in the event of a reunion, the Catholic is to remain in undisputed possession of his beliefs, whereas the Protestant is to abandon and even deny those truths which are characteristic of his religion and especially dear to him? . . . The question of reunion stands or falls by our answer to it.[76]

The question itself poses the possibility of the irrevocability of five hundred years of German history. It is almost as if Adam were saying "one cannot unring a bell." Yet another question is inherent here. Was anyone listening to Karl Adam? The answer is yes. Lorenz Jaeger was listening.

75. Jaeger to Bea, March 19, 1951, *op. cit.*
76. Cited in Tavard, *op. cit.*, p. 136.

Chapter V

The Letter

Introduction

This chapter presents the important letter of Archbishop Jaeger to Pope John XXIII of March 4, 1960. This is the letter that precipitated the foundation of the Secretariat for Promoting Christian Unity. It was indeed the collaborative effort of Archbishop Jaeger and Cardinal Bea. Cardinal Bea, together with Father Stakemeier, definitely drafted the letter. Jaeger signed the letter as a diocesan bishop and the head of the Möhler Ecumenical Institute. This letter is *the* formal document of petition. It is presented here in English for the first time, and is taken from the original Latin draft as located in the Vicar General's Archives at Paderborn.

However, the bulk of the responsibility was Bea's activity. *He* drafted the letter. He presented the letter. He accompanied the letter with his own petition. Unfortunately, his draft lies in the secret archives of the Vatican and is not yet available. It is known that Bea, through conversation, directed the purpose and scope of the new Curial body. It would be known, ultimately, as the Secretariat for Promoting Christian Unity. Archbishop Jaeger was directed by Pope John XXIII to prepare a statute, i.e., a document of constitution, which would serve as a mission statement and a provisional *modus operandi*, regarding the membership and function of this new body. What follows below is the narrative of events and the presentation of the text, as delivered into the hands of the pontiff.

Preparations for the Letter

In the time between his nomination and the actual ceremonies of his elevation, Bea wrote on 30 November to Archbishop Jaeger, renewing the pledge of his support for their common task. On 1 January 1960, Bea wrote to Jaeger's assistant, Professor Stakemeier, at the Johann Adam Möhler Institute, drafting his services to prepare the formal request, suggesting the creation of a special commission at the Vatican, to supervise issues associated with the Ecumenical Movement. In that same letter, Bea suggested that the best approach would be to address this request through recourse to the Pre-preparatory Conciliar Theological Commission with a special reference to the Cause of Ecumenism.[1]

On 6 January 1960, Archbishop Jaeger wrote to Bea that it would be "very fortunate" if "YOU would be entrusted with the leadership of the *commissio pro promotione oecumenica* [The Commission for the Promotion of Ecumenism] by the Holy Father."[2] On 9 January, Bea was finally received in private audience, for the first time, by Pope John XXIII. On this occasion, he expressed his ecumenical interest to Pope John. In fact, when he emerged from the audience with Pope John, Bea remarked to his awaiting secretary: "We understood each other perfectly."[3]

It was, however, to Jaeger that Bea confided the details of his conversation: "I have therefore instructed the Holy Father about the relationships that I formerly had with Catholic and non-Catholic circles of the Ecumenical Movement, and I asked him if I should serve further. He was very interested in it, and encouraged me also to work in this area in the future. He will remember it at the appropriate time, and thanked me greatly for the intervention. — So, that I am confirmed by the Highest Office to engage in the cause of reunion, and, I shall do this to the best of my ability."[4] Bea was

---

1. Schmidt, *op. cit.*, p. 323.

2. Jaeger to Bea, 6 January 1960, Vicar General's Archives, Paderborn (emphasis mine). "Recht glücklich würde ich sein, wenn Sie mit der Leitung einer Commissio pro motione oecumenica [*sic*] vom Hl. Vater beauftragt würden."

3. Schmidt, *op. cit.*, p. 324.

4. Bea to Jaeger, 13 January 1960, Vicar General's Archives, Paderborn. "Ich habe den HL. Vater auch unterrichtet über die Beziehungen, die ich bisher mit den Kreisen der ökumenischen Bewegung, katholischen und nicht-katholischen hatte und ihm grfragt, ob ich sie weiter pflegen solle. Er hat sich sehr dafür interessiert und mich ermuntert, auch in Zukunft auf diesem Gebiet zu arbeiten. Er werde sich bei gegebener Gelegenheit daran erinnern und danke mir sehr für die Mitteilung- somit bin ich also auch von höchster Stelle ermächtigt, mich mit den Anliegen der Wiedervereinigung zu befassen und werde dies tun, soweit es mir nur möglich ist."

thus moved to fulfill what had previously been expressed, between himself, Jaeger, Höfer and Stakemeier. "Already, there are so many Pontifical Commissions that it is not unusual if a Pontifical Commission will also be established for this area of concern."[5]

Bea's reference to a relationship between Catholic and non-Catholic circles was a direct reference to his time spent in the Holy Office.[6] During those ten years, he followed not only German affairs, *vis-à-vis* the Catholic Church, but also developments within German Protestant theology, which were pastoral and creative. Thus it could be said of him that he was generally aware of the state of theology in the principal German-speaking countries of Austria, Switzerland and Germany itself. Likewise, he was aware of the ethical and theological implications of collaborative religious resistance to the Nazis during the Hitler Era. Naturally, too, as has been demonstrated, he was aware of the developments of the *Una Sancta* Movement, which preceded the Second World War, and in the course of the War became associated with the Fulda Bishops Conference, and its ecumenical desk. Of course, without pronouncing the words, he was indicating his contact with the foremost ecumenical spokesperson for Catholic Germany, Lorenz Jaeger.

Perhaps Pope John recalled on 9 January 1960 that he had met Augustin Bea once before. This was during a *pro forma* visit to the Holy Office, where the members, consultors and staff assembled for the pope's brief *allegato* (review). On that occasion, when Pope John met Father Bea, he asked him: "Are there two Fathers Bea?" "No," replied the Jesuit, "I am the only one." "Eh," the Pope stated, "I thought there were two. There is so much writing. Keep up the good work!"[7]

Encouraged by his audience with Pope John, Bea wrote again to Stakemeier on 20 January, directing him to address the letter now to the desk of the Pope. He delivered a telling sentence: "The Holy Father knows I am deeply involved in the ecumenical question and he is very much in favour."[8]

On 28 January, Bea wrote yet again, proposing the inclusion of a title for the prospective Curial body. He wanted Commission for Promoting Christian Unity. The title *Christian* came to him from Article 381 of the *Acts of the Roman Synod* of 1960: "By Baptism, a man is a member of the Mystical Body of Christ the Priest, of the general title 'Christian.'" The article

---

5. *Ibid.* "Es gibt schon so viele 'Pontificiae Commissiones,' dass es nichts Besonderes ist, wenn auch für dieses Anliegen eine pontificia Commissio geschaffen wird."

6. Bea to Jaeger, 28 February 1960, Vicar General's Archives, Paderborn.

7. Schmidt, *op. cit.*, p. 307.

8. *Ibid.*, p. 324.

of the Synod of Rome, in turn, was inspired by the 1947 encyclical of Pope Pius XII, *Mediator Dei,* which stated that at Baptism, "through the general title as *Christian,* man becomes a member of the 'Mystical Body of Christ the Priest'" (No. 104). As a former member of the household of Pope Pius XII, indeed as his Confessor, Bea was thoroughly familiar with the language of that Pontiff's writings.[9] In commenting about the appropriateness of this appellation, the phraseology avoided the question of "return," which would be highly offensive to Protestants and Orthodox. The immediate and practical reference at hand is the terminology of Pope John's encyclical *Ad Petri Cathedram:*

> This prayer of Jesus that: "All may be one, even as thou, Father, in me and I in thee; that they also may be one in us (Jn 17:21)" was without a doubt accepted and heeded, because of its deep reverence. By this, we are given the most gratifying hope and assurance that, at some time, all the sheep that are not of this fold, will eventually desire to *return* to it. (No. 33)[10]

According to Peter Hebblethwaite, at first the leadership of the World Council of Churches found Pope John's terminology of *return* in *Ad Petri Cathedram* offensive. Knowing it not to be the intention of the Pontiff to alienate the World Council of Churches' leadership, especially at the very threshold of the Council, Bea devised a more appropriate application of language.[11] Certainly, according to Schmidt, Bea had followed closely the reports regarding Conciliar preparation, from his daily reading of *L'Osservatore Romano:*

> As concerns the celebration of the Ecumenical Council, the Holy Father does not intend it only as a means of building up the people for Christ, but also as a call to the separated communities for a search for unity, which so many souls today are yearning for in every part of the world.[12]

By use of this term, *Christian Unity,* Bea was providing the identification of *mutuality,* indigenous to Christian Unity, which is based upon the richness of that Baptismal Grace, which is already at work among all Christians,

---

9. *Ibid.*

10. (emphasis mine).

11. Hebblethwaite, *op. cit.,* pp. 323-33.

12. *Osservatore Romano,* 26/27 January 1959; cited in Schmidt, *op. cit.,* p. 293.

since, by Baptism, all are "in Christ." "God has put all things under His feet and made Him as the Ruler of Everything, and the Head of the Church, which is His Body, the fullness of Him, who fills the whole creation (Eph. 1:22-23)." In light of the above, Bea was seeking to exhibit that certain sensitivity which would comfort the apprehensions of those non-Catholic Christians who themselves were following the details of the Council's preparations.[13]

At this point, Lorenz Jaeger took over the project. As was cited above, Bea was in search of support from the Fulda Bishops Conference for the projected Rome bureau for Ecumenism. In place of the German Conference, Jaeger, as its ecumenical spokesperson, along with his role of archbishop of a local church, and the founder of the Möhler Institute, took on the burden. It was decided that the letter would bear his signature. It was a team effort. The draft, begun by Stakemeier, amended and refined by Bea, was signed by Jaeger, who by that act, bore the responsibility for its contents. It then became Jaeger's proposal, although Stakemeier appended his name and the support of the Möhler Institute to the request, in order to give it academic substance. The letter was dated 4 March. Jaeger formally submitted the entire package to Cardinal Bea on 5 March. His intermediary was Monsignor Josef Höfer at the German Embassy to the Holy See. It must be remembered that Höfer was a priest of the Archdiocese of Paderborn and a participative member of the Jaeger-Stählin Group. Furthermore, Höfer was actively affiliated with all the activities of the Möhler Institute. As a diplomat and ecclesiastic, as well as a valued ecumenical scholar in his own right, he now served as the very valuable agent for Jaeger, Stakemeier and Bea in this incident, facilitating communication and providing theological advice.[14]

In a kind of diplomatic mode, Jaeger took the formal role, i.e., the bishop who brought the project to fulfillment for pastoral reasons, involving the whole Church. By his reference to the Möhler Institute and the dignity of its credentials, he manifested the authenticity needed to convince the Pope. Jaeger's letter to Pope John was delivered by Cardinal Bea personally on 11 March.[15]

The letter, which is cited below, first of all, listed the existence and the work of various European ecumenical centers. Then the petition went on to

---

13. Schmidt, *op. cit.*, p. 324.

14. *Ibid.*, pp. 322-29.

15. *Ibid.*, p. 253. This methodology is in conformity with Bea's expectations. He always placed a priority on the role of the local Church and most especially the obligation of the bishop toward the fostering of unity.

state: "It is easy to appreciate that in an arduous field, such as this, these and similar bodies need the supreme concern and vigilance of the Apostolic See."[16] Jaeger maintained that a Pontifical Commission was needed, and should be established, to engender harmony among the various efforts to promote the unity of Christians in a variety of countries and regions. Furthermore, recommendations and directives were required to promote the endeavor. A Pontifical Commission would provide that special objectivity which is peculiar only to the Holy See, to facilitate gatherings and to delineate the differences indigenous to the specific goals associated with every project. Such a body would bring comfort, even joy, to Catholics, and it would make it easier for "non-Catholics of goodwill" to find the right path.

Bea's letter to the Pope accompanied Jaeger's request.[17] Through notes, and the Schmidt biography, one can observe that Bea both introduced and supported the words of Jaeger, calling the question of Christian Unity "complex." Bea referred to the Incident at Rhodes, in which a simple invitation to the Orthodox delegation created an unfortunate misunderstanding, and even hostility in the non-Catholic world. Drawing upon his experience as a longtime Roman, and as a member of the Papal Household of Pius XII, Bea indicated the interest of the Holy See in these matters, i.e., *per competenza* (competence) pertaining to the Holy Office, the Sacred Congregation of Rites, and the Sacred Congregation for the Oriental Churches. Harmony and balance were needed here as well. A permanent Curial body could thus provide the necessary orchestration, regarding these ecumenical issues, and offer a genuine ministry from within the Roman Curia.[18]

Bea's letter also addressed the needs of the forthcoming Vatican Council. Something was needed to pave the way for closer contacts between Roman Catholics, Orthodox, Anglicans and Protestants, and to serve as a catalyst to encourage initiatives of greater understanding and trust: "On the Protestant side, a great deal has been written about the hopes and also the fears that are felt, concerning the Council; but an office is needed in order to collect all this material, sift through the suggestions offered, and provide a clear response to the criticism and the difficulties expressed. This office would systematically collect all the relevant material,

---

16. See letter, below.

17. Upon his death, as is customary for a Cardinal, Bea's apartment was shut and sealed, and his letters and papers were carried to the Secret Archives of the Vatican, and are currently unavailable. What exists in this text, is gleaned from the uncatalogued archives of the Vicar General in Paderborn.

18. Schmidt, *op. cit.,* p. 393.

examine it, or have it examined by experts in these matters, and take or propose necessary and appropriate measures."[19]

It is clear that Jaeger and Bea consulted in regard to the appropriate manner of approaching the establishment of a Curial body for promoting the cause of Christian Unity. The only effective means of obtaining results for the cause of ecumenism would have to be an appeal to the highest authority. Conscious of the sad implications of the Rhodes Incident, which might occur again and again, Jaeger and Bea decided upon a direct approach to Pope John XXIII. Bea advised in practical terms that not only should the Incident be mentioned, but also there was just as great a need for good communications about these matters between the Vatican dicasteries. Bea spoke of the forthcoming Council in terms which implied the inauguration of dialogue with non–Roman Catholic Christians. He mentioned the feasibility of collecting material and addressing suggestions and criticisms offered by Protestants and Orthodox, in regard to the Council. In the mutually collaborative effort, Bea and Jaeger addressed a point of almost immediate urgency, one especially contained in the explication of the Council's goals, through *Ad Petri Cathedram*.

This, Pope John's first encyclical, spoke of the cause of unity; but it did so in general terms, including such themes as unity within the family, unity between employer and employee and unity among the nations. However, in light of continual friction in the world of religion and within the international sphere, it was indeed necessary to address the cause of Christian Unity in the middle of the twentieth century.[20] Drawing from the already existing pre-history of the Roman Catholic Ecumenical Movement, Jaeger and Bea presented John with the theory, already operative among those engaged in this work, and they asked him to address it in terms of the preparation for the Second Vatican Council. Pope John *would respond positively* to both prelates. Below, the official letter, signed by Archbishop Jaeger, is cited in full.[21]

---

19. Cited in *ibid.*, p. 326.

20. See Flamini, *op. cit.*, pp. 85-87. It is the observation of Roland Flamini that the fructification of John's pontificate is found in the encyclical *Pacem in Terris*, of 11 April 1963. John, as the son of farmers, had never grown above the land. It is he who gave pontifical expression to the term "active solidarity." Because John did not separate religion from the international order, he wrote and spoke of the "common good of the entire human family" (no. 98). Also, he admonished that all "have the right and duty therefore to live in communion with one another" (no. 100).

21. The Latin text draft is located in the Vicar General's Archives in Paderborn. The author obtained the photostatic copy of the original on 15 October 2001. The translation, editing, and format is done by the author. The original is presented in the Appendix of this thesis.

The Text of the Letter

4 March 1960
Paderborn

Most Holy Father:

Humbly prostrate at the feet of Your Holiness, I, the Archbishop of Paderborn, and the President of the Institute named after Johann Adam Möhler, together with the Vice Rector and the directors of the Institute, eagerly request Your Holiness to deign to establish a Pontifical Commission to Promote Christian Unity. The role of this Commission would be to observe and to help those meetings and projects, which would unite all those who were baptized, and believe in Christ the Lord into One, Holy, Catholic, and Apostolic Roman Church. (1)

Such a Commission, founded and directed by the Apostolic See, would be of great importance in fostering and promoting that inclination toward the Apostolic See, which, under the inspiration of the Holy Spirit has already risen up in many countries and which has overcome and rooted out many false, prejudicial opinions in the search for truth, as Your Holiness so clearly explained in your encyclical *Ad Petri Cathedram*. (2)

For indeed it is important to foster and nourish all those favourable tendencies, above all, those which emerge from Biblical Studies, according to the norms of the Instruction from the Holy Office, of 20 December 1949 (*A.A.S.* 42, 1950, 12-147), especially from the discussions of the learned theologians, both in oral exchange, as well as in their Biblical and dogmatic writings. Already many theologians, supported by the authority of their bishops, have begun this difficult work in various countries, especially among those people, whose Catholics live together with Protestants. The Institute, which I mentioned above and which aims at inquiring into Protestant doctrine and its evolution, was established four years ago by the Archbishop of Paderborn. It has already been able to work effectively in overcoming many prejudicial opinions of Protestants, concerning Catholic matters, and to strengthen the longed-for desires for that unity, that Our Lord Jesus Christ desired, and which the Church really based on the foundation of Peter. (3)

St. Robert Bellarmine, supported by the authority of Pope Gregory XII, successfully discussed this matter in his *Disputationibus de controversiis fidei adversus huius temporis haereticos,* according to the circumstances of that age, so that many Protestants were convinced, indeed to such a point that Theodore Beza, successor to Calvin and the Prince of the "Reformers," would consider that work of Holy Bellarmine (to be) of the highest value and would fear that it would destroy the causes of the separation. Johann Adam Möhler, an illustrious Catholic theologian at the turn of the (nineteenth century) in his work, *Symbolica vel controversia inter catholicos et protestantes vigentium exposito,* adapted and refined, somewhat, the suggestions of Saint Bellarmine, according to the changed conditions of the times. The Director of the Institute, which derives its name from the same distinguished Möhler, and his advisors, who are professors of many Catholic Theological Faculties, adhering to the very clear indications of these suggestions of Möhler, strive by word and writing to overcome the false, prejudiced opinions of the Protestants and to support their inclination toward the traditional Catholic Truth. Besides this Institute, which is important, especially for prevailing Protestantism in Germany, other similar Institutes have been founded in other countries as, e.g., The Catholic Conference for Ecumenical Questions in the Netherlands, the Roman association *Unitas,* a certain center in Switzerland (under the protection of His Excellency, Bishop Charrìer), and certain Circles instituted in Paris; the monks of the Abbey at Chevetogne, who publish the periodical called *Irenikon.* (4)

All of these studies and works, which have been successfully initiated, and which should be adapted to the conditions of times and places, need the greatest care of the Apostolic See. Indeed, this care should serve and promote the dependence of each of the works, begun, by, either the Ordinary of the place, or by the Episcopal Conference, existing in the various countries, and, should, not only, *not* take away their conferences nor supplant the direction of their Bishops; but, should especially *serve and promote,* by *very serious study,* the *specific character* of each of them, *appropriate* to the various *needs and conditions of the areas.*[22] (5)

However, it is easily understood that the individual endeavours, even in such a specialized field, (and) in a matter of such great importance, are indeed so difficult that they need a certain supreme care and vigilance by the Apostolic See. Further, that care should be ex-

---

22. Here Jaeger/Bea is exercising the Leonine (XIII) precept of subsidiarity. The sentence reflects the attitude of Bea that Rome itself can also be the source of confusion in these matters (emphasis mine).

tended to the various projects already existing in various regions and countries, so that all the works may move harmoniously toward the same final end, *namely Christian Unity;* and, that they will help each other by their advice and experience, and that they would work among themselves whole-heartedly. All of these things, as is evident, can only be done truly and effectively, *under the authority of the Apostolic See.* (6)

Therefore, this Pontifical Commission must be vigilant to take great care of these efforts in the Ecumenical Movement, i.e., in the initiatives, studies and works in the various nations, and to achieve Christian Unity *among themselves,* in whatever way it can. Any Catholics who are responsible for ecumenical matters in the individual regions, let them know these things, examine and direct the way and the method of proceeding, *according to the norms and mind of the Holy See.* Let them correct the less proper and less appropriate things with fraternal charity. Let them suggest also the ways and means, derived from the experience of other places. Having established these premises, *the Pontifical Commission could thus be practically established for the unity of Christians.* (7)

I. The Direction of the Commission

(1) Its President is one of the eminent Cardinals living in Rome. All matters of major importance must be referred to him.

(2) The (executive) Secretary to the President should be skilled, above all, in ecumenical matters. He plans and directs the ordinary work of the Commission according to the norms, given by the President and, according to his mind, disposes and directs the normal work of the Commission.

(3) The Members of the Commission are the Consultors or Officials of those Sacred Congregations more intimately associated with the questions of Christian Unity, who possess a special competence in ecumenical matters.

(4) The Consultors of the Commission are men, eminently qualified in ecumenical matters, whether residing in Rome or elsewhere. The latter can be bishops, or Moderators of Institutes, which deal with ecumenism in a particular way.

(5) The Secretary, as well as the Consultors, should be nominated by the Holy See, in consultation with the Cardinal President. In the case of the Consultors, who reside outside the City, the *votum* is sought from the appropriate Ordinary. (8)

II. Consultations occur as follows:

(1) The General Consultation: Its Members and Consultors reside in the City. It should be held several times a year, particularly in reference to grave and serious matters. [This process evolved into what is now known as the *Plenarium,* and is held once a year in the Council for Promoting Christian Unity. In 1960, some dicasteries of the Roman curia met more often for a supervisory general review of the ongoing work, drawing from the academic resources of professors already residing in Rome. — Author's note.]

(2) THE Ordinary Consultations: The Consultors reside in the City. (This type of consultation) should be held at least once a month, and/or whenever conditions necessitate it.

(3) Consultations may be held several times, even outside of Rome, where a special programme is being held on the question of unity. Members and Consultors, who are present in the same place, may also meet with them, if they can do so conveniently.[23] (9)

We humbly recommend these proposals to Your Holiness, knowing how precious this matter of Christian Unity is to Your heart. We ask Your Holiness to receive these proposals in a kindly way and, if you see it as opportune, to bring the work to fruition. Such a Pontifical Commission will be greeted by non-Catholics with great joy. Even more, it will show Protestants, who are inclined towards the Holy See, *how much the Roman Church desires and studies to promote the unity of all Christians.*[24] Besides, all Catholics will be encouraged by this action of the Holy See, so that they will pray and work fervently for Christian Unity. Non-Catholics, who are of good will, will be more effectively helped to find the right way. Evil persons

---

23. The letter followed the pattern of Curial consultations then *en vogue* at Rome. In particular, the outline herein listed follows the methods of consultations used by the Holy Office and the Propaganda Fidei (now known as Congregation for the Promotion of the Doctrine of the Faith). General Consultations were held for specific problems and involved experts *(periti)* teaching in Rome. Ordinary Consultations took place once per week. This is still the practice since there is a *congresso* within each dicastery every week in which specific issues are prepared by the staff for discussions by the staff. Extraordinary consultations could be held annually, or for specific tasks, and need not be held in Rome. General consultations now involve participative members and consultors who travel to Rome, usually for the annual November meeting. The agenda is prepared by the Secretariat's staff.

24. (emphasis mine).

will be prevented from saying, as they often do, that the Roman Church is in no way concerned with ecumenical studies to unite the Churches. Thus we think it best to prepare, so that the desire of Christ: "that there be one flock and one Shepherd (Jn. 10:16)," may be daily more and more realized. (10)

Prostrate at the feet of Your Holiness, I ask your Apostolic Benediction. I am your most humble and obedient servant.

+ Lorenz Jaeger, Archbishop of Paderborn

According to the oral testimony of Archbishop Capovilla, then Secretary to Pope John, Jaeger was already known to the Pontiff by reputation, and he was held in high esteem by the Pope. Therefore, the "author," Jaeger, and the "bearer," Bea, were readily accepted. In summary, Jaeger asked for a permanent Curial body. Already he had in mind the idea of a "Commission," which implied a certain permanent juridical status within the family of the Roman Curia. Although it would take many years, Jaeger's idea would become a reality in 1988.[25] The letter does not contain the idea of a Press Office nor does it mention the forthcoming Council. Jaeger left that material to be handled in Bea's private conversation and in his personal letter. He does ask for pontifical confirmation for the work already begun, either locally, individually, or through spontaneous initiative. The involvement of the Holy See in these matters would have two principal goals. Jaeger's first goal was to address the issue of prejudice which, while unstated, had affected the Catholic Church in Germany and indeed the entire Christian community, not only throughout Jaeger's lifetime but since the unfortunate events associated with the Classical Reformation itself. Jaeger's second goal was the facilitation of collaborative ecumenical efforts either in Rome or worldwide. Much has been unsaid in this letter, but perhaps the most poignant of all conclusions is that such a body *would bring comfort, even joy, to Catholics and it would make it easier for non-Catholics of goodwill to find the right path.* Papal involvement would bring confirmation and prestige to the Ecumenical Movement. This point is important because it in-

---

25. *Annuario Pontificio Per L'Anno 1997*, p. 1831. This historical note records the decision of Pope John Paul II to elevate the Secretariat to the staus of a Pontifical Council. In his encyclical letter *Ut Unum Sint* of 1995, Pope John Paul II declared: "At the Second Vatican Council, *the Catholic Church committed herself irrevocably* to following the path of the ecumenical venture, thus heeding the Spirit of the Lord, who teaches people to interpret carefully the *'signs of the times'*" (No. 3.1, emphasis mine). The term "irrevocable" confirms the permanence sought originally by the Jaeger-Bea Letter.

dicates that the origins of the Secretariat for Promoting Christian Unity are grounded in pastoral concern, as well as scholarship.

The formal letter did not contain reference to the all-provoking Incident at Rhodes. Discreetly, this was left to Cardinal Bea. Jaeger's letter also did not refer to the Orthodox or Eastern Christians, although the Rhodes Incident involved them and was the immediate catalyst to the project. Yet, for the record, this project was designed to be Jaeger's. Bea contributed to the formulation and the communication of the message. Because of his Curial expertise, his academic prestige, and his general, all-round Roman experience, Bea could claim more than a partial ownership to the success of the project. He truly was simultaneously the major inspiration to both parties in the correspondence, i.e., Pope John and Archbishop Jaeger. Herein lies his uniqueness. He was no mere facilitator. He was a bridge *(pons)*.

The Pontiff's Response

Since the original and central missive bore Jaeger's signature, the first implication found in Pope John's memo to himself was scribbled in the margin of the letter in his own hand, and dated March 14, 1960. It was a directive that Bea should collaborate with Archbishop Lorenz Jaeger. He should respond to him on behalf of the Pope. John authenticated this *pro memoria* (memo) with his signature, "John XXIII." Thus the Supreme Pontiff displayed his authentic respect for the role and dignity of a diocesan bishop, working, out of pastoral concern, in collaboration with the Bishop of Rome and the other members of the Episcopal College, for the sake of the Universal Church.[26]

Hence, the immediate task, which impacted Bea, was to provide a response to Jaeger, the Archbishop of Paderborn. Jaeger was recognized herein both as a leader of a diocesan family and as a scholar with ecumenical creativity. Thus did John show himself to be responsive to the counsel of bishops to which Monsignor Antonio Bacci already alluded in the pre-Conclave speech, immediately prior to John's election: "He will finally receive and welcome the bishops whom the Holy Spirit has chosen to rule over the Church of God (Acts 20:28). He will be prepared to give them counsel in their doubts to listen to and comfort them in their anxieties, *and to encourage their plans.*"[27]

26. Schmidt, *op. cit.*, p. 327.
27. Hebblethwaite, *op. cit.*, pp. 280-81 (emphasis mine).

In various letters Jaeger acknowledged that this was needed. On 21 October 1959, he had already written to Bea: "I am distraught . . . the first sorrow is that there is neither sufficient knowledge of the German situation nor of the psychological constitution of German Protestantism in Rome." This anguish motivated Jaeger.[28] He later wrote on 8 November: "The Vatican should . . . establish an official *Gutachterstelle* (an association of experts) in Rome, which must be equipped with a Press Office . . . the Secretariat must at least have a head who can really represent the office and fully carry out its tasks. . . . A single person cannot run such an office *(Amt)* by himself; he needs, therefore, immediate contacts such as, for example, those that occur in the German realm, with the Johann Adam Möhler Institute . . . for the French realm, the *Istina Centre* etc. . . . It is necessary that he can verify or correct all important incoming news within a couple of hours, by recourse to official organs within the originating countries, so that perhaps he can attain the judgment and point of view from the individual countries."[29] Jaeger, through his incessant correspondence with Pius XII, Bea and Höfer, as well as with other Vatican officials, manifested his continued deference to Rome and his personal reverence for the office of Pope. At the same time, he could not be judged *Ultramontane;* the very subject matter of his March 4 letter proves his concern for local, pastoral and ecumenical matters. Yet, given the times, he did not hesitate to call for a strong central body at Rome, to keep abreast of information and to prevent incidents, which are fraught with friction. Even to this day, Johannes Willebrands recalls the Incident at Rhodes and the anguish of Father Dumont, who, thinking himself to be gracious by inviting the Orthodox to tea on the Island of Rhodes, unthinkingly broke the protocol of the World Council of Churches. Dumont was not even aware of such a protocol. Obviously, there was a need for sensitivity and a common understanding of the rules of procedure.

28. Jaeger to Bea, 21 October 1959, Vicar General's Archives, Paderborn. "Mich bedrückt nur die ernste Sorge, dass in Rom keine genügende Kenntnis der deutschen Situation und der psychologischen Gegebenheiten im deutschen Protestantismus vorhanden sind."

29. Jaeger to Bea, 8 November 1959. "Der Vatikan sollte . . . eine offizielle Gutachterstelle in Rom einrichten, der eine Pressestelle angegliedert sein müsste. . . . Es müsste auf jeden Fall in das Sekretariat hineingenommen werden ein Kopf, der das Amt wirklich repräsentiert und voll ausfüllen kann. . . . Ein einzelner Mann kann überhaupt ein solches Amt nicht verwalten. Er braucht dazu unmittelbare Drähte, z.B. für den deutschen Raum zum Johann Adam Möhler-Institut . . . zu Centre d' Istina u.s.f. Es ist notwendig, dass er alle bedeutenderen ein laufenden Nachrichten durch eine Rückfrage in den einzelnen Ländern innerhalb weniger Stunden verifizieren oder korrigieren kann, evtl. die Beurteilung und Stellungnahmen dazu aus den einzelnen Ländern einholen kann."

Interestingly enough, in organizing his letter, Jaeger did not call upon his almost twenty years of experience as bishop. Instead, he authenticated his "submission" to Pope John as the head of the Ecumenical Institute of his diocese. That he did so consciously is found in this testimony: "Therefore, as President of the Möhler Institute of Paderborn, I have made a direct statement to John XXIII: this statement was the immediate cause of the Secretariat for the Unity of Christians, whose president was Cardinal Bea."[30]

The strategy worked. Bea wrote to Jaeger immediately, on March 14, after his meeting with Pope John the day before. He stated that he detected in John "*a sign that the cause lay close to his heart.* . . .[31] He, Pope John, said to me that he had *completely* understood the plan and wished it to be executed as soon as possible, so that the Commission could begin its work before the Council, and *he commissioned me along with Your Excellency* to prepare a statute for the Commission. Cardinal Tardini has also approved the plan."[32] Bea then requested Jaeger to draw up a *progetto* (draft) concerning the aims of the anticipated Commission. Bea was exuberant: "We have, with the help of God, made a good step forward. From my talk with the Holy Father, I have the impression that he is very interested in the question of unity and will do all from his side to further it."[33] Jaeger wrote back to Bea, on 23 March 1960, expressing his joy that the Pope had given an affirmative response to his *Gesuch*, i.e., petition: "This decision of the Holy Father supports our entire efforts to construct something that fulfills the highest expectations of the Holy Father. . . . I trust that the contribution

---

30. Schmidt, *op. cit.*, p. 324. "This information clarifies Bea's role in the institution of the Secretariat for Promoting Christian Unity. It was he who instigated the proposal from the Möhler Institute and worked on it. Archbishop L. Jaeger was only too happy to take over the project, and could do so all the more easily in as much as the formal petitioner was the Archbishop of Paderborn, while the Möhler Institute simply appended its name to the text." This is Schmidt's opinion. Wittstadt, *op. cit.*, p. 183, on the other hand claims Jaeger as the instigator.

31. Bea to Jaeger, 14 March 1960. Vicar General's Archives, Paderborn. Note the influence of Maximos IV, who confided the cause of ecumenism to the great heart of the Pontiff. This is an Arabic expression already indicated which would have been understood readily because of his diplomatic career. "ein Zeichen, wie sehr ihm die Sache am Hertzen liegt. . . ."

32. *Ibid.* "Er sagte mir sofort, er sei ganz mit dem Plan einverstanden und wolle ihn möglichst bald verwirklichen, damit die Kommission schon vor dem Konzil arbeiten könne und er beauftragte mich sofort mit Excellenz ein Statut für die Kommission auszuarbeiten. Auch Kardinal Tardini hat den Plan gebilligt. . . ."

33. *Ibid.* "Wir sind mit Gottes Hilfe einen guten Schritt vorwärts gekommen. Aus meinem Gespräch mit dem HL. Vater habe ich die Gewissheit, das er für die Frage der Einheit zutiefst interessiert ist und von seiner Seite alles tun wird, sie zu fördern."

of my endeavours to the establishment of the Papal Commission can be clearly appreciated; if not, I am happily prepared to give explanations for it."[34]

In fact, the idea of an ecumenical contribution to the forthcoming General Council of the Church nowhere appeared in Jaeger's March 4 letter, which historically must stand as the official request for the permanent body, the *Gutachterstelle*. Yet, Jaeger was acknowledged by the pope and charged by him with the task of drafting as a bishop-participant the fundamental ecumenical material for the pre-preparatory work for the Council. In an attempt to pierce the veil, it would seem that Bea's courtesy letter and his conversations with Pope John effected this outcome for Jaeger, who, of course, was delighted. Here it is possible to detect Bea's effectiveness by tracing the events of March 11-13, when Bea ultimately stood at the papal window and prayed the Sunday *Angelus* with the Pope and those faithful who were gathered together in St. Peter's Square. Through the days of this small drama it became clear that Bea possessed an impeccable sense of timing, but then so did Pope John.

From the evidence of previous correspondence, it is possible to determine exactly what Jaeger was looking for. His text about ecumenical initiatives and ecumenical institutions marks the specifics. Definitely, and above all else, Jaeger wanted an official, permanent, *Gutachterstelle* within the Roman Curia. This bureau should be peopled by experts with a sensitivity for history and who possess appropriate credentials in some credible ecclesiastical discipline. The *Gutachterstelle* should be equipped with a competent press office. The implication here is the need for a presentation of facts and developments with such clarity that ongoing events within the Catholic Church could be explained. Such a press office should not be a mere propaganda machine. Finally, Jaeger was looking for a *Fachmann,* whom he defined as "a head" who represents the office and fully carries out its tasks.

Jaeger was writing from a German point of view. While reference was made, in the earlier correspondence of October-November 1959, to the relations of the Orthodox to the World Council of Churches, Jaeger's letters stressed particularly the needs of the Church in Germany, both in regard to the Classical Reformation and the present day, post-War Evangelical Church. Therefore, the proposal in regards to the Pontifical Commission,

---

34. Jaeger to Bea, 23 March 1960. Vicar General's Archives, Paderborn. "Dieser Entschluss des HL. Vaters fordert allerdings auch unsere ganze Anstrengung, etwas zu schaffen, das die hochgestecken Erwartungen des HL. Vaters erfüllt. . . . Ich hoffe dass mein Entwurf meines Überlegungen zu der zu gründenden päpstlichen Kommission deutlich erkennen lässt, wenn nicht, bin ich gerne bereit, noch Erläuterungen dazu zu geben."

when seen against that setting, had a definite German cast. This fact facilitated the collaborative effort between the two. Until 1959 Bea held the Holy Office desk for all questions of German theology, whereas Jaeger had manned the *Una Sancta* desk for the Fulda Bishops Conference since 1943. Both prelates therefore played their part in proper order. A diocesan bishop articulated the need, and the Curial Cardinal facilitated the process and the response.

Furthermore, their exchange affirmed the impact of the already existing Ecumenical Movement, as exemplified in the work of the World Council of Churches. Jaeger was deeply concerned about it, having followed its activity personally since its very inception, particularly by recourse to the Catholic Conference for Ecumenical Questions and its President, Monsignor Willebrands. A unique man, Lorenz Jaeger was endowed with experience, love of the Church, a sense of history, a breadth of vision, ecclesiastical sensitivity, and a kind of holy daring, which recognized the need to build up the whole family of Christ.

Although suspicious about Willem A. Visser 't Hooft, General Secretary of the World Council, and about his motives, Jaeger willingly entered into mutual collaboration with Bea in order to repair the misunderstanding at Rhodes, already cited above, including the hurt feelings and the cancellation of Willebrands' proposed Venice meeting with the Orthodox. The mutual desire of both Jaeger and Bea was to avoid any further misfortune, misunderstanding and, above all, embarrassment to the Church. Their collaboration expressed sensitivity to the work and activity of the World Council of Churches. Their sense of *Realpolitik* acknowledged the irreversible Ecumenical November. Hence a department of the Roman Curia itself was proposed by them to address these issues.

Decisions in Pope John's Own Hand

The 4 March letter was dated and signed and was in Bea's hands the next day. Fr. Schmidt, Bea's secretary, telephoned the papal office. The letter was delivered by hand to the study of Pope John at an appointed time on 11 March.

Pope John's answer came two days later, on Sunday, 13 March. The pontiff approved the project and entrusted Cardinal Bea with the task of organizing the new Papal Commission.[35] The details of this decision would

---

35. Stransky in Stacpoole, *op. cit.*, pp. 63-64.

be worked out later. In his own hand, Pope John left two pieces of evidence: The first quote is from the Pope's diary.

> Yesterday evening's visit to Cardinal Tardini: good. May the Lord preserve him and grant him life. This morning I received Cardinal Bea here in the private apartment, and entrusted him with the task of organizing a commission to promote the union of Christians, of which he was to be the head, nominated by me.

The second piece of evidence appeared in the margins of the 4 March letter of Archbishop Jaeger, in the form of a memo to himself.[36]

> Consulted with the Cardinal Secretary of State and Cardinal Bea (12-13 March). The suggestion is to be implemented. Cardinal Bea to be president of the proposed pontifical commission, and to answer and take up contact with the Archbishop of Paderborn. Everything is to be organized, but any official announcement is to wait until after Easter, in line with the other commissions that will be appointed for the various subjects of the Council.[37]

On the previous Friday afternoon when Cardinal Bea left his letter in the hands of Pope John's secretary, Monsignor Loris Capovilla, Pope John opened the letter and examined its contents immediately, as was his custom. No one expected that Pope John would give an immediate and positive response as soon as Sunday, March 13. Schmidt recalls that Bea met Pope John after the mid-day *Angelus*. He was astonished to learn the pope had read all the material submitted and *was in agreement*. Pope John invited the Cardinal for this audience in order to discuss some details. The speed with which the proposal was submitted, and accepted, must be something of a record for the twentieth-century Roman Curia. In the light of the evidence, it is obvious that already a mutually appreciative spiritual chemistry existed between Cardinal Bea and Pope John.[38]

The details of the conversation can only be surmised from the conclusions. According to Bea's suggestion, the pre-Conciliar atmosphere would indeed be the appropriate environment to inaugurate this body, because the immediate task, given to it, would be to facilitate the presence of non-Catholic observers at the Second Vatican Council. It was also the in-

---

36. Schmidt, *op. cit.*, p. 327.
37. *Ibid.*
38. *Ibid.*, p. 326.

tention of Pope John to expand the visibility and the scope of this body gradually.[39]

No name was given at this time, although the designation "Secretariat" would emerge within days, according to the suggestion of the Cardinal Secretary of State, Domenico Tardini, who thought that should such a project fail, it could easily be suppressed.[40] John placed this suggestion in a positive light.[41] Since there was practically no precedent for this title in the Roman Curia, Pope John confided to Cardinal Bea that the vagueness of the designation "Secretariat" provided ample space for creativity, i.e., adaptation to the new and unique circumstances of relations with non-Catholic Christians.[42] No announcement, nor any publicity was to be given to this decision of the Pope until after Easter because the Pope determined to end the pre-preparatory phase with the disclosure of the Preparatory Framework for the Council at that time.[43] However, as President of the yet unnamed body, Bea would be of equal rank with the chairman of the other Preparatory Commissions, in that he was a Cardinal with a special expertise.[44] Obviously, Bea had demonstrated to Pope John his already long-standing interest and ability; besides the task of approaching Jaeger, Pope John charged Bea with the task of privately drawing up lists for the nomination of staff, members, and Consultors.[45]

One small victory was that Bea emerged with Cardinal Tardini on his side. Tardini had the reputation of being jaded at innovation. Tardini obviously approved, according to the evidence of the pope himself. About Bea, Tardini was heard to remark: "Yes. Cardinal Bea is a peaceful man. He will

---

39. *Ibid.*, pp. 350-51. Schmidt says that the announcement of the Council and its ecumenical aim had been "incarnated" with the creation of the Secretariat for Promoting Christian Unity. Cardinal Ottaviani was not going to be happy with this new body for it brought about a new situation in the Curial family. Ottaviani's first displeasure was shown in the question of Catholic observers to the New Delhi General Assembly of the World Council of Churches. Ottaviani simply did not like the concept of observers.

40. *Ibid.*, p. 327.

41. *Ibid.*, p. 329.

42. *Ibid.*

43. *Ibid.*, pp. 329-30.

44. *Ibid.* As is demonstrated in the text, Bea's credential is rooted in his German national origin, his biblical education at German universities under a joint Protestant and Catholic faculty, through his position at the Holy Office, and his consistent contact with developing trends in German theology. This included awareness and understanding of the Churches of the Classical Reformation. Let it be recalled here that Bea's initial mandate did not include the undertaking of ecumenical activities with Orthodox Christians.

45. *Ibid.*, p. 342.

not cause us any problems."[46] Of course, as has been cited above, the two witnesses Capovilla and Schmidt both remarked that Bea's *Germanness* was the factor in the swift and easy decision. They had in mind the Germany of the Reformation, the Nazi era and the Cold War aftermath. Pope John's sense of discernment allowed him the opportunity to view from his perspective the value of *Realpolitik*.

Having written to Jaeger on 14 March charging him with the task of establishing the statutes for the forthcoming pre-Conciliar Body, vaguely put as "an office for Christian Unity," Bea awaited Jaeger's recommendations.[47] This was a highly unusual situation which was constructed by Pope John, for until the official announcement, Jaeger was Bea's principal collaborator.[48] Jaeger first recommended the search for a member of the Congregation of the Code of Canon Law, "since Protestants and Orthodox wish to understand Church law and about the formulation of certain canons." Jaeger also emphasized emphatically the need for a *sala stampa*, i.e., press office. He wrote to Bea: "The public meaning must be in the forefront of the forthcoming Council. By recourse to the sophistication of modern people, it emerges that when something is said it not be lost but rather that it be accepted. *There must be some possibility to correct false accusations, to set aside misconceptions, and to awaken a more ample openness, understanding and communication. . . .* If this Commission truly wishes to build bridges, which will lead the Separated to the Church, it cannot disavow the work of opening-up." Obviously, Jaeger's first concern is shattering the walls of bias, prejudice and ignorance. His method was by a positive attitude and collaboration with world media. His sanguine approach in this regard has consistently given a fresh and optimistic light to the work for Christian Unity by the press and electronic communications.

Confidentially, to his consultors in Paderborn Jaeger defined the goal as "the service of reuniting the Separated Christians with the Catholic Church." He also stated to them, "only the best candidates should be elected as consultors, who are experts in their fields and who are prepared to make a priority the work of the Papal Commission."[49] Jaeger actively

46. *Ibid.*, p. 327.

47. Jaeger to Bea, 14 March 1960. Vicar General's Archives, Paderborn.

48. Wittstadt, *op. cit.*, p. 197.

49. Cited in *ibid.*, p. 196. "Da der Protestantismus wie auch die Orthodoxie mancherlei Wünsche an das Kirchenrecht sowohl nach Inhalt als auch hinsichtlich der Formulierung gewisser Canones haben. . . . Die öffentliche Meinung muss, namentlich im Hinblick das kommende Konzil, vorbereitet werden. Bei der Überempfindlichkeit des modernen Menschen

entered into the process of nominating candidates to serve on the first board of Consultors, who would see to the goal, as stated above, especially regarding the invitations to Christian leaders of other traditions. Naturally, Josef Höfer and Professor Stakemeier were among them, so were many other Germans, such as Church History professor Herbert Jedin of Bonn, Otto Semmelrath, S.J., of Frankfurt, Monsignor Herman Volk of Münster, Heinrich Fries of Munich, Johannes Hirschmann, S.J., of Frankfurt.

At Easter time Jaeger wrote to Bea that he was working through the Fulda Bishops Conference to make sure that his nominations were accurate. In a note dated 3 April 1960, Jaeger wrote to Bea: "I want you to understand that I have prepared a part of the common work of the German Episcopate, in preparation for the Council, since I have worked from the standpoint of reunion."[50] According to Wittstadt, in the days after the approbation of the project of March 13, Jaeger and Bea labored untiringly for the establishment of an ecumenical commission. Bea also thought about the time after the Council, when "the *after life* of the Commission" should be secured.[51] With those goals they sifted through the proposed names and ultimately laid them on the desk of Pope John. Most notable of them all was French professor Yves Congar, O.P., who had been himself ostracized in the 1950s for his ecumenical ideas.[52] Finally Bea wrote to Jaeger: "Last Thursday, after the concert, when the Holy Father greeted the Cardinals in the Hall of Benedictions, he said to me 'I have received and read your *Gutachtern* (panel of experts).' '*Sta bene!*' I said, 'is it so?' He answered, 'Yes, it is truly so!' Thus we have the first positive result."[53]

---

kommt es sehr darauf an, wie etwas gesagt wird, damit es nicht verletzt, sondern angenommen wird. Es muss eine Möglichkeit bestehen, falsche Auffassungen zu korrigieren, Missdeutungen zu widerlegen, kurz, in breitester Öffentlichkeit Verständnis und Bereitschaft zu wecken. . . . Wenn diese Kommission wirksam Brücken bauen will, die die Getrennten zur Kirche hinführen, kann sie auf die Öffentlichkeitsarbeit nicht verzichten. . . . Dienst an der Wiedervereinigung der getrennten Christen mit der katholischen Kirche. . . . Als Konsultoren dürfen nur beste Fachleute erwählt werden, die wenigstens für ein Spezialgebiet zuverlässige Experten sind und die die betreffende Arbeitssparte der päpstlichen Kommission zu betreuen vermöchten."

50. Jaeger to Bea, 3 April 1960. Vicar General's Archives, Paderborn. "Ich wollte Sie vorher verständigen davon, dass ich den Teil der gemeinsamen Eingabe des deutschen Episkopats zur Vorbereitung des Konzils fertiggestellt habe, den ich vom Standpunkt der Wiedervereinigungsfrage aus erarbeitet habe."

51. Wittstadt, *op. cit.*, p. 195.

52. *Ibid.*, p. 197.

53. *Ibid.*, p. 198. "Am vergangenen Donnerstag, als der HL. Vater die Kardinäle nach dem Konzert in der Aula Benedictionum begrüsste, sagte er mir: "Ich habe Ihr Gutachten

In the meantime, Jaeger was working within the Fulda Bishops Conference on his own panel of experts, expediting on 27 April 1960 the following news: Cardinal Julius Döpfner of Munich had the responsibility for the anthropological section and Bishop Michael Keller of Trier accepted ecclesiology responsibilities.[54] Jaeger himself would speak to ecumenical questions. Jaeger stood before the assembled bishops to make his intervention. It was breathtaking: "The doctrine about the Church of Christ should be rewritten by the Council, so that it can answer the question of the Separated (Brethren), from the sources of Revelation and thus afford them an invitation to Catholic Unity."[55] The assembled bishops, the composition of which was quite different from 1942, applauded Jaeger's proposition and endorsed the idea of establishing a commission for Unity in Faith. Bea remarked: "I truly congratulate, from my heart, the Episcopate for this magnificent accomplishment and I add my joy that the one (Pope John XXIII), who enjoys the most elevated position, rejoices over the *votum* and has praised it immensely. When I spoke with the Holy Father the last time, it lay upon his desk and he had read most of it."[56]

On 30 May 1960, Bea had announced in an assembly of Cardinals the official establishment of "a Secretariat in reference to the question of Unity." At the same time Pope John announced Bea to be the first and new President of the Secretariat for Promoting Christian Unity. In reference to duties of the president, he should provide a place to which the *fratelli separati* could turn with all their desires and questions.[57] Bea reflected that he was very happy and thought that the announcement represented an escalation along the way of reunion. Bea also confided to Jaeger that the news of his naming was not yet public and he requested Jaeger to handle his information discreetly.[58] The public announcement came on June 5 in the form of a *motu proprio,* entitled *Superno Dei nutu,* while Bea was in New York.[59] When the Secretariat was finally a matter of the public do-

---

bekommen und gelesen — sta bene": ich frage noch: "Geht es also so?. Er antwortete: "Ja, es ist recht so." Damit haben wir also das erste positive Ergebnis."

54. *Ibid.*

55. *Ibid.*

56. *Ibid.* "Ich kann wirklich dem Episkopat zu diesen hervorragenden Darlegungen von Herzen gratulieren und ich darf zu meiner Freude hinzufügen, dass man auch an allerhöchster Stelle sich sehr über das Votum gefreut und es ausserordentlich gelobt hat. Als ich das letzte Mal beim HL. Vater war, lag es gerade auf seinem Arbeitstisch und er hatte es schon zum grössten Teil gelesen."

57. *Ibid.*, p. 199.

58. *Ibid.*

59. Schmidt, *op. cit.*, p. 330.

main, Jaeger pronounced his own accolade, showing due deference to Bea and expressing every confidence in Bea's ability.

Yet at the same time, Jaeger was privately critical of *Superno Dei nutu*. While the papal pronouncement presented the organizational structure of the preparatory work of the Council, *there was no overarching theory of application*. This had yet to come. *It* would constitute the ecumenical endeavor of Cardinal Bea, who would, gradually and opportunely, carry out that specific responsibility. Jaeger prodded Bea to elucidate the theological premise upon which the new Secretariat would be based. Drawing from the pre-occupation of Monsignor Höfer regarding Church membership, in the light of *Mystici Corporis*, Bea as we shall see chose Baptism as the *locus theologicus* of ecumenism.[60] Jaeger said he had seen the same thing in the discussions of the Fulda Bishops Conference. *Let it be recalled that it was Jaeger himself who laid the ecumenical burden on Bea's shoulders and set him to the task that can be called, justifiably, "his ecumenical endeavor."* Jaeger wrote to Bea: "It will require very intensive effort of your Secretariat to place the conditions that the Separated Brethren can be interiorly moved by the Council and won over."[61]

Having channelled the thoughts and ideals of Archbishop Jaeger to Pope John XXIII, having consulted with Jaeger about a panel of experts to form the first cabinet of consultors, having followed the directive of Pope John and Cardinal Tardini that the proposed Commission accept the critical pathway of first serving the Council, Cardinal Bea now made his own choice. On 29 July he wrote to Jaeger that he was nominating Monsignor Johannes Willebrands, of the Netherlands, as his Secretary of the Secretariat. One could scarcely find a more knowledgeable, well-known *alter-Fachmann*.[62]

60. *Ibid.*, p. 201.

61. *Ibid.*

62. The original Secretariat consisted of sixteen voting members and twenty consultors. The Secretariat would operate in two phases, a standing commission and a Conciliar phase which would also embrace all the participants of the standing commission and add more experts during the time of the Council. The task in both phases was the delineating of the theological themes to be presented to the floor of the Council as well as the preparation of *vota* which would be filtered through the *Beratungsgegenständ* (offices of counselors). The *vota* would be the theological opinion of each participant, i.e., whether member or consultor. The status of the Secretariat, always tentative in the eyes of the general observer, was in fact guaranteed of pontifical stability by Pope John. At the time of the Council itself it did not require approval by the Council Fathers. This information is taken from the undated and personal notes of Archbishop Jaeger. They are fragmented bits of advice and recommendation for Cardinal Bea, and are located in the Vicar General's Archives, Paderborn. Also, please refer to Wittstadt, *op. cit.*, in full, for the full development of the process.

According to Johannes Willebrands, who was to succeed Bea as Cardinal President of the Secretariat for Promoting Christian Unity, Bea had already embodied through his contacts and his study, all the history of the pre-Ecumenical Movement. Through collaboration with the wisdom of Jaeger, Bea transformed the course of the pre-Ecumenical Movement to the Roman Catholic Ecumenical Movement.

A German Comprehensiveness

Pope John XXIII and Cardinal Bea are pictured together in history as intimate collaborators in the cause of Christian union. In speeches, sermons and discourses prior to the Council, both Pope and Cardinal piped a tune that proved to be a symphony. But they did so as point and counterpoint. Giancarlo Zizola, a shrewd observer of contemporary papal history, wrote of John: "This vision of the pope's was explicit in several speeches of those first months subsequent to the announcement of the Council: He augured that the Council *might procure to the Church a progress so notable that our brothers and our sons, separated from this apostolic Seat thus receive, thanks to the renewal we are hoping for, of all the Christian virtues, an invitation and a healthy excitement.*"[63] At the same time Zizola portrayed Bea as the facilitator of a process of gradualism which included *rapprochement*, reconciliation and union. Bea pronounced: "The Council, even though not intending to realize immediately the union of all Christians, can and does intend to prepare for it in the long run, bettering the atmosphere between Catholics and non-Catholics, creating conditions more favourable to union and resolving some problems connected with it."[64] A politician, a shrewd observer, a journalist and very much a man of the twentieth century, Zizola discerned "the originality of the ecumenical prospect indicated by John." Like his contemporary, Flamini, Zizola saw the summoning of the Council within the context of international, political affairs. When it came to the comparison of ecumenical intentions, Zizola and Flamini applauded John as innovative. Zizola saw the ecumenical component of the Council as an "anthropological leap" (for the concept of communion assumed a new priority). This mandate was designed to take up the very concept of community where it had been broken off.[65]

63. Giancarlo Zizola, *op. cit.*, p. 242.
64. *Ibid.*
65. *Ibid.*

Such an analysis makes no sense unless it be placed in a cultural setting. It is the conventional wisdom that "all politics is local."[66] It is not hard to pierce the corporate veil in this situation, given the history that has been traced to this point. The evidence leads to Jaeger. Without him John and Bea would not have labored in a relationship that was patently "hand in glove." In the year 1960, the politics of a divided Berlin and a divided Germany was the politics of the world: "A living organism, a major city, and a cultural center, has been cut in half. Despite the French adage, *ce n'est que le provisiore qui dure* ('Only the provisional lasts'), interim solutions must come to an end. . . . Beyond Berlin an educational effort is necessary, stretching all the way from the Baltic to show that the division of Europe cannot last indefinitely."[67]

While the author of those words analyzed the terrible dilemma of Germany in language of politics, economics and sociology, Jaeger, the Churchman, indicated that he, too, was keenly aware of the dark specter which had fallen over the history of his land. Unlike politicians, he looked both backward *and* forward to find the solution in the transcendent reality of the Church, through memory and hope. Jaeger accepted the datum of history that there was indeed a tear in the seamless robe of Christ, and that it could be perceived in modern Germany. It could be said of him that the consistency of his cause was the mark of the man; and it was Jaeger's charism to lay down his own destiny, as well as that of his people, alongside the destiny and the life of the Church.

If a man is to be judged by the cause he aspires to embrace, he must be judged too by the motive for which he embraces it, and the manner in which he embraces it. The importance of Jaeger is found in the transparency of his unselfishness, in the consistency of his ecumenical platform. Herein he was not alone. Others stood beside him, as one by one they came to recognize ecumenism as, not only appropriate, but urgent. Among those who could thus be numbered would be Max Metzger (first of all), Karl Adam, Joseph Lortz, Josef Höfer, Paul Simon, Romano Guardini, Karl Rahner, Adolf Herte, Max Pribilla, Eduard Stakemeier. In the personal and academic lives of all these individuals there is clear evidence of the search for truth, the desire for justice and the recognition of holiness as the basis for communion. In sum, these are the components of ecclesiology. The evi-

66. This reference, in the U.S.A., is most often associated with Thomas (Tip) O'Neill.

67. Stefan T. Possony, "Berlin, Focus of World Strategy," in David Collier and Kurt Glaser (eds.), *Berlin and the Future of Eastern Europe* (Chicago: Henry Regnery Company, 1963), pp. 26-27.

dence of history likewise points to the recognition of one man by another. The consistent figure who linked each individual to the other was Jaeger himself. Thus there came a time when someone else would represent him, and that representative was Bea.

Thus at this point one must leave Jaeger. When asked about Pope John's reasoning for his selection of Bea, so quickly, as president of the new Secretariat, Monsignor Capovilla said of Pope John, as we have seen so often, that he selected Bea because he was a German. John also was accustomed to looking backward in order to go forward. He thus saw in this retired German Jesuit all of the German comprehensiveness that was imported by Jaeger's mentality. Jaeger had studied the Reformation, its causes and its polemics. He had lived through the collapse of the Reformation's primary principle, the *modus vivendi* of four hundred years of German life, *Cujus regio, ejus religio*. He had experienced at first hand the nightmare struggle of the twentieth-century German *Kampf* (e.g., inter-War, Nazi and Cold War). He found his solution to every problem in the priority of the Church in history, for he believed it to be the vessel containing the Presence of God. The life of Jaeger, as lived on the German stage, provides an understanding for the firmness of resolution displayed by Bea in accepting the responsibility for inaugurating the ecumenical movement at Rome. Jaeger, too, was a German.

Conclusion

Two important points are evident from the above text. The first of these is the Germanness of the project. This is evident not only from the fact that it originated from the German experience and was husbanded by Germans, e.g., Bea, Jaeger, Stakemeier, and Höfer, but also that the first membership of the new body as nominated by Jaeger included Germans such as Jedin, Semmelroth, and Volk. Naturally, reference was made to other members of the Catholic Conference for Ecumenical Questions, but Jaeger's choice reflected the attitude of his fellow countrymen and women who were so personally familiar with the details and aftermath of the Classical Reformation. Finally, there is the evidence of Pope John himself. His secretary testifies to this day that Bea was chosen as captain of this enterprise because he was a German.

The second aspect, one of many, which can be drawn from the letter itself, is the identification of the primacy of scholarship. Paragraph five of the letter refers to "all of these studies and works." This is a direct reference to already existing ecumenical projects, all of them academic in nature. Paragraph six of the Letter of Petition refers to ecumenism as "such a specialized field . . . a matter of such great importance . . . so difficult that they need a certain supreme care and vigilance by the Apostolic See." Paragraph nine states "the Roman Church desires and *studies* to promote the unity of *all* Christians."[68] Here, the concept of the *Gutachtersteller*, so evident in the last chapter, was placed before the pontiff with subtlety and precision. Jaeger's letter places much emphasis on consultors and members who came to the table armed with rich knowledge and experience, and indeed wisdom. Ecumenism had become, therefore, a *métier*. By his positive response to that fact, i.e., the already-existing and vital impetus to intra-religious activity and dialogue, Pope John XXIII initiated a new and active apostolate as well as an academic discipline within the field of Roman Catholic theology.

68. (emphasis mine).

Chapter VI

The Ecumenical Endeavor of Cardinal Bea

Introduction

At this point, it is important to review the information that has been gleaned thus far in order to ascertain the historical foundations of what would be the ecumenical endeavor of Cardinal Bea. First, Jaeger's dispute with Archbishop Gröber (1942-1943) uncovered a burgeoning Roman Catholic interest in Reformation studies, in general, and in the origins and development of Luther's thought specifically. Adolf Herte had produced ample research to indicate that Roman Catholic studies of Church history in Germany basically reproduced, over four hundred years, the *same* critical analysis of Johannes Cochläus, from the sixteenth century itself. Joseph Lortz published, even during the early years of the War when paper was scarce, a critical study of Luther's spirituality and theological thought against the background of the time in which Luther himself lived. Karl Adam represented the ongoing interest of German theology regarding the subject matter, *De ecclesia,* a topic which had been of relevance in the midst of the German nineteenth- and twentieth-century history, in fact, since the Napoleonic Age. Adam was to indicate through his writings that the time was ripe for the development of the topic of ecumenism. On the local level, Max Metzger was already organizing dialogues between Protestant pastors and Roman Catholic priests. We have seen that Bishop von Galen studied Reformation subjects, almost daily, as a matter of personal interest and discipline.

Secondly, after 1945, the climate of the times was that of a Germany broken in its identity, its resources and its morale. Cardinal Jaeger's *Open*

Letter of 1946, describing the material needs of his own diocese, went so far as to attempt to solicit fundamental household goods and domestic facilities. The poverty of defeat was apparent at every level. That same public letter called for a reinstatement of a sense of community.

Thirdly, during the entire time of the Hitler regime (1933-1945), the Catholic life of Germany functioned more and more in a moral blackout. The leadership stemming from the Bishops Conference only presented the German Catholic Church with a riddle. The above-mentioned Bishop von Galen denounced Hitler from the pulpit and then courageously stared down his imminent arrest. On the other hand, even in the early days of May 1945, when the President of the Fulda Bishops Conference, Cardinal Adolf Bertram, learned of Hitler's suicide, he ordered all the churches of his archdiocese to "celebrate a solemn requiem Mass for the Fuhrer."[1] Thus we can see how disparate was the membership of the Bishops Conference of Greater Germany in this regard.

The Fulda Conference obviously was terrorized into immobility. In the aftermath of the War, it was completely stripped of any possibility of hiding from accusation in the face of the evidence. Because of their claim to be servants of God, they were, therefore, devoted to living moral lives. All leaders, so ran the charge, have a greater responsibility to act morally, especially to defend those who need defending.[2] These same accusations were likewise hurled at the Lutheran hierarchy. In consequence not only of the *lacuna* of leadership but also as a result of twelve years of a paganized propaganda, Germany now possessed a substantial population of religiously skeptical and secularized citizens. Today, they would simply be called the "unchurched." The pain of such knowledge is easily identified in the long and consistently pastoral administration of Archbishop Jaeger.

Finally, in 1960, cognizant of all these realities, Cardinal Bea approached Pope John for his first substantial conversation. He found in Pope John an historical scholar and a man cognizant of a world divided by rapid social change, instant nuclear threat, and the Cold War confrontation between the Soviet Union and the nations of the West. It was Bea's concerted opinion that the time was ripe for Pope John XXIII to act and to address the question of Christian unity.

---

1. Daniel Goldhagen, *A Moral Reckoning* (New York: Alfred A. Knopf, 2002), p. 200.
2. *Ibid.*, p. 122.

The Evidence of the Foregoing

The evidence of the foregoing provides ample opportunity to draw several conclusions. The first of these is that the exchange between Archbishop Jaeger and Cardinal Bea provided a moment of grace and profound insight into the nature of the Church. The Church itself is the beneficiary of this collaborative effort on the part of these two German prelates. Fr. Schmidt and Fr. Stransky, C.S.P., the American member of the first staff of the Secretariat for Promoting Christian Unity, both argue that the laurels for this effort belong to Bea. Klein and Wittstadt have presented ample evidence that Jaeger was the predominating figure.[3] Jaeger himself believed this to be true and even said so, at Bea's funeral, in 1968. Schmidt even recorded in a footnote that Höfer claimed that *he* had so conditioned Bea as to make an ecumenist out of him.[4]

After analyzing the documents, one would have to say that under the Holy Spirit, this was a Providential moment, when the activities of several figures coalesced and were evident primarily in the initiative of Cardinal Bea. Realization of the seriousness of the Rhodes Incident had dawned on both prelates simultaneously, as is evidenced by the correspondence. They did not sit down and decide this is yours, mine, and ours. From the start, the ecumenical project was a collaborative effort between Bea, Jaeger, Höfer and Stakemeier. It is appropriate to refer to the letter of 4 March as the Bea/Jaeger letter, in which a proposal for the establishment for the Secretariat for Promoting Christian Unity was laid before Pope John XXIII. Bea predominates in this scenario because he was the Curial Cardinal whose ready access to Pope John, his past experience in ecumenical matters and in Curial procedure, and his biblical scholarship gave him the appropriate opportunity to provide the Pontiff with an authentic vehicle to address the need of fostering Christian Unity at a critical moment in the Church's history.

That critical moment was highlighted by several events in twentieth-century history, including national and international consciousness of the

---

3. Schmidt, *op. cit.*, p. 322. Thomas Stransky, "The Foundation of the Secretariat for Promoting Christian Unity," in Stacpoole (ed.), *op. cit.*, p. 64. Klaus Wittstadt, *op. cit.*, p. 203. From the very first day of the author's meeting in 1979 with Monsignor Klein, he indicated that Cardinal Jaeger was the motivating and driving force in the collaboration. Wittstadt demonstrates that, in the letters of 1 and 20 January 1960, Bea gave his consent to the plan of Archbishop Jaeger. It is difficult to determine where the efforts of one man ends and the other begins, and vice versa.

4. Schmidt, *op. cit.*, p. 404.

effects of World War II, the Cold War between East and West and a remarkable period of rapid social change in which communications became instant, news became readily accessible and former colonies took their place among the nations of the world as social and economic entities, in their own right. Pope John would address all of these issues in future encyclicals, *Mater et Magistra* (1961) and *Pacem in Terris* (1963).[5] The theme of unity and its grounding in religion had already been addressed by John's first encyclical, *Ad Petri Cathedram* (1959), and it had been enunciated within the context of the forthcoming Council, which he had convoked earlier in that same year. The evidence of Pope John's intimate thoughts in the years of his pontificate can only come from one man, John's secretary, Monsignor Loris Capovilla. Capovilla explained that the pontiff accepted the contents of the Jaeger/Bea proposal from Bea and appointed him first President of the Secretariat for Promoting Christian Unity, *because he was a German.*[6] In John's mind, according to the evidence of Capovilla's witness, Bea represented the dividedness of contemporary Cold War Germany, the aftermath of World War II Germany, and the relevance of Reformation Germany. In this last category Bea brought his skills as a prominent biblical scholar of the Church, one who assisted Pius XII in the drafting of the landmark encyclical *Divino Afflante Spiritu* (1943).[7] Bea, it must be remembered, received his basic training in philology, archeology, and hermeneutics not in the Roman schools, but in Berlin. Those who first conditioned his biblical aptitudes were *Protestant* and *German*. Therefore, even in his professional career it could be said of him that *he was a German.*[8]

If Bea was the voice, Jaeger was the content of his speech. Jaeger represented the history and the exigency of a Germany yet divided by the Classical Reformation of the sixteenth century. Bea handed Pope John XXIII Jaeger's letter, which in essence was a valid representation of communal interest to the Supreme Pontiff of the universal Church by the shepherd of a local Church. As history has proven, this was a beneficial moment for the entire Church. History has also recorded that this missive was not a lone article of reporting, although that fact was unknown to Bea and Jaeger. As

---

5. Flamini, *op. cit.*, p. 9. Flamini defines John's purpose as the search to lead the Church in ways of more direct relation with modern life.

6. Ralph Wiltgen, *The Rhine Flows into the Tiber* (New York: Hawthorn Books, 1967), p. 5. Surprisingly enough this author, while he sees adequately enough the presence of the German ethos in the Council, makes no effort to see the ecclesiological theme. Jaeger's name is mentioned only once in the entire book.

7. Schmidt, *op. cit.*, pp. 202-5.

8. Leeming, *Kardinal Bea*, p. 4.

already stated in the first chapter, Patriarch Maximos IV Saigh had written to the pope independently and from an Eastern viewpoint, and presented a document of proposal on 23 May 1959. There is remarkable consensus between the two letters, and some points can be addressed when a comparison of the two is made. These are: (1) the practicality of the local Church, or the *vox episcopatis;* (2) the *sensus coetus,* i.e., the mystery of the Church as community; (3) the competence of *periti;* (4) the ministry of the Secretariat for Promoting Christian Unity.

The Practicality of the Local Church or the *Vox Episcopatis*

The directive of the Conciliar decree, *Christus Dominus,* on the Pastoral Office of Bishops in the Church, describes the historicity of the bishop's particular apostolate: "Since it is the mission of the Church to maintain close relations with the society in which she lives, the bishops should make it their special care to approach men and to initiate and promote dialogue with them (No. 13)." Men do not live in a vacuum but rather are conditioned by their society and their culture, which is historically based. According to the Council, bishops should facilitate understanding, and their own actions should be marked by humility and courtesy. Thus, "truth may be combined with charity, and understanding with love . . . by promoting friendship conducive to a union of minds (No. 13)." It can be said that in the separate actions of Jaeger and Maximos, they demonstrated the practicality of ecclesiology and dramatically highlighted the role of the local Church and its bishop. His task is not merely cerebral. Instead the local Church, which is identified with the bishop, is based upon historical circumstances, cultural experiences, and ecclesiological principles.

During the Second Session of the Second Vatican Council, Auxiliary Bishop Eduard Schick of Fulda made this intervention:

> We neglect that concept of the equally primitive term *ekklesia* which is the Church as a community of Christian believers. . . . Therefore, although local Churches do not make up the universal Church, by the mere fact of being externally gathered together, at the same time, they are not mere administrative divisions of the Church. We must rather say that each local Church is a true representation of the total and universal Church, which itself *carries on its own life* in these local Churches.[9]

9. In Küng et al., *op. cit.,* p. 36.

Bea prioritized this specific understanding of the role of a bishop. Even before he received news of his call to the Sacred Purple and the concomitant responsibility of serving as a leading Father of the Council, never anticipating the role that would be his, Bea wrote in 1959 that the role of the local Church and the responsibility of its bishop *must be the very first item* to be addressed by the Council.[10] Bea claimed that everything in this regard is contained in the Great Commission of Matthew 28:19: "Go therefore and make disciples of all nations." According to the evidence, Jesus did not give this mandate only to Peter. He did not say, you, Peter, go, make disciples of all nations, and tell the other eleven to do the same. The Great Commission was entrusted to the College of the Apostles together.[11] As he was writing to colleagues and friends, Bea was expressing his appreciation for the particularity, the unique identity and the cultural conditioning of the local Church, all of this founded in the exigencies of history. The local Church reflects its particular experience, one that is unique, relevant and factual, and quite capable therefore of displaying its integrity as well as the clarity of its vision, its goals and its methodology.

The language of the letter of Maximos Saigh is simple and straightforward in this regard. He wished "to create a new Congregation or a special Roman Commission for all that concerns relations with the Christian Churches who are not *in communion* with the Holy See and all that has to be done to advance union."[12] Note the important words "communion" and "to advance union." The consideration of the East, with its rich historic, patristic and liturgical treasury, broadened the cause of ecumenism from the start, because it, perforce, included "the imperative of charity." As early as 1920 the Orthodox had brought to the already decade-long ecumenical movement, which had begun with the Edinburgh Conference of 1910, an Eastern ecumenical charter. This is, *de facto,* the Encyclical of the Ecumenical Patriarchate at Constantinople, which sounded the first clarion call to unity, within the *entire* Christian family, in the twentieth century: "Above all, love should be rekindled and strengthened among the churches so that they, no more, consider one another as strangers and foreigners, but as relatives, and, as being part of the household of Christ and fellow heirs, members of the same Body and partakers of the promise of God in Christ (Eph. 3:6)."[13]

10. Schmidt, *op. cit.,* p. 295.

11. *Ibid.,* p. 367.

12. *Le Lien, op. cit.,* p. 65.

13. The Encyclical of the Ecumenical Patriarchate, 1920. Cited in Michael Kinnamon and Brian E. Cope (eds.), *The Ecumenical Movement: An Anthology of Key Texts and Voices* (Geneva: WCC Publications, 1997), p. 14.

Maximos always approached the question of Christian Unity from the perspective of ecclesiology. He eventually would clarify his language on the floor of the Council, when on 27 November 1962, he explained that the Oriental Churches were completely distinct from the Latin Church. They owed their origins directly to Christ and the apostles, and received their traditions and rites from the Greek and Oriental Fathers. He concluded his first Conciliar intervention with words of high drama, already cited above: "For us Oriental Catholics this separation from our Eastern brethren is a terrible agony that touches the very core of our hearts. *Reunion is our greatest desire* and for this very purpose we are willing to make great sacrifices. *We form one family with them,* hence we want to forget past quarrels and human considerations and join them in Christ to realize his wish."[14]

Maximos' Council speech gave life to the words which he had first penned to "the great heart of His Holiness the Pope, John XXIII," according to Arabic style.[15] He brought forward then the quest for union, not "return," according to the centuries-old theology of the East — that the Church *is* a communion, a family, a fellowship of believers. On the other hand, Jaeger pragmatically sought a Rome clearinghouse.

Jaeger's proposal was different because his experience was different. He had been a German Division Commander and there was something of precision in the way in which he handled Church matters. Therefore it comes as no surprise that his letter to Pope John is compartmentalized and juridical in both tone and content: in other words, all of these ecumenical organizations (Chevetogne, Paris, Paderborn, etc.) are active everywhere; they *need* to be organized and supervised. Jaeger's career as a bishop suggests a Field Marshall with a mitre, in contact with the bunker of the Commander of the Campaign. This is not to portray Jaeger negatively. The evidence of the foregoing should indicate that Germany was indeed throughout the twentieth century a theologically vibrant theater envisioning speculative ecclesiology, as it impinged on ecumenism. On the Evangelical side, traditional Reformation concepts such as the theology of the "Word-forming community" and the "Priesthood of all Believers" had found a new vitality in the multifold German religious movements of the twentieth century.[16] On the other hand, especially through careful atten-

14. Rynne, *Letters from Vatican City, op. cit.,* p. 196.

15. *Le Lien, op. cit.,* p. 65.

16. The significance of the Holy Bible, on both sides of Catholic and Protestant Germany, was begun in the Reformation in the renewed veneration of St. Jerome, the translator of the Vulgate. This veneration returned in the twentieth century. Eugene F. Rice, Jr., *St. Jerome and the Renaissance* (Baltimore: Johns Hopkins University Press, 1985), p. 179.

tion paid to the doctrine of the Mystical Body, according to the evidence of Jaeger's personal correspondence, the biblically based themes of the Mystical Body itself, its relationship to the Holy Spirit and the concept of the Royal Dominion of Christ the Priest were all ripe for theological attention within the deliberations of the forthcoming Second Vatican Council. While Jaeger's language of petition is formal, the evidence of his letters, as well as his supervision of the theological projects, undertaken for the Council by the Fulda Bishops Conference indicate that Jaeger was, in fact, highly attentive to the authenticity of the theological endeavor behind the statute.

It could therefore be said that each bishop represented a unique ethos. Maximos spoke in terms of a communion theology while the concept of the Mystical Body affected Jaeger. Yet in essence the two gave the same proposal, and in so doing demonstrated the principle of episcopal collegiality and the relevance of the concept of the "local Church." In fact, Maximos said as much in regard to the general cause of Christian unity in the 26 November 1962 speech cited above: "The treatment of Christian unity should first mention a *collegial character of the Church's pastorate,* the bishops being the successors of the College of the Apostles."[17]

It is the evidence of Edward J. Kilmartin, S.J., the noted American scholar, that the witness of a common faith formed the original Church both locally and universally, built on the teaching of the apostles — Jesus is Crucified, Risen, Glorified and Ascended. "Jesus is Lord!" By the second century, a mono-episcopal form of government had emerged and the bishop was defined as the center of unity of his own local Church and "the visible point of contact with the other Churches." In other words, the bishop is the touchstone, by which "the one and the many" come together ecclesiologically! The bishop is the channel of connectedness between the parochial need and the universal cause. The bishop is responsible for faith and order, and, as such, is an extension of the personal mission of the Holy Spirit to the Church. Trust and reverence for the bishop, as expressed by the members of the local Church, is an essential element for his pastoral office, which bespeaks the sacramental reality, bequeathed to the Church by the Holy Spirit. It is the testimony of the Fathers of the Church that the Church itself is the continuation of the mission of the Holy Spirit to Christ rather than simply a continuation of the Incarnation.[18]

17. Rynne, *Letters from Vatican City, op. cit.,* p. 196.

18. Edward J. Kilmartin, S.J., *Toward Reunion: The Roman Catholic and the Orthodox Churches* (New York: Paulist Press, 1979), p. 4. This small work synthesizes the central issues of theology at the inception of Orthodox and Roman Catholic dialogue in the twentieth century. These are "(1) knowledge of God; (2) mission of the Holy Spirit; and (3) procession of the Holy

It is a source of wonder that two venerable bishops of the Church, one from deep in the land of the Reformation and the other the Patriarch of Antioch, the Second See of Christendom, should have made what is essentially the same proposal at the same time. As such they operated from motives of hope, for the prayer of Jesus, *Ut Unum Sint,* had not *yet* been fulfilled. Finally they looked for a meeting point between the Churches as they themselves were a meeting point, as servants of the Church.

The *Sensus Coetus*

Father Joseph Ellul, O.P., of the Pontifical University of St. Thomas Aquinas has written: "As a term, *koinonia* has made a relatively recent appearance in ecumenical vocabulary; nevertheless it is today *the essence of ecumenical thinking on ecclesiology.*"[19] It was at this moment in time, within the course of the preparations of the Second Vatican Council, that both the integrity and peculiarity of the idea of the local Church began to emerge vigorously as a topic of theological conversation. This phenomenon became apparent when the reception by Pope John to the idea of a Secretariat for Promoting Christian Unity opened up a wealth of possibilities. All were focused upon the theological exploration of the significance of the Church. To draw a parallel, just as a diocesan bishop is a meeting point of ecclesial fellowship, so too could this new and distinguished "ministry" *(dicastery)* of the Pontifical Household serve as a meeting point, for the fellowship of Churches and ecclesial communions, at the tombs of Peter and Paul.

Significantly, in its erection and constitution it was given the task of inviting ecumenical guests and observers to the Second Vatican Council and providing them with hospitality. It was not very long before people such as Archbishop Ramsey of Canterbury and W. A. Visser 't Hooft of the World Council of Churches began to refer to the Secretariat as "our home in Rome." It is possible then to refer to the Secretariat as possessive of a *sensus coetus,* i.e., an acknowledged and felt meeting point whereby the Christian fellowship of Churches could be acknowledged, pinpointed, and delineated. Writing during this very period, the British ecumenical pioneer, Father Bernard Leeming, S.J., stated: "Everyone must welcome this assertion that the

---

Spirit within the Trinity." Kilmartin outlines the history of Roman Catholic–Orthodox relations in his first chapter, pp. 5-16.

19. *Id., Growth in Koinonia: Baptism and Its Relation to the Eucharist in Roman Catholic–Orthodox Perspective* (Rome: Pontifical University of St. Thomas Aquinas, 1997), p. 164.

visible unity of the Church is a necessity and that Churches must try to over-come their disunity. At the same time the passage is hard to understand. The Church has an existence 'in that divine realm where disunity is unthink-able.'"[20] The heart of the question behind the letters of Maximos and Jaeger is this: Does the Church exist in the world, at all, or does it exist in the di-vine realm where it is beyond human perception? Dr. William Temple, Arch-bishop of Canterbury during the Second World War, had pondered the ques-tion and was fond of using the term "visible and invisible Church." In the 1950s English-speaking biblical scholars drew the distinction between reality and teleology in referring to the Church as an eschatological entity. Arch-bishop Temple had declared bluntly: "I believe in the holy, catholic Church, and sincerely regret that at present it does not exist."[21]

For the Catholic, the *sensus coetus* is expressive of the uniqueness of the Church, at once a temporal and eschatological reality, which is unlike any institution as perceived sociologically or anthropologically. In the nineteenth century, Johann Michael Sailer clarified this point by a re-introduction of the theme of the Mystical Body of Christ which, as has been noted, had a life of its own as a theological topic, through the nineteenth and twentieth centu-ries. More fundamentally, however, the *sensus coetus* produces an emotion of expectation and wonder, for: "With all wisdom and insight, He has made known to us the mystery of His will, according to His good pleasure, that He set forth in Christ, as a plan for the fullness of time, to gather up all things in Him, things in heaven and things on earth (Eph. 1:8-10)."

According to Pauline terminology, the phrase "Everything in the heav-ens" *(panta epi tois uranois)* (Eph. 1:10) is found only in this letter to the Ephesians. Paul's reference is to an unseen spiritual world, behind and above the material universe. Hope is expressive of the belief that the "things in heaven" constitute the real world, which touches the reality of the things on earth. The Pauline text describes "awareness" as the meeting point, not between the heavenly reality and a separate earthly reality; rather, there is one reality with an eternal expression and a temporal one. If there is an awareness of a drawing together between a heavenly expression and a tem-poral one, the same magnet likewise is present to draw together all of the disparate entities across the frontiers of separation underneath the timeline. The Secretariat for Promoting Christian Unity was, in fact, defined in its task by Bea himself; and, thus it met the expectations of the proposals of

---

20. *Id., The Churches and the Church* (London: Darton, Longman and Todd, 1960), p. 131.

21. *Ibid.*, p. 134.

both Jaeger and Maximos, for Bea used the term *ad fovendam* — "promoting." Bea saw the work of this little group whom he would assemble, Mons. Willebrands, Mons. Arrighi, Fr. Schmidt, Fr. Stransky and the administrative assistants, Mlle. Corinna de Martini and Mlle. Josette Kersters, as a *community of active awareness* of the reconciling power of the Lord Christ among the family of believers. (N.B. Within weeks, Father Erich Salzmann, a Swiss-born priest, joined the staff as an administrative ombudsman.)

The Competence of *Periti*

In a letter dated 21 October 1959, Archbishop Jaeger confided to Father Bea his fear that there was little understanding or appreciation of the particularity of the German situation, vis-à-vis the relationship of Catholics to Protestants and the particular psychological situation in Germany: "Dass in Rom keine genügende Kenntnis der deutschen Situation und der psychologischen Gegebenheiten des deutschen Protestantismus vorhanden sind." This has been cited above. Jaeger expressed his disappointment that the exigencies of the local German Churches' (Catholic and Protestant) relations totally passed by the concern of the Roman Curia. Out of his frustration, Jaeger posited to Bea the need for an ecumenical *Fachmann,* i.e., an expert in ecumenical matters. This is a concept which Bea both appreciated and accepted.

At the same time, the two clerics identified a new religious personality in the mainstream of the life of the Church. According to them, the *Fachmann* is a specialist endowed with a particular quality of visualizing the other Churches or ecclesial communions *as they see themselves.* The concept of the *Fachmann* is an innovation that yet remains to be developed in the literature. Forty years have now passed since Jaeger first posed the concept to Bea. Yet certain elements can be identified.

The first component is scholarship. This is one which would naturally lend itself to the personality of Cardinal Bea. Especially as a biblical academic, who was wedded to exegesis through reference to the *Sitz im Leben,* he realized that ecumenical exigencies can only be satisfied by clarity, sincerity, and concern. The components of the *Fachmann,* as manifested by Herte and Lortz, require first of all a dedication to study. This must be lifelong. Bea was deemed to be an appropriate *Fachmann* because of his ability with the Sacred Scriptures, understanding their role in the structuring of the religious ethos of Germany from the time of the Reformation. Bea had been trained in Germany and had maintained his contacts with German biblical exegetes, such as Oscar Cullmann and H. H. Harms.

For his part, Bea defined the primary role of the *Fachmann* as theological investigation, saying that the first urgencies of the ecumenical question, those of Church union, can only be answered by "calm and objective study by individuals," and by "theological conversations between specialists, belonging to different denominations."[22] When asked in 1961, by the mayor of Strassburg, if he were an optimist or a pessimist about ecumenism's future, Bea replied: "I am a realist!" In other words, the *Fachmann* has to be a person of virtue, endowed not with a sense of over-optimism but instead an individual of patience, discretion, hope, veracity, understanding, sympathy, and courage. The *Fachmann* also is willing to undertake the journey, although long and complex. The *Fachmann* realizes that he is a person of history and therefore must be content not to see immediately the results of his labor: "One man sows, another man reaps (Jn. 4:36)."[23]

Bea went on to address this question at Harvard University in 1963, between the first and second sessions of the Second Vatican Council. The *Fachmann,* he indicated, is a scholar of truth in charity: "Truth and charity must be ever present in our ecumenical work, and hand-in-hand, because truth without charity is intolerant and repulsive, and charity without truth is blind and will not endure."[24] In that same lecture, Bea identified the very first task of the *Fachmann* as the identification of "what the different confessions have in common . . . besides, it is a well-known principle that in obscure questions one starts from what is clear, advancing step by step into the obscure. In the same way, the exact discovery of the Christian goods we have in common is a help in distinguishing clearly the differences, in seeing them in the right light and proportion and also in gradually overcoming them."[25]

The *Fachmann* also possesses a sensitivity to the pneumatological elements of ecumenism. Bea himself was a pragmatic man who delineated the problem and proposed elements which might be taken into consideration, in arriving at the solution.[26] But Bea was aware, in this matter, that the *Fachmann* must be prone to appreciate the singularity of this work as "a special breath of the Holy Spirit."[27] Therefore the *Fachmann* must be a

---

22. Bea, *Unity of Christians,* p. 203.

23. Schmidt, *op. cit.,* pp. 408-11.

24. Bea, "Academic Pursuits and Christian Unity," in *Ecumenical Dialogue at Harvard,* ed. Samuel H. Miller and G. Ernest Wright (Cambridge: Harvard University Press, Belknap Press, 1964), p. 33.

25. *Ibid.,* p. 32.

26. Schmidt, *op. cit.,* p. 374.

27. *Ibid.,* p. 347.

person of faith, realizing that the work of Christian unity is actually the Holy Spirit, laboring, groaning and fulfilling the prayer of Jesus: "Father, that they all may be one."

A specific problem yet remains to be examined in the future. This would be the identification of the relationship of the *Fachmann* to the bishop, the College of bishops and the Holy See. The *Fachmann* cannot be a wandering figure, charismatically endowed, but unrecognized and unappreciated in his findings and in his study. It is the evidence of Father Schmidt that Bea believed *that in all things ecumenical the supervision of the bishop is necessary*. Further ecumenism is a question of submission to the faith, to the truth of the faith, and to those who are entrusted with the responsibility of teaching the content of the faith, as well as passing on the faith. Submission therefore is not a matter of surrender; it is a matter of humility and a recognition of the Church universal, as the Mystical Body of Christ, Lord and Savior.

In the days after the acceptance of the 4 March proposal, Bea wanted a universal body of *Fachmänner*, one from every country in fact. Jaeger thought this idea ridiculous and said as much to Bea. The *Fachmann* is a *vocation* which is discernible by the sensitivity and intellectual acumen demonstrated not only to ideas but especially to people, within the community of the Church. Therefore the panel of experts at Rome, who would fulfill the expectations of the above, would be precisely dedicated to facilitating the cause of Christian unity, which is the prayer of Jesus (Jn. 17:21).

Maximos Saigh also sought expertise at Rome. While his theology was more oriented toward a communion ecclesiology, his practical conclusion was juridical. He asked for experts at Rome who were not given to centrist tendencies, but who understood the integrity of the local Church. Most especially, Maximos sought an appreciation of the Oriental Church and of the Fathers. Maximos therefore would have had to have in mind the thought of St. Cyprian of Carthage, author of the earliest treatise on ecclesiology: "We continuously live by her (Church) Spirit as children in the womb of their mothers live on the substance of their mothers."[28] Cyprian's imagery of the Church is that of spouse and dove. In this latter title, there is the note of tenderness and solicitude:

> That is also the reason why the Holy Spirit comes in the form of a dove:
> It [the dove] is a simple joyous creature, not bitter with gall, not biting

---

28. Cited in Henri de Lubac, S.J., *The Splendor of the Church* (Glen Rock, N.J.: Paulist Press, 1955), p. 161.

savagely, with vicious tearing claws; *it loves to dwell with humankind,* it keeps to one house for assembling, when they mate they hatch their young together, when they fly anywhere they keep their formation. The resorts they live in are shared in common, by their billing do they pay tribute to concord and peace, in all things they fulfil the law of unanimity. The same is the simplicity of the Church which we need to learn. This is the charity we must acquire that we may imitate the doves in our love for the brotherhood.[29]

The image of the Church as dove, analogical and poetic, uncovers in every child of the Church a sense of filial piety: "And every true Catholic will have a feeling of tender *pietas* towards her. He will love to call her *mother* — the title that sprang from the hearts of her first children as the texts of Christian antiquity bear witness on so many occasions."[30] A definition of the *Fachmann* was anticipated some five years before by the French theologian (later Cardinal) Henri de Lubac, S.J., who wrote: "History and his own experience combined to show him both the desire for the knowledge of divine things which stirs the human spirit, and the weakness that lays that spirit open to falling into every kind of error."[31] De Lubac also added: "The baptismal instinct of the child responds with a leaping joy to the demands made upon it by its mother: 'Wherever the Spirit of the Lord is, there also is its freedom.'"[32] The *Fachmann* is endowed with that specific knowledge.

The Ministry of the Secretariat for Promoting Christian Unity

In his letter of 23 May 1959, Maximos proposed that the new Vatican bureau be composed of competent members. He specifically sought participation from the Holy Office, the Sacred Congregation for the Oriental Churches and from the Vatican Secretariate of State. The other members should represent the Church in its pluriformity, especially those of an Eastern theological mentality. Maximos admitted that theologians of this ilk

---

29. St. Cyprian, *The Lapsed and the Unity of the Catholic Church,* ed. Maurice Bénot (Baltimore: Newman Press, 1957), p. 51.

30. De Lubac, *op. cit.,* p. 161.

31. *Ibid.,* p. 158.

32. Cited in *ibid.,* p. 158. St. Augustine, *De Spiritu et Littera* 16.28 (Patrologia Latina 44:218).

are few.[33] As was indicated in Chapter One, he too, therefore, did not want to see established at Rome a "watchdog" committee. Most of all, Maximos IV desired that the focus of Rome's attention should be to recognize the integrity of the Eastern Churches, in tradition, uniqueness, and dignity. No more is this clearly recognized than in the theme of the sacred liturgy. Five years previously, Sir Stephen Runciman, Britain's greatest scholar of Byzantium, affirmed the primacy of the liturgical ethos in the East:

> Right worship was really more important to the Eastern Christians. . . . They were devoted to their liturgy, although it did not become definitely fixed till after the Iconoclastic Controversy. But that very controversy had shown their attachment to their forms was growing. The liturgy was something in which the whole congregation played its part; and even the decoration of the Church building was involved in it; the icons and mosaic figures, too, were participants. They grew to resent very bitterly any criticism of their ritual and their practices, and were suspicious of attempts at innovation or alteration.[34]

At the Council itself, Bishop Hakim, who would later accede to the Patriarchate of Antioch, put it all very succinctly: "With us the liturgy is the chief means of instruction in the faith through its symbolism. Instruction is never separated from Scripture or the Fathers."[35]

In particular, the Eastern Church embraces a dynamic theology of the Holy Spirit. At the time of the convocation of the Second Vatican Council, the *Filioque* question remained a point of dispute between the East and the West as it does even to this day. However, the Eastern Churches are possessed of a dynamic understanding of the procession of the Holy Spirit from the Father and the vivifying gifts of the Holy Spirit to the Church. At the Second Vatican Council, Maximos would stand up, over and over, again and again, to enunciate that theology, so that the effect of his letter to Pope John would continue through the work of the Council. Did Pope John hear him? The answer is "Yes." On 8 December 1962, Pope John formally closed the First Session with these words: "It will be a *'new Pentecost'* indeed, which will cause the Church to renew her interior riches and to extend her maternal care in every sphere of human activity."[36] What did

---

33. "But thanks be to God there are more and more of them. . . ." [Mais Dieu merci, il y en a et de plus en plus. . . .]

34. *Id., The Eastern Schism*)Oxford: Oxford University Press, 1955), pp. 7-8.

35. Rynne, *Letters from Vatican City,* p. 159.

36. Cited in *ibid.,* p. 276.

Maximos seek from the Council? In a fairly long statement on the issue of Divine Revelation, Maximos summarized his deepest thoughts:

> What we expect is a peaceful and positive message, worthy of the attention of our Separated Brethren. The spirit of this *schema* is once again the spirit of the Counter-Reformation . . . since Vatican I only a partial and incomplete picture of the Church has been presented. The prerogatives of the Visible Head have been put in evidence in such an isolated way that the rest of the body of the Church seems dwarfish in comparison. We must re-establish the true proportions between the body and its head and thus give a truer and more complete picture. I ask once again that the schema on the Church and the hierarchy be submitted as soon as possible. Everything depends on that *schema,* because then we can take up pastoral and social questions. All of us await that moment.[37]

Clearly, Maximos' first motive was to address the expectations of all the Separated Brethren. Secondly, he saw the issue of ecumenism as intimately associated with a refined ecclesiological understanding. The Secretariat for Promoting Christian Unity would be the organ which would carry these concepts forward.

On the other hand, Jaeger's letter of 17 December 1959 was mostly functional in tone. He advised Bea of the necessity of establishing at Rome a bureau of experts, an *offizielle Gutachterstelle.* Jaeger referred to it as a corresponding Catholic organ to the World Council of Churches. The immediate task at hand would be the assembling of a body of information as well as the dissemination of facts and dates in order to provide knowledge and animation for the fostering of ecumenical activity. Clearly for Bea and Jaeger such a body was pragmatic, since it sought to forestay any further misunderstandings such as the disastrous Rhodes Incident. It definitely had the character of a Press Office. Its personnel would ferret out the truth and report it in a non-offensive way.

From the first, Bea's *Gutachterstelle* was on a shaky foundation. For example, Hebblethwaite records that by the autumn of 1960, Pope John warned Bea that the newly established body had produced negative speculation on the part of the Roman Curia, that its contacts could distract the Fathers of the Council, create disarray among them, and delay the work of preparing the Council.[38] However, that simply did not happen. Father Schmidt has reported that the ecumenical aim of the Second Vatican Coun-

37. *Ibid.,* p. 149.
38. Hebblethwaite, *Pope John XXIII,* p. 380.

cil had in fact been incarnated with the creation of the Secretariat for Promoting Christian Unity. This in fact happened over a period of time.

On 21 June 1962, a specific incident brought the matter to a head. Again, the World Council of Churches was involved. A Vatican press release occasioned an AP International news item. The Associated Press headlined its story: "Church Blasts Ecumenism." Underneath, the item narrated that the Central Commission of the Second Vatican Council had taken a strong stand against the ecumenism of Bea and his Secretariat. It went on to say:

> The word ecumenism, as used today, habitually by non-Catholics and particularly Protestants, indicates a form of understanding, almost a federation of all Christian Churches, each with equal rights. According to this theory, the different churches should consider themselves equally guilty of the separation. No church should presume to be the one true church of Christ. The future church resulting from the union of the present churches would not be identified with any existing church but would be completely new.[39]

The above information was based upon a press communiqué by Monsignor Fausto Vaillainc, who was the entire Press Office of the Second Vatican Council, but not for long. The Associated Press then gave this interpretation: "The Roman Catholic Church considers 'ecumenicalism' [*sic*] or Christian Unity as possible only by the return to the Church of the 'separated brothers.'"[40] Reading the newspaper in his apartment, Cardinal Bea decided that he had had enough. American journalist Robert Blair Kaiser reports him saying:

> "Why, when His Holiness constituted our Secretariat he called it a Secretariat for the Union of Christians — not the *reunion* of Christians?" Bea paused and let that sink in. "And when he read the bull announcing the Council, he said that he was aware that many are 'gripped by a desire for unity and peace — *unitatis et pacis assequendae desiderio teneri.*' But the *Osservatore Romano* translated this passage as 'anxious for return — *sono ansiosi di un ritorno di unità e di pace.*' Maybe the people at *Osservatore Romano* don't understand."[41]

---

39. Robert Blair Kaiser, *Pope Council and World* (New York: Macmillan Company, 1963), p. 73.
40. *Ibid.*
41. *Ibid.*, p. 74.

That was just the point. They did not understand. In exasperation, Bea pronounced: "As much confusion here as there are words." Bea's distinction is about union while so many others were confused and could not even envisage such a concept. Robert Blair Kaiser wryly remarked: "Cardinal Bea's charitable judgment is obviously the true one. The Curialist approach is rarely malicious. The Curialists just do not understand."[42]

It should be clear, from the above-cited incident, that the scope and purpose of the Jaeger/Bea *Gutachterstelle* was a presentation of a new non-Counter-Reformation Church, and the demonstration of that fact by its engagement with the life and activity of the other Churches and Christian communities. As Father Schmidt reported, the ecclesiological vision of the Second Vatican Council *was* incarnated with the creation of the Secretariat for Promoting Christian Unity. The Counter-Reformation age had come to a close. The new *Gutachterstelle* was the symbol of that fact. It was designed to meet the needs of the Oriental Churches and those of Reformation history. In so doing, it provided hope.

That hope is founded upon a premise of Archbishop Jaeger. In his letter of 21 October 1959, he wrote to Bea that there was little *Kenntnis* (knowledge) of the ecumenical situation, factual and psychological. The Secretariat is to be the center of such *Kenntnis,* and as such, should be manned by individuals who were true experts. Their *Kenntnis* is not merely conceptual. Their dignity comes from the awareness that together they are a concretization of the prayer of Jesus (Jn. 17:21). Secondly, they are capable of love. They are to be the expressions of the love of the Church of all the family of God. Without a continued reminder of the spiritual quality of their vocation, their efforts would be reduced as such to ashes. Expertise is bolstered only by prayer and acts of charity, for hope exists in the spiritual dimension. It is the provisional, the not yet, the eschatological.

Cardinal Bea: A Man of Hope

Pope Leo XIII penned these words: "Nothing is more useful than to see the world as it really is and to look elsewhere for a remedy for its troubles."[43] Writing at mid–twentieth century, the German psychiatrist Karl Stern defined the principle of hope as the dynamic inner thrust of the essence of ev-

42. *Ibid.*

43. Cited in Augustine Paul Hennessy, C.P., *Encountering Christ* (Union City, N.J.: Sign Press, 1979), p. 230.

ery man. By borrowing from concepts of St. Thomas Aquinas that man is always *homo viator,* "man on the way," tending toward *homo comprehensor,* "man reaching understanding,"[44] he stated that it is not extraneous or superficial to the human personality to hope. In 1969, Augustine Paul Hennessy, C.P., formerly president of the American Catholic Theological Society, wrote: "Hope *is the meeting ground* where Christians, Jews, and all men of good will can effectively proclaim their faith in the future of man. There is nothing tired or resigned or overwhelmed about God-given hope. It is always trying something new to free man from folly." The same author wrote: "Whether we like it or not, at this moment of history we have a yoke to bear. The People of God are captive to oppressive moods. . . . When we lose our confidence in words, we lose confidence in our own humanity."[45] All of the above enables us to make the following reflections.

The 4 November letter of Bea to Jaeger spoke about the necessity of the *Gutachterstelle* at Rome and the qualified *Fachmann* to lead it. Now, what remained was the definition of its mission. That mission was dialogue. Bea agreed with Jaeger's assessment that in Rome there was neither knowledge nor understanding of theological developments in the Protestant world. Given the exigencies of the times, the *status quo* was no longer tenable, not for pragmatic reasons, but for theological reasons. After the establishment of the Secretariat for Promoting Christian Unity, Bea began an incessant round of lectures and press conferences in which he displayed, in the words of his assistant, Jean-Francois Arrighi: "The singular witness of this attitude of fraternity in regard to the other Christians" [témoignage singulier de cette attitude de fraternité vécue à l'égard des autres chrétiens].[46] In his *Irenikon* article, regarding Cardinal Bea's reflections on baptism and Christian unity, the noted ecumenist Dom Emmanuel Lanne correctly identified the nature of the ecumenical problem facing the Catholic Church in those years. "But at this moment in time the lines had been taken, and not without human foresight" [Mais à l'époque ces lignes prenaient position et non point sans réflexion].[47] The significance of paragraph 22 of *Mystici Corporis* was the issue. Significantly, Josef Höfer had

44. Karl Stern, *Pillar of Fire* (Garden City, N.Y.: Doubleday and Company, 1959), pp. 206-7. These Latin terms are adaptations of Stern based upon the teaching of Joseph Pieper in his presentation of Thomistic theology.

45. *Id., op. cit.,* pp. 194, 230.

46. Cited in Emmanuel Lanne, "La contribution du cardinal Bea à la question du baptême et l'Unité des chrétiens," *Irenikon,* no. 55 (1982): 472.

47. *Ibid.,* p. 473.

previously advised both Archbishop Jaeger and Father Bea of its ambiguity, throughout the 1950s. It was the first theological challenge to Cardinal Bea's ecumenical task: "Who is a member of the Church?"

Dom Lanne wrote on the eve of the publication of the Joint Ortho-dox–Roman Catholic Agreed Statement of 1982, known as the "Munich Agreed Text": *The Mystery of the Church and of the Eucharist in the Light of the Mystery of the Holy Trinity*. These are his words: "The audacity of the thought of Bea (in regard to this question) only emerges with lots of evidence" [L'audace de la pensée de Bea n'en ressortira qu'avec plus d'évidence].[48] In his article, Lanne carefully noted that a few people had prepared the groundwork for answering that question, but that others had refused, for theological reasons, to address the argument concerning baptism received by Christians.[49] Bea did not shrink from the challenge.

With his appointment by John XXIII as the first Cardinal President, Bea was endowed with a "bully pulpit" to draw his argument in public and to distinguish his conclusion regarding "the incommensurable grace of baptism, which consists of indestructible bonds, stronger than all our divisions" [l'incommensurable grâce du baptême, qui a établi des liens indestrucibles, plus forts que toutes nos divisions].[50] Dom Lanne demonstrated that point through means of a summary of Bea's three major specific texts, i.e., (1) a Sacred Heart Messenger article (December 1960), (2) a press conference held at the Columbus Hotel (December 4, 1960), and (3) an Angelicum Speech commemorating the Week of Church Unity Octave on January 21, 1961. According to Lanne's judgment, Bea successfully explored the concept of baptism, and thus uncovered the possibilities for dialogue in the future. He expressed the hope of finding common ground for dialogue, which he *knew* already existed within the sacramental theology of the Christian family. So confident was Bea that by 1962 he used this language of hope in order to call the observers (Orthodox, Anglican, and Protestant) to the First Session of the Second Vatican Council: "My Brothers."[51]

While at this time Bea's language elicited aspirations of hope, primarily from the heirs of the Reformers, whose theme was the "Priesthood of All Believers," it also became an invitation to the Orthodox, who gave it a positive reception, which varied in degree from one autocephaly to another.[52] No one

48. *Ibid.*, p. 476.

49. *Ibid.*, p. 472.

50. *Ibid.*, p. 471.

51. *Ibid.* This he did on the eve of the opening session of the Council, when he met them as a group for the first time.

52. The evidence of Bea's success comes from the testimony of Robert McAfee Brown,

could ever deny that the concept of Baptism establishes the priority of holy things. The holiest of undertakings possible to all Christians is the expression of charity, for it is in love that one can imitate the selfless, worshipful generosity and obedience of Christ, who came to be the "Servant of all (Is. 42:11)." The concepts of service of generosity and of worship are all found in the Holy Thursday events (Jn. 13:1-13).[53] "Father, that all may be one, as I am in You, and You are in me . . . (Jn. 17:21-22)." *The vision was expanding.*[54]

Formal responsibility for Eastern Christians did not pass into the Secretariat's hands until the promulgation of *Humani Salutis,* i.e., the Bull of Convocation of the Council at Christmas, 1961. They were however present to the vision of the Secretariat almost from the start, with the presence of Monsignor Willebrands, who arrived in Rome to take up his responsibilities as Secretary of the Secretariat on 7 July. He carried Orthodox concerns and interests with him.

The Idea of Unity Emerges on the Council Floor

Perhaps the most succinct evidence of Augustin Bea's personal thought about the scope of his Secretariat was ultimately delivered on the Council floor, when the discussion of the subject of Christian Unity was introduced

---

who wrote of the importance of this concept to the children of the Reformation. All minister to one another: "We are all priests to one another." Cited in *The Ecumenical Revolution* (Garden City, N.Y.: Doubleday and Company, 1967), pp. 22-23. Yves Congar, O.P., *The Mystery of the Temple* (Westminster, Md.: Newman Press, 1962), p. 178, views the analogy in another way but conveyed the same thought: "It is through the maturing of a personal spiritual life, begun at baptism, a maturing and a growth brought about by the Word of God, which they both desire and receive . . . that the faithful give themselves to be built up as living stones into the spiritual edifice of the church which they then form." See Jean Daniélou, S.J., *The Presence of God, op. cit.,* p. 33: "The Temple of the Church that is thus slowly built up by charity is at the same time the fulfillment of the Mosaic Temple and of the Cosmic Temple."

53. *Superno Dei nutu,* cited thus in Schmidt, *op. cit.,* p. 330: "In order to show in a special way our love and our benevolence towards those who bear the name of Christians but are separated from this Apostolic See, and in order that they may watch the work of the Council and more easily find the way towards that unity that Jesus Christ implored from the heavenly Father with ardent prayer, we have set up a special committee *(coetus)* or secretariat."

54. Daniélou, *The Presence of God, op. cit.,* pp. 27-29, provided evidence of the reception of this ecclesiology in his above-cited book: "This presence is no longer bound to a single place. It is connected with the glorified Manhood of Christ, the final and conclusive Temple that is, with the total Christ in his individual reality and in His Mystical Body, the place of worship 'in spirit and in truth.' . . . It is the manhood of Jesus that is the Temple of the New Law but this Manhood must be taken as a whole, that is to say, it is the Mystical Body in its entirety; this is the complete and final Temple."

and taken up during the Twenty-Seventh General Congregation of the first period, on Monday, 26 November 1962. Curiously, the subject was not introduced then by Bea's Secretariat but by the Preparatory Commission for the Oriental Churches. The title of the *schema* was *"Ut Unum Sint."*[55] While this was appropriate enough, the politics of the preparation for the Council had become so embroiled that two other *schemata* were prepared on the general theme of unity. One was the property of the Theological Commission, which was concerned with Protestants of the Classical Reformation. The Secretariat for Promoting Christian Unity took as its responsibility the formulation of general ecumenical principles. At this point, even then, though at the very beginning, the Council Fathers found themselves quite confused! Almost at once, they found themselves confronted with the topics of the East, the West, the Classical Reformation, theological theory, and the need to formulate a quite precise statement about the nature of the Church. The late John Cardinal Krol, who later played a part in the Central Committee of the Council, acknowledged for the author the authenticity of these words taken from Xavier Rynne:

> A certain amount of internecine rivalry, therefore, was undoubtedly responsible for the present situation, which the Central Preparatory Commission either would not, or could not, resolve. It must be acknowledged, likewise, that Cardinal Bea's Secretariat did not at first enjoy, within the confines of the Church, the tremendous prestige which it later acquired, and the advantages of having it coordinate *all* aspects of the problem of reunion, theological as well as practical, which were not fully seen at first, although laid down in theory.[56]

At 11:10 A.M. that day, Cardinal Amletto Cicognani approached the microphone to introduce the *schema,* which took up the question of prospects for "reunion" with the Orthodox Churches. The Secretary of the Preparatory Commission, Father Athanasius Welykyj, of the Order of St. Basil of St. Josaphat, outlined the principal points of the draft. The Archbishop of Lille, Cardinal Achille Lienart, began the discussion with an expression of displeasure.[57]

Cardinal Lienart found some small merit in the presentation, but he objected to the document's insistence upon a "return to the true fold,"

---

55. Rynne, *Letters from Vatican City,* p. 190. The above-cited interview with Cardinal Krol took place at the Residence of the Cardinals of Philadelphia on February 25, 1996.

56. *Ibid.,* p. 191.

57. *Ibid.,* p. 192.

which in turn was "placing a hopeless obstacle in the way of reunion." A rather lengthy and confusing discussion followed, during which the Patriarch Maximos IV Saigh finally stepped out of the shadows, where he had remained from May 1959 until the present moment, to make *his* intervention. Maximos quoted an old Arab proverb: "When many hands prepare the cooking, the meat is sure to be burnt." Therefore, he proposed that the combination of the three separate *schemata* should be effected, before things became more confused and people became demoralized. The entire incident deserves to be quoted from Rynne:

> Patriarch Maximos IV Saigh, speaking in French, said that as the schema dealt with the Orthodox it did not concern Oriental Catholics directly. However, as it was of such great importance, he desired to point out that certain sections, particularly in the first part, would only serve to enrage rather than attract those among the Orthodox who were benevolently disposed toward Catholicism, for they were evidence of the old Roman absolutism, and gave an unbalanced picture of both the history and responsibility for the earlier split in Christendom. It must be realized, he insisted, that the Oriental Churches were completely distinct from the Latin Church. They owed their origins directly to Christ and the Apostles, and received their traditions and rites from the Greek and Oriental Fathers. Hence, even in their organization, they were not dependent on the See of Rome. Since this was the case, he asked, were Fathers such as Basil, the Gregories, Cyril and Chrysostom to be considered as Catholics of a lower rank than the Latin Fathers? The schema should speak a truly Catholic language. First it should mention the collegial character of the Church's pastorate, the bishops being the successors of the college of Apostles, and then only come to the papal primacy as the basis, foundation and center of that collegiality. Next he recommended that the three separate schemata prepared by the Theological and Oriental Commissions and the Secretariat for Promoting Christian Unity should be combined.[58]

The debate lasted for several days and at the end Cardinal Bea made *his* intervention, during which he called for the combination of responsibilities, as were outlined by Patriarch Maximos. He said that much had been introduced by the inaugural *schemata,* but what was actually the topic of debate was indeed the provenance, within the entire work of this Council, of the Secretariat for Promoting Christian Unity.

58. *Ibid.,* p. 195.

Bea then made a curious statement. He posited that the inspiration for the Secretariat "had to come to Pope John XXIII from plans of which Pope Leo XIII had for establishing, a *Concilium,* along this line, but which had to be abandoned, when that pope died."[59] Also curiously, prior to Cardinal Bea's intervention, Bea was known by his colleagues and his staff as a master of timing. When he spoke to the Bishops, within the context of the Council, he likewise did this in reference to both precedence within the history of the papacy as well as always with clear biblical, juridical, and magisterial references. Obviously, the cross-reference to the planned *Concilium* of Leo XIII *was not* the direct cause of inspiration to Pope John XXIII in regard to the question of Christian Unity. At least two other men in the *aula* knew that fact, i.e., Patriarch Maximos and Archbishop Jaeger. Bea knew quite well that *he* had presented the inspiring letter to Pope John. However, more than likely, with his grasp of the history of the contemporary papacy, he not only found, but brought, to Pope John's attention, Pope Leo's blueprint for the sake of Christian Unity. For the record, in this manner and in public, he provided the historical seal of authentication to forestay any other arguments about ecumenical *competenza.*

In the Second Session of the Second Vatican Council, the tabled *schemata* produced no better results than the first. Much discussion was followed by no real sense of resolution! Pope John XXIII died on 3 June 1963. When Cardinal Montini came to the Chair of Peter on 21 June 1963 as Pope Paul VI, he announced the following day that the Council was reconvened under his own authority and in his own name. During the period between the two sessions, Bea's overall thought had much opportunity to mature. Therefore, in the midst of a chaos of ideas regarding the purpose and scope of ecumenism, he took the floor and made this brief intervention under the title "Clarifications."[60] He was confident of the security of his efforts at the dawn of the new pontificate.[61]

---

59. *Ibid.,* p. 208.

60. Cardinal Augustine Bea, "Clarifications," in Yves Congar, O.P., Hans Küng, and Daniel O'Hanlon, S.J. (eds.), *Council Speeches of Vatican II* (Glen Rock, N.J.: Paulist Press, 1964), pp. 165-69.

61. Peter Hebblethwaite, *Paul VI* (London: Harper Collins, 1993), p. 370. Pope Paul VI took over Pope John's Council, giving it direction by clarifying its goals: "The renewal of the Church, the promotion of Christian Unity, and dialogue with the modern world. He treated the Council with great respect, assuring it the greatest freedom of discussion by not assigning a date for its conclusion and not seeking to anticipate its results by its decisions."

Bea's "Clarifications" in Light of a New Pontificate

Having heard the deliberations regarding the cause of unity, through two sessions, Cardinal Bea expressed himself in the clearest possible terms in his second speech:

> The primary requirement of all ecumenical activity is that we have an accurate knowledge of them [our non-Catholic brothers], sincere admiration, and genuine Christian love. For this reason the Sovereign Pontiffs, beginning with Leo XIII, have repeatedly shown what "traces of Christ and gifts of the Holy Spirit" are found among our non-Catholic brothers, and this because of their baptism itself and the graces, which flow from Baptism. And anyone who assails this way of acting automatically attacks the Sovereign Pontiffs from Leo XIII to Paul VI.[62]

Bea had already cited Leo XIII in his previous intervention at the first session. Specifically his reference was to Leo's encyclical about the Holy Spirit, *Divinum Illud*, of 4 May 1897:

> So He, Who is the Divine goodness and the mutual love of the Father and Son completes and perfects, by His strong yet gentle power, the secret work of man's eternal salvation.[63]

That encyclical spoke of the Holy Spirit as being the soul of Christ's Body. As has been indicated, the concept of the Mystical Body of Christ became a major ecclesiological pre-occupation of Roman Catholic theologians in the twentieth century, especially those from northern Europe. One example of this trend is Karl Adam, who wrote about it in his seminal work in the mid-1920s, *The Spirit of Catholicism*: "But the Church is not only invisible because she is the Kingdom of God, she is no haphazard collection of individuals, but an ordered system of regularly subordinated parts and because the Church is the Body of Christ she is essentially an organism, with its members purposely interrelated, and a visible organism."[64]

---

62. *Ibid.*, p. 168.

63. Cited in Fremantle, *op. cit.*, p. 159 (emphasis mine).

64. *Id., The Spirit of Catholicism, op. cit.*, p. 34. See also p. 59. "The Pentecostal experience of the first disciples, because it was effected by God, has two characteristics: its comprehensive catholicity and its compact unity. Catholicity, universality, belongs properly to God's redemptive activity. Where God is at work there can be no respect of persons." This book first appeared in English in 1929, and was written in Germany between 1925 and 1927. For the history and evolution of Adam's thought, see Krieg, *op. cit.*, pp. 1-27.

Having cited the pneumatic insight of Leo XIII, Bea then concluded with Paul VI, who, in *his* opening address to the Second Session of the Council, spoke of the "unity" challenge previously put before the Council Fathers by Pope John XXIII. Pope Paul called this challenge "one, which in the order of spiritual realities is most grave. It concerns *the other Christians* — those who believe in Christ but whom we cannot happily number among ourselves in the perfect unity of Christ, which only the Catholic Church can afford them. *This unity, objectively speaking, should be theirs by Baptism.* It is something which they already desire."[65] In effect, Paul VI in his opening speech from the Chair acknowledged two new facts, (1) the sad death of John XXIII and the beginning of his own reign as pontiff, and (2) *the unity of all Christians* in the one Church of Christ as *one of the main aims of the Council.*[66]

In style, Cardinal Bea was a true Roman. For him, it was all in the timing! Furthermore, he conveniently used language which could be stylized as Ultramontane. However, at the heart of his reasoning, as will become clear, is the focus of his attention on the significance and the irrevocability of the Sacrament of Baptism, by which the grace of "Adopted Sonship" and the ever active fructifying dynamic of the Holy Spirit is showered upon "all who are baptized (and who) are indeed baptized in Christ Jesus (Eph. 3:6)."[67]

Bea ended his intervention with these words: "My conclusion is that what has been said seems to show how important it is for all Catholics to have a correct understanding of the ecumenical movement, which the Sovereign Pontiffs from Leo XIII to Paul VI desire and promote ever more enthusiastically."[68]

The Twin Components of Unity

Bea acknowledged therefore a particular character of the Ecumenical Movement that had been disclosed in the death of Pope John, who died with the words *"Ut unum sint"* upon his lips. That character is also evident in the attitude of Pope John regarding "doing the truth in charity."[69] The two necessary components of that background are "truth" and "charity."

65. Küng, *et al., op. cit.,* p. 145.
66. Schmidt, *op. cit.,* pp. 462-63.
67. *Ibid.*
68. *Ibid.*
69. *Ibid.,* p. 462.

The phraseology is not mere jargon. Bea said the primary requirement of all ecumenical activity is "that we have an accurate knowledge of them, sincere admiration and genuine Christian love."[70] There is precedent for this concept of "truth" and "charity" as prerequisites for the Ecumenical Movement, drawn from the worldwide Ecumenical Movement itself.

In a small article on the antecedents of the Roman Catholic entry into the Ecumenical Movement, Étienne Fouilloux wrote about the philosophical agitation within the first decade of the twentieth century; a trend toward "a return to the sources" emerged. Fouilloux posited that this trend was a necessary antidote, at once, to fundamentalism, Liberal politics and even Darwinian science, all evident in the nineteenth century. Naturally, ecclesiastical studies were likewise affected. This was especially true of biblical studies. The remarkable contribution of linguistics and archaeology at the same time had affected Catholics, Orthodox, Anglicans and Protestants, to varying degrees. Among the latter, the movement of *ressourcement* (return to the sources) was present at the groundbreaking Ecumenical Assembly in Edinburgh in 1910. There, the word *agape* (love) arose as the mandate of the Savior and would never be absent again.[71] The motive of charity was expressed in 1920, through the encyclical of the Greek Patriarchate of Constantinople, drafted by Metropolitan Germanos: "Above all, love should be rekindled and *strengthened among the churches,* so that they no more consider one another as strangers and foreigners, but as relatives, and, as being a part of the household of Christ and fellow heirs, members of the same Body and partakers of the promise of God in Christ (Eph. 3:6)."[72]

While precedent towards "truth" and "charity" was contained in examples from the worldwide Ecumenical Movement, Bea brought his expertise as a biblical scholar to the discussion of this very concept. From 1955 to 1959, he wrote many personal letters on the topic of ecumenism, ac-

---

70. *Ibid.*

71. *Id.* "Église Romaine et Chrétientés non Catholiques de la grande guerre au concile Vatican II" (The Roman Church and the non-Catholic Christendoms during the Great War of the Second Vatican Council), in *Paolo VI e L'ecumenismo* (Brescia: Istituto Paolo VI, 2001), pp. 24-25.

72. Schmidt, *op. cit.* pp. 246-47, describes the commitment of Bea to a dialogue of truth and charity in practical terms vis-à-vis an explanation of the doctrine of the Assumption to Protestants during his teaching career. He described the components of arrival at such a teaching: illumination by the Holy Spirit, contemplation of truth, the evidence of Sacred Revelation, *sensus fidei,* and confirmation by the Magisterium. This description also takes in Bea's sense of patience, understanding, and a desire to show compassion and provide comfort.

cording to the biography by Father Schmidt. Schmidt recorded that in a letter of 1956:

> He [Bea] explained that it is certainly not true that there is nothing but error *on the other side;* nor can we *a priori* be sure that our understanding of the viewpoint of others is always correct. "Only the Lord possesses the absolute truth." And here we see how this applies to our subject: in such a complex matter as ecumenical work, there are obscure points that can be clarified only if we proceed calmly and objectively. In conclusion, as we shall see, he (Bea) says that doctrinal differences must be frankly noted, but that we must always show the *maximum respect and charity for the others,* and leave the necessary time for grace and intelligence to operate, just as the Lord does.[73]

Bea's understanding of ecumenism, at this point in the first Conciliar activities, indicates that demands for submission give way to invitations for mutual exploration in grace. Reconciliation between brothers and sisters is the goal, not conviction through argument. Unity does not mean uniformity. Truth is associated with a kind of *vestigia* theology whereby the discovery of the "impress" of the Church is associated with gifts, given through the Holy Spirit. One of those gifts is Baptism. It can truly be said that the catholic gift, otherwise universally apparent throughout the entire Church, had over time become muddled by reason of the separation of Churches and ecclesial communions. Furthermore, the very fact of separation had become mingled with other factors, viz., political, cultural, and personal. But, as Pope Pius XI declared: "Pieces broken off from gold-bearing rock, themselves bear gold" [Massi staccati da una roccia aurifera sono auriferi anche essi].[74] As Bernard Leeming has stated, all those "who have been baptized and draw their inspiration from the Gospel, possess something very precious which must be acknowledged by all fellow believers."[75]

---

73. *Ibid.,* p. 249. Schmidt also notes that the correspondence of Bea contains over 180 letters dealing with ecumenical questions prior to his being made Cardinal, p. 237. Bea's correspondence also reveals that in July of 1959 he wrote: "The developments of the last months show with sad clarity how far we are from unity" [Gli sviluppi degli ultimi mesi monstrano con triste chiarezza come ora siamo piú che mai lontani dall' unità]. This is the original sentence as written in Italian in S. Schmidt, *Agostino Bea* (Rome: Città Nuova Editrice, 1987), p. 258.

74. Found in the 9 January 1927 "Allocution on the Eastern Churches," *Osservatore Romano,* 10/11 January 1927.

75. Leeming, *The Churches and the Church, op. cit.,* p. 255.

Baptism: The Heart of the Matter

When the author first spoke to Father Schmidt about the thought of Cardinal Bea (1978) regarding his specifically ecumenical contribution to, and his blueprint for, the future for the Secretariat for Promoting Christian Unity, Father Schmidt immediately mentioned that "Baptism" was the key. Father Schmidt had not yet written his memoir of Cardinal Bea, which contained the important references to the January 1960 letter to Stakemeier, the Roman Synod of 1960, and Pius XII's encyclical *Mediator Dei*. At that time, Father Schmidt did make reference to the text of a 1961 speech for the Dominican Faculty of the Pontifical Athenaeum, now the University of St. Thomas in Rome (Angelicum), in which Cardinal Bea discussed the components of an ecumenical *a priori*. For a long time, this author thought that that particular speech was the most significant in the drafting of an ecumenical blueprint.

However, a more recent visit to Father Schmidt revealed that, in truth, "Il Cattolico" is actually the third text of three seminal works, as had been indicated by Dom Emmanuel Lanne.[76] The first of these three was composed for the Italian version of the *Sacred Heart Messenger,* and entitled "Gli ostacoli all' unione dei cristiani." The second text, which was delivered before the first text was even published, concerns the visit of Archbishop Geoffrey Fisher, Anglican Archbishop of Canterbury and Primate of all England, which occurred in 1960. This text was entitled "A proposito della visita di S.G. il dott. G. Fisher." Both texts, two and three, were published in *La Civiltà Cattolica*. Schmidt's comment about "Bea's blueprint" characterized his thought as "a work in progress."

Having persuaded Pope John of the necessity of a Secretariat for Promoting Christian Unity, Bea took the Pontiff's sage advice seriously. *He should move slowly!* As the Executive Secretary of the Secretariat, Monsignor Willebrands was often given to comment that the bishops who were familiar with the Ecumenical Movement, or even inclined to a mild interest, were few indeed. As has already been cited, neither Bea's momentum nor that of his Secretariat had sufficient velocity to take off until the Second Session of the Vatican Council, when Pope John XXIII was already dead. The Secretariat itself was innovative. By the time when Bea prepared to deliver his "Clarifications," it had become very popular.[77] Among the

76. In an interview on 5 October 2001, Father Schmidt indicated that all three works should be taken together. Also cf. Lanne, *op. cit.*, pp. 472ff.

77. Bea, "Clarifications," in Küng, *op. cit.*, p. 65. Bea's biblical scholarship is particu-

Council Fathers, Bea's task was, however, much more lonely and profoundly more contemplative. His obligation was to present compelling arguments to the bishops of the world concerning the very basis of the Ecumenical Movement. In doing so, three considerations should be kept in
mind:

1. The advice to the author from Father Schmidt, who had the opportunity to observe Bea, during this time, and at very close range, maintained that the formulation of Bea's argument was indeed a *work of
   process,* primarily through 1960-1961.
2. Cardinal Bea was a biblical scholar of the first order, whose academic
   work had *already* enabled him to transcend denominational lines,
   with the explicit permission of, indeed the support of, Pope Pius XI
   and Pope Pius XII, to whom he reported on his meetings with
   Protestant biblical scholars of Germany.
3. Instead, Bea was mandated to oversee the preparation of a statute,
   that is, a theological premise upon which the Secretariat for Promoting Christian Unity should operate before, during and after the
   Council. Jaeger was to collaborate with Bea, according to the 13
   March directive of Pope John. However, Jaeger had already advised
   Bea that besides the Clarifications, regarding the *Fachmann,* the
   Gutachterstelle, and the Press Office, he must also provide *"an overarching theory"* upon which he must direct the work of the Secretariat. Bea chose Baptism. *It is not as if he pulled it from the air* or drew
   a conclusion after a period of research among dusty tomes of papal
   encyclicals. In fact, Bea had been intricately involved for several years
   in the draft of a reform of the Paschal Liturgy which highlights, in
   sign and Word, the significance of the sacraments. In this context, **the
   sacrament of intense explication is, of course, Baptism.** Biblically, liturgically and academically, without any reference or further study,
   Bea was more than qualified to address the fundamental theological
   premise. By reference to it, he fulfilled the expectations of Pope John
   and Archbishop Jaeger for that overarching theory of operation.

---

larly noted by Hebblethwaite, who praises him for his ability to spotlight the monumental importance of baptism in his seminal works. Speaking of "the Catholic attitude to the problem
of Christian unity," he indicated "that it was a boring and rather conventional article that did
not yield up its meaning straightaway." Addressing Bea's conclusions, Hebblethwaite, *Pope
John, op. cit.,* pp. 380, 382, said: "More than twenty years later these are banalities, blunted by
endless repetition. In the early 1960's they were liberating discoveries, enlightening truths."

Message to the Laity

In order to facilitate the search for "Bea's Blueprint," each text will be taken in chronological order, one by one. Cardinal Bea's first audience was the laity. The *Sacred Heart Messenger* text, which was entitled "The Obstacles to Christian Unity," was originally intended for the celebration of Church Unity Octave, January 18-25, 1961. It was fitting that Bea began to establish a public program for Christian Unity, by providing a substantial commentary for popular use during those eight days. The *Sacred Heart Messenger,* published internationally by members of Bea's own Order, solicited the text. For the sake of widespread diffusion and grassroots support, as well as from his initial impetus to make use of the media, Bea willingly accepted the offer of publication.

The article began in Bea's style: "Our prayer for January, is, that the *truth and charity* of Christ may remove the obstacles that still stand in the way of the reunion of all Christians in the one Church of Christ."[78] The second part of his introduction links the cause of unity with the motive of the Passion of Jesus: "The union of all those who bear the name of Christ is, after all, the greatest desire of Our Lord. In the last hours of his life, he prayed for all those whom the Father had given him, that is, for all those who believe or will believe that the Father had sent Him."[79]

A further paragraph states sadly: "This desire of Our Lord is unhappily far from fulfillment." The rest of the article is filled with a description of disharmony, first among the Orthodox Churches themselves, and of Orthodoxy with Rome. In this regard, Bea saw not only deterioration in the possibilities of conversation because of incidents in history, he also understood that history had exacerbated attitudes of bias and prejudice on all sides.[80] While Bea's references, in this article, to Protestants may seem brief, perhaps even dismissive, he had something positive to say:

> Even in their separation, they [the Churches of the Classical Reformation] have kept in varying degrees, much of the rich inheritance of truth and devotion which derives from the Mother Church, and indeed, in many cases, they were originally cut off from this Church, not of their own choosing, but on account of the absolute power of prince or the bad example of worldly prelate. Those among them who hold faithfully

78. Bea, *op. cit.,* p. 38.
79. *Ibid.*
80. *Ibid.,* p. 42. Schmidt records that Bea had the Fourth Crusade and the seizure of Constantinople (1204) in mind.

to the doctrines inherited from their Catholic ancestors and try to live according to them, easily come to recognize that they do not possess the whole truth and that they lack many aids which our Lord has promised to his faithful.[81]

Clearly Bea had espoused a *vestigia* theology which came from the secret meeting of World Council of Churches officials and certain Catholic scholars at Istina in 1949, about which he had been briefed by Monsignor Willebrands. Therefore in this same text, Cardinal Bea spoke positively of the World Council of Churches and of the Christological basis of this body, which represents the worldwide movement for Christian Unity: "Jesus Christ is recognized as God and Our Saviour." The text likewise states that, while promises of unity are part of our vocation of hope, obstacles must not dismay nor discourage. History and theology are at issue and, when looked upon with the naked eye, may seem impossible: "The historical fact is too complicated to be the object of human judgment — God alone can unravel the threads of that tangled skein of history."[82]

Of greatest importance is Bea's statement regarding "Baptism," a statement that previously arose in his first personal conversations with Pope John and his preparatory draft letter with Stakemeier in January 1960:

> All those who are validly baptized, from the fact of their Baptism, have the status of "persons in the Church of Christ," and have the full rights and duties of Christians, except where an obstacle prevents the exercise of rights, as laid down in Canon Law (cf. Canon 87).

> [Baptismate homo constituitur in Ecclesia Christi persona cum omnibus christianorum iuribus et officiis, nisi, adiura quad attinet, obstet obex ecclesiasticae communionis vinculum impediens, vel lata ab Ecclesia censura (Canon 87)].[83]

Basically, this was the same doctrine as was taught by the Apostle, St. Paul (cf. I Cor. 12:13; Gal. 3:25ff.; Eph. 1:5ff.). The encyclical *Mediator Dei* (On the Sacred Liturgy) explicitly and categorically confirms this: *"By reason of their Baptism, Christians are in the mystical Body* and become, by a common title, members of *Christ the Priest."* The reference here is not only

---

81. *Ibid.*, pp. 42-43.

82. *Ibid.*, pp. 39-40. At the time of the Jaeger-Bea 1959 Correspondence, the Catholic Conference on Questions for Christian Unity was engaged in contributing to a WCC document on "the Lordship of Christ."

83. *Ibid.*, p. 39.

to a pontifical document, by way of *"precedent,"* say, in the field of Canonical Jurisprudence. The biblical-liturgical work of Father Bea in the 1950s, within the context of the Pian Commission, presented clear evidence regarding the significance of *the renewal of the liturgy in light of the concept of the Mystical Body of Christ.*[84] Because of this doctrine, Bea intended to motivate and improve human actions outside the church building. In the *Sacred Heart Messenger* article, although almost casually, one can find in Bea a link between the Ecumenical Movement, the liturgical movement, the missionary movement, and the lay apostolate.[85]

In every instance a recall of the Royal Priesthood of Christ and the call of all the baptized to share in it has motivated the organization, the promotion and the success of these great twentieth-century movements. Promotion of the privilege and responsibility of the baptized to participate in the worship of Christ to the Father had clearly been enunciated by St. Thomas Aquinas.[86] Baptism concerns worship. By baptism, all Christians are deputed to the worship of God. This obligation is shared by all who have experienced the generosity of the Father's love, by recourse to the action of the Son and the outpouring of the Holy Spirit.

It was at this precise moment in time that the issues of Liturgy were being drawn to the top of the list of items for consideration by the forthcoming Vatican Council. Therefore, Bea's wording comes as no surprise, since it epitomizes the three major trends of spirituality of the twentieth century, as listed above: "If, therefore, we wish to be loyal to the will of Christ, we ought to pray and work for the removal of all obstacles, so that

---

84. Bugnini, *op. cit.* p. 7.

85. Schmidt, *op. cit.,* p. 353. Interestingly Bea prioritized issues raised by these same movements in the twentieth century as the first work of his new Secretariat (the significance of the Royal Priesthood of Christ, the role of the laity, the relationship of all the baptized), outlining them in his inaugural speech to the first plenary of the new Secretariat.

86. *S.T.* III, q. 69, art. 10. Cardinal Bea would ultimately argue that the sacramental character is granted to all the baptized. He based his argument upon the evidence of St. Thomas Aquinas: "In like manner when a man is baptized, he receives the character, which is like the form; and he receives in consequence its proper effect, which is grace whereby all his sins are remitted. But this effect is sometimes by insincerity" [Et similiter quando aliquis baptizatur, accipit characterem, quasi formam, et consequitur proprium effectum, qui est gratia remitens omnia peccata. Impeditur autem quando que perfectionem]. Bea's argumentation pertaining to sincerity and insincerity includes the whole of Question 69 of *Pars Tertia.* The central theme of the question is incorporation into the Passion of Christ and the Resurrection of Christ, and the baptized is thus conformed to Christ. Bea would argue that those who are presently separated from the Church as a result of either the Classical Reformation or the schisms between East and West are not in a state of insincerity.

every single baptized person may enjoy to the full all the privileges and rights conferred on him *by Baptism,* in the unity of the one holy, and visible Church."[87]

In concluding the article for the *Sacred Heart Messenger,* Bea insisted once more upon the achievement of "truth in charity" which he characterized as follows: "One especially good work is the practice of true, deep and creative Christian charity toward our separated brethren. . . . A good Catholic illustrates what Jesus means when he says that our good works are a light by which we shine before the eyes of men so that seeing them they glorify Our Father who is in heaven (cf. Matt. 5:16)."[88] He goes on to warn: "A further obstacle to union, unfortunately, is the kind of lives which some Catholics lead." In order to placate those who were his ideological enemies within the Curia, Bea gave this assurance:

> About Catholic dogma we are obliged to be "uncompromising." Yet this intransigence, joined to memories of the struggles of the past and of the *injuries* inflicted during them has too often tended to narrow and harden the minds and hearts of separated brethren and to lead them, if not to hatred, at least to lack of any real interest. *Nevertheless, they are still brethren and must be treated as brethren.*[89]

In synthesizing his message, having already cited Pope Pius XII, he then recalled the recent words of Pope John XXIII in *Ad Petri Cathedram:* "Rightly did the Holy Father recall to us the striking words of St. Augustine: 'Whether they will it or not, they are our brethren.' They will cease to be our brethren when they cease to say: 'Our Father.'" As regards to style, Bea's text, no matter how brief or personally reflective, is vividly peppered with biblical references particularly from the Pauline Corpus, e.g., Corinthians, Galatians, Ephesians, and Romans. Here, as later, Bea had demonstrated his overwhelming facility with the evidence of Sacred Scripture.[90] By reference to "the kind of lives" the people lead, Bea directed his remarks not to theologians and Cardinals. He was concerned with the value and importance of the lives of ordinary Catholics, which not only are taken up with the consecration of the world but also with the profound Evangelical quality of the Christian vocation. Eastern spirituality refers to the life of the layman as "the liturgy after the liturgy." Bea's remarks dovetail with this

---

87. Bea, *op. cit.,* p. 39 (emphasis mine).
88. *Ibid.*
89. *Ibid.*
90. *Ibid.*

contemporary comment by Martin H. Work: "As Christ prayed in His last days for unity, so should we all — laymen and clergy alike. Until we make prayer for unity a part of our individual daily life as laymen and include it in our collective prayers in meetings and in parishes, we really aren't taking the unity movement seriously."[91]

The Purpose of the Secretariat and Its Ministry

The evidence, as cited above, indicates that Bea took seriously the issues, raised for the forthcoming Vatican Council, by the four prominent twentieth-century movements of ecumenism, missionary activity, lay apostolate and liturgy, with which he was personally familiar. At this very time, Bea began the work of the Secretariat. In addressing the first plenary of the Secretariat for Promoting Christian Unity, and after devising a plan in conjunction with Archbishop Jaeger and with his own staff, including the body of Consultors, Bea called for approval of the Secretariat's statute, i.e., its mandate, its content and its methodology. Bea listed, for the seventy-five prelate-members, the most urgent item of all, that of Church membership of non-Catholic baptized people. Those present for the occasion of this inaugural meeting, conducted in the presence of Pope John XXIII, approved his working order, for it accurately represented the *status quaestionis* at the time. The prioritization of this item, of the baptized non-Catholic Christian, emerged because, with the assistance of Pope John, the definition of the Secretariat's work came more clearly into focus.[92]

It had now become clear that the first work of the Secretariat would not exactly be what was initially intended by Jaeger — a Press Office, to clarify the news.[93] In fact, Schmidt recorded that Bea refuted the categorization that his task would be the supervision of a Catholic Bureau of Infor-

---

91. Michael Greene (ed.), *The Layman and the Council* (Springfield, Ill.: Templegate, 1964), p. 89.

92. Schmidt, *op. cit.*, pp. 354-55. "In mid-November, the real preparatory work for the Council began, in accordance with the Pope's wishes. . . . Just like the Preparatory Commissions, the Secretariat had the task of studying the subjects put forward by the Pope in the light of the suggestions of the Roman Curia, and drawing up drafts to be submitted to the Council." Again see Schmidt, p. 343. Bea therefore addressed letters to the seventy-five members of the Secretariat before their first Plenary which would take place a year later!

93. *Ibid.*, p. 346. This is not to refute the intention of Archbishop Jaeger, but Bea also wanted to confirm that in light of the forthcoming Council, the Secretariat had the right to prepare and present certain *schemata*. This is especially true of issues such as religious freedom and the Jewish people.

mation. No, the first work of the Secretariat would be to fulfill the intentions of the Pontiff, that it should address itself to the work of the Council. Bea and his staff were to provide the Council with an ecumenical conscience, given the expressions of expectation from the Curia, the bishops of the world and the various leaders from the non-Catholic world. This required the highest level of precision. Perhaps most importantly of all, it was clear to Bea, from the evidence of events, that the permanence of the life of this body was being questioned.

First, Cardinal Tardini thought that it would be best that Bea's bureau labor under the title of "Secretariat" in case it should fail.[94] With such a title it could easily be explained away as an experiment. Secondly, there was agitation if not outright friction between Bea and Cardinal Ottaviani, about the scope of the Secretariat's mandate and its protocol.[95] Finally, Pope John himself informed the Plenary that the life of the Secretariat, after the Council, was reserved to the decision of the Pope.[96] Bea realized that he was, at first, on a shaky platform. Through theological explication he sought to strengthen it.

There were also several pastoral considerations to be taken up within the context of the Council. Monsignor Willebrands was given to say, over and over, that most of the bishops of the Council had given little or no consideration to any ecumenical matter previously.[97] Any thought about these issues had come under the shadow of polemical invective. Bea also had to consider that the Doctrinal Commission of the Council was charged with the task of filtering through the foundational question of theory. Thus Bea's responsibility was the introduction of the subject of ecumenism, in terms that were, appropriately, theological *materia*.[98] Also, invitations had to be extended to non-Catholic observers. This was perhaps the most delicate of all items and with a history! The Council of Trent invited Lutherans to the Second Session of its convocation; the politics of the time were sufficiently weighty that these came to the Council and went, like snowflakes in

---

94. *Ibid.,* p. 329. The *schemata* in fact had already been handed to the Pre-preparatory and Preparatory Commissions as early as April 1961. First among these items was Church membership of non-baptized people. Also, Pope John's decision contravened any possibility of the presentation of a mandate to the Secretariat by the Council. It seems clear that this body was, at this time, on its way to becoming a true dicastery, i.e., a ministry of the Chief Shepherd of the Roman Catholic Church.

95. *Ibid.,* p. 351.

96. *Ibid.,* p. 354. The Plenary took place in November 1961.

97. *Ibid.,* p. 341.

98. *Ibid.,* p. 354.

a Texas summer.[99] Vatican I also offered invitations to Protestants and Orthodox, but the wording of the invitation could only invite the response of refusal or decline. Now, the publicity of Vatican II elicited the expectation that Protestants, perhaps, might join in the deliberations. When it was explained that the proposed Vatican Council would be an internal matter to Roman Catholics, there was much unhappiness from the non-Catholic world. Bea therefore had to walk a fine line. Skepticism came at him from two directions, the Curia and the non-Catholic world. Many saw the invitation to Protestant and Orthodox observers as a mere humanitarian gesture, an act of public relations, a sociological decision of Pope John, an act of courtesy devoid of real substance. Bea's concern, however, was to demonstrate the invitation as a genuine outreach from the depth of a burgeoning ecclesial sensitivity and understanding.

A Press Conference at the Columbus Hotel

The visit of Archbishop Fisher to Rome and to Pope John XXIII, on 1 December 1960, occasioned the further opportunity for Cardinal Bea to expand the blueprint for a paradigm of the unity of Christians. Like so many turns in the road, in the history of ecumenism, this particular event was fraught with conflicting possibilities. Bea's words, therefore, are best seen in the setting in which they were placed by history! Monsignor William Purdy was a part of the visit. In his book *The Search for Unity,* published after his death, he left a narrative which, when taken together with Bea's testimony, indicates the depth and significance of the words which Cardinal Bea put together for that occasion. What follows here outlines the events and the stark contrast between current Roman Catholic and Anglican attitudes toward ecumenism at the time, and the *de facto* enunciation of the ecumenical cause, which Bea preached.

The idea of the Canterbury visit to Rome dated back to April 1959,

---

99. Schmidt, *ibid.,* recorded that "the Ecumenical aim . . . had then been incarnated with the creation of the Secretariat for Promoting Christian Unity." This produced a certain resentment from Ottaviani. The protocol issue emerged with Ottaviani's refusal at first to allow five official Catholic observers to attend the WCC assembly at New Delhi (1961). He wanted them to go as journalists. Bea disputed this at once. He won the argument, but as a true diplomat he learned that gestures and words can perdure. Hence he searched for something that was at once concrete and transcendent as a bond for forging relationships. For the history of invitations to Trent and Vatican I, see Thomas Stransky, "Council of Trent," in Lossky et al., *op. cit.,* p. 1019, *id.,* "Vatican Councils I and II," pp. 1053-55.

when the Anglican bishop of Southwark, Mervyn Stockwood, wrote to Archbishop Fisher, reporting on his own semi-private audience with John XXIII. On that occasion, Pope John forwarded to Fisher a simple communiqué: "Two souls can meet in prayer, though distance divides." At this time, Fisher, who was keenly interested in Anglican and Orthodox questions of reunion, had planned a trip to end his ministry as Archbishop of Canterbury, which would include Istanbul, Rome and Geneva. On 3 November 1960, a press release was issued from Lambeth Palace which outlined Fisher's forthcoming itinerary. The announcement of a Rome stopover was met by the Italian secular press with enthusiasm. The Catholic papers were cool. Behind the scenes, Bea's Secretariat made an inquiry for "deep background" from Father Bernard Leeming. Leeming's details filtered in. An English Jesuit, Leeming had both an Oxford background and some contact with Archbishop Fisher's family. On 24 November, some six days before Fisher's projected arrival, he reported: "Fisher's *first* wish was to visit the Pope." Such an announcement was not well received within the Curia:

> But there was nothing that he [Willebrands] could do at this time to improve the predominant attitude in the Roman Curia. For them, polite paper exchanges at a thousand miles were one thing; top-level visits were another. The SPCU was only a few weeks old and was already seen as up to antics which the old guard viewed with grave disapproval. Prudence dictated drawing heavy purple curtains.[100]

Doctor Fisher arrived at the old airport, at Rome, at Ciampino, on 1 December 1960, a mere six months after the foundation of the Secretariat for Promoting Christian Unity. Father Stransky, the American attaché of the Secretariat, recalled that at the time the Secretariat was so poor that he had to take the paperwork regarding this visit to his home at the rectory of Santa Susanna. There he used the parish typewriter, since there were not enough typewriters to go around during working hours at the Vatican. Further, hectograph copies of speeches and news reports were run off and hand dipped in one of the Secretariat's many bathtubs. The pages were hung on clotheslines, secured with paper clips or clothespins, and left to dry.[101] While something of a frenzy went on inside the Secretariat itself, not much enthusiasm was shown outside. When Fisher's plane landed, not a

---

100. William Purdy, *The Search for Unity* (New York: Geoffrey Chapman and Company, 1996), p. 28.

101. Interview of Thomas Stransky with the author, 11 September 1987.

single Roman Catholic prelate was present to welcome him officially. Further, the British Minister to the Holy See, Sir Peter Scarlett, handed Fisher a list of protocols. These were the conditions of the visit as conveyed in Fisher's memoirs:

1. There should be no official photograph of me [Fisher] with the Pope. To make sure of this, Tardini had sent away the official photographer for a fortnight holiday. So that was off. It had never occurred to me that there would or would not be official photographs: but he, Tardini, obviously thought it was important.

2. It was stated that I should next *not* see Cardinal Bea, the Head of the department recently set up by the Pope to foster relations with other Churches. This sounded a preposterous thing, but there it was.

3. There was to be no kind of press release after my meeting with the Pope. That was a little odd as I had already drafted one.

4. This Minister was not to invite to meet me at his house any of the Vatican officials.[102]

Despite the rub, Fisher continued to respond with optimism. That night, at Evensong in the local Anglican Church of All Saints, Fisher stated that "history . . . has brought it about that the Orthodox Churches have found their greatest strength in their withdrawal into worship, while the Churches of the Roman Communion have found their greatest calling in the strength and authority of their witness to the world."[103]

The second expression of his optimism came the next morning with his actual visit with the Pope. Again, Fisher recorded the event:

The Pope read, in English, a passage [from an address of his], which included a reference to "the time when our Separated Brethren should return to the Mother Church." I at once said: "Your Holiness, not *return*." He looked puzzled and said "not return? Why not?" I said, "none of us can go backwards. We are now running on parallel courses; we are looking forward until in God's good time, our two courses approximate and meet." He said, after a moment's pause, "You are right." . . . Somewhere in our conversation I thanked the Pope for

---

102. Purdy, *The Search for Unity, op. cit.*, p. 29.

103. *Ibid.*, p. 30. Schmidt is slightly critical of his homily, stating: "The Archbishop himself had not helped matters," for he drew a comparison between "the conception of an imperialistic church and the more ancient and apostolic conception of a commonwealth of churches." *Op. cit.*, p. 348.

what he had done in setting up the new department under Cardinal Bea. He then said with a smile and a twinkle: "Yes, and this afternoon you shall see Cardinal Bea." I realized that Tardini had been overruled by the Pope, revealing a little of the breaking of the barriers and the icy wastes of the Vatican Curia.[104]

Indeed, despite the earlier prohibitions, that afternoon Archbishop Fisher took tea with Cardinal Bea and Monsignor Willebrands at the Brazilian College on the Via Aurelia. By the time of Fisher's departure, the atmosphere in Rome had brightened considerably. According to Purdy, "the Catholic *Il Quotidiano,* in a dignified paragraph, summed up the better Roman feeling":

> There will not be lacking discorded voices, unwarranted pessimism. We prefer to record the event as a page of good will, which looks to God, to the Redeemer, to the Gospel, to the Church, to the Salvation of the human race. If non-Catholics, English or other, have their own views of the event, if they do not see beyond the particular aspects of it, if indeed it produces no tangible effect, we know about the vicissitude of time and space: God watches over all, echoing the Redeemer's wish *Ut Sint Unum.* . . . The Christian world is in movement. God grant it be towards better things.[105]

According to Purdy, and the evidence of the little band of six who comprised the Secretariat staff: "Fisher's visit to Rome was an epoch-making event, which faced the Secretariat for Promoting Christian Unity at a moment when it was undergoing its baptism."[106]

In light of the above history, Bea's speech to the press at the Hotel Columbus appears in something of an apologetic cast. A serious overview of the text indicates that it was intended to invite a new mindset on the part of the media towards the cause of unity within the Church: "How could one expect a mother to give wide publicity to these first steps toward a new *rapprochement* after so long and so sorrowful a separation!"[107] Less biblical than other texts, nonetheless, Bea relied upon the evidence of Sacred Scripture, especially citing the Gospel of Luke, the prophet Isaiah, and again from the Pauline Corpus, the Letters to the Ephesians, Romans, and Philippians.

---

104. *Ibid.,* pp. 30-31.
105. *Ibid.,* p. 34.
106. *Ibid.,* p. 37.
107. Bea, *op. cit.,* p. 70.

Again, perhaps in the face of the coldness of the Roman officials, he wished to assure that the ecumenical cause was concerned with "safeguarding Catholic dogma in its entirety."[108] He stated: "The reason for this is clear, the unity of Christians cannot be built on the betrayal of truth."[109] The nature of that truth is Christological, for the Church carries as the hallmark of its faith, its "fidelity," that is, "its loyalty to the person of Christ, her divine Founder. It is not the Church's task to preach her own discoveries, the fruit of her own reflections, but to propound what Jesus has taught her; her office is to bear witness to him, to hand on the sacred deposit of faith confided to her by her divine Master."[110] Some people may see this as inflexibility and, therefore, may be surprised or even antagonized. Yet the Church can do no other, for it is endowed by the Savior with the mission of preserving the unity of the faith and safeguarding the truth. However, Bea did not leave this principle isolated.[111]

The exercise of truth is always balanced by the obligation to charity. It was Bea's point, in the second section of his treatise, that all are obligated to charity. Bea made the transition from the term "Christians," by which he meant "fellow believers," to that of brothers, "even though separated from the Catholic faith." As once again, based upon Pope Pius XII's encyclical, *Mediator Dei,* Bea states explicitly that those validly baptized are in the Mystical Body and become, by common title, members of Christ the Priest. As before, Bea cited Canon 87 of the 1917 Code, which declared that a person, validly baptized, becomes a member of the Church of Christ, with all the rights and duties of Christians, save only in those cases where an obstacle prevents a person enjoying the use of these rights. It is almost certain that the contents of Canon 87 did not come to the attention of most Catholic ministers, and, therefore, would have been overlooked in theory and in practice. From the promulgation of the Code until the publication of new Liturgical instructions in 1967, some fifty years later, by the *Concilium* of Pope Paul VI, following the Second Vati-

---

108. *Ibid.,* p. 65. Hebblethwaite, *Pope John, op. cit.,* pp. 381-83, records: "The Curia was hostile to this hob-nobbing with 'dissidents.'" Hebblethwaite also states that Peter Nichols, the English journalist, referred to it as a "guilty secret." Ottaviani was nonplussed at Bea's press conference. He could find nothing wrong with Bea's explication of biblical references and suspected a catch somewhere. "Ottaviani is reliably reported to have joked that St. Paul, although undoubtedly inspired, was so confused that his works would not have got through the Holy Office censorship."

109. *Ibid.*

110. *Ibid.,* pp. 55-56.

111. *Ibid.*

can Council, the pastoral practice was that baptism of converts was *sub conditione.*[112]

Bea's statement, by reference to the twentieth-century ecclesiastical documents and directives, pierced the hard shell of opposition, which was prevalent in Rome at the time of the visit of Dr. Fisher.[113] As a renowned biblical scholar, Bea was a master at the harmonization of texts. One might have expected to find here the Pauline soliloquy to charity, which predominates in First Corinthians 13; however, Bea identified, autobiographically, instead, with the anguish of Paul's love for his own people, the Jews: "For I could wish that I myself were accursed and cut off from Christ for the sake of my own people, my kindred, according to the flesh (Rom. 9:3)." The focus on this text, perforce, drew a clear distinction between human love and that particular bond of love, which is identified as *agape.*[114] Here, Bea again drew from similes, which found their precedence in the inaugural Johannine encyclical *Ad Petri Cathedram:* "Allow us to express our affection for you and to call you sons and brothers . . . address you, then, as brothers, even though you are separated from us. For as St. Augustine said: *Whether they like it or not they are our brothers.* They will only cease to be *our* brothers when they cease to say *Our* Father."[115]

Here, in a more profound demonstration, the simile of father and children and Holy Mother Church and her babies was, once more, employed to demonstrate the strength of the bond, as being greater than the long fracture:

> By Baptism they have become members of the mystical Body of Christ and, by that very fact, the Church's children; even though some are deprived of the full use of their rights because they are separated from her. The love of the Church for them is a love full of deep sorrow and grief, and of a heart-felt affliction because of the separation that prevents them enjoying so many privileges and rights, and makes them lose so many graces. The words of God in Holy Scripture, "Can a woman for-

112. *Ibid.,* pp. 67-68.

113. Schmidt, *op. cit.,* pp. 348-49. See *Directory concerning Ecumenical Matters,* Part One, *Ad Totam Ecclesiam,* 14 May 1967, No. 14. "Indiscriminate conditional baptism of all who desire full communion with the Catholic Church cannot be approved. The Sacrament of Baptism cannot be repeated." Austin Flannery, O.P., trans. *Vatican Council II: The Conciliar and Post-Conciliar Documents* (Northport, N.Y.: Costello Publishing Company, 1981), p. 489.

114. Bea, *op. cit.,* p. 66. "A charity so magnificently described by St. Paul . . . and possessed by him to such a heroic degree that he was willing to be separated from Christ for the sake of non-believing Jew."

115. *Ibid.,* p. 67 (emphasis mine).

get her child that is still unweaned, pity no longer the son she bore in her womb," (Is. 49:15), refers to this love.[116]

Within the second point of this particular text, Bea seemingly employed the biblical category of a doublet, wherein the same point is made twice, as if in a two-sided picture frame. At the beginning of a long paragraph which focused upon Baptism in terms of the family of faith, with oft-cited references to mother, father, child, brother and kinsman, Paul anguishes in love over those of his race, superseded now by the Church, whose effect, upon each and every member, is without question: "If for any reason a child does not know and hence does not recognize his own mother, she nevertheless does not cease to be his mother nor he the fruit of her womb; it is impossible for her not to have for her child a mother's love and tenderness."[117] This particular text must be viewed in the specificity of the Anglican character of the visit. First the initiative for this visit was taken by Dr. Fisher. Secondly, such a visit would have been impossible, according to Bea, a short time before. While renouncing the opportunity to field the opinions and interpretations of the press, nor to impugn the motives of Archbishop Fisher, Bea proceeded to break his own rule:

> Far from wishing to underestimate the merits of the man to whose initiative we owe this visit, we would, on the contrary, point out that the importance of his action can best be appreciated, *in the light of the principles outlined above.* It was Dr. Fisher who sensed the change of atmosphere; pointed it out; realized the obligations entailed and took the necessary steps to bring the public to a greater awareness of the new atmosphere, and to further their interests.[118]

There are some necessary corollaries which Bea felt compelled to draw. In the first instance, Bea reiterated that purity of faith, clarity of faith and the enunciation of faith constitute the avoidance of the false irenicism and indifferentism, so unnecessarily feared. In other words, "doing the truth" is the necessary obligation to remain loyal to Christ, the Spouse of the Church and the essence of the Mystical Body, into whom all are incorporated by Baptism. The second corollary flows from the principle of love itself, which is to be identified with the Blessed Trinity. Love it-

---

116. *Ibid.*

117. *Ibid.*

118. *Ibid.*, p. 71 (emphasis mine). The dynamic of the Secretariat has always been based upon "invitation" and "response."

self is not to be confused with friendship or purely human acts of kindness. Bea's words here are powerful. Baptismal love is thus identified as *"loyalty to Christ,* whereby we must realize that we are treading on most holy ground. Such sacred matters should not be offered in the open marketplace to the casual passerby like merchandise to the gaze of profane eyes, nor considered as a means to satisfy men's curiosity or to amuse them." Furthermore, there are these words from a master diplomat, "They cannot even be compared to diplomatic negotiations, however important these may be."[119] Bea refers to this attitude toward the new *rapprochement* as discretion. There is a certain isolation, even a certain bereavement, involved. "We are, as it were, gazing in upon the private sorrow of a mother and her shame for a stigma which has brought disgrace and dishonour to her great Christian family. How could one expect a mother to give wide publicity to these first steps towards a new *rapprochement,* after so long and so sorrowful a separation?"[120]

Here, then, Bea presented the mindset of "reverence" which flows from this sense of "discretion." In language which approximates the teaching of his countryman and contemporary, the phenomenologist Dietrich von Hildebrand, these would be called the *Fundamental Moral Attitudes* of ecumenism. There would have to be profound humility, charity, prayer, and sacrifice.[121]

Having thus outlined the significance of the visit, as well as the theological implications, including the ethical and historical considerations, Bea pleaded the cause for a press office, which both he and Jaeger had foreseen as being vital almost one year before. In light of the *très négatif* Rhodes Incident, he was conscious now that one more ecumenical encounter created publicity which could not be ignored. He expressed these sentiments: "It is a question of combining genuine prudence with the real necessity of satisfying the legitimate curiosity of world opinion."[122]

Thus did Bea refer to the delicacy of the meeting between Pope John and Archbishop Fisher. "We are thus presented with a practical problem of the utmost delicacy, and one which does not permit of easy solution: how

---

119. *Ibid.,* p. 69.

120. *Ibid.,* pp. 69-70.

121. Dietrich Von Hildebrand, *Fundamental Moral Attitudes* (New York: Longmans, Green and Company, 1950), pp. 1ff., defines this attitude as "reverence." He calls it the most basic Christian attitude of all, the *a priori,* without which there can be no system of morality. The author lists as the fundamental moral virtues reverence, faithfulness, awareness of responsibility, veracity, and goodness.

122. *Ibid.,* p. 70.

far can we satisfy the public's desire to know all the details of a meeting of this sort, and where should a prudent silence begin?"[123]

The day that Archbishop Fisher and Pope John had their meeting, the atmosphere was one of intense silence. The Jesuit, Father Giovanni Caprile, recorded the all-telling heaviness: "On that afternoon of 2 December, the Vatican was almost deserted and strangely quiet, but behind the scenes, the eyes of all the court, and especially of the curia, were fixed on this sprightly old gentleman in his strange half-lay, half-clerical dress, who moved, with a small following towards the Pope's apartment, and whom John XXIII left his throne to greet with open arms and with all the warmth of an old friend who had constantly waited the day and the hour of this meeting."[124]

Incredibly, Cardinal Bea's Secretariat had been given the responsibility of arranging the details of the visit, including the hospitality, as is noted above in the comments of Monsignor Purdy and Father Stransky. Yet Cardinal Bea was not to participate in the visit, according to the protocol of Secretary of State Tardini. Complying with the etiquette without complaint was to Fisher's credit. Bea, as cited above, affirmed that the initiative was "wholly from the Anglican side." Yet for his part, "Fisher in turn attributed the change of atmosphere to John. He was responding to *John's* persistent expression of a desire to improve the relations of the Roman Church with the other Churches."[125] When Pope John accepted Fisher's proposal, he pierced the corporate veil of the Roman Curia and threw it into consternation. Behind that veil stood a phalanx of opposition to the new body of Bea's Secretariat.

Bernard Bonnot, an early expert in the ministry of Pope John XXIII, identified the members of the opposition as Cardinal Alfredo Ottaviani and his Holy Office, Cardinal Domenico Tardini and the Secretariate of State, as well as the faculty of the Lateran University.[126] Also Cardinals Pizzardo, Ruffini, and Browne were "conservative and proud of it!"[127] Pizzardo later would, under Pope John's direction, be compelled to write a letter of apology to Cardinal Bea for embarrassments caused to him in the press. Bea had an atmosphere of intransigence and suspicion thrust upon him. The

123. Bea, *op. cit.*, p. 70.

124. Carlo Falconi, *The Popes in the Twentieth Century* (London: Wiedenfeld and Nicolson, 1967), p. 333.

125. Bernard Bonnot, *Pope John XXIII: An Astute Pastoral Leader* (New York: Alba House, 1968), p. 182 (emphasis mine).

126. *Ibid.*, pp. 184-87.

127. Hebblethwaite, *Pope John, op. cit.*, p. 411.

day after the meeting with Archbishop Fisher, Bea returned to Gazzada, to confer with World Council of Churches officials about accepting their invitation to send five delegated observers to the Third General Assembly of the World Council of Churches, which was targeted for November 1961, at New Delhi. As has been noted above, when he returned and placed his protocol on Ottaviani's table, the vote of the members of the Holy Office was negative. This was personally hurtful to Bea, since he had formally been an insider of the Holy Office family. Only by referring the matter to Pope John did Bea find happier results. The atmosphere was clear; Bea was living in a hostile world.

At this point "gradualism" became a part of contemporary ecclesiastical jargon.[128] Pope John was to refer to it in his encyclical *Pacem in Terris,* when he said: "*To proceed gradually* is the law of life in all of its expressions; equally is it true of institutions . . . (No. 162)" (emphasis mine). In 1964, Pope Paul's first encyclical, *Ecclesiam Suam,* borrowed freely from the concept.[129] While the popes used the phrase, Bea actually demonstrated its value in the manner of a true pedagogue — "teach and reteach!" By this time, in the preparatory phase of the Council, Bea knew that he would be a boon to the worldwide agenda of Pope John if he were to assume the role of expositor or publicist for the ecumenical perspective, which in Rome was seen as an "alternative vision of the Church."[130] The Church of the *status quo* was a juridical model. In this preparatory phase, not only did he undertake an immediate and intensive lecture tour in Germany, Austria, Switzerland, France, Great Britain, and the United States, but he published 240 articles which later emerged into ten books.[131]

While he did all this on behalf of Pope John, his great historical mind

128. Schmidt, *op. cit.,* p. 360, reports that Bea insisted on proceeding by degrees.

129. This is especially true of the rules of the Church's dialogue with the circles or, if you will, spheres of relationship between clusters of "faith entities" and the Church. It would be fair to say that Paul VI's personal assessment of the Church was carried on in terms of missiology: "The dialectic of this exercise of thought and of patience will make us discover elements of truth also in the opinion of others. It will force us to express our teaching with great fairness, and it will reward us for the work of having explained it in accordance with the objections of another or despite his slow assimilation of our teaching. The dialogue will make us wise. It will make us teachers (No. 83)." It is the comment of Cardinal Willebrands to the author that Paul VI drafted this encyclical entirely on his own and that the circular theory was entirely Pope Paul's. It was not readily understood by others and the content of the above-cited quote never gained popularity. For further information see Peter Hebblethwaite, *Paul VI* (London: Harper Collins Religious, 1993), p. 2.

130. Bonnot, *op. cit.,* p. 189.

131. Leeming, *Men of the Council, op. cit.,* pp. 16, 26.

and his all-encompassing vision took in the significance of his little company in the corner of the Palazzo Convertendi, the Secretariat for Promoting Christian Unity. The Council was attracting interest from other Churches, yet those same ecclesial communions were historically repelled by the idea of the Roman Curia. The Secretariat's public image, from the first, as a Conciliar organ, invited freedom, spontaneity, creativity, and exchange. At the same time, Bea needed to do a little internal ecumenical work as well. He needed the advice if not the outright support of representative Curial officials vis-à-vis canon law, sacraments, catechetics, doctrine, to name but a few. With the title "Secretariat" imposed upon this new entity, by Pope John, Cardinal Bea and *his associates* (staff members and consultors) were free to travel, consult and invite for the sake of forming a family of Consultors and guests, at the Council.[132]

Bea's chief assistant, Johannes Willebrands, was the "mightiest of the mighty" in this regard. By now a seasoned ecumenist, having stayed with this work since 1948, when the World Council of Churches held its first General Assembly in Amsterdam, Willebrands, who was then a seminary professor at Warmond in the Diocese of Haarlem, not only followed the work of the World Council, but founded the Catholic Conference for Ecumenical Questions. Willebrands' skills were at once human, academic, and refined. Endowed with an ability to speak fluently practically every language in Western Europe, he made contact with Church leaders, especially those of the World confessional families, and he made every effort to obtain the collaboration of Europe's finest theologians in this regard. Furthermore, Willebrands was a friend and confidant of the Archbishop of Paderborn, Lorenz Jaeger. In a way, his enthusiasm, and that of his early colleague, Frans Thijssen, reflected, and reflects still, the manner in which the Dutch people grasped with wonder the fact that the initiative of organized ecumenical activity should have had its inception on Dutch soil. When she renounced her throne in 1952, Dutch Queen Wilhelmina did so with the express intention of dedicating the remainder of her life to the chief hope of the future, the Christian Ecumenical Movement.[133] The presence of Willebrands, who was at once so talented, so energetic, and so flexible, was the main hallmark of the title "Secretariat" as opposed to "Commission." Commissions merely study, report, and recommend. In this case,

---

132. Hebblethwaite, *Pope John XIII*, p. 377.

133. Louis de Jong, *The Netherlands and Nazi Germany* (London: Harvard University Press, 1990), p. 72. For an account of the abdication, see Cees Fasseur, *Wilhelmina: Krijgshaftig in een vormeloze jas* (Amersfoort: Uitgeverij, Balans, 2001), pp. 538-43.

the feedback from the non-Catholic constituency went from Cardinal Bea's lips to the Pope's ears.

At the same time, Pope John charged Bea with getting the message from the Pope's heart to the public's vision. Bea himself wrote that it was his specific task to see to the "general mobilization of all ranks in the Catholic Church, in favour of these brethren."[134] So Bea had more to do than publicize. Tardini saw the Council in terms of an "internal event." Bea had to counterbalance this concept; therefore, he needed a science and a method. The scientific basis which he chose, for the new atmosphere that he was seeking to create, was the presentation of Baptism as the *essential* experience for all Christians. Further it is the basis of all unity. As far as contacts and relations, all else is secondary. His many, many lectures were intended to state that the Catholic Church had a deep and compelling obligation to care for all baptized Christians and to care *about* them, because the bonds of grace are nothing less than the life of God through the action of the Holy Spirit. In fact, as a result of this pre-preparatory phase of the Second Vatican Council, Bea was never to let up on the primacy of Baptism. He would go so far as to say that, no matter what Church or ecclesial communion was the opposite number in dialogue, here there was an even greater responsibility than that of a white-habited missionary, evangelizing among the non-baptized.[135]

The Lecture at the Angelicum: The Quest for Truth

All of these points may be found in the lecture entitled "The Catholic Attitude towards the Problem of the Unity of Christians" (Il cattolico di fronte al problema dell' unione dei cristiani), which Emmanuel Lanne identified as Bea's panoramic lecture.[136] Within the text of the oft-cited address, Bea stated that this mobilization of the Church should have recourse to the invocation of two principles: *Celui de verité et celui de charité* (That of truth and that of charity). Judgment regarding this talk by such authors as Emmanuel Lanne, O.S.B., the late Jean Marie Tillard, O.P., and the late Monsignor Jean-Francois Arrighi is that this talk stands as the clearest, most comprehensive expression of Bea's thought. According to Dom Lanne, "[Arrighi] referred to this overture [by Bea] in the premier address to the

---

134. Cited in Bonnot, *op. cit.*, p. 179.
135. *Ibid.*, pp. 179-80.
136. Bea, *op. cit.*, pp. 19-37, and Lanne, *op. cit.*

[non–Roman Catholic] Observers as a singular testimony to this attitude of fraternity, which had sprung up in regard to other Christians" [S'est référé à cette ouverture de la première allocution aux observateurs comme témoignage singulier de cette attitude de fraternité vécue à l'égard des autres chrétiens].[137]

The doctrine, which he presented at that time, had ripened, as he had hoped. The occasion for this talk was the Week of Church Unity Octave, which was then being celebrated within the Dominican Faculty of the Athenaum of St. Thomas Aquinas (the Angelicum) in Rome. The date was 21 January 1961. Here, Bea took the occasion to present his position in language which he was certain would be published. He was right. The microphone did not function and his voice was too soft.[138] The article was more successful than the lecture. While the Secretariat was engaged in facilitating many contacts, Bea had not yet been charged by Pope John with the task of issuing the formal invitations to the Vatican Council, either to the World Council of Churches, the leaders of the world confessional families or the special guests. Bea's *apologia* for the life and work of the Secretariat was oriented to the task of addressing doctrine. Not only was the Secretariat charged with the examination of doctrine, but was founded upon doctrine.

In order to clarify his point, Bea cited St. Augustine in the terse memorable phrase "odisse errores: diligere errantes" [Hate errors: love those who err].[139] In order to clarify the strength of his argument, Bea appended a litany of New Testament references. The first of these was from the First Letter to the Corinthians in which St. Paul spoke of himself as having a unique relationship to the Corinthians: "Choose, then; am I to come to you rod in hand, or lovingly, in a spirit of forbearance? (I Cor. 4:21)." Here the reference made St. Paul an icon of both harshness and love. The rest of the texts, cited by Bea, under the principle *odisse errores* are also Pauline. Paul's writing herein is apodictic, harsh and terse, in order to enunciate the strength of his belief, that what was given to the early Christians must be cherished and practiced in the integrity of truth (I Cor. 4:21). The letter to Titus contains these frightening words: "It was one of them, their very own prophet [the Cretan poet Epimenides (*circa* 600 B.C.)], who said: 'Cretans are always liars, evil beasts, slothful bellies.' " Paul believed that testimony to be true. For this reason Titus was to rebuke them sharply, so that they may be sound in the faith, not paying attention to Jewish myths or to the

---

137. *Ibid.*, p. 472.
138. Schmidt, *op. cit.*, p. 383.
139. Bea, *op. cit.*, p. 21.

commandment of those who reject the truth (Titus 1:12-13). The warning was just as strong in another citation from First Corinthians: "If anyone who is counted among the brethren is debauched, or a miser, or an idolater or bitter of speech or a drunkard, or an extortioner, you must avoid his company; you must not even sit at table with him (1 Cor. 5:11)." The reason for this Pauline dictum is that immoral people are bound to be met in society but do not have to be accepted as brothers or sisters.[140]

Membership in the community of the believers *ipso facto* protects one from Satan's destructive power; but the immoral person, in this case, a man living with his father's wife, is not holy, does not seek holiness, and, therefore, should be handed over to Satan's destructive power, which is the destruction of the flesh, i.e., slow disease and death. However, there is some hope for the spirit of the individual after judgment day: "Call an assembly at which I will be present in spirit, with all the power of the Lord Jesus Christ, and so, in the name of our Lord Jesus Christ hand over the person named to Satan for the overthrow of his corrupt nature, so that his spirit may find salvation in the day of Our Lord Jesus Christ (I Cor. 1:4-5)." Before the instruction on the Eucharist, after warning the Corinthians that there are divisions among them, and knowing them as he does, Paul believed the division to be true to some extent. This dictum was delivered: "Indeed, there have to be factions among you, for only so will it become clear who among you is genuine." Finally, St. Luke put these words in Paul's mouth in the discourse to the Elders of the Church of Ephesus, who assembled to greet Paul at Miletus. Paul's tone is that of an elder statesman: "I know that after I have gone, savage wolves will come in among you, not sparing the flock. . . . Keep watch over yourselves and over all the flock, of which the Holy Spirit has made you overseers, to shepherd the church of God that he obtained with the blood of his own Son (Acts 20:28-29)."[141]

The above references from the Pauline Corpus are corroborated by the words of Jesus, as found in the Synoptic Gospels: "Woe to the world because of stumbling blocks! The occasions of stumbling are bound to come, but woe to the one by whom the stumbling block comes (Mt. 18:7)!" A Lukan account calls for the one scandalizing little children to have a millstone tied around his neck (Luke 17:2). A member of the assembly who refuses reproof or instruction, he is to become marginalized in Jerusalem society. "If he will not even listen to the Church, then count him all one with heathen and the publican (Mt. 18:17)."

140. *Ibid.*, p. 22.
141. *Ibid.*

Bea presented compelling evidence. Indeed, within his talk, the list of his references, almost all taken from the Pauline Corpus, is monumental. He said: "The Apostle's severity can be sometimes terrible!" Yet, on the basis of Scripture he provided testimony, which was meant to show his colleagues in the Curia that he too was as zealous as they for the purity of the doctrine of the faith. Citing the Pastoral Epistle to Timothy, he declared: "Some, through refusing this duty, have made shipwreck of the faith; among them, Hymenaeus and Alexander, whom I have made over to Satan, until they are cured of their blasphemy (1 Tim. 1:19-20)."[142]

The conclusion of Bea's discourse spoke of "the general mobilization" of Christians and, like so many of the other 240 articles, lectures, and sermons, Bea stated that "the Holy Father (Pope John) has definitely designated union as the *ultimate* aim of the Council, even if it not be the immediate aim."[143] In this particular presentation, Bea clearly delineated that he was conscious about where he was in history, having stated before that his was a time of rapid social change. The Church of Christ is now faced with a secularized, technological, and materialistic world; in countries that used to be called missionary, the past few years had seen the development of a decisive situation for the place of Christianity in those lands. The Church of Christ, today, more than ever, needs to be strong and its strength will depend on its unity. Having laid down the gauntlet, Bea outlined the tools necessary to achieve that goal: "One man sows; another man reaps (Jn. 4:37)." Here he was speaking of the long-term work necessary to attain a real meeting of minds, to eliminate prejudices, to enlighten and deepen faith, to achieve closer and closer collaboration in fields not directly concerned with the faith. That is the goal! Here is the method: "This preparatory work obviously requires, in those engaged in it, a sound knowledge of their own beliefs, clarity of ideas, firm adherence to their own faith, and, above all, the holiness that comes from humility, charity, prayer and sacrifice, and the example of a good Catholic life."[144] This is love, a love that rises from the wellspring of faith in God, commitment to Christ, and openness to the prompting of the Holy Spirit. Yet, while the boat may float

---

142. Bea, *op. cit.*, pp. 21-25.

143. *Ibid.*, p. 36.

144. *Ibid.*, p. 37. See also *Ibid.*, p. 49. Bea was addressing this fundamental ecumenical attitude first of all to the bishops in a conference at Ferrara. On 9 November 1960 he stated: "The principal part in the work of union falls to *the hierarchy of the Church herself*. The hierarchy must pave the way for union, on their side doing what they can to remove obstacles and dealing officially with our separated brethren or their authorized representatives" (emphasis mine).

upon an open sea, it carries the anchor of an unmitigated adherence to truth. Cardinal Newman was aware of all the faults of Churchmen and all the blots on the record of Church history. Still under the detritus of the ages he perceived the light of holiness. Magnetic "holiness" draws men to itself. People grow tired of cleverness, beauty, prestige, even frankness, but they never grow tired of holiness.

In light of Bea's stated goal it is now possible to see the significance of this all-important sentence: *"Strange as it may seem, the cause of this severity, when all is said and done, is love."*[145] To support this sentiment, Bea used no less than eighteen quotes from the New Testament.[146] For example: "But you will receive power when the Holy Spirit has come upon you; and you will be my witnesses in Jerusalem, in all Judea and Samaria, and to the ends of the earth (Acts 1:8)." The use of this text, though not specifically spelled out, is interesting in that it has an ecumenical cast. The Apostles, once filled with the Spirit of the risen Lord, would evangelize first in Jerusalem, in the very place of Jesus' teaching, his execution and his resurrection. All Jerusalem knew the events, as is stated in St. Luke's Gospel by the two characters on the way to Emmaus. The evangelization would pass to Judea and its countryside, where the Jewish faith was said to be pure; and then to Samaria, where those Hebrew ideas and practices that were still existing were syncretized with paganism; and finally to the purely pagan world. This text contained within itself a mandate of priority. By reference to it, Bea was already groping toward a concept of a hierarchy of relationships and hierarchy of truths, which would ultimately manifest itself in 1964, with the promulgation of *Unitatis Redintegratio:*

> Furthermore, in ecumenical dialogue, catholic theologians, standing fast by the teaching of the Church yet searching together with separated brethren into the divine mysteries, should do so with love for the truth, with charity, and with humility. When comparing doctrines with one another, they should remember that in Catholic doctrine there exists an order or "hierarchy" of truths, since they vary in their relation

---

145. *Ibid.*, p. 23.

146. It is not surprising that Bea should use this number of citations. It is part of the human experience to express love in a variety of ways. In a recent novel of awakening, Sue Monk Kidd, *The Secret Life of Bees* (New York: Viking Penguin, 2002), p. 140, an older Black woman speaks to a young White girl: "Did you know there are thirty-two names for love in one of the Eskimo languages? . . . And we just have this one. We are so limited, you have to use the same word for loving Rosaleen as you do for loving a Coke with peanuts. Isn't that a shame we don't have more ways to say it?"

to the foundation of the Christian faith. Thus the way will be opened whereby this kind of "fraternal rivalry" will incite all to a deeper realization and a clearer expression of the unfathomable riches of Christ. (No. 11)[147]

The same rubric of love comes from an awareness that grace is the prompting by the Spirit toward goodness. In this regard Bea quoted St. Peter: "Yet always you must remember this, that no prophecy in scripture is the subject of private interpretation. It was never man's impulse, after all, that gave us prophecy; men gave it utterance, but they were men whom God had sanctified, carried away as they spoke by the Holy Spirit (2 Pet. 1:20-21)." The love of the faith and the love of Christ are one and the same. This conviction is based upon the immutability of the Lordship of Jesus. Flight from the truth provides no haven: "If anyone refuses to listen to what we have said in our letter, he is to be a marked man; avoid his company until he is ashamed of himself . . . (2 Thess. 3:14)."

On the basis of this early Pauline text, Bea incited his listeners with what he hoped would be a zealous love, because it is love of Christ. Where such love, *agape,* is present, there is also the Holy Spirit.[148] The fruit of this love is love itself, love of truth, love of unity, love of the souls of the faithful, and also those of the wanderers. As if the theological argument were not compelling, Bea herein cited his own time as a necessary reason to be faith-filled and faithful: "Love of the faithful and those who go astray does not, perhaps, cause us any difficulty, but it is not so with this zealous love of truth and purity of doctrine. Living, as we do, in a world teeming with ideas, and with all kinds of philosophical systems with vainness with one another we are perhaps too inclined to acquiesce, to adopt an attitude of indifference, to be ashamed of the intransigence of Catholic dogma, as of something niggardly, unmodern, out of touch with reality, and almost fanatical."[149] As if to assuage the fears of his Curial confreres, Bea's next sentence showed his own sense of caution regarding a false security: "Further-

147. This instruction calls for discernment and a scientific understanding of the Church or ecclesial communion which may be the dialogue partner. It also calls for an ecumenical compassion whereby the *Fachmann* sees the ecumenical partner as it sees itself, in its own ethos.

148. Gottfried Quell and Ethelbert Stauffer, "Love," in G. Kittel, *Bible Keywords* (New York: Harper and Brothers, 1951), p. 66. "*Agape* among the Greeks meant the mutual respect and sympathy of equals. Christian *Agape* is charged with a twofold consciousness, viz., a sense of unworthiness before God and a realization of his mercy. The sense of charity sets the tone of the brotherhood in all its ways."

149. Bea, *op. cit.,* p. 24.

more, an ill informed love for unity and for our separated brethren may drive us, at times, to a false kind of eirenicism."[150] Then Bea reached a crescendo, which he took directly from one more Pauline writing. "We are to follow the truth in a spirit of charity, *and so grow up* in everything, into him, Christ, who is our Head (Eph. 4:13-15)."

Regarding his love of those who err, Bea again relied heavily on Pauline biblical references to make his point. Bea used five biblical quotes in order to argue his conviction that there is no contradiction in hating the error and loving those who are in error. Attitudes can be different expressions of the same charity, e.g., "tough love" and the "gentle caress." These are both expressions which are rooted in love and grow in love. Bea's argument is strongly based herein on papal texts, e.g., from Pope Pius XII, Pope John XXIII and the 1949 *Instructio de promotione oecumenica* of 20 December. Those who *"individually and consciously withdraw themselves* from the true faith, this is certainly *not* the case of all those now separated from us."[151] Referring to Pope John, who in his first "Speech from the Chair" on 29 October 1958, the day after his election, and in his first encyclical, *Ad Petri Cathedram,* used phrases such as "sons and brothers": "May all return; with full and tender longing, we beseech them to return . . . they will not enter a strange or unfriendly home but their own home."[152] By these Johannine references, Bea dared to make an innovation which he derived from history.

Within Greater Germany, the Churches of the Classical Reformation, as well as the Roman Catholic Church, were bound by the mandate *Cujus regio, ejus religio.* That historical fact was more than three hundred years old. Within the twentieth-century experience it was part of the jargon of pluralistic Christian neighborhoods to say: "You are what you are born to." According to Bea's speculation, neither the present-day Protestant communities nor the Orthodox Churches have made any effort to concoct heresy or promote schism. Children of their families are also children of history. They were in fact born into their current religious traditions. As the date of the Council approached, Roman Catholics should have willingly acknowledged reality: *"Accepting in good faith the inheritance handed on by their parents, these non-Catholics can sincerely believe that they are on the right path."*[153]

---

150. *Ibid.,* p. 25.
151. *Ibid.,* p. 26 (emphasis mine).
152. *Ibid.*
153. *Ibid.* (emphasis mine).

Based upon this stark point of history, Bea cleverly stepped over the injunctions of *Mystici Corporis* (No. 22).[154] Not only are these individuals separated from the wider Church by a severance of history, rather than by self will, but they have persevered tenaciously, and are in search for the *vestigia ecclesiae,* which were so often the reference of the early European ecumenical activity. In the Evangelical experience, of course, these include the place of the community, the profound reverence for the Sacred Scriptures as the Word of God, the devotion to the Crucified, the obligation to charity and the celebration of the sacraments, the first of which is, of course, Baptism: "Nor should we forget that, in spite of all the differences in doctrine and worship, our separated brethren still have much in common with us."[155] The hallmark of Protestants is the genuine piety, noticeable especially among the ordinary faithful, and the desire to attend to the commandments of God in ordinary lives. Above all, however, Bea was anxious to showcase the irrevocability of the gift of Baptism upon which all else is based. The Orthodox Churches of the East are particularly close because they possess the unbroken succession of their bishops, the valid sacraments and the Holy Eucharist which forms the center of their piety. They not only preserve both the ancient Apostolic Tradition and the Patristic Tradition, but they enrich the Universal Church by their cultural expressions. Most especially a great veneration of the Word of God, common to Orthodox and Protestant Traditions, i.e., the biblical tradition is calling *all* members of the household of God to find identity in Christ, and with one another.[156]

Citing once again the 20 December document of 1949 from the Holy Office, Bea made reference to the "signs of the times."[157] Bea declared: "The present time has witnessed in different parts of the world a growing desire among many persons outside the church for the reunion of all those

---

154. Hebblethwaite's (*Pope John XXIII*, p. 382) comment is as follows: "The syntax [of Bea's speech] was tortured but the meaning clear: this was a decisive move from an ecclesiology that *excluded* other Christians to one that *embraced* them; it was based on an older tradition that regarded baptism as the common bond between all who invoke the name of Christ; it by-passed *Mystici Corporis* and left it stranded in the pages of Denzinger, a curious historical monument from 1943" (emphasis mine).

155. Bea, *op. cit.*, p. 27. Luther left a sacramental heritage to the Evangelical Church of Germany for the presence of God is discerned in nature and is discernible because of the Word. God therefore is *absconditus et revelatus* (hidden and revealed). According to Bernard M. G. Reardon, *Religious Thought in the Reformation* (London: Longman House, 1995), p. 77, Luther himself was noted for his trust in divine providence as a principal characteristic of his personal piety throughout his life.

156. *Ibid.*

157. Hebblethwaite, *Paul VI*, p. 2.

who believe in Christ."[158] Bea illustrated this point first by reference to literary figures who manifested a particularly religious sensitivity, both before and during a moment of conversion to Catholicism: John Henry Newman, Thomas Merton, Sigrid Undset, Gilbert Keith Chesterton, Johannes Jörgensen, Gertrude von le Fort, Edward Schaper, Bruce Marshall, and Graham Greene.[159] He also cited the restoration of ancient liturgies among Protestant communities, as well as exchanges between the Churches which "for so long were of a polemical nature but which now have become genuine dialogues."[160] Finally, he cited the unity of Christians in the World Council of Churches, "which brings together about 180 religious groups, recognizing as the condition for membership, Jesus Christ as God and Saviour."[161]

The above-cited examples give dramatic witness to what Bea called "a great change; and this change is due not to mere human and natural motives, but to supernatural influences."[162] Then Bea made a plea:

> Since, then, Our Lord himself bestows such graces on so many of our separated brethren who are in good faith, and since the Church exhorts us to help them by heartfelt prayers, ought we not to feel an obligation to hold them dear with that true and sincere supernatural charity of which the Holy Father gives us so magnificent an example.[163]

To the question then, "What ought we to do?" Bea provided the answer. The concluding paragraphs of this text deserve to be quoted in full. In the year and a half since the Incident at Rhodes, Bea had come to realize, as Father Schmidt instructed this author, that the action of the Holy Spirit in the matter of "Unity" is *always* a work-in-process:

> The (other) three great movements in the life of the Church during the last fifty years have been the Liturgical Movement, the Lay Apostolate, and the Missions. At the same time the movement in favour of Separated Brethren has steadily grown and has now reached vast proportions. *One can almost speak of a general mobilization of all ranks in the Church in favour of these brethren.* The plain fact is that the Holy Father has definitely designated *union as the ultimate aim of the Coun-*

158. Bea, *op. cit.,* p. 28
159. *Ibid.*
160. *Ibid.*
161. *Ibid.*
162. *Ibid.*
163. *Ibid.,* p. 29.

cil, even if it is not the immediate aim, and has asked the whole Church to make a united effort for prayer and purification in preparation for it. But the Council cannot reach the finishing point even if it is a point of departure. The concern is to *foster more frequent and wider contacts* with separated brethren, inspired by the greatest possible *frankness and charity.* Only in this way will it be possible, by *slow* and *hard work,* to attain a real meeting of minds, to eliminate prejudices, to enlighten and deepen faith and charity, and to achieve closer and closer collaboration in fields not directly concerned with the faith. The Holy Father himself, speaking of union with brethren of the Eastern Church has defined the stages of this persevering work as, "first of all, an approach, a drawing together and only then complete union." It is clear then that at the moment there is no question of spectacular results, nor of successes in the near future, but of long, patient preparation, to which can be applied the proverb quoted by Our Lord himself: "One man sows, another reaps (John 4:37)." This preparatory work obviously requires, in those engaged on it, a sound knowledge of their own beliefs, clarity of ideas, firm adherence to their own faith and, above all, the holiness which comes from humility, charity, prayer and sacrifice, and the example of a good Catholic life.[164]

Since this work of preparation has joined to it the grace of the Holy Spirit which Our Lord implored on the night of his death, and which he himself implores each day through the celebrant of each Holy Mass, we may have serene confidence that the day draws ever nearer when there will be "one fold and one shepherd" (John 10:16) for all who bear witness to the name of Jesus.[165]

Bea's motto of "doing the truth in charity" would remain, in effect, the work of the Council which was the first fruit of the Secretariat for Promoting Christian Unity. It was neither an example of religious jargon nor a meaningless expression of pious poetry. Every ounce of "Germanness," either from the sixteenth century or the twentieth, is contained in Bea's legacy. For those who worked with him or who immediately came after him, the first imperative of Bea's addresses, either to the press, his curial colleagues, or to the separated brethren themselves, implied facing hostility in order to eradicate historical prejudice. Secondly, the topic of discourse was always Baptism and the study of doctrine; faith in Christ and the integrity

164. *Ibid.,* p. 36 (emphasis mine).
165. *Ibid.*

of dogma are so intimately associated, that it is impossible to separate them. Finally, since the goal is the discovery of unity, the method is authenticity, remembering that one must be "absolutely faithful to the internal truth taught by Christ and his Spouse the Church." Therefore, according to Bea, the ecumenists' motto will always be "*veritatem facientes in caritate* (Eph. 4:15.)."[166]

The Evidence of the Foregoing: Concluded

As the work of preparing for the Second Vatican Council deepened, Bea now found himself addressing a wide variety of tasks confided to him, and to his Secretariat. The most important of these was to clarify for himself and for others the theological statute upon which the work of "promoting Christian Unity" is based. As Emmanuel Lanne has written, Bea's organization was "founded upon doctrine" [mais comme un organisme fondé sur une doctrine].[167] In order to do this, he relied upon two dynamics, "Word and Sacrament" (a Reformation principle) and his motto "truth and charity." As a Scripture scholar, his field of expertise was fundamental biblical methodology, i.e., the principle of the hermeneutic. Relying upon the data of the primitive Church of the New Testament, Bea assembled a monumental stack of texts, especially taken from the writings of St. Paul, in order to present "the weight of the evidence." In so doing, he profoundly affected the entire Christian world with regard to the image of the Church.

As the world anticipated the Council Fathers to soon assemble at Rome, the prevailing imagery of the Church, among them, was that of the Mystical Body which served, *ad intra,* as a functioning ontology, a kind of reification of the mystery of *ekklesia*.[168] This was a time of ecclesiological isomorphisms, as various experiences of Church came to find expression.[169] In the days of the Council itself, the Fathers would ultimately

---

166. *Ibid.,* p. 29.

167. Lanne, *op. cit.,* p. 478.

168. John Francis Kobler, C.P., *Vatican II and Phenomenology* (Dordrecht: Martinus Niejhoff Publishers, 1985), p. 116.

169. Avery Dulles, S.J., *Models of the Church* (Garden City, N.Y.: Doubleday and Company, 1974), p. 21. "When an image is employed reflectively and critically to deepen one's theoretical understanding of a reality it becomes what is today called a 'model.' Some models are also images — that is, those that can be readily imagined. Other models are of a more abstract nature, and are not precisely images. In the former class, one might put temple, vine, and flock; in the latter, institution, society, community."

adopt the image of the "People of God." "*Hence the universal Church is seen to be a people brought into unity from the unity of the Father, the Son and the Holy Spirit (Lumen Gentium, 4).*" This image was used by St. Cyprian of Carthage, the earliest Patristic ecclesiologist.[170] It was reintroduced into the English-speaking world by Dom Ansgar Vonier, Abbot of Buckfast, who purposefully sought, as a theologian, to meet the challenges proposed by Nazism, Fascism, and Communism, all of which sought to fashion a new people. The commodity in question is that of "solidarity." Vonier found that the testimony of Sacred Scripture delivered up the very real paradigm of the "People of God" which bypassed any purely spiritual popular impression which might stem from the model of the Mystical Body. The "People of God" terminology is rational on the vertical and horizontal level alike. It is material and spiritual, it is personal and social, it is moral and worshipful, etc. The dynamism of this terminology is based upon the "obediential capacity" of all the children of God to be conformed to Christ.[171]

The anguish of the age of the emergence of ecclesiological isomorphisms was to be epitomized in the encyclical *Ecclesiam Suam* (6 August 1964). It is perhaps the most heartfelt encyclical ever composed to that date. Paul VI was a student of European philosophy and was particularly affected by the teachings of the French school of *Personalism*. In turn, he envisioned a world populated by individuals who were yearning for fulfillment and the satisfaction of a hunger for meaning:

> We see these men serving a demanding and often a noble cause, fired with enthusiasm and idealism, dreaming of justice and progress, and striving for a social order which they conceive of as the ultimate of perfection and all but Divine. This, for them, is the Absolute and the Necessary. It proves that nothing can tear from their hearts their yearning for God, the first and final cause of all things. (104)

Paul VI based his vision of ministry, as pope, on principles of self-awareness, the hunger for transcendent concepts of purity, holiness, strength, and authenticity. The Church offered both a message, contained in Divine Revelation, and a mission, which could be identified with what

---

170. St. Cyprian, *De oratione Domini* 23; J. P. Migne, *Patrologia Latina* 553.

171. For a full discussion, refer to Karl Rahner, S.J., *Potentia Obedientialis,* in Karl Rahner et al., *Sacramentum Mundi* (New York: Herder and Herder, 1970), p. 66. "Human nature is a *potentia oboedientialis* for the radical self expression of God which is actualized in Jesus Christ."

he termed a vogue word, "dialogue." In his own words: "The Church *must* enter into dialogue with the world in which it lives. It has something to say, a message to give, a communication to make" (*Ecclesiam Suam,* No. 65, emphasis mine). To the context of the new ecclesial paradigm, posited by Pope Paul VI, Bea provided the ecumenical conscience.[172]

For this endeavor, Bea brought the genius of his ability to interpret biblical texts. To some he has appeared only as a well-meaning scholarly careerist. He manifested Christian sentiments such as hospitality, solicitude, and inclusiveness. Divorced from either a biblical or theological grounding, such an attitude could certainly appear as ephemeral or as a kind of religious superficiality, a mere sociological exercise. However, he indicated that the reality of the Church *is* founded *on the evidence* of Divine Revelation. Therefore he did not plunge into an analysis of medieval Scholastic tracts but dedicated his earliest ecumenical efforts to an analysis of Divine Revelation. That analysis provided both the Council and the Church with the possibility of going forward. The best manner of proceeding was to find that starting point which is the well-spring of the question — Sacred Scripture itself.

That question is: Are the Orthodox, Anglican and Protestant Churches endowed with any kind of ecclesiological foundation, or are they sociological, anthropological units, condemned to gestures, which, at best, are expressions of idolatry? Attendance at Protestant services in those days was judged to be participation in false worship. Or is there something of Christ in every Christian assembly? Bea's answer was a wholehearted **YES**. His task was the presentation of eidetic imagery regarding the meaning of the Church. How was he to accomplish this?

Whether wittingly or unwittingly, Bea did bypass potentially paralyzing questions of ecclesial ontology, either theoretical or functional. Still, he took seriously the datum of Pope Pius XII, the imagery of the Mystical Body. Josef Höfer had advised him of the seriousness of that conspicuous paragraph and the problematic it imposes: Who is a member of the Church? All the baptized are members of the Church unless through an unhappy act they cut themselves off from membership through heresy and schism. Therefore, are Orthodox, Anglicans or Protestants outside the Church?

To answer that question, Bea resorted to the concepts of Word and Sacrament. In basically what are his three inaugural texts, the *Sacred Heart Messenger* article, the press briefing regarding Archbishop Fisher and the Angelicum discourse, the new President of the Secretariat identified the

---

172. Hebblethwaite, *Paul VI, op. cit.,* p. 380.

ecclesial elements which are shared by all Christians: Sacred Scripture and the celebration of the sacrament of Baptism as the fundamental rite of Christian initiation. Thus it could be said that this disclosure of the Church, by Word and Sacrament, provided a methodology that could be viable in the future, as the topic of ecclesiology moved from the floor of the Council to the table of theological conversation between many denominations of the Christian family in the form of dialogues (usually bilateral in scope) which emerged as the heart of ecumenical activity, after the Council, beginning in 1966.

By emphasis on "what we share," Bea avoided holding anyone up to the standards of objectivized reality, as it were, a theological extrinsicism. Instead, he operated from a twofold intrinsicism, to resolve the problem of *Mystici Corporis,* No. 22, by recourse to his understanding of the hermeneutical principle: clarity is found in the evidence of a New Testament author. Father Schmidt's biography of Cardinal Bea reveals his measure of research and interpretation. Sometime in 1959, well before he received word of any sort of possible involvement with the Council, he wrote: "In ecclesiology, the question of Christ's royal dominion seems to me important. Apart from this, the idea of the Holy Spirit as the leading and illuminating principle of the life of the Mystical Body of Christ needs considerable development to justify the Church's teaching from within."[173] This was Bea's first priority, the analysis and emphasis of the significance of the "Lordship of Christ." One must look for this theme in all of Bea's theological pre-occupations at the Council's inception.

A Jesuit Christology

It must be remembered that Bea was first and foremost a Jesuit. As such, he was possessed of Ignatian sensibilities regarding the process of theological investigation or, if one will, "discernment."[174] He was also taken up with a Jesuit theme of Christic priority.[175] In emphasizing the Lordship of Christ,

173. Schmidt, *op. cit.,* p. 295.

174. David Lansdale, "The Serpent's Tail: Rules for Discernment," in *The Way of Ignatius Loyola,* ed. Philip Sheldrake, S.J. (London: SPCK, 1991), p. 172.

175. *The Ignatian Theme:* An individual comes into "at-one-ness of his whole being" with Christ, in Gerard W. Hughes, "Forgotten Truths," in Sheldrake, *op. cit.,* p. 30. Also see Charles Davis, *Sacraments of Initiation, Baptism and Confirmation* (New York: Sheed and Ward, 1964), p. 95. This baptismal identity with Christ had been explicated by Charles Davis: "Our personal relation to the Son is that of brothers. He is the model of our life of grace, the

Bea likewise resorted to the image of the Christ of the Paschal Mystery, at once Crucified and Glorified. Inherent in this concept is an essential Christocentrism. Bea carried his Christic concerns to the continued debate on the Church and contributed in no small way to the development of the image of the People of God and the identification of the Christ of the People of God as the Shepherd/Logos.[176] The renowned German theologian Joseph Cardinal Ratzinger (now Pope Benedict XVI) said: "The Council is 'pastoral' in its fusion of truth and love, 'doctrine' and pastoral solicitude: It wished to reach beyond the dichotomy between pragmatism and doctrinalism, back to the biblical unity in which practice and dogma are one, a unity grounded in Christ, who is both *Logos* and the Shepherd; As the *Logos* he is our Shepherd, and as our Shepherd he is the *Logos*."[177]

Let it be recalled here that, even in 1959, Bea's words were: "In ecclesiology, the question of Christ's royal dominion seems to me important."[178] In his autumn 1959 letters, Bea identified, in fact, three ecclesiological themes, viz., (1) "the royal Lordship of Christ," (2) "the Holy Spirit as the leading and illuminating principle," and (3) "laying the groundwork for gradual reunion."[179] This is how Bea proceeded. At rock bottom, however, is identity with Christ and incorporation into Christ through Baptism. "All you who have been baptized in Christ's name have put on the person of Christ; no more Jew or Gentile, no more slave or freeman (1 Cor. 12:13)." According to the American theologian Avery Cardinal Dulles, S.J.: "The unity for which Christians pray is not something to be manufactured out of whole cloth but rather *a coming to consciousness of a unity that in germ we already have* thanks to the oneness of God, Our Father, Christ our Savior and the Spirit who is their mutual communion with each other and with us."[180] It is Bea's argument that the entrance to the Trinity is through Christ: "We are all only one in Christ Jesus (Gal. 3:27)."[181] Finally Bea

---

pattern after whom we are formed, when we are given a share in the divine life. Since he took our nature and thus put himself on an equality with us, we can call him our brother. We are joined to him, so that it is his life we possess, his relation to the Father we share. Our personal intimacy with him must be expressed in terms of identity, though our distinct personality is not absorbed . . . union of Father and Son in the life of the Trinity is sealed by the Spirit . . . since we enter the union between Father and Son, we receive the Spirit as gift."

176. See Schmidt, *op. cit.* pp. 364-65, 465 and 670.

177. Cited in Herbert Vorgrimler, *Commentary on the Documents of Vatican II*, vol. 1 (New York: Herder and Herder, 1967-1969), p. 299.

178. Cited in Schmidt, *op. cit.*, p. 295.

179. *Ibid.*

180. Dulles, *Models*, *op. cit.*, p. 138.

181. Bea, *op. cit.*, p. 30.

stated: "Now notice that the teaching of *Mediator Dei* and St. Paul is un-qualified; It states what is always effected by the actual reception of bap-tism, provided, of course, that it is valid."[182] The foundation of ecumenism is ecclesiology; the basis of ecclesiology is Christ. Both are the necessary components of the ecumenical endeavor of the Church. The *realization* of the action of Christ in the Church and the mission of the Holy Spirit to the Church produced the effect of a Kantian categorical imperative, if the Ecu-menical Movement were going to be credible.

Ecclesio-consciousness is always Christocentric. Christ in this sense is the model of unity. Not only is the Church to be conformed to that grace, which is Christ, it must be open to the action of God to receive that grace even if its promptings be on the fringe of consciousness. When Christians look at the Church, they see only human beings and deal with them intel-lectually through noetic characterization and judgments. Yet, the action of God is effected sometimes through an infra-human way and even in a non-human way. These promptings toward conformity to Christ are the work of the Holy Spirit: "You made of them a kingdom and priests to serve our God, and they shall reign on the earth (Rev. 5:10)," and "God has given us the wisdom to understand fully the mystery the plan he was pleased to de-cree in Christ, a plan to be carried out in Christ in the fullness of time, to bring all things into one in him, in the heavens and on the earth (Eph. 1:9-10)." Ecclesio-consciousness is also pneumatic.

Bea's theology opened up the sensitivity of many all over the world. His words were heard in every Church and ecclesial communion. It was his genius to resort to the texts of Scripture, his own field of expertise, to ex-press his insight. Bea's pneumatology cannot herein be developed, for in the primitive texts, cited above, the action of the Holy Spirit is identified but not developed. Certainly, however, it was a priority to him in the pre-Council days, as is evidenced by his letters. Since not all of the documents of that time are yet available, therefore, the subject of the Holy Spirit must be tabled. The theme of Baptism as the constitution of the Christian life and the entrance of all Christians into the ecumenical endeavor is indige-nous to the thought of Cardinal Bea. It was his major theological theme, in the explication of his ecumenical mission.

Several theological topics remain for further examination. These top-ics include: (1) the centrality of *koinonia* in the ecclesiology of the Roman Catholic Church, since the Second Vatican Council; (2) the local bishop as teacher of ecumenism, and the importance of the local Church as *locus* of

---

182. *Ibid.*

theology; (3) the ecumenical significance of the relationship between the local and universal Church, particularly in reference to development of doctrine; (4) the specific ongoing function of the Pontifical Council of Christian Unity and of international ecumenical research centers and how the two interact; (5) the "life of holiness" in an ecumenical context; (6) confident reliance on the Holy Spirit as the agent of unity; (7) ecumenism as an ongoing ecclesiological imperative; (8) the effect of a particular deleterious culture upon the life of the Church, e.g., the Fascist era, Communism, the twenty-first-century world after 11 September 2001; (9) the Church and inculturation, specifically with reference to liberation theology; (10) the emergence of the concept of a "World Church," and the impact of the "New Churches"; (11) Baptism and Evangelization; (12) the study of sacred texts and documents of convergence, and the principle of hermeneutics in the worldwide ecumenical effort; and (13) the possibilities inherent in the necessary task of ecumenical education.

This task grew out of research, first undertaken to reach an understanding of the significance of Cardinal Bea's German origins and the theological importance of his ongoing personal cultural and professional ties to his homeland. The study revealed that Bea was a man of the Church, like no other in his day. Yet he must be viewed historically between two other figures, good Pope John and historically minded Archbishop Jaeger. While Jaeger and Bea were not alike, they were both endowed with the same ecumenical charism. It is difficult in some instances to determine where the work of one man ended and the efforts of the other began. Together they addressed the issue of the Rhodes Incident, viewing it as a serious symptom of the still un-addressed question of ecumenism at Rome. They also developed a document of request for papal attention to this matter. Together they developed the concepts of the *Fachmann* (the ecumenical expert) and the *Gutachterstelle* (the bureau of experts) and *Kenntnis* (ecumenical knowledge and wisdom).

Jaeger's letter, like the earlier one from Patriarch Maximos IV Saigh of Antioch, demonstrated the vitality and authenticity of the *voice of the local Church*. In this, the East and West converge. Bea was possessed of a genius which indicated that he did not forget his lifetime work of Biblical study. Höfer had warned Bea in the 1950s of the ambiguity of paragraph 22 in *Mystici Corporis*. Bea did not tear down the image of *Mystici Corporis* but built upon it by reference to the Pauline biblical texts. His priorities were Christological, pneumatological, and ecclesial. By his efforts he helped pave the way for a new and inclusive reference to the Church as the "People of God." Most especially Bea was a true prophet. He affected what he preached. To recall the words of Karl Adam, "We do not know what is in the divine plan of salvation. However, we do know that we ourselves though we cannot create any final unity in Christendom must do everything possible to prepare the way for dynamic unity, a unity of hearts and minds."[183] Adam prescribed a remedy when he said that faith leads to love. What does love mean in this instance? Bea's answer is clear. From the certitude of ecumenical *Kenntnis*, love means acceptance of anyone who has been chosen by Christ, who has believed in Christ and who has been baptized in Christ, for like it or not, we are together in the family of Christ.

Bea heroically challenged the status quo of Vatican procedure. He dared to dream of and effect a Secretariat for Promoting Christian Unity. He was a kind of ecclesiastical "New Frontiersman." When all the borders of the world had been crossed by missionaries, *he brought the Church to yet one more frontier to be crossed, that of ignorance, bias and suspicion.* Through his discourses, he made the Church see the Evangelical possibilities of Jesus' High Priestly prayer (Jn. 17:21). Since 1910, the worldwide Ecumenical Movement, which began at Edinburgh, could not penetrate the ambiguous language of the Roman Church. Without bombast but with the steadiness of his quiet consistency, Bea opened a new door, in order to let in the light of realization of Jesus' mission and prayer — "that all may be one."

183. *Id., One and Holy, op. cit.*, p. 78.

Conclusion

In substance, through the course of this study, I have attempted to research a confined historical era in order to target the significance of the dates March 11-13, 1960, and the letter of Cardinal Jaeger to Pope John XXIII on 4 March of that same year. The documentation and the events of those days are at the very heart of the foundation and the mission of what was to become known as the Secretariat for Promoting Christian Unity. The three central figures of that drama were Cardinal Augustin Bea, Archbishop (later Cardinal) Lorenz Jaeger of Paderborn and, of course, Pope John XXIII. The *dramatis personae* cannot exclude the Patriarch (later Cardinal) Maximos IV Saigh, whose own correspondence with Pope John provided the overture to the ecumenical drama.

In order to achieve my goal, I examined a circumscribed era, primarily, that of twentieth-century German Church history. While many figures appear within the time frame of 1940 to 1960, the relevant dates, Lorenz Jaeger is the consistent protagonist. Further, while the time frame of the Second World War and its aftermath forms the immediate scenario, necessary references have had to be made to events preceding the War, and also to the days immediately preceding the Second Vatican Council of 1962. This work does not take up either Conciliar deliberations or Conciliar conclusions.

This essay does, however, attempt to render further insight into the thought of the renowned and effective ecumenical pioneer Augustin Bea, who in the years between 1960 and 1962 opened up for the Catholic world the theological field of ecumenism. He accomplished this through the disclosure of the doctrinal and biblical foundations of the ecumenical endeavor itself. He also addressed ecumenism's future by pointing out the necessity of Christian contact and conversation. Bilateral and multilateral exchanges eventually would provide the road map for reconciliation and Christian Unity. As such, that quest is based upon that particular unity inherent in the Sacrament of Baptism. It is also a thoroughly Christian endeavor. The process, later prompted by Pope Paul VI, has become known as "dialogue."

As is clear from his correspondence with Archbishop Jaeger, Bea wanted a structure in which both the intellectual and pastoral dimensions of ecumenism would flourish. Bea, too, wanted a specific place in which ecumenical experts would be schooled, as it were, in the diplomacy of dialogue. This was his first aim as the designated President of the Secretariat for Promoting Christian Unity.

As such, Bea believed that all ecumenical activity is not an option. As outlined in the Gospel (Jn. 17:21), it is an imperative. As was for Christ in his anguished prayer to the Father on the eve of his Passion, "that all may be one," so too, in this context, for every Christian and for the Church, it involves suffering. The ecumenical endeavor also requires conversion. What does that concept mean? According to Cardinal Willebrands, who, as it were, was "present at the creation," Bea intentionally required an awareness of spiritual ecumenism, i.e., "prayer." Prayer, said Willebrands, implied that no human activity can bring this about. Unity and peace are the "gift of God." Through prayer, the Church retreats to silence to be attentive to the plans of Providence and the promptings of the Spirit. To acknowledge these points, let us look back to a summary of the narrative of the events, personalities, movements and ideas which are the components of this study.

The stage for this examination is the German nation, which, since the Reformation, is unique in its complexity and in its secular and religious sphere. Michael Stürmer, a renowned historian of twentieth-century Germany, made this reflection:

> Four months after the fall of the Berlin Wall in 1989, Margaret Thatcher convoked a colloquium of learned historians from Great Britain and the United States and put to them the question: "Have the Germans changed?" In the defining moment after the Cold War, Mrs. Thatcher wanted to know where Germany was going and by implication, how Europe would be affected. The questions revealed deep-seated anxieties about Germany's past as much as about her present and future.[1]

---

1. Michael Stürmer, *The German Empire (1870-1918)* (New York: Modern Library, 2000), p. 131.

Having cited Lady Margaret Thatcher, Professor Stürmer went on to cite the importance of architecture as representative of *Sturm und Volk:* "Berlin has a collection of buildings with resonances far beyond their immediate presence. . . . The neo-Classical Brandenburg Gate, erected just before the French Revolution, has witnessed events from Napoleon's triumphant entry in 1806 to the victorious return of the Prussian Guards from Paris in 1871; from the bitterness of Civil War in 1918-1919; to the torchlight parade of Hitler's Storm Troopers on the evening of January 30, 1933; from the blockade of Berlin by Stalin in 1948-1949; to the building and dismantling of the Wall in 1961 and 1989, respectively."[2] These latter events surround the twenty years which are the focus of this examination. One other event must likewise be cited. It is that of the Reformation itself, dating from that particular Halloween when Luther nailed his Ninety-five Theses to the Church door at Wittenberg, in 1517. Leslie Slote, a minor character in the American version of *War and Peace,* Herman Wouk's *The Winds of War,* described Luther as possessing the unique genius of the German who "saw through the rot of the Catholic Church and broke its back."[3]

For four hundred years, the influence of Luther predominated the German landscape. Within the first hundred years, the clash between princes and peasantry *(Bundschuh),* while wearing a religious mask, in fact was generated by political motives, only to be resolved by the Peace of Westphalia, in 1648. That so-called compact imposed, within the Holy Roman Empire and within Germany itself, the principle: *Cujus regio, ejus religio,* empowering, especially in the Protestant world, secular rulers with the prerogatives of Catholic bishops. For four hundred years, Germany was composed of a common people, *Volk,* who were divided not by political ideologies, philosophical tendencies, nor by cultural peculiarities, but rather by the scandal of confessional boundaries. In substance, the Evangelical Church of Germany and the Roman Catholic Church were pitted against each other; their only words were polemical and their only methods were by nature "Procrustean."

All of that changed with the collapse of the Second Empire in 1918, in "a landscape saturated with history and littered with monuments to human folly."[4] As the throne of the Kaiser tumbled, and the blueprint of Otto von Bismarck crumbled, so too did the principle *Cujus regio, ejus religio.* As the next twenty years unfolded, there arose the quest for "Church."[5]

---

2. *Ibid.,* p. 132.
3. *Id.* (London: Little, Brown & Co., 1971), p. 10.
4. Stürmer, *op. cit.,* p. 131.
5. As evidence, see the following from Bendiscioli, *op. cit.,* pp. 7, 128-29: "The religious

The Empire was succeeded by the short-lived Weimar Republic and, finally, by the outrageous government of the Hitler era, which sought to eradicate matters of religion. Yet, almost miraculously, despite so many upheavals going on at the time, many ecclesiological issues were coming forward for enunciation in the German forum. For example, on November 7, 1933, Cardinal Karl Josef Shulte of Cologne (1871-1941) handed a letter to Pius XI from a gathering of German Lutheran pastors, which contained these words:

> It was an error that in German Lutheran Protestantism, in contrast with the Augsburg Confession of the Church, some of Luther's ideas were affirmed as being absolutely binding, including that of the complete break away from the Catholic Church. In this respect we have not quite forgotten that Luther was originally desirous for a Reformation within the bosom of the Catholic Church, but today we must recognize the fact that the development of Lutheranism — not without pressure from outside — has followed a false path, always drifting further and further from the Church, and that in this way it has also drifted away from the positive desire for reform of Luther himself, merely emphasizing its negative aspects. For this reason we wish to turn aside from this path which led us apart from the One Holy Catholic and Apostolic Church and we desire to beg humbly to be restored to its bosom.[6]

Amidst these cataclysmic events of multiple outbursts of violence, chaotic government and minor revolutions, various expressions of the search for "Church," particularly from the various German Lutheran communities, flourished. Karl Thieme published a book entitled *Evangelical German Christians on the Way to the Catholic Church: Deeds and*

---

question in Germany has occupied, in recent years, the position of primary importance in the minds of the public. The new political and doctrinal claims which have been advanced in its domain in connection with national socialism have clashed in the strenuous manner in which they have been put into operation with conscientious convictions, secular organizations and cultural and legal traditions. This is not a new phenomenon in Germany. The *Jus Reformandi,* the rite of reforming the Church, which the Lutheran leaders, in their hierarchical role, had held from the beginning of the religious revolution in their attitude which was more political than theological, entailed stubborn resistance both in the Catholic and Protestant camps. . . . Bismarck tried to weaken the autonomy of German Catholicism with his famous *Kulturkampf* during the period from 1871 to 1886." In 1918-1930, the Republic "forced the churches to seek a reason for their autonomous existence, independent of the state, and based on their own religious office, in the same way as Catholicism. One liberal protestant wrote in dismay, 'Protestantism in Germany was on the way to Rome.'"

6. Cited in *ibid.,* pp. 139-40.

Debates.[7] According to Mario Bendiscioli, as was cited above, it was at this time that many Protestants discovered Catholicism.[8] Thus, above everything else, the Church is the Mystical Body of Christ. If the Church is thus to be identified so intimately with Christ and Christ is the center of worship for Christian vitality and ethical teaching, then the Church, as it was originally intended, must not only be *re*-discovered, but it must be re-embraced.[9] High Church Lutheran movements began to emerge with a renewed emphasis upon liturgical ceremony. The words of the Credo were re-examined in private study sessions; and, among Evangelical Christians, a renewed consciousness of the duty of keeping the legacy of the faith intact, and in its entirety, burgeoned. It was Max Pribilla, as was cited above, who recorded these changes in his 1930 book, *Um Kirchliche Einheit.*[10] The political, social and economic exigencies of the times dulled the sharp bite of confessional arguments, which in the face of the attack of materialism, secularism and German neo-paganism, seemed almost meaningless. In the past, abstruse and even remote questions such as "Justification," the ontology of grace, and the significance of apostolic authority were at the heart of Reformation and post-Reformation arguments and discord.

The post-War era of 1918-1922, and the ensuing upheaval of society, reiterated for all Christians in Germany that the Church is both historical

7. (Zurich: n.p., 1934). Dr. Thieme had made a statement to the press in October 1933 in which in the current crisis he and a small body of pastors and laymen were convinced that the doctrine as the result of which Luther had broken away from the Curia in the sixteenth century could not now be preached rightly except through the medium of the Roman Catholic Church. Cited in Bendiscioli, *op. cit.*, pp. 126-27. This press statement made historical precedent, thus facilitating initiatives by Max Metzger and Archbishop Jaeger.

8. *Ibid.*, p. 127.

9. Karl Adam, *op. cit.*, p. 270.

10. Bendiscioli, *op. cit.*, p. 131. Bendiscioli also noted as a firsthand witness that during the period Catholics did not consider themselves absorbed by Nazism. They stood sufficiently aloof, according to his judgment, as not yet to be docile. *Ibid.*, p. 153. By 1935, the Nazi government had begun a full-swing persecution of the Jesuits. Besides his position as editor and ecumenist, Max Pribilla had, as we have stated, become an outspoken critic of Hitler. His associate Fr. Bernhard Stempfle, S.J., was assassinated during the Night of the Long Knives. Therefore, he raised his voice: "Silence has its limits. There are moments when without any tangible utility, something has to be said for no other reason but that it is true. If it is not said, the moral order of the world suffers a blow that is harder to overcome than its violation by brute force, and this principle is valid also for the silence 'to prevent worse.' For ultimately, the worst that could really happen is that truth and justice would no longer find spokesmen and martyrs on earth." Cited in Vincent A. Lapomarda, *The Jesuits and the Third Reich* (Lampeter, Dyfed, Wales: Mellon House, 1989), p. 13.

and eschatological, and, for that reason, stands in apposition to the prioritization of German causes, government and ideology. Therefore, with its tradition of *Landkirche,* local communities were attempting to grapple with the sense of the essence of the Church. This realization led the young Dietrich Bonhoeffer to reflect:

> Perhaps Protestantism should never have aimed to becoming an established church but should have remained one of the large sects, which always have things easier — and perhaps then it would not be in the present calamity. . . . Now where the official ties between church and state have been dropped, the church is confronted by the truth; for too long it has been a refuge for homeless spirits, a shelter for uneducated enlightenment. Had it never become an established church, things would be very different. It would still have a significant number of enthusiastic supporters, in view of its size it could hardly be described as a sect, and it would present an unusual phenomenon of religious life and seriously profound piety. Thus it would be the ideal form of religion that is so sought after today . . . or is the whole game up? Will it shortly return to the bosom of the only saving church, that is, the Roman church, under the semblance of fraternity? One would like to know.[11]

The answer to that question would be found in the hands of Lorenz Jaeger. Although not an academic, he was at once a scholar and a pastor, endowed with an uncanny sense of discernment. Chosen to serve as Archbishop of Paderborn in 1941, he was able to determine that somehow Germany had special needs. It would be safe to say that his vision, which encompassed the depth and the seriousness of the times in which he was designated to serve, bespoke a corporate and ethnic responsibility, which could not rest, until the Church was somehow brought back into unity.

As was indicated, the theme of the Mystical Body of Christ had been a perennial topic of theological conversation in the first half of the twentieth century. It was even a subject for discussion at clandestine ecumenical meetings before the Hitler era. With the coming of Hitler in 1933, there also arrived a concerted Nazi effort to control religion with such concepts as the *Reichskirche* and *Reichsbischof*. Because of the system of *Landeskirche* and other expressions of Protestant pluriformity, Lutheranism fell into a life-and-death struggle with the Reich over the issue of *Völkische,* i.e., the national or racial element of the German Christian program: "Only one peo-

11. Eberhard Bethge, *Dietrich Bonhoeffer: A Biography* (Minneapolis: Fortress Press, 2000), p. 61.

ple, only one state, only one Church."[12] As contemporary history has shown, Hitler made every attempt to compromise the Catholic Church. Pope Pius XI counter-challenged with his encyclical *Mit brennender Sorge* (With Burning Anxiety) of 1937.[13] Efforts to compromise the successor, Pope Pius XII, especially through the creation of ambiguous diplomacy, compelled the Pontiff to elevate the situation to higher ground, through the promulgation of the encyclical *Mystici Corporis*.[14]

In 1943, while the War was at its height, Pius wrote of the transcendent nature of the Church: "And thus: to return to Our theme: as the Son of the Eternal Father came down from heaven for the salvation of us all, He likewise established the body of the Church and enriched it with the Divine Spirit to ensure that immortal souls should attain eternal happiness according to the words of the Apostle: 'All things are yours; and you are Christ's; and Christ is God's.' For the Church exists both for the good of the faithful and for the glory of God and of Jesus Christ whom He sent" (*MC*, No. 61). Pius XII, who previously had never been considered as interested in ecclesiology, issued the encyclical, which is the papal *prolegomenon* to today's contemporary ecclesiology. When probably not at all expected, Pius introduced again something that had not been pronounced for several centuries. He re-introduced the concept of the pneumatological dynamic source of the Church, which in remarkably *kerygmatic* terms he described as imbedded in the essential Christocentric framework of the total faith community:

12. Gurian, *op. cit.*, p. 85. In his novel *Winds of War, op. cit.*, p. 538, Herman Wouk wrote of the distorted sense of unity: "This was what now made Berlin completely intolerable. The Germans had balled themselves into one tight fist. The little tramp had his 'one Reich, one people, one leader,' that he had so long screeched for. Victor Henry [the protagonist], a man of discipline, understood and admired the stiff obedient efficiency of these people, but their mindless shutting out of facts disgusted him. It was not only stupid, not only shameless; it was bad war making. The 'estimate' of the situation — a phrase borrowed by the Navy from Prussian military doctrine — had to start from the facts."

13. Ronald J. Rychlak, *Hitler, the War, and the Pope, op. cit.*, p. 59.

14. A discussion of the efforts of Foreign Minister Joachim von Ribbentrop and the Vatican can be found in the introduction to Saul Friedländer, *Pius XII and the Third Reich* (New York: Alfred A. Knopf, 1966), pp. xv-xxv. Of particular interest is the author's assessment of German Ambassador Baron Ernst von Weizsäcker, who was transferred from the position of State Secretary within the foreign ministry to Ambassador for the Reich to the Vatican. Because of his aloofness, Weizsäcker was not particularly well understood. However, the collaborative memories of Weizsäcker's friends and associates indicate that he was personally hostile to the National Socialist Regime and "he was involved at various times in plans of the German resistance directed against Hitler." Weizsäcker was embarrassed to be chosen to be placed in the humiliating position of having to confuse the Pope.

Although the juridical principles, on which the Church rests and is established, derive from the divine constitution given to it by Christ and contribute to the attaining of its supernatural end, nevertheless that which lifts the Society of Christians far above the whole natural order is the Spirit of our Redeemer who penetrates and fills every part of the Church's being and is active within it until the end of time as the source of every grace and every gift and every miraculous power. Just as our composite mortal body although it is a marvelous work of the Creator, falls far short of the eminent dignity of our soul so the social structure of the Christian community, though it proclaims the wisdom of its divine Architect, still remains something inferior when compared to the spiritual gifts which give it beauty and life, and to the divine source whence they flow. (*MC*, No. 63)

Archbishop Jaeger was assisted by historians and by historiography in his assessment of the Catholic Church in Germany at the end of the Wartime era. Historians, Herte and Lortz, appeared at his side as did historical theologians, such as Romano Guardini and Josef Höfer. Armed with this revolutionary charter of the Church, i.e., Pius XII's encyclical, and with the very capable assistance of scholars of the Reformation, Jaeger was well equipped, paradoxically, to look backward toward a new, relevant understanding of the historical Church in Germany.

Prior to this time, the study of history was considered to be nothing more than the composition of a list of facts. At best, it could be said to be the assemblage of a series of cause and effect events. In the early twentieth century, German religious historians began to apply a new method to the study of the Reformation of the sixteenth century.[15] This type of study, contextualization, i.e., the application of the relevant texts to the details of the period, was applied successfully by Adolf Herte, whose story has been told above. Herte cut through the polemic of post-Reformation history to uncover the fact that a single biography of Luther had affected the whole of the Catholic evaluation of the life and theology of that central Reformation figure.

While Herte concentrated on the source and manner by which German ecclesiastical history had conducted itself for four hundred years, Joseph Lortz made the same journey by an attempt to discover, through primary documentation, the German landscape onto which the Reformation spilled. Through his study of history, Jaeger concluded that, while Hitler

---

15. Swidler, *op. cit.*, p. 25.

might attempt to constrain the Lutheran churches, it was less easy to co-opt the Church at Rome, due to its international composition.[16] As a diocesan Bishop, he detected a great fundamental yearning, noticing that, especially among the ecclesiastically sophisticated, there was a desire to consider the Church of Rome as home. Further, someone had to address those needs in order to find the presence of Christ in a Germany which expressed itself in terms of *Volk*, who were divided, alas, through the dictates of history, into confessional boundaries. The political restraints of more than four hundred years, expressing themselves now in Fascist symbols, provided the proverbial Procrustean bed of this unique history. Jaeger's diocese, for example, is a key to understanding the man ecumenically.

As already stated in Chapter Two, part of the Archdiocese centered around the Cathedral City, Paderborn, while part of it centered around the Protestant town of Magdeburg. The Archdiocese was divided in two, by another whole diocese, that of Hildesheim.[17] Historically conscious, endowed with remarkable gifts of practical, almost political, discernment, and confronted with a nightmare existence under the Nazi flag, Jaeger privately decided that enough was enough! From his own place at the table of the Fulda Bishops Conference, he espoused cause after cause that spoke to the need to discover anew the already existing Holy and Catholic Christian presence within the German nation. Most especially, Jaeger, from the time that he first received the mitre, established contact and remained in correspondence with Pope Pius XII, as well as other important officials at Rome.[18] This was because he was wedded to the concept of tradition and to the Petrine Office in which he found security, direction, and comfort. For this reason, this study has centered around the years of his episcopal

---

16. Cf. Gruss, *op. cit.,* p. 126, for an example of this differential, refer to the German Evangelical protest of 1941 and the reflections of Cardinal Bertram, President of the Fulda Bishops Conference, in his attempt to protest the integrity of Catholicism on behalf of the German bishops, in November of that year.

17. Link and Slominski, *op. cit.,* p. 13. As Archbishop of Paderborn, Jaeger was also Diasporavikar der Protektor und interessierte Förderer des Bonifatius Vereins für das katholische Deutschland, i.e., Jaeger held responsibility for support both for German Catholics and indeed for German Christians scattered throughout the world as well as for mission-sending societies and for German benevolent causes. He thus had continuous information about collaborative efforts within the Christian family worldwide.

18. Jaeger to Pope Pius XII, May 12, 1945, Vicar General's Archives, Paderborn. For example, herein Archbishop Jaeger informed Pius XII about developments, within German Protestantism, highlighting the very admirable role of a certain Dr. Asmussen who, despite his attempts to unite various branches of Lutheranism within the Evangeliche Kirche Deutschland (EKD), was dismissed.

ministry, since for Jaeger, modern events had rendered the long-standing post-medieval marks of German demarcation as less binding and as less meaningful for the mission of the Church. Karl Adam, immediately after the War, drew his nation's attention to the frontiers of the Deutsche Demokratische Republik (DDR) with its atheist roots, now planted in German soil and guarded by the Russian military.[19] Atheism, secularism, and materialism loomed large against an unresolved four-hundred-year religious history. It was Jaeger's genius to discern this new and critical pastoral problem.

In the meantime, at the Pontifical Biblical Institute, Augustin Bea was concluding his long and fruitful service within the ambience of both Roman academic life and the shadows of the Apostolic Palace of the popes.[20] It never occurred to him to do as Jaeger had done, i.e., to attempt to approach and view other ecclesial communities, i.e., the churches of the Classical Reformation, as they would see themselves. He never had to! For him, the magisterial map had long been plotted and the occasion to address Protestantism rarely occurred, except through the tools of biblical studies.[21] Although a German, he was physically removed from the pastoral problems of his nation, even though they were dramatic and immediate. When he was approached by Jaeger, he received, through the exchange of correspondence, a rich schooling, which enabled him to transfer his biblical and historical proclivities to the pastoral scene of his native Germany, now divided many times over. Bea's nomination as a Cardinal provided him with the rich opportunity to accomplish what Maximos IV Saigh could not. One of the reasons was his obvious proximity to the Pope; another reason was his age, which was precisely that of John XXIII. The mutual understanding that developed between these two men and their prioritization of the cause of unity was more than serendipitous. For his part, Pope John had already opened the door to Bea's transmission of the letter of Archbishop Jaeger, asking for a permanent Curial body to coordinate and monitor ecumenical organizations, which already were in existence. *Ad Petri Cathedram,* Pope John's inaugural encyclical, sounded the lyric to the tune that was to be continuously played through the first days of the life of the Secretariat for Promoting Christian Unity, which

19. Adam, *op. cit.,* pp. 3-4.

20. Schmidt, *op. cit.,* p. 289.

21. *Ibid.,* p. 97. On this occasion, "two respected Evangelical German scholars, Johannes Hempel and Paul Polz, were organizing the first International Congress of Old Testament exegesis, to be held in Göttingen in 1935, and, for the first time in history, the Pontifical Biblical Institute was invited to such a meeting."

John, in a characteristically spontaneous but well-reasoned gesture, placed under the direction of the old German cardinal, Augustin Bea: "They are our brothers. They will not cease to be our brothers until they cease to say, 'Our Father.'"

The immediate ecumenical task, which Cardinal Bea faced, came to him as a result not only of Reformation history, but as the result of German history within his own lifetime, i.e., the collapse of the Imperial Reich, the Hitler Era, the Cold War. The challenge, indeed the endeavor, of his immediate theoretical undertaking was to trace back through the 450-year history, since Luther nailed his Ninety-five Theses to the Church door. Were all these people who called themselves Lutherans, Calvinists, Evangelicals or Reformed, Zwinglians, Waldensians, Baptists, Dissenters, all "formal" heretics? Jaeger reminded him, if not explicitly, then subliminally: "We have to try to approach and visualize the other communities as they see themselves."[22] Since the constituents of his undertaking were initially those people who had been affected by the politics of a *Landgraf* for generations, they lived under the principle *Cujus regio, ejus religio*. Somehow, Bea had to remove the title "formal heretics" from the judgment of the Roman Catholic Church. Bea found his ally in a most unpredictable source — Pope Pius XII, who, in 1947, promulgated the encyclical on the Sacred Liturgy, *Mediator Dei*, in which he identified the heart of the Church's worship, indeed its very being, as Christ the Priest: "The sacred Liturgy is consequently the public worship which our Redeemer, as head of the Church, renders to the Father as well as the worship which the community of the faithful renders to its Founder and through Him to the Heavenly Father. It is, in short, the worship rendered by the Mystical Body of Christ in the entirety of its head and members . . . (*MD*, No. 20)." In an encyclical, dedicated to the practicalities of liturgical celebration, Pius XII, in fact, thought to restore reverence for the Sacred Liturgy in its historical setting, beginning with the rituals of the primitive church. Theologically, he has been judged to be, above all, the Pope of the Mystical Body, and that concept is also consistently evident within the text of his 1947 encyclical.[23] As has been noted above, even before the presentation of Bea's letter to Pope John XXIII, Bea had traced the importance of the Sacrament of Baptism as the gateway to many things, but most especially, as the gateway to understanding the Church. In writing to Professor Stakemeier, while helping him draft Jaeger's formal letter to Pope John XXIII, Bea took up the conclu-

---

22. Interview of Monsignor Aloys Klein with the author, October 15, 2001.
23. In Fremantle, *op. cit.*, p. 263.

sions of the Roman Synod, which in turn were based upon the words of Pius XII:

> Let the faithful, therefore, consider to what a high dignity they are raised by the Sacrament of Baptism. They should not think it enough to participate in the eucharistic sacrifice with that general intention which befits members of Christ and the children of the Church. . . . (*MD*, No. 88)[24]

Even before the Secretariat for Promoting Christian Unity became a reality, Bea provided John with an understanding of the ecumenical possibilities of such a title by recourse to the use of the specific word "Christian," as it was used by Pope Pius XII, in the encyclical *Mediator Dei*. Citing various references from that encyclical, Bea concluded that Pius was teaching that, through Baptism, everyone who receives the saving waters is constituted *Homo Christianus*, a person in Christ: "Through the general title of Christian, man becomes a member of the Mystical Body of Christ the Priest." Since all share this identity, Pius disclosed the priestly dignity of human life, human experience and human work, "in Christ": "Nor should Christians forget to offer themselves with their cares, their sorrows, their distresses, and their necessities, in union with the Divine Saviour upon the cross (*MD*, No. 104)."

Later, in his famous speech for the Church Unity Octave of 1961, delivered for the Dominican Faculty at the Angelicum, Bea bolstered his arguments from *Mediator Dei* with continued references to the Apostle Paul. In consequence, he declared:

> Now notice that the teaching of *Mediator Dei* and St. Paul is unqualified; it states what is always effected by the actual reception of Baptism, provided, of course, that is valid. So this must somehow hold good for our separated brethren also, even though they are separated from the Holy See as a result of heresy or schism *inherited from their ancestors.*[25]

Of special note in this statement is the concluding conditional phrase, "inherited from their ancestors." Bea did not ascribe responsibility nor condemnation to the results of history. He was saying, as Aloys Klein recalled aloud: "It is a fact. We can not go back . . . we can not go back. . . . The present is our circumstance; it is not our challenge to undo history and

---

24. *Acts of the Roman Synod, op. cit.*, No. 381.
25. Bea, *The Unity of Christians, op. cit.*, p. 30 (emphasis mine).

components thereof are beyond the scope, even of the Church. It is the task of the present to disclose or uncover the unity that is already there. This is a spiritual burden. It is futile to start anew and pretend that the past is not with us, nor that its descendants are guilty of crimes and errors for which, or in which, they played no part, and about which they, in fact, care little or nothing today."[26]

Now it remains to be seen as to what can be done for the future. The idea of dialogue on either a multivalent or a bilateral level had not yet crossed Bea's imagination. The immediate practicality was to begin that necessary first contact which would hopefully end up in a series of invitations for representative Christians of various denominations to attend the sessions of the General Council of the Church. The *raison d'être* for this task would be to cut through already existing circumstances of bias, misunderstanding, and outright prejudice. To accomplish this task, he once again borrowed from his collaborator, Lorenz Jaeger, and employed those all-Christian tools of "truth and of charity." Therefore, the final implications of the work of Bea, biblical scholar-turned-ecumenist, are rooted in those terms which are precious to the Greek New Testament, *agape* (love) and *aletheia* (truth).

In what sense, therefore, did Bea employ the term *truth?* Let it not be forgotten that Bea spent his entire priestly ministry in the study of Holy Scripture, and not only of Scripture itself, but the nature of its origin, transmission and exegesis. In consequence thereof, it is not unreasonable to borrow from Karl Barth, Bea's contemporary, who wrote extensively, and at the same time synthetically, about the topic of the centrality of Biblical Truth within the work of theology:

> If we accept the witness of Holy Scripture, then implicitly we accept the fact that, quite irrespective of the way in which they were humanly and historically conditioned, its authors were objectively true, reliable and trustworthy witnesses. It is not merely that we recognize their opinions to be good and pious, or appreciate their part and significance in religious history. We perceive rather that it pleased God the King of Israel, to whom the power of their witness is pledged as to the Lord, to raise up these true witnesses by his word and work. In this fact, at the very beginning of the history of Scripture, and at the heart of world-occurrence, even while the fact itself is a moment in occurrence generally, what we see is not merely a moment in occurrence generally, and in religious occurrence in particular, but a trace of the governance of

26. Interview of Monsignor Aloys Klein with the author, October 15, 2001.

God as the one and only true God, a trace of this God as the lord of all world-occurrence.[27]

As Johannes Willebrands, Bea's right-hand man, affirms, this Barthian synopsis reiterated an essential principle of Cardinal Bea: "Let there be no doubt about it, the Secretariat for Promoting Christian Unity was aimed at the study of doctrine and therefore aimed at the discovery of truth. Truth, in this sense, comes from God and is found in the Sacred Texts."[28] Barth put it rather succinctly when he wrote: "The only likelihood is that we may misunderstand the character and aim of the bible, by reading into it our own vacillations."[29] In another quote, Barth expressed himself strongly and existentially: "What the Bible has to offer us is *insight* to the effect that the knowledge of God is the eternal problem of our profoundest personal existence, that it is the starting point at which we begin and yet do not begin, from which we are separated and yet are not separated. From the Bible we may learn to soften the affirmations of our belief or unbelief, and perhaps to keep silence, until we perceive the true relation between God and ourselves."[30]

By resorting to Barth, in order to clarify Bea's claim to the primacy of Biblical Truth, it is possible to envision a Christian anthropology in which the baptized individual stands under the content of Divine Revelation and in the shadow of its record, the Holy Bible. In this very sense, Truth comes from Revelation and the task, indeed, the ethic is, first of all, "to listen." We come across Truth in all aspects of life, but as we try to assimilate Truth as best we can, it is only possible to turn to Christ Jesus, who is the ultimate expression of God's authorship.

---

27. Karl Barth, *Church Dogmatics: A Selection* (Edinburgh: T&T Clark, 1961), No. 32, p. 77.

28. Interview of Cardinal Johannes Willebrands with the author, August 2, 2000.

29. Karl Barth, *The Word of God and the Word of Man* (New York: Pilgrim Press, 1928), p. 75.

30. Karl Barth, *ibid.,* p. 59. In 1964, after the Second Vatican Council had in fact begun, Barth penned a series of essays for the Ruth Nanda Anshen series entitled *Religious Perspectives.* The series included some of the most famous theologians of the time, including Paul Tillich, Martin D'Arcy, Helmut Thielicke, as well as historians Christopher Dawson and Herbert Butterfield. The goal and purpose of the series states: "*Religious Perspectives* attempts to show the fallacy of the apparent irrelevance of God in history." Therefore, along with the above authors, Karl Barth, *God Here and Now* (New York: Harper & Row, 1964), p. 59, stated: "The *ecumenical unity* of the Christian Church and its theologians is a *truth* or an illusion in so far as the authority of the Bible as defined is respected or not respected." This can be identified as a convergence point between the thought of Barth and that of Bea.

The secondary mandate is one of judgment, in which all things are subjected to the light of the Christological point of view, and *not only* all things but all activities. The Barthian perspective, from which I borrow, in order to illuminate Bea's position, could be identified as "reactionary," for Barth rejected the Liberal Theology of the nineteenth century with its ideas of conformity to "this world."[31] A bourgeois congregation had formerly listened to preachers posit that mankind does not have a soul. In that sense, religion could be said to be "demonic," for it placed more faith in "progress" than in grace.[32] But the adherence to truth, in the sense shared by Barth and Bea, is that God has *revealed himself in Jesus*. There is a truth and that Truth is *Jesus*. Having called that Truth *phos* (light), Barth also recognized Truth as soteriological, eschatological, and practical. In short, he associated Truth with the practice of religion; but then he warned, "for *at the moment when religion becomes conscious of religion, when it becomes a psychologically and historically conceivable magnitude in the world, it falls away from its inner character, from its truth, to idols. Its truth is its other-worldliness, its refusal of the idea of sacredness, its non historicity.*"[33] By representing a renewal of the Biblical Movement, Barth and Bea together cautioned against a genuflection to the dictates of history but indicated, through Word and Sacrament, that the Church, especially in its holiness, is greater than history, yet of necessity must exist in history.

By baptism the Christian is not only incorporated into "Christ the Royal Priest," as Pius XII had taught, but the Christian is also awakened to Christ's teachings and, metaphysically speaking, to an identity with

31. Livingstone, *op. cit.,* pp. 324-39.

32. Herbert Butterfield, *Writings on Christianity and History* (New York: Oxford University Press, 1979), p. 40. "The services of religion to the cause of mundane progress were great, particularly as there were some religious valuations that had a mundane reference and effected the conduct of life."

33. Karl Barth, *The Word of God and the Word of Man, op. cit.,* pp. 68, 69 (emphasis in original). Cf. also: "The Church, together with its Commission with respect to the world, stands or falls with the presence and lordship of Jesus Christ in the form of the authority of the bible as defined." Barth, *God Here and Now, op. cit.* p. 58. According to Cardinal Willebrands, the thinking of Barth became very important in the ecumenical movement among Catholics at this time. For one thing, Jerome Hamer and Hans Küng had produced studies on the possibilities of his thought for theological reconciliation between Protestants and Catholics. Secondly, Barth placed strong emphasis on biblical theology making it possible to define a common methodology for dialogue in that the Bible was a sacred treasure held in common by Protestants and Catholics alike. Finally, Barth, as a leader in the Barmen protest against Hitler, was viewed as a pure and unsullied religious thinker, and was admired as a hero by the Christians of Europe for his open and consistent protest against Hitler.

Christ.[34] If each individual is made one with Christ and accessible to Christ, specifically as the Word, then Truth binds all into oneness.[35] In this sense, envisioning Truth is neither a sociological, anthropological, psychological nor any other kind of human endeavor. Christological truth is both necessary and fundamental.[36] Bea's theology, although possibly unintentionally, presented the image of the Christian, whether apostle or disciple, not as the expositor of Truth but as "the listener" to Truth. By way of summary, Bea prepared a theology of dialogue, in which the Word has content; the Word reveals something of the character of the speaker; and the Word evokes a response from the listener, no matter how subtle or even imperceptible.[37] This last point is all-important for the motto, "Doing the truth

34. Edward Schillebeeckx, O.P., synthesized this insight in a groundbreaking volume entitled *Christ, the Sacrament of the Encounter with God* (New York: Sheed and Ward, 1963), pp. 6, 8, 10: "In general we can therefore say that there is no religion if there is no Church. Grace never comes just interiorly; it confronts us in visible shape as well. To separate religion from Church is ultimately to destroy the life of religion. If one is to serve God, to be religious, one *must also live by Church and sacrament*" (emphasis mine). In his book, Schillebeeckx stated his purpose: "we are directing our attention to sacramentality in religion in order to arrive eventually at the insight that the sacraments are the properly human mode of encounter with God." While acknowledging "the world of creation then becomes an actual part of the inner yet still anonymous dialogue with God," the author also stated, against the paganism, neopaganism and secularity of the twentieth century: "Even religion itself was striving to give outward shape to its inner expectations."

35. Killian McDonnell, O.S.B., *The Baptism of Jesus in the Jordan* (Collegeville, Minn.: Liturgical Press, 1996), pp. 6-7. The source of that oneness is "the status of God's Son established in the power of the Spirit." McDonnell calls this "The Universalizing Content" of Baptism.

36. "Christ is our High Priest in his sacramental manifestation of salvation and through his preaching of the word." *Ibid.*, p. 99.

37. The theology of dialogue reached its climax in the middle years of the twentieth century. Avery Dulles, S.J., in *The Assurance of Things Hoped For* (Oxford: Oxford University Press, 1994), p. 139, thus described the ambience of Bea's demonstration: "The personalist phenomenology of faith gave added force to what many theologians since Newman had been saying about the radical difference between faith and scientific demonstration. If faith was a grace-filled response to the loving self-gift of God, it should be approached by some other route than rational apologetics. The prospective believer must be prepared to welcome the good news with interior joy and gratitude and to dwell within the Church as the community of faith. By displacing the centrality of faith from purely intellectual assent to a total personalist relationship, these theologians called into question the then-dominant Scholastic view that the formal object of faith could be adequately described as the truthfulness of God. Although they did not question the official teaching of the Church, the personalists made room for the supposition *that someone may have authentic faith without being able to assent sincerely to every dogma*. The new spirit of this theology would find its legitimization at the Council announced by Pope John XXIII, in 1959."

in love," for it posits the urgency not of abstractions or bureaucracy, but of sensitivity.[38]

In Bea's own words, this sensitivity was quite specific.[39] The conclusion to his *Athenaeum* (Angelicum) speech defines that sensitivity as: "The concern to foster more frequent and wider contacts with Separated Brethren, inspired by the greatest possible frankness and charity. Only in this way will it be possible, by slow and hard work, to attain a real meeting of minds, to eliminate prejudices, to enlighten and deepen faith and charity, and to achieve closer and closer collaborations in fields not directly concerned with the faith."[40] This sentence may very well be called Bea's *mandatum*. The very concept of "charity," or love, is expressed again from Bea's biblical experience. Most especially, it is based upon the Christian use of the Greek word *agape*, and its history.

While I have relied upon Barth in an attempt to achieve a like understanding of truth, I rely here upon Anders Nygren for an attempt to approximate Bea's understanding of *caritas* (love). Nygren, the Swedish Lutheran Bishop of Lund who produced the classic treatise *Agape and Eros*, gave a cohesive cast to the Catholic understanding of love, which he defined as: "The bond which ultimately holds the whole together."[41] In the history of Christian philology, the concept of love in the Christian sense emerged "in the twilight of the mystery cults,"[42] and stands in apposition to *eros* which is, of its nature, an acquisitive love.[43] The *mandatum* is the

---

38. *Ibid.* "The love of truth, without love, becomes intolerant and repels. Love without truth is blind and cannot last. . . . Indeed, what greater union is possible than when one spirit sparks off the other and one is lit by the flame of the other, when one heart warms another and is warmed by the spirit of the other and by his love." Cited in Schmidt, *op. cit.,* p. 587. Schmidt's own comment: "The Cardinal could therefore conclude that truth and love are unifying virtues *par excellence,* provided that they are both united in a well-based balance."

39. *Ibid.* Despite the specificity of love, through the eradication of bias, Bea's three inaugural talks do not develop the meaning of New Testament love. This remained a lacuna until the mid-1960s when Bea's addresses to three *Agape* Conferences were delivered at Rome. Some of Bea's insights are recorded above.

40. Bea, *Unity of Christians,* pp. 36-37.

41. *Id.* (Philadelphia: Westminster Press, 1953), p. 739.

42. Quell and Stauffer, in Kittel, *op. cit.,* p. 67.

43. Paul Tillich, *Love, Power, and Justice* (London: Oxford University Press, 1954), p. 33, identified love, *agape,* as radical in its very essence: "The quality of love . . . dominates the New Testament . . . because *agape* enters from another dimension into the whole of life and into all qualities of love. One could call *agape* the depth of love or love in relationship to the ground of life. One could say that in *agape* ultimate reality manifests itself and transforms life and love. *Agape* is love cutting into love, just as revelation is reason cutting into reason and the Word of God is the word cutting into all words."

new demand for *agape,* which is unconditional; for example, in Matthew 5:43ff. and Luke 6:32ff.: "You have heard it said . . . but now I say. . . ." Jesus is authoritative but Jesus is not a utopian. He does not provide the fantasy of universal love in a better world. In a sober, objective, serious manner, knowing full well the world as it is, Jesus provides a new way and treats the matter of love as being obviously self-evident "in the new way."[44]

God's love, which, in Christ, broke into the world at a great moment of history, is a *pardoning* love. The *agape* preached by Jesus possesses two qualities. Thus, it is the specifically conscious sense of unworthiness before God, and the petition for His mercy and, secondly, it sets the tone for brotherhood in all ways.[45] In the Apostolic and the sub-Apostolic Age, *agape* denoted "Christian piety as a whole": "See how these Christians love one another."[46] Piety is a familial term! Classically used, say in the language of *The Aeneid,* it depicts the attitude of a son's tenderness toward his father, wherein *"pious Aeneas"* carried Ancheises, his feeble father, in his own arms from the burning city of Troy. This sense of *pietas* and love is, indeed, what Nygren had concluded.[47] Terms of cohesive bonding apply to the love of God and to the love of the brethren. The *mandatum* of Holy Thursday is constituted by components of forgiveness, peacemaking, servanthood, and friendship. *Agape* among the Greeks meant the mutual respect and sympathy of equals.[48] Therefore, by Christians it was adopted to express the affectionate solidarity that constituted "the Brethren!" In the Apostolic and sub-Apostolic Age, letters of Christian origin began with the salutation *agapatos,* "beloved."[49] Naturally, there is no single New Testament concept of love.[50] Instead, there is a Pauline, a Johannine, a Mat-

---

44. Quell and Stauffer, in Kittel, *op. cit.,* pp. 50-53 and p. 63. "The new way is epitomized by the act of pardon." Mercy is concomitant with generosity, whereby bonds of division are not allowed to be perpetrated and therefore take on a life of their own. Further, love is even to the death.

45. *Ibid.,* p. 58.

46. *Ibid.,* p. 64.

47. Nygren, *op. cit.,* p. 412. "The human is raised up to the divine — Irenaeus shares this idea with Hellenistic *piety* generally. The raising is not man's, but from first to last, God's work — so the Agape motif proves, after all, determinative of his thought. Fellowship with God rests wholly on the miracle of the Incarnation on the fact that in His love, God has come down to us in Christ — here all is consistently conceived according to the scheme of agape. And yet this fellowship is regarded as a fellowship on God's own level, on the level of holiness and perfection."

48. Quell and Stauffer, in Kittel, *op. cit.,* p. 66.

49. *Ibid.*

50. Ethical directives in the New Testament are founded upon the concept of the King-

thean, Lukan, and Markan presentation. However, there is no doubt that love is the *fundamentum* of the faith of the New Testament, according to the evidence of the whole New Testament taken together.[51] Thus also did Martin D'Arcy, S.J., express the depth of interior love and the depth of ecclesial love.[52] Father D'Arcy drafted the foremost response to the Nygren book. As a literary philosopher and former Master of Campion Hall, Oxford, his contribution to the subjective structure of the philosophy of love is considered one of the most noteworthy treatises on the subject in the twentieth century.

For his part, as a biblicist, Bea did not hesitate to state: "Non-Catholic Christians must not, therefore, be put on the same plain as the non-baptized; for they always bear, not only the name of Christ on their

---

dom of God *(basilea)*, and conversion *(metanoia)*. Cf. Eduard Lohse, *Theological Ethics of the New Testament* (Minneapolis: Fortress Press, 1991), pp. 3, 27: "All the writings of the New Testament are directed to a specific situation within the early Christian congregations, and are not systematic essays or tractates devoted to specific themes. . . . Ethical statements are found primarily in the hortatory parts of the New Testament letters, but are also found in sections of the Gospels and in the Apocalypse as well as in the Acts' depictions of early Christian life." "Where words of the Lord are clearly identified by an introductory formula, their binding authority with regard to their ethical content is emphasized. They are thereby consistently couched in such a way that they address the present situation of the community. Thus in Acts the responsibility of attending to the needs of the weaker members of the community is made more pointed by appealing to a saying of Jesus: 'It is more blessed to give than to receive' (Acts 20:35)."

51. Martin C. D'Arcy, S.J., *The Mind and Heart of Love: Lion & Unicorn* (New York: Meridian Books, 1956), pp. 348 and 371. In this remarkable treatise on the medieval Christian tradition, D'Arcy cited two *loci* to indicate the total disinterestedness and generosity of authentic love: "Wisely hath Helen done in setting the cross (the symbol of love) above the Kings' heads that the Cross of Christ may be adored in Kings (from St. Ambrose on St. Helen)." Secondly, D'Arcy wrote: "But better perhaps than any of the others save St. John of the Cross does the . . . author of *The Mirror of Simple Souls* give us the first effect of love and its relation to the desire to know God. In the sixth and highest stage of union upon this earth, he tells us of the soul that 'pure and clarified,' she sees nor God nor herself: but God sees this of Him in her, for her, without her, that shows her that there is none but He. Nay, she knows but Him, nor she loves but Him, nor she praises but Him, for there is but He. And the Seventh keeps He within him, for to give us in everlasting glory. If we wit it not now, we shall wit it when the body, our soul leaves." It will be noticed here that love insists in being so united with God that the soul feels and thinks in the divine life and love. It belongs utterly to its lover.

52. *Ibid.* "The definitive statement of this new love is given in the Fourth Gospel in the discourse at the Last Supper. The doctrine of disinterested love which comes into its own, first chivalrously in all personal friendships and then finally in divine love, is no more than a paraphrase of the love declared by Christ on the eve of His Passion 'I am the vine, and you the branches; he that abideth in me and I in him the same beareth much fruit, for without me you can do nothing.'"

foreheads, but his actual image in their souls, deeply and indelibly imprinted there by baptism."[53] This was the occasion of Bea's speech before the *Athenaeum Angelicum* on January 22, 1961. As was cited above, the importance of the speech was universally recognized from the date of its publication. This text marked the first time that Bea spoke about baptism and its consequences for the Church membership of other Christians.[54]

The effect of such a vision was overwhelming to the listeners of Bea's exposition. Without realization, certainly without conscious effort, he provided a new and irreversible image of the Church Universal. Not by argumentation, but rather by harmonization of texts and by demonstration did he achieve this goal. By citing Pius XII's two encyclicals, *Mystici Corporis* and *Mediator Dei,* as well as a brief passage of Canon 87 of the 1917 Code of Canon Law, Bea led his listeners back to the simplicity of the primitive Pauline letter to the Galatians: "You are all sons of God through faith in Christ Jesus, for all of you who were united with Christ in baptism, have been clothed with Christ. There is neither Jew nor Greek, slave nor free, male nor female, for you are all one in Christ Jesus (3:25-28)." The key phrase of this exhortation is the putting on of clothing, *enedusásthe.* This is the traditional paschal symbol whereby the neophyte, having been baptized, through immersion into the pool of water, re-emerged and was clothed in a pure white garment, which did not denote rank. In the Pauline environment, clothing meant so much more than would be recognized today. At that time, it was symbolic of rank, family, education or trade. The pure white robe symbolized not only innocence, but unity, indeed *familialness.*[55]

Citing Pope John, Bea declared: "One great point to be held firmly by *'every baptised person'* is that 'the Church remains forever *his* Mystical

---

53. *Id., op. cit.,* p. 32.

54. Schmidt, *op. cit.,* p. 383.

55. See Max Zerwick, S.J., and Mary Grosbenor, *A Grammatical Analysis of the Greek New Testament* (Rome: Editrice Pontificio Istituto Biblico, 1996), pp. 570, 571. Cf. also, Kilian McDonnell's treatment of St. Ephrem, *op. cit.,* 197. The use of the term *enedusásthe,* "put on," is derived from the Greek *eneduo,* "I clothe myself." Here, it is in the aorist middle tense and therefore has a reflexive quality. The environment of the Pauline reference was definitely hierarchical, in the secular sense with several versions of class distinction, i.e., noble, equestrian, slave, etc. The distinction in clothing was in the Hellenistic world and in the Roman world quite important. In the Christian world, especially after the inception of monasticism, the wearing of distinctive garb indicated the "putting on" of Christ and was a radical witness to the awareness of one's own baptism. In baptism, one put on the new clothing of Christ as a conscious recall that in baptism, one was clothed in pure white after standing up from the pool of water as a symbol of death and resurrection.

Body [Christ's]. He is the Head, to it, each of us believers is related, to it, we belong.' Why should this point have to be held firmly by *every* baptized person and consequently by Separated Brethren if they do not belong there in any way whatever?"[56] In virtue of Baptism, all are subjects and members of the Church, who have been baptized in Christ with the Trinitarian formula.[57] The effect is not removed by either heresy or schism. Those who have had the same experience are to be called "Brothers." Bea's allusion is to the famous Augustinian refrain, used by Pope John: "Whether they will it or not, they are *our* brethren. They will cease to be our brethren when they cease to say: '*Our* Father'" (emphasis mine). In the history of theology, this was the principal contention of St. Augustine during the Donatist Controversy of the fourth century.[58]

For Bea, the *mandatum* of love is so intimately associated with the all-pervasive "New Creation" of baptism that the very realization compelled him to move forward in history. This vision did not mean that he irresponsibly ceased to look backward, for indeed the challenge to unravel the skein of division implied knowledge, understanding, compassion, sensitivity, experience and wisdom, all of these, gifts of history! But the goal was clothed in glory, since it is identified with the Lordship of Christ, and the Creation, as envisioned in the *eschaton*. One reads in the Letter to the Colossians: "Seek the things that are above. Set your minds on things that are above, not on things that are on earth. . . . Put to death therefore what is earthly in you: immorality, impurity, passion, evil desire, and that covetousness which is idolatry. . . . But now put them all away: anger, wrath, malice, slander, and foul talk from your mouth. . . . Put on then as Christ's chosen ones, Holy and Beloved, compassion, kindness, lowliness, meekness and patience (3:1-12)."[59] The joy is found in the fact that the unraveling of

56. Bea, *op. cit.*, pp. 32, 33 (emphasis mine).

57. Aidan Nichols, *Epiphany: A Theological Introduction to Catholicism* (Collegeville, Minn.: Liturgical Press, 1996), p. 289. "Baptism is entrance into fellowship with the Holy Trinity. As the Trinitarian Persons ceaselessly give themselves to each other in eternity, so in the love they communicate in time do they unfold the baptized Christian in their own communion."

58. For a complete treatment, see Frederic Van der Meer, *Augustine the Bishop* (London: Sheed and Ward, 1961), pp. 79-128, and J. E. Merdinger, *Rome and the African Church in the Time of Augustine* (New Haven: Yale University Press, 1997), pp. 50-65. Augustine's teaching is found in his *De Baptismo Contra Donatistas*.

59. The text continues, "clothe yourselves with compassion" and "above all clothe yourselves with love, which binds everything together in perfect harmony." The presence of the word *endusámenoi*, used in the aorist imperative "to put on or wear," is twice used in conjunction with *sundesmos*, "bond," and *telos*, "perfection." Zerwick, *op. cit.*, p. 610, identifies all this with the significance of love, for "love insures the presence of all the virtues that go to

the skein is the work not of the few, but of the many who find the identity of Christ in one another, and who allow themselves to feel that natural, grace-impelled yearning for the "holy kiss," which is the seal of Christian Unity.[60] It was Bea's clear vision, derived from his biblical scholarship, that the unity yet to come is so totally new, unimagined, and unanticipated that it is grasped only in a shadowy form through the theological virtues of faith, hope and love. This is God's work.

This expresses the ecumenical endeavor of Cardinal Bea. This is what he meant by his motto: "Doing the truth in charity!" This is the significance of the phrase *facientes veritatem in caritate!* Let us conclude with Bea's own words:

> It is a question, then, of the charity which must exist among brothers, and a love which the Holy Father, the Father of all, feels for His children. This love is correlative to the maternal love of holy mother Church for her children. And hence it follows that it is the duty of the Church not only to preserve intact the integrity of the Catholic faith, but also to show a mother's love for all her children. By baptism, they have become members of the Mystical Body of Christ and, by that very fact, the Church's children: even though some are deprived of the full use of their rights, because they are visibly separated from her. . . . The words of God in holy scripture, "Can a woman forget her child that is still unweaned, pity no longer the son she bore in her womb (Is. 49:15)," refers to this love. The Church can not possibly forget these children of hers, because her motherhood is of supernatural origin, inspired by the

---

make up perfection." According to Geoffrey Wainwright, *Doxology* (New York: Oxford University Press, 1980), p. 129: "These passages reveal an eschatological tension: holiness, for the new life, is a gift of God already given, and yet its realization still has to be striven for, because of the power of sin; for the present, there is a danger of a relapse into the ways of the old eon that is now passing away." Wainwright, p. 130, calls the Colossians text, cited above, a *"Christological text and example for the conduct appropriate to the new age"* (emphasis mine).

60. In his last Easter message, Pope John XXIII delivered these words: "The lamb led to the slaughter opened not his mouth before his persecutors; in his death he reveals to us the secret of true fecundity. . . . May this law find its response in the hearts of all who bear responsibility for the rising generation: Parents and teachers and all those who, being vested with authority, must regard themselves as being at the service of their brethren. May it be a special invitation, in the harmony of obedience, brotherly discipline and common aspirations, to all who labour to spread through the world the light of the Gospel, the reflection of Christ's resurrection." Cited in Yves Congar, O.P., *Power and Poverty in the Church* (Baltimore: Helicon Press, 1964), p. 146.

infinite love of the Blessed Trinity itself. So she has the right to say, using the words of God: "Let her forget; I will not be forgetful of thee *(ibid.)*." If for any reason a child does not know and hence does not recognize his own mother, she nevertheless does not cease to be his mother nor he the fruit of her womb; it is impossible for her not to have for her child a mother's love and tenderness. In the same way the Church never fails to have a deep and tender affection for all her children, though they may be visibly separated from her, and this affection can never be belied.[61]

The overall discourse is notable for two salient characteristics. First, Bea expressed in the speech what *he* meant by charity, i.e., "to act with the most perfect courtesy."[62] Second, this text was taken from the "press conference" regarding Archbishop Fisher's visit.[63] While Bea addressed a congenial constituency there, of media representatives, he had at his back a hostile and uncompromising Roman Curia. As was indicated above, it was not even foreseen that Bea would be allowed a commentary on Archbishop Fisher's visit. Therefore, from this point in time, one can picture him in characteristic pose with his heavy Waterman pen in hand, writing spontaneously and comfortably through the night, in order to have a presentable handout for those who came to hear him. These words which contain sentiments of sustenance, nurture and undying fidelity, based upon his Jesuit dedication to the "infinite love for the Blessed Trinity" itself,[64] his firm belief in Providence, as well as his masterful control of the Isaian text for which he was famous, in his teaching days,[65] represent the spontaneity and the wisdom that was the seal of recognition that he was the right man for the time. Proverbially speaking, he was the right man for the assignment. He was the man to pick up the staff of Moses (Ex. 4:2) to forge the way for all the Pilgrim People of God into the promised land of unity, harmony, family, and peace.

---

61. Bea, *The Unity of Christians*, pp. 67-68.

62. Charity, in fact, constitutes one of the two essential principles which Bea outlined in his speech regarding Archbishop Fisher's visit. The other principle, of course, is personal and ecclesial integrity in matters affecting the truth of the faith. *Ibid.*, pp. 66-67.

63. Purdy, *op. cit.*, p. 31.

64. *The Spiritual Exercises of St. Ignatius*, ed. Puhl, *op. cit.*, No. 102, p. 49.

65. Schmidt, *op. cit.*, p. 90.

Bibliography

Author's Note on the Sources

First and foremost, the following bibliographical material is based upon original documentation contained in the sealed archives of various dioceses of Germany. Through the kindness of the late Monsignor Aloys Klein and the late Cardinal Johannes Degenhardt, the following material has been retrieved from the Archdiocese of Paderborn.

1. Correspondence between Pope John XXIII, Lorenz Cardinal Jaeger and Augustin Cardinal Bea of March 1960.
2. Pastoral letters of Cardinal Jaeger regarding the wartime and postwar situation in his diocese from 1945 to 1960. These documents also included pastoral references to the ecumenical, i.e., *Una Sancta,* activity. Some correspondence was sealed by the German government, under its agreement with the Allied authorities, in the aftermath of the Second World War and therefore has been unreviewed until the present.
3. Correspondence of Patriarch Maximos V Hakim to Pope Paul VI upon the death of Cardinal Bea, November 1968. This correspondence comes to the author through the Vicar General's Archives of the Archbishop of Paderborn. Commentary upon its relevance came from Archbishop Loris Capovilla, former Secretary to the late Pope John XXIII. The unavailability of primary resource material makes it difficult to construct a viable paper trail. The active memory and notes of Archbishop Capovilla bridged many gaps so that it was possible to project a cause and effect sequence. For example, he alone,

now, can provide an answer as to why the original petition of Patriarch Maximos IV Saigh was not carried forward. Cardinal Johannes Willebrands, Father Stjepan Schmidt and Monsignor Klein all admit that they had no direct knowledge of this matter.

The original letter of March 4, 1960, of Cardinal Jaeger and the drafted texts of Cardinal Bea were removed to the Secret Archives of the Vatican, upon the deaths of these two prelates. Through the kindness of Monsignor Klein, photostatic copies of the original Latin draft were provided by the Vicar General's Archives in Paderborn. Fragments of correspondence between Jaeger and Bea can be found there, dating from 1947 until 1959. A fuller portfolio of their original correspondence from 1959 to 1965 remains for further examination.

To fill out each scenario, the author conducted interviews with Monsignor Aloys Klein on 13 March 1983; 28 March 1983; and 7 June 1989 at Rome. Interviews with Archbishop Loris Capovilla took place at Sotto Il Monte on 28 April 2000, 9 September 2000 and 7 October 2001. The earliest interview regarding this subject was undertaken by the author with Father Walter Abbott, S.J. It took place at Assumption College in Worcester, Massachusetts, on 22 August 1980, in the presence of Cardinal Johannes Willebrands. The subject of that interview was Bea's reception of the Red Hat. Abbott lived with Bea at the Biblicum and remembered well the details of the notification of Bea that he was to be a cardinal, as well as the sentiments of Bea regarding his first interview with Pope John XXIII. Notes were taken on the above occasions.

Cardinal Johannes Willebrands continues to remember the events associated with the foundation of the Secretariat for Promoting Christian Unity. In particular, he provided the details of the painful misunderstanding which occurred at Rhodes. He reviewed this material as recently as April 4, 2003, providing refinements and further insights.

Father Schmidt continues to reside at the Jesuit headquarters in Rome. Besides the keenness of his memory and the wealth of his research, ecumenism must always be grateful for his book: *Augustin Bea: A Cardinal of Unity*. Father Schmidt reviewed this material as recently as September 30, 2002.

On 28 April 2000, Archbishop Loris Capovilla presented the author with a photocopy of a page of his unpublished notes and memoirs. With his permission, the author published a portion of it in *A Joyful Soul* (see publishing information below). The author is grateful for the insights provided by the four Secretaries cited above: Willebrands, Schmidt, Klein, and

Capovilla. The fragment presented to him indicates the ongoingness of the ecumenical endeavor of Cardinal Bea and how precious it was to the dying Pope John XXIII.

Letters — Vicar-General's Archives — Paderborn

1.	Jaeger to Bea	6 January 1960
2.	Bea to Jaeger	15 September 1959
3.	Bea to Jaeger	3 November 1959
4.	Jaeger to Bea	16 November 1959
5.	Jaeger to Bea	8 November 1959
6.	Jaeger to Bea	21 October 1959
7.	Bea to Jaeger	30 November 1959
8.	Jaeger to Bea	16 November 1959
9.	Bea to Jaeger	30 November 1959
10.	Jaeger to Bea	17 December 1959
11.	Bea to Jaeger	1 January 1960
12.	Bea to Jaeger	13 January 1960
13.	Jaeger to Bea	6 January 1960
14.	Bea to Stakemeier	20 January 1960
15.	Jaeger to Pope John	4 March 1960

Sources

Books by Cardinal Bea

Bea, Augustin Cardinal, S.J. *On Christian Unity.* New York: St. Paul Publications, Derby, 1961.
———. *The Unity of Christians.* New York: Herder and Herder, 1963.
———. *St. Paul on the Essence and Importance of the Interior Life.* Mequon, Wis.: Notre Dame of the Lake Press, 1963.
———. "Clarifications." In *Council Speeches of Vatican II,* edited by Yves Congar, O.P., Hans Küng, and Daniel O'Hanlon, S.J. Glen Rock, N.J.: Paulist Press, 1964.
———. *Unity in Freedom.* New York: Harper and Row, 1964.

Documents

Anonymous. *Daten zum Lebenslauf von Josef Rudolf Höfer* (Data for a curriculum vitae of Josef Rudolf Höfer). Vicar General's Archives, Paderborn.

Annuario Pontificio per L'anno 1997. Vatican City: Libreria Editrice Vaticana, 1977.

Aquinas, Thomas. *Summa Theologica.* English trans. New York: Benzinger Brothers, 1928.

Augustine. *De Spiritu et Littera* 16.28. Patrologia Latina 44:218.

Benedict XV. *Ad Beatissimi.* 1 November 1914. N. 64.

Faith and Order. *Baptism, Eucharist and Ministry.* Geneva: World Council of Churches, 1982.

Flannery, Austin, O.P., ed. *Documents of the Second Vatican Council.* Vols. 1 and 2. Northport, N.Y.: Costello Publishing Company, 1982, 1983.

Hakim, Patriarch Maximos V. *Le Lien.* Bulletin du Patriarcat Grec-Melkite Catholique 33, no. 5-6 (Nov.-Dec. 1968).

Jaeger, Lorenz. *Caritasdienst in der Stadt Paderborn.* Archives of the Vicar General, Paderborn, 15 October 1945.

John XXIII. *To the Roman Synod.* Washington, D.C.: National Catholic Welfare Conference, 1960.

———. *Ad Petri Cathedram.* In *Encyclicals of Pope John XXIII,* pp. 3-50. Washington, D.C.: National Catholic Welfare Conference, 1963.

John Paul II. *Ut Unum Sint.* In *The Encyclicals of Pope John Paul II,* edited by J. Michael Miller, C.S.B. Huntington, Ind.: Sunday Visitor Press, 1996.

Leo XIII. *Militantis Ecclesiae.* 1 August 1897.

———. *Mirae Caritatis.* May 1902.

Pius XII. *Mediator Dei.* 1947 *(On the Sacred Liturgy).* Enlarged and revised edition of 1954. New York: America Press.

———. *Mystici Corporis.* In *Four Great Encyclicals of Pope Pius XII.* New York: Paulist Press, 1961.

Shaw, Russell, ed. *The Ministry of Bishops: Papers from the Collegeville Assembly.* Washington, D.C.: National Conference of Catholic Bishops, 1982.

Vatican Documents on the Eastern Churches: Papal Encyclicals and Documents. Fairfax, Va.: Eastern Christian Publications, 2002.

Articles

Bea, Augustin Cardinal. "Academic Pursuits and Christian Unity." In *Ecumenical Dialogue at Harvard,* edited by Samuel H. Miller and G. Ernest Wright. Cambridge: Harvard University Press, Belknap Press, 1964.

Berger, Teresa. "Worship in the Ecumenical Movement." In *Dictionary of the Ecumenical Movement,* edited by Nicholas Lossky et al. Geneva: WCC Publications, 1991.

Biggar, Nigel. "Barth's Trinitarian Ethic." In *The Cambridge Companion to Karl Barth,* edited by John Webster, p. 213. Cambridge: Cambridge University Press, 2000.

Bibliography

Blancy, Alain. "Ecumenical Institute of Bossey." In *Dictionary of the Ecumenical Movement,* edited by Nicholas Lossky et al. Geneva: WCC Publications, 1991.

Bouwen, Frans. "Ecumenical Conferences." In *Dictionary of the Ecumenical Movement,* edited by Nicholas Lossky et al. Geneva: WCC Publications, 1991.

Clapsis, Emmanuel. "Eschatology." In *Dictionary of the Ecumenical Movement,* edited by Nicholas Lossky et al. Geneva: WCC Publications, 1991.

Congar, Yves, O.P. "Amica Contestatio." In *Inter-Communion,* edited by Donald Baillie and John Marsh. London: SCM Press, 1952.

Fouilloux, Étienne. "Église romaine et Chrétientés non catholiques de la grande guerre au concile Vatican II." In *Paolo VI e l'ecumenismo, Istituto Paolo VI.* Brescia, 2001.

Görres, Ida Friederike. "Open Letter on the Church." *Frankfurter Hefte.* 1946.

Griener, George E. "Herman Schell and the Reform of the Catholic Church in Germany." *Theological Studies* 54 (1993).

Heschel, Abraham. "No Religion Is an Island." In *No Religion Is an Island: Abraham Joshua Heschel,* edited by Harold Kasimow and Byron L. Sherwin. Maryknoll, N.Y.: Orbis Books, 1991.

Höfer, Josef. "Die katholische Wirklichkeit im Licht der Enzyklika, 'Mystici Corporis,' im Ergebnisbericht der Werktagung des 74." *Deutschen Katholikentags Passau in Altötting.* Vicar General's Archives, Paderborn 1950.

Hughes, Jerald W., S.J. "Forgotten Truths." In *The Way of Ignatius Loyola,* edited by Philip Sheldrake, S.J. London: SPCK, 1991.

Hünermann, Peter. "Perspectives toward the Future in the Dogmatics of the Tübingen Theologians." In *The Legacy of the Tübingen School,* edited by Donald J. Dietrich and Michael J. Himes, pp. 21-37. New York: Crossroad Herder, 1997.

Kiefl, Franz Xavier. "Martin Luthers *religiösepsyche als Wurzel eines neuen philosophischen Weltbildes*" *(Martin Luther's religious psyche as the root of a new philosophical worldview). Hochland* 15 (1917/1918).

Klein, Aloys. "Adolf Herte (1887-1970). Eine Episode aus seiner Lutherforschung." *Theologie und Glaube* (Paderborn), no. 4 (1989): 568-75.

———. "Es begann mit der Una — Sancta — Bewegung." In *Surrexit Dominus vere, Die Gegenwart des Auferstandenden in seiner Kirche,* edited by Josef Ernst and Stephan Leimgruber. Paderborn: Bonafatius, 1995.

Krieg, Robert Anthony, C.S.C. "Romano Guardini's Theology of the Human Person." *Theological Studies* 59 (1998).

———. "Karl Adam, National Socialism and Christian Tradition." *Theological Studies* 60 (1999).

Ladous, Regis. "Spiritual Ecumenism." In *Dictionary of the Ecumenical Movement,* edited by Nicholas Lossky et al. Geneva: WCC Publications, 1991.

Lanne, Emmanuel, O.S.B. "La contribution du cardinal Bea à la question du baptême et l'unité des chrétiens." *Irenikon* 55, no. 4 (1982).

Lansdale, David. "The Serpent's Tail: Rules for Discernment." In *The Way of Ignatius Loyola,* edited by Philip Sheldrake, S.J. London: SPCK, 1991.

Martina, Giacomo, S.J. "The Historical Context in Which the Idea of a New Ecumenical Council Was Born." In *Vatican II Assessment and Perspective,* vol. 1, edited by René Latourelle, S.J. New York: Paulist Press, 1988.

McDonald, Kevin. "Anglican–Roman Catholic Dialogue." In *Dictionary of the Ecumenical Movement,* edited by Nicholas Lossky et al. Geneva: WCC Publications, 1991.

Pelland, Gilles, S.J. "A Few Words on Triumphalism." In *Vatican II Assessment and Perspective,* vol. 1, edited by René Latourelle, S.J. New York: Paulist Press, 1988.

Possony, Stefan. "Berlin — Focus of World Strategy." In *Berlin and the Future of Eastern Europe,* edited by D. Collier and K. Glaser. Chicago: Henry Regnery Company, 1963.

Pribilla, Max. "Um das katholische Lutherbild" (Concerning a Catholic portrait of Luther). In *Stimmen der Zeit.* CXL 1947. Original pagination not available. In off-print, p. 4.

Quell, Gottfried, and Ethelbert Stauffer. "Love." In G. Kittel, *Bible Keywords.* New York: Harper and Brothers, 1951.

Rahner, Karl. "Potentia Obedientialis." In Karl Rahner et al., *Sacramentum Mundi.* New York: Herder and Herder, 1970.

Rausch, William G. "Baptism, Eucharist, and Ministry." In *Dictionary of the Ecumenical Movement,* edited by Nicholas Lossky et al. Geneva: WCC Publications, 1991.

Rondeau, M. J., and B. Van Hove. "Jean Daniélou." In *The New Catholic Encyclopedia,* vol. 17. Washington, D.C.: Catholic University of America Press, 1981.

Seinfels, Peter. "Beliefs." *New York Times,* 20 July 2002, section A-10.

Staples, Peter. "Catholicity." In *Dictionary of the Ecumenical Movement,* edited by Nicholas Lossky et al. Geneva: WCC Publications, 1991.

Stransky, Thomas F., C.S.P. "The Foundation of the Secretariat for Promoting Christian Unity." In *Vatican II: Revisited by Those Who Were There,* edited by A. Stacpoole. Minneapolis: Winston Press, 1986.

———. "Council of Trent." In *Dictionary of the Ecumenical Movement,* edited by Nicholas Lossky et al. Geneva: WCC Publications, 1991.

———. "Roman Catholic Church and Pre-Vatican II Ecumenism." In *Dictionary of the Ecumenical Movement,* edited by Nicholas Lossky et al. Geneva: WCC Publications, 1991.

———. "Lambert Beaduin." In *Dictionary of the Ecumenical Movement,* edited by Nicholas Lossky et al. Geneva: WCC Publications, 1991, 1992.

Winfield, Nicole. "Vatican Speeds Up Opening WWII Archives." *Pittsburgh Post-Gazette,* February 14, 2003.

Wittstadt, Klaus. "Die Verdienste des Paderborner Erzbischofs Lorenz Jaeger um die Errichtung des Einheitssekretariat." Vicar General's Archives, Paderborn.

Bibliography

Zahn, Gordon C. "Catholic Resistance? A Yes and a No." In *The German Church Struggle and the Holocaust,* edited by Franklin H. Littell and Hubert C. Locke. Detroit: Wayne State University Press, 1974.

Books

Achtemeier, Paul J. *Bible Dictionary.* San Francisco: Harper Collins, 1996.

Adam, Karl. *The Spirit of Catholicism.* New York: Macmillan, 1929.

———. *Christ Our Brother.* New York: Macmillan, 1931.

———. *Saint Augustine: The Odyssey of His Soul.* New York: Macmillan, 1932.

———. *The Son of God.* New York: Sheed and Ward, 1934.

———. *One and Holy.* New York: Sheed and Ward, 1951.

Anonymous. *Die Erzdiözese Paderborn.* Schöningh: Verlag Ferdinand, 1930.

Barry, Colman J., O.S.B. *Worship and Work.* Collegeville, Minn.: St. John's Abbey, 1956.

Barth, Karl. *The Word of God and the Word of Man.* Brookline, Mass.: Pilgrim Press, 1928.

———. *God Here and Now.* New York: Harper and Row, 1964.

———. *Ad Limina Apostolorum.* Richmond, Va.: John Knox Press, 1968.

Beasley-Murray, George Raymond. *Baptism in the New Testament.* Exeter, U.K.: Paternoster Press, 1972.

Begnini, Mario, and Goffredo Zanchi. *John XXIII: The Official Biography.* Boston: Pauline Press, 2001.

Bell, George. *The Church and Humanity.* New York: Longmans, Green and Co., 1946.

Bendiscioli, Mario. *Nazism versus Christianity.* London: Skeffington & Son, 1938.

Benoit, André, Boris Bobrinskoy, and François Coudreau. *Baptême, Sacrement d'unité.* Tours: Mame, 1971.

Bethge, Eberhard. *Dietrich Bonhoeffer: A Biography.* Minneapolis: Fortress Press, 2000.

Bliss, Frederick M., S.M. *Catholic and Ecumenical: History and Hope.* Franklin, Wis.: Sheed and Ward, 1999.

Boegner, Marc. *The Long Road to Unity: Memories and Anticipation.* London: Collins, 1970.

Bonhoeffer, Dietrich. *Life Together.* San Francisco: Harper & Row, 1954.

Bonnot, Bernard. *Pope John XXIII: An Astute Pastoral Leader.* New York: Alba House, 1968.

Bornkamm, Heinrich. *The Heart of Reformation Faith: The Fundamental Axioms of Evangelical Belief.* New York: Harper and Row, 1965.

Bouyer, Louis, C.O. *Dom Lambert Beauduin: L'homme d'Église.* Paris: Casterman, 1964.

Braaten, Carl E., and Robert W. Jenson. *Church Unity and the Papal Office: An Ec-*

umenical Dialogue on Pope John Paul II's Encyclical "Ut Unum Sint." Grand Rapids: Eerdmans, 2001.

Brown, Peter. *The Making of Late Antiquity.* Cambridge: Harvard University Press, 1978.

Brown, Robert McAfee. *Observer in Rome.* Garden City, N.Y.: Doubleday, 1964.

————. *The Ecumenical Revolution.* Garden City, N.Y.: Doubleday, 1967.

Buchmuller, Maria, ed. *Augustin Kardinal Bea: Wegbereiter der Einheit.* Augsburg: Verlag, Winfried-Werk, 1972.

Bugnini, Annibale. *The Reform of the Liturgy: 1948-1975.* Collegeville, Minn.: Liturgical Press, 1990.

Burleigh, Michael. *The Third Reich.* London: Macmillan, Pan Books, 2000.

Busch, Eberhard. *Karl Barth.* Grand Rapids: Eerdmans, 1994.

Butterfield, Herbert. *Writings on Christianity and History.* New York: Oxford University Press, 1979.

Cahill, Thomas. *Pope John XXIII.* New York: Lipper/Viking Book, 2001.

Cammadini, Giuseppe, ed. *Paolo VI e l'ecumenismo: Colloquio Internazionale di Studio.* Brescia: Istituto Paolo VI, 2001.

Capovilla, Loris. *John XXIII: Witness to the Tenderness of God.* Sherbrooke, Quebec: Médiaspal, 2001.

Chacour, Elias. *Blood Brothers.* Grand Rapids: Chosen Books, 1984.

Charles, Conrad, C.P. *The Foundation of the Passionists in England: 1840-1851.* Rome: Pontifica Universitas Gregoriana, 1961.

Coleman, John A. *The Evolution of Dutch Catholicism, 1958-1974.* London: University of California Press, 1978.

Congar, Yves, O.P. *Chrétienes désunis: Principes d'un oecuménisme catholique.* Paris: Les editions du Cerf, 1937.

————. *The Mystery of the Temple.* New York: Newman Press, 1962.

————. *Power and Poverty in the Church.* Baltimore: Helicon Press, 1964.

————. *I Believe in the Holy Spirit.* New York: Crossroad, 1997.

Cope, Brian E., and Michael Kinnamon, eds. *The Ecumenical Movement: An Anthology of Key Texts and Voices.* Geneva: WCC Publications, 1977.

Cornwell, John. *Hitler's Pope: The Secret History of Pope Pius XII.* New York: Viking, 1999.

Corrêa de Oliveria, Plino. *Nobility and Analogous Traditional Elites in the Allocutions of Pope Pius XII.* York, Pa.: American Society for the Defence of Tradition, Family and Property, 1993.

Croghan, Patrick A. *The Peasant from Makeyevka.* Worcester, Mass.: Augustinians of the Assumption, 1982.

Curtis, Geoffrey. *Paul Couturier and Unity in Christ.* London: SCM Press, 1964.

Cyprian. *The Lapsed and the Unity of the Catholic Church.* Edited by Maurice Bévenot. Baltimore: Newman Press, 1957.

————. *De oratione Domini* 23. In J. P. Migne, *Patrologia Latina,* p. 553.

Cyril of Jerusalem. *Lectures on the Catholic Sacraments.* Crestwood, N.Y.: St. Vladimir's Seminary Press, 1995.

Daniélou, Jean. *The Salvation of the Nations.* London: Sheed and Ward, 1949.

———. *The Presence of God.* London: A. R. Mowbray, 1958.

———. *The Dead Sea Scrolls and Primitive Christianity.* Baltimore: Helicon Press, 1958.

D'Arcy, Martin C., S.J. *The Mind and Heart of Love: The Lion and the Unicorn.* New York: Meridian Books, 1956.

Davidson, Clarissa S. *God's Man.* Westport, Conn.: Greenwood Publishing, 1979.

Davis, Charles. *Sacraments of Initiation, Baptism, and Confirmation.* New York: Sheed and Ward, 1965.

De Gruchy, John W. *The Cambridge Companion to Dietrich Bonhoeffer.* Cambridge: Cambridge University Press, 1999.

Deissmann, Adolf. *Una Sancta.* Gütersloh, 1936.

de Jonge, Louis. *The Netherlands and Nazi Germany.* London: Harvard University Press, 1990.

de Lubac, Henri, S.J. *Catholicism: The Study of Dogma in Relation to the Corporate Destiny of Mankind.* New York: Sheed and Ward, 1950.

———. *The Splendor of the Church.* Glen Rock, N.J.: Paulist Press, 1963.

———. *At the Service of the Church.* San Francisco: Ignatius Press, 1993.

Dickens, A. G. *The German Nation and Martin Luther.* London: Edward Arnold, 1974.

Dragas, G. D. *John Henry Newman as a Starting Point for Rediscovering the Catholicity of the Fathers Today.* Rome: Center of Newman Friends, 1975.

Driscoll, Martha. *A Silent Herald of Unity.* Kalamazoo, Mich.: Cistercian Publications, 1990.

Dulles, Avery Cardinal. *Models of the Church.* Garden City, N.Y.: Doubleday, 1974.

———. *The Assurance of Things Hoped For.* Oxford: Oxford University Press, 1994.

———. *The Splendor of Faith: The Theological Vision of John Paul II.* New York: Crossroad, 1999.

Durrwell, F. X. *In the Redeeming Christ.* London: Sheed and Ward, 1963.

Eastman, A. Theodore. *The Baptizing Community: Christian Initiation and the Local Congregation.* New York: Seabury Press, 1982.

Ehrenstrom, Nils. *Mutual Recognition of Baptism in Inter-Church Agreements.* Geneva: World Council of Churches, 1978.

Elert, Werner. *Law and Gospel.* Philadelphia: Fortress Press, 1967.

Ellul, Joseph, O.P. *Growth in Koinonia: Baptism and Its Relation to the Eucharist in Roman Catholic–Orthodox Perspective.* Rome: Pontifical University of St. Thomas Aquinas, 1997.

Fackre, Gabriel J. *Baptismal Encounter.* Lancaster, Pa.: Lancaster Theological Seminary, 1962.

Fahey, Michael A., ed. *Catholic Perspectives on Baptism, Eucharist, and Ministry.* Lanham, Md.: University Press of America, 1986.

Falardeau, Ernest, S.S.S. *That All May Be One.* New York: Paulist Press, 2000.

Falconi, Carlo. *The Popes in the Twentieth Century.* London: Wiedenfeld and Nicolson, 1967.

Feldman, Christian. *Pope John XXIII: A Spiritual Biography.* New York: Crossroad, 2000.

Fittkau, Gerhard A. *My Thirty Third Year: A Priest's Experience in a Russian Work Camp.* New York: Farrar, Strauss and Cudahy, 1958.

Flamini, Roland. *Pope, Premier, and President.* New York: Macmillan, 1980.

Fontenelle, R. *His Holiness Pope Pius XI.* London: Catholic Book Club, 1939.

Forte, Bruno. *The Church: Icon of the Trinity.* Boston: St. Paul Books and Media, 1991.

Frederich, Otto. *Before the Deluge.* New York: Harper Perennial, 1972.

Fremantle, Anne. *The Papal Encyclicals in Their Historical Context.* New York: G. P. Putnam's Sons, 1956.

Friedländer, Saul. *Pius XII and the Third Reich.* New York: Alfred A. Knopf, 1966.

Gade, John A. *The Life of Cardinal Mercier.* London: Charles Scribner's Sons, 1934.

Gallin, Mary Alice, O.S.U. *German Resistance to Hitler,* pp. 26-79. Washington, D.C.: Catholic University of America Press, 1961.

Ganoczy, Alexandre. *Becoming Christian.* New York: Paulist Press, 1976.

Gaspari, Antonio. *Gli Ebrei Salvati da Pio XII.* Rome: Logos, 2001.

Gassmann, Günther, ed. *Documentary History of Faith and Order.* Geneva: World Council of Churches Press, 1993.

Gilman, Sander L. *Jews in Today's German Culture.* Bloomington: Indiana University Press, 1995.

Goldhagen, Daniel. *A Moral Reckoning.* New York: Alfred A. Knopf, 2002.

Grave, S. A. *Conscience in Newman's Thought.* Oxford: Clarendon Press, 1989.

Greene, Michael, ed. *The Layman and the Council.* Springfield, Ill.: Templegate, 1964.

Gros, Jeffrey, F.S.C., Eamon McManus, and Ann Riggs. *Introduction to Ecumenism.* New York: Paulist Press, 1998.

Gruppo Misto Per Lo Studio. *Una Catechesi Ecumenica: Quel Desiderio Di Unitá.* Padova: Edizioni, Messaggero, 2000.

Gruss, Heribert. *Erzbischof Lorenz Jaeger als Kirchenführer im Dritten Reich.* Paderborn: Bonifatius, 1995.

Guardini, Romano. *The Spirit of the Liturgy.* New York: Sheed and Ward, 1951.

Gurian, Waldemar. *Hitler and the Christians.* London: Sheed and Ward, 1936.

Gwynn, Denis. *The Second Spring: 1818-1852.* London: Catholic Book Club, 1944.

Häring, Bernard. *Priesthood Imperiled.* Liguori, Mo.: Triumph Books, 1996.

Hatch, Alden. *A Man Named John.* New York: Hawthorn Books, 1963.

Hatch, Alden, and Seamus Walshe. *Crown of Glory.* New York: Hawthorn Books, 1957.

Hebblethwaite, Peter. *Pope John XXIII*. Garden City, N.Y.: Doubleday and Company, 1985.

———. *Paul VI*. London: Harper Collins Religious, 1993.

Hellman, John. *Emmanuel Mounier and the New Catholic Left, 1930-1950*. Toronto: University of Toronto Press, 1981.

Hendrix, Georges. *The Westminster Confession for Today: A Contemporary Interpretation*. Richmond, Va.: John Knox Press, 1960.

Hennessey, Augustine Paul, C.P. *Encountering Christ*. Union City, N.J.: Sign Press, 1979.

Holmes, Augustine, O.S.B. *A Life Pleasing to God: The Spirituality of the Rules of St. Basil*. Kalamazoo, Mich.: Cistercian Publications, 2000.

Holmes, J. Derek. *The Triumph of the Holy See*. London: Burns and Oates, 1978.

———. *The Papacy in the Modern World: 1914-1978*. New York: Crossroad, 1981.

Hughes, John J. *Absolutely Null and Utterly Void*. Washington, D.C.: Corpus Books, 1968.

Hughes, Kathleen, R.S.C.J. *The Monk's Tale: A Biography of Godfrey Diekmann, O.S.B*. Collegeville, Minn.: Liturgical Press, 1991.

Hughes, Philip. *Pope Pius XI*. New York: Sheed and Ward, 1937.

———. *Popular History of the Catholic Church*. New York: Doubleday, 1954.

Ignatius of Loyola. *The Spiritual Exercises of St. Ignatius*. Edited by Louis J. Puhl. Chicago: Loyola Press, 1951.

———. *St. Ignatius of Loyola: The Spiritual Exercises and Selected Works*. Edited by George E. Ganss. New York: Paulist Press, 1991.

Jaeger, Lorenz Cardinal. *The Ecumenical Council: The Church and Christendom*. New York: P. J. Kennedy and Sons, 1961.

Jung, E. M. *Kardinal Bea, Sein Leben und Werk*. St. Ottilier: Inglessis Eos Verlag Erzabtei, 1994.

Kaiser, Robert Blair. *Pope, Council, and World: The Story of Vatican II*. New York: Macmillan, 1963.

Kelly, J. N. D. *The Oxford Dictionary of Popes*. Oxford: Oxford University Press, 1986.

Kendall, Daniel, S.J., and Stephen T. Davis, eds. *The Convergence of Theology: A Festschrift Honoring Gerald O'Collins, S.J.* New York: Paulist Press, 2001.

Kerr, Ian. *John Henry Newman*. New York: Oxford University Press, 1988.

Kertzer, David I. *The Popes against the Jews: The Vatican's Role in the Rise of Modern Antisemitism*. New York: Alfred A. Knopf, 2001.

Kidd, Sue Monk. *The Secret Life of Bees*. New York: Viking Penguin, 2002.

Kilmartin, Edward J., S.J. *Toward Reunion*. New York: Paulist Press, 1979.

Kittel, G., Gottfried Quell, and Ethelbert Stauffer. *Bible Keywords*. New York: Harper and Brothers, 1951.

Klein, Kasper. *Die Erzdiözese Paderborn Festschrift aus Anlass der Erheburg des Bisturs*. Paderborn: Paderborn Zur Erzdiözese, Verlag, Ferdinand, Schöningh, 1930.

Kobler, John Francis. *Vatican II and Phenomenology.* Dordrecht: Martinus Niejhoff Publishers, 1985.

Korolevsky, Cyril Charon. *History of the Melkite Patriarchates.* Vols. I, II, III. Fairfax, Va.: Eastern Christian Publications, 1998.

Kreig, Gordon A. *The Germans.* New York: G. P. Putnam's Sons, 1982.

Krieg, Robert Anthony, C.S.C. *Karl Adam.* Notre Dame: University of Notre Dame Press, 1992.

Kuhrt, Gordon W. *Believing in Baptism: Christian Baptism — Its Theology and Practice.* London: Mowbray, 1986.

Küng, Hans. *The Council, Reform and Reunion.* New York: Sheed and Ward, 1961.

Lackmann, Max. *The Augsburg Confession and Catholic Unity.* New York: Herder and Herder, 1963.

LaFarge, John. *Reflections on Growing Old.* Garden City, N.Y.: Doubleday, 1963.

Lapomarda, Vincent A. *The Jesuits and the Third Reich.* Lampenter, Dyfed, Wales: Mellon House, 1989.

Larere, Philippe. *Baptism in Water and Baptism in the Spirit: A Biblical, Liturgical, and Theological Exposition.* Collegeville, Minn.: Liturgical Press, 1993.

LaVerdiere, Eugene, S.S.S. *Eucharist in the New Testament and the Early Church.* Collegeville, Minn.: Liturgical Press, 1996.

Lazareth, William Henry. *Growing Together in Baptism, Eucharist, and Ministry: A Study Guide.* Geneva: World Council of Churches, 1982.

Leeming, Bernard J., S.J. *"Augustin Cardinal Bea," in (Männer des Konzils).* Würzburg: Echter, 1965.

————. *The Churches and the Church.*

Leslie, Sir Shane. *Cardinal Gasquet: A Memoir.* London: Burns and Oates, 1953.

Lewy, Guenter. *The Catholic Church and Nazi Germany.* New York: McGraw-Hill Book Company, 1964.

Link, Joseph G., and Josef A. Slominski. *Kardinal Jaeger.* Paderborn: Verlag, Bonifatius-Druckerei, 1966.

Littell, Franklin Hamlin. *The German Phoenix.* Garden City, N.Y.: Doubleday, 1960.

Livingston, James C. *Modern Christian Thought: From the Enlightenment to Vatican II.* New York: Macmillan, 1971.

Löhr, Dame Aemiliana, O.S.B. *The Mass through the Year.* London: Longmans, Green, 1958.

Lohse, Edward. *Theological Ethics of the New Testament.* Minneapolis: Fortress Press, 1991.

Lortz, Joseph. *The Reformation: A Problem for Today.* Westminster, Md.: Newman Press, 1964.

————. *The Reformation in Germany.* Vols. 1, 2. New York: Herder and Herder, 1968 and 1969.

Mannheim, Karl. *Ideology and Utopia.* New York: Harcourt, Brace and Company, 1985.

Marshall, Bruce D. *Trinity and Truth*. Cambridge: Cambridge University Press, 2000.

Martimort, Aimé Georges. *The Church of Prayer: Introduction to the Liturgy*. Collegeville, Minn.: Liturgical Press, 1992.

McCabe, Herbert, O.P. *The People of God: The Fullness of Life in the Church*. New York: Sheed and Ward, 1964.

McDonnell, Killian, O.S.B. *The Baptism of Jesus in the Jordan: The Trinitarian and Cosmic Order of Salvation*. Collegeville, Minn.: Liturgical Press, 1996.

McInerny, Ralph. *The Defamation of Pius XII*. South Bend, Ind.: St. Augustine Press, 2001.

McNeill, J. T. *Unitive Protestantism*. Richmond, Va.: John Knox Press, 1964.

Meioni, Anthony J., Jr., ed. *The Popes against Modern Errors: Sixteen Papal Documents*. Rockford, Ill.: Tan Book Publishers, 1999.

Merdinger, J. E. *Rome and the African Church in the Time of Augustine*. New Haven: Yale University Press, 1997.

Meyendorff, John. *Catholicity in the Church*. New York: St. Vladimir's Seminary Press, 1983.

Miller, Samuel H., and G. Ernest Wright. *Ecumenical Dialogue at Harvard: The Roman Catholic–Protestant Colloquium*. Cambridge: Harvard University Press, 1964.

A Monk of the Eastern Church. *Orthodox Spirituality: An Outline of the Ascetical and Mystical Tradition*. 2nd ed. Crestwood, N.Y.: St. Vladimir Seminary Press, 1987.

Moody, Dale. *Baptism; Foundation of Christian Unity*. Philadelphia: Westminster Press, 1967.

Newman, John Henry. *Apologia Pro Vita Sua*. New York: Catholic Publication House, 1890.

———. "Tamworth Reading Room." In *Discussions and Arguments on Various Subjects*. London: Longmans, Green and Co., 1891.

———. *On Consulting the Faithful in Matters of Doctrine*. New York: Sheed and Ward, 1961.

Nichols, Aidan, O.P. *Yves Congar, O.P.* Wilton, Conn.: Morehouse-Barlow, 1989.

———. *Rome and the Eastern Churches*. Collegeville, Minn.: Liturgical Press, 1992.

———. *Epiphany: A Theological Introduction to Catholicism*. Collegeville, Minn.: Liturgical Press, 1996.

Niebuhr, H. Richard. *Theology, History, and Culture: Major Unpublished Writings*. Edited by William Stacy Johnson. New Haven: Yale University Press, 1996.

Niemöller, Martin. *God Is My Führer*. New York: Philosophical Library, n.d.

Nygren, Anders. *Agape and Eros*. Philadelphia: Westminster Press, 1953.

Osborne, John. *Luther*. New York: Plume Imprint-Dutton-Plume, 1994.

Pahlke, Georg, and Wilhelm Hardehausen Pohlmann. *Wir Gehen Durch das alte Kloster*. Paderborn: Bonifatius, 1998.

Passelecq, Georges, and Bernard Suchecky. *The Hidden Encyclical of Pius XI*. New York: Harcourt Brace & Company, 1997.

Paul VI (pope). *Pope John XXIII*. New York: Herder and Herder, 1965.

Penco, Giovanni Battista. *Il Cardinal Andrea Ferrari: Arcivescovo di Milano*. Milan: Instituto, Propoganda Libraria, 1987.

Perkins, Pheme. *Jesus as Teacher*. New York: Cambridge University Press, 1990.

Perthe, Fredereich. *Leben von Clemens Theodor Perthes*. Vol. II. Hamburg: Herder, 1851.

Peters, Walter H. *The Life of Benedict XV*. Milwaukee: Bruce Publishing Co., 1959.

Phayer, Michael. *The Catholic Church and the Holocaust: 1930-1965*. Bloomington: Indiana University Press, 2000.

Phillippe, Paul Cardinal. *The Ends of the Religious Life according to St. Thomas Aquinis*. Athens: Fraternity of the Blessed Virgin Mary, 1962.

Pollard, John F. *The Unknown Pope*. London: Geoffrey Chapman, 1999.

Portmann, Heinrich. *Cardinal von Galen*. London: Jarrolds, 1957.

Pribilla, Max. *Um kirchliche Einheit*. Freiberg: Herder, 1930.

Purdy, W. A. *The Church on the Move*. New York: John Day Co., 1966.

———. *The Search for Unity: Relations between the Anglican and Roman Catholic Churches from the 1950's to 1970's*. London: Geoffrey Chapman, 1996.

Quitslund, Sonya A. *Beauduin: A Prophet Vindicated*. New York: Newman Press, 1973.

Rahner, Hugo, S.J. *Ignatius the Theologian*. San Francisco: Ignatius Press, 1964.

Rahner, Karl, S.J. *I Remember*. New York: Crossroad, 1985.

Reardon, Bernard M. G. *Religious Thought in the Reformation*. London: Longman House, 1995.

Rhodes, Anthony. *The Vatican in the Age of the Dictators: 1922-1945*. New York: Holt, Rinehart and Winston, 1973.

———. *The Power of Rome*. New York: Franklin Watts, 1983.

Rhodes, Richard. *Masters of Death*. New York: Alfred A. Knopf, 2002.

Rice, Eugene F., Jr. *St. Jerome and the Renaissance*. Baltimore: Johns Hopkins University Press, 1985.

Richards, Richard, A.A. *The Assumptionists*. New York: Assumption Provincial House, 1980.

Root, Michael, and Risto Saarinen, eds. *Baptism and the Unity of the Church*. Grand Rapids: Eerdmans, 1997.

Runciman, Sir Stephen. *The Eastern Schism*. Oxford: Oxford University Press, 1955.

Rychlak, Ronald J. *Hitler, the War, and the Pope*. Columbus, Miss.: Genesis Press, 2000.

Rynne, Xavier. *Letters from Vatican City*. New York: Farrar, Straus and Co., 1963.

———. *The Second Session: Debates and Decrees of Vatican Council II*. New York: Farrar, Straus and Co., 1964.

Sabatier, Auguste. *Esquisse d'une philosophie de la religion*. Paris, 1897.

Bibliography

Sachs, John R., S.J. *The Christian Vision of Humanity: Basic Christian Anthropology*. Collegeville, Minn.: Liturgical Press, 1991.

Savon, Hervé. *Johann Adam Möhler, the Father of Modern Theology*. Glen Rock, N.J.: Paulist Press, 1966.

Scheeben, Matthias. *Die Mysterien des Christentums*. Freiburg: Herder and Herder, 1865.

Schillebeeckx, Edward, O.P. *Christ the Sacrament of the Encounter with God*. New York: Sheed and Ward, 1963.

Schleiermacher, Friedrich. *Aus Schleiermachers Leben im Briefen*. London, 1860.

Schmidt, Stjepan, S.J. *The Augustin Bea Prize: Unity of Mankind in Freedom*. Lugano: International Foundation/Humanism, 1971.

———. *Augustin Bea: The Cardinal of Unity*. New Rochelle, N.Y.: New City Press, 1992.

Schnackenburg, Rudolf. *The Moral Teaching of the New Testament*. New York: Herder and Herder, 1965.

Schoof, T. M. *A Survey of Catholic Theology: 1800-1970*. Amsterdam: Paulist Newman Press, 1970.

Schutz, Roger. *Unity, Man's Tomorrow*. London: Faith Press, 1962.

———. *His Love Is a Fire*. Collegeville, Minn.: Liturgical Press, 1990.

Sheerin, John B. *Never Look Back*. New York: Paulist Press, 1975.

Smith, Dennis Mack. *Italy and Its Monarchy*. London: Yale University Press, 1989.

Spencer, Charles. *The Spencers*. New York: St. Martin's Press, 2000.

Spink, Kathryn. *A Universal Heart: The Life and Vision of Brother Roger of Taizé*. San Francisco: Harper & Row Publishers, 1986.

Stehlin, Stewart A. *Weimar and the Vatican, 1919-1933*. Princeton: Princeton University Press, 1983.

Stein, Leo. *Hitler Came for Niemöller*. Gretna, La.: Pelican Publishing, 2002.

Stern, Karl. *Pillar of Fire*. Garden City, N.Y.: Doubleday, 1959.

Stookey, Laurence Hull. *Baptism, Christ's Art in the Church*. Nashville: Abingdon Press, 1982.

Stürmer, Michael. *The German Empire (1870-1918)*. New York: Modern Library, 2000.

Suhard, Emmanuel. *Priests among Men*. Notre Dame: Fides Publishers, 1960.

Sundkler, Bengt. *Nathan Söderblom: His Life and Work*. Lund: Gleerups, 1968.

Swidler, Leonard. *The Ecumenical Vanguard*. Pittsburgh: Duquesne University Press, 1966.

Tavard, George F. *Two Centuries of Ecumenism*. Notre Dame: Fides Publishing Co., 1960.

———. *Petite Histoire du Mouvement Oecuménique*. Paris: Editions Fleuerus, 1960.

Teresa, Mother, and Roger Schutz. *Seeking the Heart of God*. San Francisco: Harper, 1993.

Thieme, Karl. *Evangelical German Christians on the Way to the Catholic Church: Deeds and Debates, Ignotus.* Zürich, 1934.

Thurian, Max, ed. *Visible Unity and Tradition.* Baltimore: Helicon Press, 1962.

———. *The Consecration of the Layman.* Dublin: Helicon, 1963.

———. *Ecumenical Perspective in Baptism, Eucharist, and Ministry.* Geneva: World Council of Churches, 1983.

Thurian, Max, and Geoffrey Wainwright, eds. *Baptism and Eucharist: Ecumenical Convergence in Celebration.* Geneva: World Council of Churches, 1983.

Tillich, Paul. *Love, Power, and Justice.* London: Oxford University Press, 1954.

Torrance, Thomas F. *Royal Priesthood.* Edinburgh: T&T Clark Limited, 1993.

Touveneraud, Pierre. *Emmanuel d'Alzon: 1810-1880.* Rome: Congregation of the Augustinians of the Assumption, 1980.

Vanden Bussche, Jozef, C.P. *Ignatius (George) Spencer Passionist (1799-1864).* Leuven: University Press, 1991.

Van der Meer, Frederic. *Augustine the Bishop.* London: Sheed and Ward, 1961.

Vegnini, Mario. *John XXIII: The Official Biography.* Boston: Pauline Books and Media, 2001.

Vereb, Jerome M., C.P. *Apostle of Christian Unity.* Sutton, England: Passionist Press, 1978.

———, ed. *A Joyful Soul.* Kansas City, Mo.: Andrews McMeel Publishing, 2000.

Visser 't Hooft, Willem A. *Does the Ecumenical Movement Have a Future?* New York: Crossroad, 1974.

———. *Memoirs.* Geneva: WCC Publications, 1987.

von Hildebrand, Dietrich. *Fundamental Moral Attitudes.* New York: Longmans, Green and Company, 1950.

von le Fort, Gertrude. *Hymns to the Church.* New York: Sheed and Ward, 1953.

Vorgrimler, Herbert. *Commentary on the Documents of Vatican II.* Vol. 1. New York: Herder and Herder, 1967-1969.

Wainwright, Geoffrey. *Doxology.* New York: Oxford University Press, 1980.

Weber, Eugen. *Action Francaise.* Stanford: Stanford University Press, 1962.

Webster, John. *The Cambridge Companion to Karl Barth.* Cambridge: Cambridge University Press, 2000.

Weigel, George. *Witness to Hope.* New York: Cliff Street Books, 1999.

Weitz, John. *Hitler's Diplomat.* New York: Ticknor and Fields, 1992.

Weymar, Paul. *Adenauer.* London: Andre Deutsch, 1957.

Whitaker, Edward Charles. *Documents of the Baptismal Liturgy.* London: Alcuin Club Collections, SPCK, 1960.

Wigginton, F. Peter. *The Popes of Vatican Council II.* New York: Franciscan Herald Press, 1983.

Willebrands, Johannes Cardinal. *Emanuel D'Alzon and John Henry Newman: The Road to Christian Unity.* Worcester, Mass.: Assumption College, 1980.

Wills, Gary. *St. Augustine.* New York: Viking Group, 1998.

Wiltgen, Ralph. *The Rhine Flows into the Tiber.* New York: Hawthorn Books, 1967.

Bibliography

Wistrich, Robert A. *Hitler and the Holocaust.* New York: Modern Library, 2001.

Wouk, Herman. *The Winds of War.* London: Little, Brown, 1971.

Wright, N. T. *The Crown and the Fire: Meditations on the Cross and the Life of the Spirit.* Grand Rapids: Eerdmans, 1995.

Yee, Gail A. *Jewish Feasts and the Gospel of John.* Wilmington, Del.: Michael Glazier Publishing, 1989.

Zerwick, Max, S.S., and Mary Grosvenor. *A Grammatical Analysis of the Greek New Testament.* Rome: Editrice Pontificio Istituto Biblico, 1996.

Zizola, Giancarlo. *The Utopia of Pope John XXIII.* Maryknoll, N.Y.: Orbis Books, 1978.

Appendix

*   *   *

Beyrouth le 19-11-68

Très Saint Pere,
    La nouvelle du décès de feu le Cardinal Augustin Bea, que nous avons lue dans la presse, nous a causé une douleur profonde. Nous

nous sommes tout de suite représenté la peine que Votre Sainteté a dû éprouver devant la perte de cet éminent collaborateur de Votre apostolat œcuménique, qui était si bien entré dans les vues de Votre Sainteté et celle de Votre saint prédécesseur, Jean XXIII, fondateur du Secrétariat pour favoriser l'union des Chrétiens. Aussi, est-ce bien sincèrement qu'en mon nom et au nom de tous les membres de l'Episcopat grec-melkite, je présente nos condoléances émues à Votre Sainteté. La cardinal Bea, il est vrai, était âgé de 87 ans, mais il avait la clarté et la vigueur de pensée d'un homme en pleine maturité; l'activité et l'esprit de sacrifice d'une jeunesse prolongée. Sa science, sa sainteté de vie, son obéissance, sa compréhension, faisaient de lui un excellent instrument entre les mains des Papes dans leur action pour le rapprochement des Chrétiens.

Notre patriarcat qui, déjà en mai et en août 1959, avait proposé à Jean XXIII l'instition d'un organisme spécial permanent pour s'occuper des questions œcuméniques au sein de la curie romaine, avait été très heureux de la création du Secrétariat et depuis, a entretenu avec le Cardinal Bea et ses collaborateurs les relations les plus cordialement confiantes, les aidant dans la mesure de nos faibles moyens et recevant d'eux des encouragements éclairés dans notre attitude pendant et apres le Concile.

Aussi, est-ce de tout ceuer que nous nous unissons aux prières que Votre Sainteté élève vers Dieu pour accorder à l'âme vaillante de notre cher défunt le repos et la récompense qu'il a si bien mérités.

Renouvelant l'expression de nos sincères condoléances, nous prions Votre Sainteté de nous bénir.

> \+ Maximos V Hakim
> Patriarche d'Antioche et de tout l'Orient,
> d'Alexandrie et de Jérusalem

*　　*　　*

PONTIFICO INSTITUTO BIBLICO
Via Della Pilotta, 25
Roma (204)
November 30, 1959
His Excellency Reverend Dr. Lorenz Jaeger
Archbishop of Paderborn
PADERBORN

Your Excellency! Most Reverend and Dear Archbishop,

Since I have a little free time, I wish at least to thank you for your informative letter of November 8. To my joy I perceive that we are completely united in the adjudication about the matter. Geneva endeavors to "make good weather again," at least as Professor Willebrands had the impression, since he was personally there. Now, much depends upon who takes the place of Dr. Harms (who by the way, as Willebrands says) should not give up his department entirely. The most important thing is the question of the advocacy of the ecumenical movement in Rome. When the vacation is over, I shall speak with the Holy Father directly about it. Just as a "Commissio pro Russia" was formed, now one can be established "pro motione oecumenica." The most important thing is that it is set up well. Your Excellency is right that a single person cannot do all these things. We hope and pray then to find the right way. After I have spoken with the Holy Father, I shall bring forward your missive so that the Bishops Conference, in all events, will not be damaged unnecessarily.

About all other things, then, later. You understand that, at this time, I am overburdened with thousands of matters and other cares. But my letter should at least be a signal that my interest in the issues which has concerned us to now, will continue in the future. I shall be always very grateful for any information.

The answer to the kind letter of the 16th, which your well wishes brought me, are enclosed (with "Schema F" of the Secretariat!). I have to answer hundreds of telegrams and letters. Heartfelt thanks and God's blessing to all!

With most respectful greetings,

Your Excellency,
Most Respectfully in the Lord,
Aug. Bea S.J.

*   *   *

Rome
January 13, 1960
Via Aurelia 527
Cardinal Augustin Bea
The Most Reverend Dr. Lorenz Jaeger
Archbishop of Paderborn
PADERBORN

Your Excellency!
Most Reverend and Dear Archbishop!

I thank you sincerely for the kind letter of January 6, with the enclosure concerning the ante-preparatory Commission. I have read the enclosure with great interest, and greatly rejoice that you have, in a special way, laid out the teaching of the Church so forcefully, in accentuating the considerations, which are of particular importance to separated Christians. I should be very happy if I ever have the opportunity, to lend vigorous support, particularly in matters of writing.

At my audience on last Thursday, I also discussed with the Holy Father, the relationship that I formerly had with circles of the Ecumenical Movement, both Catholic and non-Catholic, and I asked him if I should foster it further. He was very interested in it, and encouraged me to work, in the future, in this area. He was reminded of similar eventuations, and thanked me for the intervention. Thus, I am fortified by the highest office to continue with the work of reunion, and I shall do this in so far as it is possible. I shall always be very grateful for your pertinent interventions and information.

In regard to the "Pontifica Commissio pro rebus oecumenicis," Professor H. H. Stakemeier gave me a draft of a statement that he would direct to the Holy Father. I very carefully examined the extract, enlarged it somewhat, and I shall send it back to Professor Stakemeier today. It would perhaps be easier, if you were to send me the statement due to the Holy Father; then I, on my part, will give it again, with warm recommendations, to the Holy Father who is so interested in it. There are so many Pontifical Commissions. (cf. Annuario Pont. p. 1897, 1959) that this request for the establishment of a Pontifical Commission is not unusual as e.g., the Pontifical Commission *pro-Russia,* or for Latin America. Therefore, I would especially point this out in my covering document. Praise God that the intervention will come to a good end. I shall especially think of it at the altar.

Your interventions, in reference to the "storm in the teapot against Rome," were interesting. You have completely confirmed my impression, which I had reached some months ago. In certain circles people do not *want* unity, and set themselves to do all in their power to hinder it. All the friendly words and gestures which have been made by Geneva cannot however delude one. I rejoice that, in your preaching in reference to the Unity Octave, you desire to address the Council from the ecumenical point of view. If you send me the text early, I would see if I could reproduce something, immediately, in regard to it, on Vatican Radio, on Monday.

So much for today. I am still under pressure, but gradually the tempo of daily life passes (as long as it is possible to be engaged in many obligations). Many thanks for the New Year's greetings, which I repeat from the heart.

With most respectful greetings,

Yours truly,
Aug. Card Bea

Index